Linguistic Resistance in Pakistan

LINGUISTIC RESISTANCE IN PAKISTAN

Punjabi Language Movements After Independence

JULIEN COLUMEAU

COLUMBIA UNIVERSITY PRESS *NEW YORK*

Columbia University Press
Publishers Since 1893
New York Chichester, West Sussex
cup.columbia.edu

Library of Congress Cataloging-in-Publication Data
Names: Columeau, Julien author
Title: Linguistic resistance in Pakistan : Punjabi language movements after independence / Julien Columeau.
Description: New York : Columbia University Press, [2026] | Includes bibliographical references and index.
Identifiers: LCCN 2025037033 (print) | LCCN 2025037034 (ebook) | ISBN 9780231219815 hardback | ISBN 9780231219822 trade paperback | ISBN 9780231562911 ebook
Subjects: LCSH: Language policy—Pakistan—Punjab | Panjabi language—Political aspects—Pakistan—Punjab | Social movements—Pakistan—Punjab | Punjab (Pakistan)—Languages—Political aspects | Pakistan—Politics and government—1947–1971
Classification: LCC P119.32.P18 C65 2026 (print) | LCC P119.32.P18 (ebook)
LC record available at https://lccn.loc.gov/2025037033
LC ebook record available at https://lccn.loc.gov/2025037034

Cover design: Noah Arlow

GPSR Authorized Representative: Easy Access System Europe, Mustamäe tee 50, 10621 Tallinn, Estonia, gpsr.requests@easproject.com

Contents

Note on Transliteration vii

Introduction 1

ONE Pakistan's Linguistic Landscape: Urduization and Language Movements 11

TWO The Linguistic Situation in Punjab 28

THREE Lahore's Intellectual Landscape 55

FOUR The Marxist Punjabi Movement (1947–1959) 64

FIVE The Conservative Punjabi Movement (1950–1960) 120

SIX The Punjabi Modernist Movement (1957–1959) 186

Conclusion 210

Notes 215
Bibliography 255
Index 267

Note on Transliteration

The Punjabi and Urdu texts quoted in the following pages were written in the Arabic-Persian *nastaʿlīq* script. They have been transcribed according to the pronunciation in standard contemporary Punjabi and Urdu, but consonants have been strictly transliterated in order, for instance, to differentiate the four Arabic letters ذ, ز, ض and ظ, to which only the sound /z/ corresponds in Punjabi/Urdu.

ا	a, u, i	جھ	jh	ڑھ	ṛh	ک	k
آ	ā	چ	c	ز	z	گ	g
ب	b	چھ	ch	س	s	ل	l
بھ	bh	ح	ḥ	ش	š	م	m
پ	p	خ	x	ص	ṣ	ن	n
پھ	ph	د	d	ض	ẓ	ں	ṁ
ت	t	دھ	dh	ط	ṯ	ݨ	ṇ
تھ	th	ڈ	ḍ	ظ	ẕ	و	v, w, o, au, ū
ٹ	ṭ	ڈھ	ḍh	ع	ʿ	ھ	h
ٹھ	ṭh	ذ	ż	غ	ġ	ی	ī
ث	ṡ	ر	r	ف	f	ے	e, ai
ج	j	ڑ	ṛ	ق	q		

Introduction

DURING MY FIVE-YEAR stay in Lahore, I came in contact with Urdu writers such as Intizar Hussain, M. Salim-ur-Rahman, Zahid Dar, Ikramullah, and Abdullah Hussain, as well as Punjabi writers such as Mushtaq Soofi, Zubair Ahmad, Manzur Ejaz, Shuja ul-Haq, Mazhar Tirmizi, Saeed Bhutta, Iqbal Qaiser, Maqsood Saqib, and Ahmad Salim. It was soon clear to me that a gulf separated Urdu and Punjabi writers. Their language ideologies were antagonistic: Most Urdu writers treated the Punjabi language with contempt or condescension, considering it an undeveloped language, while most Punjabi writers considered Urdu to be a foreign language, imposed by the country's intelligentsia through a conspiracy aimed at depriving Punjabis of their identity and their cultural heritage.[1] There were also notable political differences between Urdu and Punjabi writers: While the former were often conservative in outlook, or exhibited a dubious "apoliticism," the latter were often Marxist (and a good number of them had been associated with leftist organizations in the past). Finally, there was among Punjabi writers the feeling of being involved in an ongoing language movement that was fighting for the restoration of Punjabi rights: They would demonstrate every February 21st in front of the Lahore Press Club to demand recognition of Punjabi as the official language of the province of Punjab. Although a few bilingual writers (Zahid Hassan, Ghulam Hussain Sajid) tried to establish a link between the Urdu and Punjabi groups, there was virtually no contact between these two groups. Urdu and Punjabi writers generally avoided using each other's language and moved, so to speak, in two different, though geographically adjacent, universes. The circles and organizations to which they belonged were different. The publishing houses and journals that published them were also different. Urdu writers met during the sessions of the *Ḥalqa-e Arbāb-e Żauq* (Circle of the Men of Good Taste); their latest texts were published in journals such as *Saverā* and *Adab-e Laṯīf* and their latest books by *Sang-e-meel Publications*, *Nigarishat*, or *Fiction House*. Punjabi writers met during the sessions of the *Sangat* (the familiar name given to the *Panjābī Adabī Sangat*, the Punjabi Literary Association), which were held at Najm Hosain Syed's residence on Jail Road; their texts were published in *Pancham* and *Ravail* and their books by *Suchet* or *Sanjh*. Intizar Hussain's residence, where senior Urdu literati met every evening, and Najm Hosain Syed's residence, where the sessions of the *Sangat* took place, were separated by a simple road (Jail Road), but this road seemed to be as wide as a continent.

Jail Road physically separated not only two groups of supporters of two languages but also two literary traditions, of which the literary salon of Intizar Hussain and that of Najm Hosain Syed were the embodiments. The genealogy of the *Dabistān-e Lāhore* (Lahore Literary School), to which most of the Urdu writers claim to belong, could be readily traced through numerous books and articles.[2] It emerged in 1860–1870 with the relocation of Urdu Migrant Literati to Lahore and, after going through different phases, adopted social realism and modernism in the 1930s with the establishment of a branch of the *Anjuman-e Taraqqī-pasand Muṣannifīn* (Progressive Writers' Association) in 1936 and the foundation of *Ḥalqa-e Arbāb-e Żauq* in 1939. The Punjabi literary school seemed relatively new in comparison: it revolved around the *Panjābī Adabī Sangat*, founded in 1963. "Regulars" of the sessions of the *Sangat* began to attend them at the beginning of the 1970s, and the publishing houses and journals that were active in publishing new Punjabi texts were founded at the end of the 1980s. The question that often came to my mind was: what organizations, journals, and personalities had preceded them?

Documents proved that Lahore's pre-Partition Punjabi literary scene had been very vibrant, a multidenominational scene with which were associated Sikh and Hindu writers such as Amrita Pritam, Pr. Mohan Singh, Kartar Singh Duggal, I. C. Nanda, Balwant Gargi, and Gurbaksh Singh Pritlari; Christians such as Joshua Fazal Din and Bhola Nath Waris; and Muslims such as

Qazi Fazl-e Haq, Faqeer Mohammad Faqeer, Ustad Hamdam, Ustad Daman, and Ustad Ishq Lehr. One could find also documents regarding some Punjabi literary journals (*Prītam*, *Prītlaṛī*, *Hitkārī*) that were published in Lahore before Partition as well as some literary organizations, such as the *Lahore Singh Sabhā* (Lahore Society of Singhs) or the Punjabi Society of the Government College of Lahore, that were active in the city before Partition. But Partition disrupted Lahore's Punjabi literary scene, forcing Sikh and Hindu writers to emigrate and dismantling the network of organizations and journals they had established. What happened to this scene between Partition and the establishment of the *Sangat* in 1963? Documents and accounts of this period were rare, and when I asked contemporary Punjabi writers about it, they often replied that it was a "poor" period. The best informed among them mentioned two Punjabi writers active during these postindependence years—Ahmad Rahi and Abdul Majeed Bhatti—and two Punjabi books published during those years: Rahi's *Tirinjan* (The Assembly of Women), published in 1953, and Bhatti's s Punjabi novel *Ṭheḍḍā* (A Blow), published in 1960.[3] Was it possible that during the sixteen years that passed between the disappearance of the city's multidenominational scene and the foundation of the *Sangat*, Punjabi-language activity was limited to only two writers and produced only two books? This seemed unlikely. It was also hard to believe that no one was promoting Punjabi language and literature before the establishment of the *Sangat*. One could surmise that a Punjabi literary corpus, even if limited, had been produced before 1963—of which *Tirinjan* and *Ṭheḍḍā* were the only works contemporary writers wanted to remember—and that some individuals had been involved in promoting Punjabi in Lahore before the foundation of the *Sangat*. Who were the writers involved in the production of this pre-*Sangat* literature? What were the characteristics of their literature? What was the motivation of these pre-*Sangat* Punjabi activists? Their program and their strategy? Their political affiliation and social background? And to which extent was their movement influenced by language movements going on in other provinces of Pakistan at the same moment (in East Bengal and Sindh)? These were the questions that motivated the research project of which this book is the outcome.

This research seemed necessary because the period from Partition in 1947 to the creation of the *Sangat* in 1963 has been generally neglected by historians of the Punjabi movement, including Christopher Shackle, Alyssa Ayres, Vrinder Kalra, Waqas Butt, and Sara Kazmi. These scholars have documented in detail the activities of the *Sangat* and the movement it initiated. The first published text regarding its activities is Christopher Shackle's "Punjabi in Lahore," an essay written after the author's stay in Lahore between 1967 and 1968, during which time he observed the activities of the *Panjābī Adabī Sangat*.[4] Alyssa Ayres, in her book *Speaking Like a State*, examined the discourse of "Punjabiness" (*Panjābiyat*) in Najm Hosain Syed, Shafqat Tanvir Mirza, Hanif Ramay, and Fakhr Zaman's works and analyzed the evolution of this discourse between the end of the 1960s and the 1990s, highlighting the role of the *Majlis-e Šāh Ḥussain* (a sister organization of the *Panjābī Adabī Sangat*, founded in 1964) in the development and propagation of this discourse.[5] Virinder Kalra and Waqas Butt's article " 'In One Hand a Pen in the Other a Gun' "[6] focused on Major Ishaq and Mian Saleem Jahangir and examined the role played by the Mazdoor Kisan Party in the Punjabi movement of the 1970s. Sara Kazmi, in her lengthy essay "The Marxist Punjabi Movement: Language and Literary Radicalism in Pakistan,"[7] focused on the same personalities discussed by Alyssa Ayres and Virinder Kalra and Waqas Butt—Major Ishaq and Najm Hosain Syed—and discussed their role in the Punjabi movement of the 1970s as well as their dramatic production. The common points among these texts is that they do not mention any promotion of Punjabi before 1960s and they all stress the idea that Punjabi was promoted only by left-wing intellectuals.

Four texts examine the Punjabi movement in the years preceding the establishment of the *Sangat*: Tariq Rahman's essays "The Punjabi Movement" and "Punjabi"; Kanwal Mushtaq's lengthy essay serialized in 1997–1998 in the Punjabi journal *Saver*; and an interview of Shafqat Tanvir Mirza included in Maqsood Saqib's *Puchāṃ dasāṃ*, a collection of interviews with early Punjabi activists.[8] Rahman devotes a few pages in his two essays to the activities of Punjabi activists in the 1950s, but he focuses mainly on the activities of Faqeer Mohammad Faqeer and his group and does not mention the activities, equally important, of Marxist and modernist groups. Mushtaq's essay includes information roughly similar to that included in Tariq Rahman's two essays but also highlights the role of two organizations founded in Lahore after independence: the Punjabi Cultural Society and the *Panjābī Majlis* (Punjabi Society).

Shafqat Tanvir Mirza's interview is a very important document on the activities of promoting Punjabi in postindependence Lahore.[9] In discussing the Punjabi literary landscape in Lahore after independence, he divides the

Punjabi writers into three groups: (1) the traditionalist group (Faqeer Mohammad Faqeer, Joshua Fazal Din, Maula Bakhsh Kushta), supported by nationalist figures such as Hamid Nizami and Shorish Kashmiri; (2) the progressive group (Ahmad Rahi, Sharif Kunjahi), supported by Marxist literary figures such as Faiz Ahmad Faiz and Ahmad Nadeem Qasmi; and (3) the *Panjābī Majlis* group, a composite group of senior writers (Sufi Ghulam Mustafa Tabassum) and young writers (Anis Nagi, Salim ur-Rahman) led by Safdar Mir.[10] This account, unlike others, suggests that Pakistan's postindependence Punjabi literary landscape was severely polarized, mirroring the country's intellectual/literary field in that it was divided into groups formed on a political basis.

I decided to retrace the history of the three Punjabi groups mentioned by Shafqat Tanvir Mirza. It seemed to me that, for this history to be complete, I should situate these groups in the intellectual/literary field of their times and analyze their language ideology, the social background of their members, and their literary production. My model was, initially, Khizar Humayun Ansari's study of Indian progressive writers (*The Emergence of Socialist Thought Among North Indian Muslims, 1917–1947*), which examines in separate chapters the literary and political activities of progressive writers, their social background, and their literary production.[11] But there were many challenges ahead. First, unlike an Urdu organization like the *Ḥalqa-e Arbāb-e Żauq*, which kept a record of its activities, members of Punjabi groups did not record the activities of their organizations. Retracing the history of these groups required a cross-referencing of all the documents I could find on postindependence Punjabi literary circles (periodicals, memoirs, PhD dissertations, and master's theses). Second, most of the Punjabi texts published during the 1950s appeared in newspapers (like *Daily Imroz*) or in literary journals (like *Monthly Panjābī* and *Panjdaryā*) and were therefore difficult to trace because such documents are usually scattered and often incomplete. It took me several trips to Pakistan to gather archives, browsing through periodicals kept in Lahore's Government College Library and Punjab Public Library, as well as through the private archives of Junaid Akram, Ahmad Salim, Prof. Khalid Humayun, and Iqbal Qaiser.[12] Third, while many of the gaps created by the unavailability of documents could have been filled by interviewing some of the Punjabi activists/writers of the 1950s who were still alive, their number was dwindling. The writers Shafqat Tanvir Mirza, Saleem Kashir, Shafi Aqeel, Anis Nagi, Shehzad Ahmad, Afzal

Ahsan Randhawa, Akmal Aleemi, and Munnu Bhai, whom I intended to interview, passed away in the course of this research. Nevertheless, I managed to carry out long interviews with some activists/writers who had been active in those years.

This work relies on the following documents:

1. Periodicals: *Monthly Panjābī* (the first Punjabi journal published in Pakistan after independence), *Saverā* (which published texts in Punjabi between 1950 and 1951), *Daily Imroz* (which had a weekly section devoted to Punjabi between 1951 and 1959 and also published numerous articles in Urdu on Punjabi language and literature), *Panjdaryā*, *Panjāb Rang*, *Panjābī Adab*.
2. Books and pamphlets: poetry collections, radio play collections, literary anthologies, and communist pamphlets.[13]
3. PhD dissertations and master's theses discussing Punjabi writers of the 1930s, 1940s, and 1950s (Joshua Fazal Din, Talib Jalandhari, Sehrai Gurdaspuri etc).[14]
4. Memoirs and reminiscences: memoirs of Raja Risalu, Anis Nagi, and Intizar Hussain; reminiscences of Ahmad Rahi, Shorish Kashmiri, Ahmad Nadeem Qasmi, K. K.Aziz, Akmal Aleemi, and Hameed Akhtar.[15]
5. Interviews: Najm Hosain Syed, Zafar Iqbal, and Shahbaz Malik declined to give me interviews, but I was able to interview Rauf Malik, Abid Hassan Minto, Anver Sajjad, Zahid Dar, Dr. Kanwal Feroze, Raza Kazim, and Ahmad Salim, as well as Junaid Akram, great-nephew of activist Faqeer Mohammad Faqeer and custodian of his legacy.[16]

After collecting these documents, I decided to focus predominantly on the activities of Lahore-based groups. My initial plan had been to document activities of promoting Punjabi throughout Pakistan, since some Punjabi organizations were active also in Sahiwal, Lyallpur, and Karachi, but it turned out that the activities of these organizations were extremely limited and were not recorded by any members.[17] Furthermore, they did not publish any journals or any books. Punjabi writers associated with these organizations preferred to send their contributions to Lahore-based newspapers and journals (*Daily Imroz*, *Monthly Panjābī*, *Panjdaryā*, *Panjābī Adab*), as Lahore was an important center for Punjabi literature and language; the activities and literary productions emanating from it had an impact and were discussed all over the Punjabi-speaking world (as far as Karachi and Indian Punjab). Soon after Pakistan was created, Pothohari, Siraiki, and Hindko-speaking intellectuals strived to promote their respective dialects (a Pothohari program began to be aired on Radio Pakistan, Rawalpindi, a Siraiki literary journal was launched in Karachi, and an organization for the promotion of Hindko was established in Peshawar), but as my research was focusing on the promotion of standard Punjabi (based on the Lahore/Amritsar variant), I did not examine initiatives aiming at promoting these distinct dialects of Punjabi. I nevertheless mentioned and analyzed all the references to these dialects that I encountered in the Punjabi texts published during the studied period. I also decided to examine the activities of the Punjabi groups between 1947 and 1960—not 1963, the founding date of the *Panjābī Adabī Sangat*—because I realized that 1960 represented, even more than 1963, a pivotal date in the history of the Punjabi movement in Pakistan. It was between 1959 and 1960 that the three groups whose activities I studied in this work disappeared, and it was in 1960 that two important literary personalities emerged (Shafqat Tanvir Mirza and Najm Hosain Syed), who not only established the *Panjābī Adabī Sangat* in 1963 but also played a key role in the Punjabi literary scene for decades to come. A page was turned in 1960, and a new chapter in the history of Punjabi in Pakistan began.

This study is divided in two distinct sections. The first section analyzes the background in which the Punjabi movements emerged on two levels: the national and the provincial. On the national level (chapter 1), it examines the development of the pro-Urdu state policy, the different dimensions of Maulvi Abdul Haq's Urdu movement (which represented a section of civil society backing up Urdu imposition), and the various language movements that emerged in different provinces (Bengali, Sindhi, Pashto, Balochi movements) in reaction to them. It highlights the similarities among these movements in terms of strategies: creation or consolidation of a literature, foundation of journals and organizations, organization of conferences, and demand for/establishment of a state-sponsored academy. Moving to the provincial level, chapter 2 examines the stages of the adoption of Urdu in Punjab during the colonial era, as well as the movements for the defense and promotion of Punjabi that developed during this period. Then it analyzes the language policy of the province of Punjab at the creation of Pakistan and the status of Punjabi in the society of the province before and after independence, its sphere of use, and its perception. This first section shows that four elements were instrumental in the genesis of the Punjabi movements: the aggressive state policy of Urdu imposition, the awakening of a linguistic awareness across the provinces, the legacy of the Christian-Muslim Punjabi activism of the 1920s, and the low status and stigmatization of Punjabi in the very province where it was the majority language.

The second section of this study retraces the history of the three Punjabi movements going on between 1947 and 1960. It starts, in chapter 3, with a depiction of the intellectual field as the backdrop against which they emerged, a field torn between Marxists, conservatives, and modernists, each group competing to dominate it. Chapters 4, 5, and 6 retrace the history of a movement launched by each of these groups, presenting the activists' initiatives in chronological order, examining their language ideology, their program, and their literary production, as well as the structure of each group and the trajectory of some of their key members: Who were they? What was their background, and what were their motivations? Each chapter ends with an assessment of the activities of the studied group and of the impact of its movement. Reading the Punjabi periodicals of the 1950s, one is surprised not to find anything written by great modern Pakistani writers such as Saadat Hasan Manto and Faiz Ahmad Faiz. Why did these Punjabi-speaking writers not contribute to Punjabi literature during this period? We will also attempt to answer this question in this section.

This second section argues that there was no unified movement for Punjabi, and that the division of the Punjabi subfield in Pakistan in those years mirrors the division of the Urdu subfield, which was also structured around the opposition among three groups. This was to be expected, as in those years the Urdu and Punjabi subfields shared the same space within the same literary capital—Lahore—and many writers were bilingual, moving freely from one subfield to the other. This section reconstructs the controversies and debates that took place among the Marxists, conservatives, and modernists and challenges the ways some scholars have thought about the issue of national language in Pakistan. Previous studies have usually viewed Punjabi language movements as opposed to the idea of Pakistan, situating them within the framework of regional "separatism" or of *Punjabiyat*, but these notions have developed on the false assumption that it was only through Urdu and English that the idea of Pakistan was promoted and popularized. As this second part shows, many advocates of Punjabi did not reject the Pakistani state but, in fact, used various Punjabi literary and linguistic platforms to circulate the idea of Pakistan across the Punjab province. Some others also used them to circulate Marxist ideas challenging the state.

Methodologically, this study combines history, sociology, sociolinguistics, linguistics, and literary criticism in order to highlight the various dimensions and contributions of the Punjabi movement. Some of the specific concepts used have rarely been applied in South Asian studies, such as Bambi Schieffelin's concept of language ideology and Pierre Bourdieu's concepts of linguistic market and literary/intellectual field.[18] Drawing upon Pierre Bourdieu's analysis of the configuration of literary fields, this study highlights the hierarchy structuring the Punjabi literary subfield, as well as the hierarchy that operates within the different groups active in it. In light of this analytical framework, we differentiate the "dominant" from the "dominated" writers according to their degree of notoriety (an opposition that often coincides with the rift between "old" and "young"). We also differentiate between them according to the type of notoriety they enjoyed: on one hand, notoriety of a temporal order (institutional consecration, editorship, and association with well-known newspapers/journals); on the other, notoriety in the symbolic order (peer recognition). This study also draws on Gisèle Sapiro's analysis of the process of politicization and polarization of literary fields, closely examining some literary trajectories in order to understand to what extent social properties and political affiliations have conditioned the commitment of some writers to Punjabi and the type of discourse and literature they have produced.[19]

A recent resurgence of interest in the role of Marxists in Pakistan's early political, social, and cultural history has generated a number of works by Kamran Asdar Ali, Sadia Toor, Ali Raza, Anushay Malik, Ali Usman Qasmi, and Irfan Wahid Usmani. This study—which also highlights the role played by Marxists in the promotion of Punjabi and of other Pakistani regional languages after independence—can be situated as a continuation of their work, while simultaneously calling attention to a wider set of political affiliations among those who were committed to Punjabi in the opening decades of the postcolonial period.

A revival in Punjabi studies has also taken place in the past two decades, decades during which Tariq Rahman, Alyssa Ayres, Farina Mir, Anne Murphy, Virinder Kalra/Waqas Butt, and Sara Kazmi have produced groundbreaking works in the field of Punjabi studies. My own work owes a lot to theirs. Nevertheless, I must acknowledge that my main inspiration has been the work of my mentor, Dr. Denis Matringe, whose insights I have benefited from in the course of my research. His essay "Disguising Political Resistance in the Sufi Idiom: The Kafian of Najm Husain Sayyid of Pakistan" made me realize the relevance of Pierre Bourdieu's notion of "field" in the analysis of the Punjabi literary landscape, but above all made me understand to what extent the Punjabi movement was a matter of linguistic resistance.[20] Punjabi was used by activists as a tool for challenging and undermining the hegemony of Urdu in Pakistan's postcolonial context. They reclaimed and redefined their language, challenging the stereotypes/dominant discourse connected to it ("Punjabi is the Sikhs' language," "Punjabi is a dialect of Urdu"), redefining social meanings associated with it, and criticizing the cultural imperialism of which Urdu's dominance was the manifestation.

ONE

Pakistan's Linguistic Landscape

Urduization and Language Movements

WHEN IT WAS created, Pakistan—whose population was estimated at 75,636,100 inhabitants during its first census in 1951—was made up of two parts: East Pakistan (or East Bengal) and West Pakistan. Ninety-eight percent of East Pakistan's 41,932,000 inhabitants spoke Bengali, whereas West Pakistan's 33,704,000 inhabitants spoke Punjabi and its various dialects (Pothohari, Hindko, and Siraiki), Sindhi, Pashto, Balochi, Brahui, Shina, Khowar, and other languages. Bengali was the first language of Pakistan by the number of its speakers (55.4 percent of the population), and Punjabi the second (28 percent). Pashto was third (6.6 percent), Sindhi fourth (5.3 percent), and Urdu fifth (3.3 percent, spoken mainly by migrants from northern India, or *Mohajirs*). Punjabi was the majority language of West Pakistan (spoken by 62.84 percent of West Pakistan's population).

The use of these languages varied from one province to another as a result of British colonial language policy, which was not consistent. While Bengali and Sindhi had been used for decades as administrative languages and languages of instruction in the provinces where they were majority languages, this was not the case with Punjabi, Pashto, and Balochi. Urdu had been used in Punjab, North West Frontier Province (NWFP), and Balochistan for administrative and educational purposes since the start of British rule.

The issue of official language had arose soon after Pakistan's creation. The central government did not want English to be used anymore as the country's official language and wanted to replace it with a local vernacular. Urdu was chosen to fulfil this role, despite being a minority language, and this choice was formalized in the various draft constitutions that emerged after independence. It was not until the promulgation of the 1956 constitution that Urdu was adopted as an official language, alongside Bengali.

The promulgation of Urdu and Bengali as official languages barely affected the status of English, which continued to be used by the civilian and military elites and in the schools where they were educated and trained. English remained the language of high administration, high courts, and higher and scientific education. Ironically, it was in English that the debate concerning the official language took place in the Constituent Assembly, and in English that the promulgation of Urdu and Bengali as official languages was made.

This chapter will discuss how Pakistan adopted a minority language like Urdu as an official language, what kind of ideology accompanied this adoption, which status was given to local vernaculars (Bengali, Punjabi, Pashto, Sindhi, etc.), and how the speakers of these languages (apart from Punjabi, which we will deal with in the next chapters) reacted.

Adoption of Urdu

Urdu as an Official Language

The first Pakistani statesmen who expressed publicly the wish to make Urdu Pakistan's only official language were Pakistan's Prime Minister Liaquat Ali Khan and East Pakistan's Chief Minister Khawaja Nazimuddin (both native Urdu speakers). A resolution had been passed during the first session of the Constituent Assembly in Karachi, on February 23, 1948, stipulating that assembly members would debate in either Urdu or English; Dhirendranath Datta, a member of the East Pakistan Congress Party, proposed amending this resolution to add Bengali to these two languages. Liaquat Ali Khan opposed the amendment, declaring that "Pakistan has been created by the demand of 100 million Muslims of the sub-continent and their language is Urdu and therefore, it is wrong to move this amendment." His statement was supported by Khawaja Nazimuddin, who declared that the people of his province were also in favor of Urdu.[1]

A month later, the "Father of the Nation" and governor-general of Pakistan, Muhammad Ali Jinnah, reiterated Liaquat Ali Khan and Khawaja Nazimuddin's position. During the only visit he made to East Pakistan after independence, addressing a public meeting at Dhaka's Race Course Maidan on March 21, 1948, he declared: "Let me make it very clear to you that the State Language of Pakistan is going to be Urdu and no other language. Anyone who tries to mislead you is really the enemy of Pakistan. Without one State Language, no Nation can remain tied up solidly together and function. Look at the history of other countries. Therefore, so far as the State Language is concerned, Pakistan's language shall be Urdu."[2] Jinnah further clarified his position during the Dhaka University convocation on March 24, 1948: "The State language, therefore, must obviously be Urdu, a language that has been nurtured by a hundred million Muslims of this sub-continent, a language understood throughout the length and breadth of Pakistan and above all, a language which, more than any other provincial language, embodies the best that is in Islamic culture and Muslim tradition and is nearest to the language used in other Islamic countries."[3] Guided by this ideology, the Constituent Assembly initiated the process of making Urdu Pakistan's only official language. On September 28, 1950, its Basic Principles' Committee (formed on March 12, 1949) presented its initial report, which called for the state of Pakistan to be a federation with Urdu as its official language. In the meantime, a movement aimed at the recognition of Bengali as an official language had begun in 1948 in East Bengal. It intensified when this report became public and culminated in the bloody events of February 21, 1952 (discussed later in this chapter).[4] The pressure on the government was such that a new chapter was added to the report, declaring that both Urdu and Bengali would be the official languages of Pakistan. Accordingly, the 1956 Constitution of Pakistan proclaimed both Bengali and Urdu as official languages.[5]

Urdu as a Language of Instruction

The policy of Pakistan's central government regarding the medium of instruction to be used in the country's schools was an extension of its official language policy, and was marked by a strong desire to get rid of English in educational institutions—especially in higher education, where it was systematically used—and to replace it with Urdu. An educational conference was held in Karachi from November 27 to December 1, 1947 in order to design the government's policy regarding education, at the end of which the participants recommended making Urdu the first vehicular language (or lingua franca) of Pakistan and teaching it as a compulsory language all over the country.[6] An Education Advisory Council met on June 7–9, 1948 and, while agreeing that "the mother tongue should be the medium of instruction in the primary stage," announced its intention to see Urdu replace English as the language of instruction at university level.[7] It set up a committee for the promotion and development of Urdu under the chairmanship of Maulvi Abdul Haq, secretary-general of the *Anjuman-e Taraqqī-e Urdu* (Organization for the Advancement of Urdu), who was an expert in the use of Urdu in the educational sphere. In 1950, this committee decided that Urdu should be a medium of instruction in the schools of Punjab, NWFP, and Balochistan, as well as in in the Federal Capital Territory of Karachi. From 1952, Urdu became an optional medium of instruction at the intermediate level in colleges affiliated with Peshawar University, Karachi University, and Punjab University.[8] A process of Urduization had started in Sindh and Eastern Bengal. In Sindh, Urdu became compulsory from class IV to class XII, and Sindhi vanished from the University of Karachi in 1957, which chose Urdu as its medium of instruction.[9] Urdu was introduced as an additional compulsory subject from class V in 1950–51 in East Bengal. In 1953–54, Urdu was introduced from class IV as a compulsory subject in some parts of East Bengal and as an optional subject in others.[10] These measures only affected state-run educational establishments. English-medium private schools such as Burnhall in Abbotabad, Lawrence College in Murrie, and Aitchison College in Lahore did not adopt Urdu, and continued to produce English-speaking elites.[11]

In order to train teachers capable of teaching Urdu, Urdu departments were established in universities all over the country. The first Urdu department opened in Dhaka University in April 1948, where for the first time in the history of the subcontinent an MA Urdu was introduced.[12] Urdu departments opened in Lahore's Punjab University in October 1948, in Hyderabad's University of Sindh and Peshawar University in 1953, and in Quetta University in 1963.[13] Karachi University, soon after its foundation in 1951, incorporated the Urdu College that had been established in 1949 by Maulvi Abdul Haq, on the model of the Osmania University of Hyderabad.[14]

Field Marshall Ayub Khan, who seized power on October 8, 1958 and imposed martial law, continued the policy of Urduization carried out by previous civilian governments. He appointed a National Education Commission on December 30, 1958 (known as the Sharif Commission), which submitted its report on August 26, 1959. The Sharif Commission followed Ayub Khan's centralizing policy, proposing to strengthen the position of Urdu and Bengali, the country's two official languages.[15] The commission decided that Urdu and Bengali would become the languages of instruction from class VI in government schools. Nevertheless, the commission did not recommend replacing English with Urdu and Bengali, stating, "While we feel that English must yield to the national languages the paramount position that it has occupied in our educational system so far, we are at the same time convinced that English should have a permanent place in that system."[16]

The Role of the Anjuman-e Taraqqī-e Urdu *in Promoting Urdu*

To promote Urdu all over Pakistan, the central government enlisted the services of the *Anjuman-e Taraqqī-e Urdu*, an organization founded in 1903 to counter Hindi supporters and advocate for Urdu to be used as an official language and taught in schools and universities. Mostly financed by the Nizam of Hyderabad, the *Anjuman-e Taraqqī-e Urdu* was headquartered in Aligarh (1903–1913), Aurangabad (1913–1938), Delhi (1938–1948), and finally Karachi after 1948.[17] Maulvi Abdul Haq (1870–1961), a famous Urdu lexicographer, translator, and grammarian, often called *Bābā-e Urdu* ("The father of Urdu"), was its secretary between 1913 and 1961. He was one of the founders of Hyderabad's Osmania University and of Aurangabad's College (both Urdu-medium institutions). After the *Anjuman-e Taraqqī-e Urdu* moved to Karachi at the end of 1948, the central government awarded it a grant of 20,000 rupees. In 1952, it received a grant of 50,000 rupees from the Punjab government.[18] Thanks to these grants, the *Anjuman-e Taraqqī-e Urdu* established an Urdu college (where all subjects were taught in Urdu) and an Urdu library and published numerous books and journals. The central government and Punjab's provincial government funded this organization so that they could benefit from its expertise in three important fields:

1. Education. The Urdu College, founded on June 25, 1949 in Karachi and run by the *Anjuman-e Taraqqī-e Urdu*, soon came to be considered a model to be emulated. Eight hundred students were enrolled during the year 1950–51, taught by forty professors. The college offered courses in economics, political science, history, mathematics, geography, philosophy, psychology, logic, business, and law, all taught in Urdu. In 1951, the Urdu College was incorporated into Karachi University.[19]
2. Creation of neologisms. The *Anjuman-e Taraqqī-e Urdu* had been working in this area for years. It had been publishing *Science*, a journal featuring articles on new scientific discoveries in Urdu, since 1928 and *Mʿaāšyāt* (Economics), a journal featuring articles in Urdu on sociology and economics, since 1946. In 1952, the *Anjuman-e Taraqqī-e Urdu* established a *Šʿoba-e Taṣnīf-o Tālīf* (Department of Texts Compilation), which compiled Urdu textbooks on sciences, commerce, economics, law, Islamic studies, political science, history, and geography.[20]
3. Language promotion. The organization became an important ally of the government in the promotion of Urdu. Soon after it moved to Pakistan, *Anjuman-e Taraqqī-e Urdu* opened branches in all the major towns of the country, maintaining a network of activists (men of letters, civil servants, and teachers) who promoted Urdu with missionary zeal, even in remote places where it was almost unknown. Branches of the *Anjuman-e Taraqqī-e Urdu* were established in Peshawar, Kohat, Mardan, Quetta, Sylhet, Chittagong, Saidpur, Comilla, and Dhaka.[21]

The Role of the Mohajirs *in the Dissemination of Urdu*

The arrival of significant numbers of Urdu-speaking *Mohajirs* accelerated Urdu's spread in Pakistan.[22] In 1948, Lahore's refugee camps hosted 1,111,800 refugees from Haryana (Karnal, Hisar, Ambala, Gurgaon, Rohtak, and Jind), 235,181 from Rajasthan (Alwar and Bharatpur) and 119,548 from Delhi and Uttar Pradesh (UP).[23] Some of them remained in Lahore or settled in other towns of Punjab, such as Rawalpindi and Multan, while others settled in NFWP (51,100) and Balochistan (28,000), but the overwhelming majority of them subsequently moved to Karachi and Sindh. The 1951 census shows that 1,491,244 *Mohajirs* lived in Karachi and in other towns of Sindh, making up 57.55 percent of the total population of Karachi, 66.08 percent of Hyderabad, 54.08 percent of Sukkur, 68.42 percent of Mirpur Khas, and 54.79 percent of Nawabshah.[24] As a consequence of this huge migration, the number of Urdu-medium schools massively increased in Sindh: in August 1948, Karachi had 57 Sindhi-medium schools and 69 Urdu-medium schools; by 1954, it had 76 Sindhi-medium schools and 187 Urdu-medium schools.[25] Karachi became a new center of Urdu culture. As Tariq Rahman writes, "The Mohajirs, who already felt that their urban Mughal culture was superior to the indigenous culture of Sindh, now got a physical locale in which that culture could take root and flourish. As Urdu was an important aspect of the aesthetic sensibility of Lucknow and Delhi, the two centers of UP culture, it assumed the role of an evocative cultural symbol in urban Sindh too."[26]

Another consequence of the huge migration of *Mohajirs* to Sindh was a massive increase in Urdu newspapers and periodicals in the province, which ended up exceeding in number those in Sindhi. In 1955, a total of 156 Urdu newspapers and periodicals were published in Sindh (11 dailies, 1 biweekly, 44 weeklies, 7 quarterlies, 86 monthlies, and 7 bimonthlies), compared with only 52 Sindhi newspapers and periodicals (2 dailies, 46 weeklies, and 4 monthlies).[27] Urdu was becoming dominant all over the province. However, the number of Urdu-speaking refugees in East Bengal was too small to further the spread of the language. Thus, East Bengal was the only province in Pakistan where newspapers and periodicals in the local vernacular (Bengali) outnumbered those in Urdu. In 1955, a total of 81 Bengali newspapers and periodicals were published in the province (7 dailies, 1 biweekly, 53 weeklies, 6 fortnightlies, and 14 monthlies), compared with only 8 Urdu newspapers and periodicals (4 dailies, 2 weeklies, 1 fortnightly, and 1 monthly).[28]

Language Movements in Pakistan

Faced with this aggressive Urduization policy, the intellectual elites of the provinces united to defend and promote the local vernaculars, launching language movements that managed to mobilize the masses more or less successfully. Some movements were politicized from the beginning (like the Pashto and Sindhi movements, initiated by political figures such as Abdul

Ghaffar Khan in NWFP and G. M. Syed in Sindh), and some became gradually politicized (the Bengali and Balochi movements). The demands of the language activists varied from maximum to minimum: Bengali and Sindhi language activists demanded that their languages be recognized as Pakistan's official languages alongside Urdu, but Pashto and Balochi activists demanded only an official status for their languages at the provincial level. Here we examine four language movements—Bengali, Sindhi, Pashto, and Balochi—that emerged in reaction to Pakistan's state-led Urduization.

The Bengali Movement

The overwhelming majority of people in East Bengal spoke Bengali (and its different dialects) as their mother tongue. Urdu was the mother tongue of the Bengali aristocracy (or *Ašrāf*, to which East Bengal's Chief Minister Khawaja Nazimuddin belonged) and of a small community of *Mohajirs* who had migrated from Bihar and Eastern UP.[29] These Urdu-speaking *Mohajirs* numbered between 115,148 (according to Papiya Ghosh) and 250,000 (according to Ian Talbot).[30]

The Bengali language movement emerged after Pakistan's first educational conference, which was held in Karachi at the end of November 1947. The conference concluded that Bengali would be excluded from the list of subjects for examination by the Civil Service Commission and would not appear in government printed materials (stamps, forms, envelopes, postcards, etc.). These decisions were immediately opposed by the East Pakistanis participating in the conference. In December 1947, a *Rāštrabhāšā Sangrām Parišad* (Linguistic Action Committee) was founded in Dhaka, and at its first meeting a resolution was unanimously adopted proposing the adoption of Bengali as the official language of Pakistan.[31] The *Raštrabhāšā Sangram Parišad* subsequently launched a protest, which a huge number of students and teachers of Dhaka University and other educational institutions joined. The protest intensified, and a general strike was observed on March 11, 1948, accompanied by huge demonstrations. About fifty demonstrators were injured in a police charge, and a large number of students and political leaders were arrested. The situation worsened in the following days, with strikes observed from March 12 to 15. The situation escalated so much that Muhammad Ali Jinnah had to come to Dhaka to appease the protesters, but the speeches he delivered at the Race Course Maidan on March 21 and at the University of Dhaka on March 24 (quoted earlier), in which he reiterated his wish to make Urdu Pakistan's sole official language, had an adverse effect. The Bengali language movement received even wider support in East Pakistan after these declarations, and protests erupted immediately after Jinnah's weeklong visit.[32]

At the beginning of 1952, the recommendation to make Urdu the only official language, issued by the Basic Principles Committee of the Constitutional Assembly of Pakistan, triggered a new wave of anger in East Pakistan. Representatives of various political and cultural organizations held a meeting on January 31, chaired by Maulana Bhashani, leader of the newly formed *Awami League*, and decided to call a strike and stage protests on February 21 across East Pakistan. As preparations for protests were underway, the government imposed Section 144 in Dhaka city, banning rallies and demonstrations. Violating this article, Dhaka University students gathered by the thousands, held a meeting on February 21 on the campus of the university, and marched on the Legislative Assembly. The police opened fire, and three students and two other people were killed. A general strike was launched to protest against these killings, and the crowd demonstrated again the next day. The police and the army retaliated, resulting in several deaths, injuries, and arrests. The February 21 killing became known as *Ekushey* (the Bengali word for "twenty-one"), a date Bangladeshis remember as their state's founding event and UNESCO proclaimed in 2000 as International Mother Language Day.

Soon after, the Bengali language movement became fully politicized. The 1954 provincial elections in East Bengal were won by the United Front, a coalition of opposition parties led by Maulana Bhashani and A. K. Fazlul Huq, which demanded that Bengali be recognized as one of the official languages of Pakistan, that instruction be imparted all over East Bengal in Bengali, and that Burdwan House (the official residence of the chief minister) be converted into a research center for Bengali language and literature (the Bengali Academy or *Bangla Akademi*).

The United Front pushed through its agenda, and the ruling elite made several concessions. First, a *Bangla Akademi* opened at Burdwan House on December 3, 1955. Its objectives were as follows:

> To translate into Bengali important books of such oriental languages as Arabic, Persian, Urdu, Sanskrit, Pali and important books of such western languages as English, French, German etc to start a committee to be known as *Paribhasha Committee* for gleaning and coining Bengali technical and scientific words and legal and official terms to ensure uniformity in the use of such terms in the books of science, art, law etc in government offices, to translate books of intrinsic merit into Urdu, English or Arabic . . . to prepare text books in Bengali for higher education with a view to facilitate an easy change over from English to Bengali as the medium of instruction.[33]

Second, the process of official recognition of Bengali was initiated at high level. It led to the promulgation on February 29, 1956 of article 214 (1) of the constitution of Pakistan, which stipulates that the official languages of Pakistan will be Urdu and Bengali.[34]

The Bengali language movement owes its success to the fact that it managed to mobilize people across East Bengal's social spectrum. Tariq Rahman writes, "The challengers were the vernacular proto-elites: the modern, educated, Bengali-speaking class, and the largely middle-class professionals, and students who aspired to join the middle class. The subordinate social forces supported the movement from time to time."[35]

The Sindhi Movement

Adopted as the language of administration by the British in 1851, shortly after the conquest of Sindh, Sindhi was the main administrative language and medium of instruction in the newly created province of Sindh (it had obtained an autonomous status after been detached from the province of Bombay in 1936).[36]

Partition caused demographic and political changes in Sindh that drastically affected its linguistic landscape. The cities of Sindh witnessed the departure of Hindus and a huge influx of *Mohajirs* from northern India, who made up a majority in the five largest cities of the province, and on July 23, 1948, Karachi—the new capital of Pakistan—was separated from the province of Sindh and became a federal territory. In Karachi, the number of schools in Sindhi decreased dramatically, the University of Sindh—which had just been established in 1946—was shifted to Hyderabad, and the newly established University of Karachi declared Urdu its language of instruction and prohibited students from answering examination questions in Sindhi.[37] In 1954, the merging of the provinces of Western Pakistan to form a single administrative unit, the One Unit Scheme, further weakened Sindhi's already fragile status, as Sindhi lost its status as a provincial language.[38]

In the meantime, a Sindhi language movement had emerged, launched by the writer and politician G. M. Syed, who, as a minister of education in the government of Sindh in the 1940s, had actively promoted Sindhi (setting up a central advisory board for Sindhi literature and making Sindhi a compulsory language in all schools in the province).[39] In 1953, Syed founded the *Sindh 'Awāmī Maḥāż* (Sindh People's Front), which won seven seats in the 1953 provincial parliamentary elections. As the *Sindh 'Awāmī Maḥāż's* elected parliamentary leader in the Sindh Assembly, Syed submitted a memorandum to the governor of Sindh demanding that Sindhi be used in all the administrative, legislative, judicial, and educational institutions of the province and be given equal status with the other languages of Pakistan.[40] In the provincial assembly, he regularly asked the government of Sindh questions regarding the protection and promotion of Sindhi.[41]

Inspired and encouraged by G. M. Syed, Sindhi intellectuals mobilized for their language and organized conferences such as that of Mirpur Bathoro in January 1956 (during which Syed made a highly remarked speech) and Larkana later in 1956 to discuss Sindhi's present status and steps to be taken to defend and promote it.[42] During the Larkana conference, the vice-chancellor of the University of Sindh, I. I. Qazi, alerted the participants to the risk of the disappearance of their culture if the Sindhi language fell into disuse.[43]

Two cultural organizations were involved in the defense and promotion of Sindhi: the *Sindhī Adabī Sangat* (Sindhi Literary Society) and the *Sindhī Adabī Board* (Sindhi Literary Committee). The *Sindhī Adabī Sangat* was founded in 1944–45 in Karachi by Subho Gyan Chandani, Gobind Malhi, Jamal Abro, and Ram Panjwani. After independence, young socialist writers such as Shaikh Ayaz, Narayan Shyam, Shaikh Razaq Raaz, and Sundri Uttamchandani joined it and brought it closer to the Marxist *Anjuman-e Taraqqī-pasand Muṣannifīn* (Progressive Writers' Association).[44] Though its activities were initially limited to Karachi, it subsequently established branches in Hyderabad and Shikarpur. In 1956, a few weeks before the country's first constitution was promulgated, the *Sindhī Adabī Sangat* circulated a petition asking that Sindhi be recognized as one of the official languages of Pakistan. This petition received considerable popular support. An article in the Sindhi language weekly *'Awām* reported that, in the big cities as well as in the small villages of Sindh, youngsters showed such enthusiasm that some went so far as to sign the petition with their blood.[45] The *Sindhī Adabī Board*, founded in 1940 by G. M. Syed to supervise and promote the publication of material in the Sindhi language, became one of the spearheads of the Sindhi movement after independence. It published the journal *Mehrān* (which featured articles defending the Sindhi language and its rights) as well as translations into Sindhi of old historical accounts such as the *Chachnama* (1953) and the *Toḥfat ul-Karam* (1957), collections of classical poets such as the *Kulyāt-e Hammal Leġārī* in 1953 and the *Kulyāt-e Ḥasan Baxš* in 1957, Bherumal Mahirchand Advani's *Sindhī bolī jī tārix* (History of the Sindhi language) in 1956, and other works.[46] It also published in 1952 G. M. Syed's *Paiġām-e Laṭīf* (The Message of Shah Abdul Latif Bhittai), which presented a Sindhi nationalist reading of the great Sindhi poet.[47] Julien Levesque writes:

> On the basis of these works, Sindhi intellectuals will appropriate the past to build a historical narrative centered on Sindh, thought of as a social, political and geographical entity that evolves and is maintained through the ages. The research work of historians provides the material for a nationalist history which insists on the continuity of the Sindhi people since the Indus civilization and exalts, even if it means mixing legend and history, the role of heroes of the resistance like Raja Dahir, Dodo Soomro and Hosh Muhammad Sheedi. The works of cultural institutions . . . oppose the historiography promoted by the state of Pakistan, which imagines a narrative of Pakistan through the ages to create unity among the Pakistani people. The Sindhī Adabī Board thus contributes to the Sindhi nationalist discourse by producing a historiography specific to Sindh.[48]

The *Sindhī Adabī Board* also initiated in 1957, under the aegis of Nabi Bakhsh Baloch, a folklore research program, which resulted in the publication in 1959 of the first volume of a series of compiled Sindhi folktales.[49]

Field Marshal Ayub Khan, who came to power through a coup on October 8, 1958, continued the policy of Urduization of Sindh initiated by his civilian predecessors. The national education commission he appointed (known as the Sharif Commission) in its report reduced the importance of Sindhi, concluding that "Urdu should be introduced as the medium of instruction from class VI from 1963 and should continue progressively in the higher classes. It is necessary to give Urdu the same position in Sindh as in the rest of West Pakistan."[50]

The Pashto Movement

In 1951, Pashto was the third language of Pakistan in terms of number of speakers, after Bengali and Punjabi but ahead of Sindhi. The British had chosen Urdu as the administrative and educational language of NWFP soon after its annexation in 1849, to hasten the unification of the provinces with the rest of British India. Tariq Rahman writes: "The idea that the Pashto-speaking people of the Frontier should look towards India, where Urdu was predominant, and not towards Afghanistan, certainly influenced the choice of the vernacular in this Region."[51] Nevertheless, since the 1920s, a Pashto language movement had been ongoing in NWFP, launched by the politician Abdul Ghaffar Khan, the founder of the anti-British and pro–Congress Party movement *Xudā'ī Xidmatgār* (Servants of God) and an advocate of *Paxtunistan.*[52] Inspired by the initiatives of Afghanistan's King Amanullah to promote Pashto, Abdul Ghaffar Khan started establishing Pashto-medium schools, known as the Azad Schools, in NWFP in 1921.[53] Thus, 57 Azad Schools opened around Peshawar between 1921 and 1923, and their number reached 134 in the 1930s.[54] In 1928, Abdul Ghaffar Khan launched *Paxtūn*, a Pashto literary journal that published Pashtun nationalist prose and poetry as well as articles on the linguistic development of Pashto, emphasizing its role as a marker of Pashtun identity and urging people and authorities to use it in all spheres of life.[55]

Independence created a new situation in NWFP. Abdul Ghaffar Khan was jailed, the literary journal *Paxtūn* was banned, thousands of Urdu-speaking *Mohajirs* were moved to NWFP, and the province's Muslim League government adopted a pro-Urdu policy. The result, reports Professor Sharar Nomani, was that "Urdu was already taught in schools and colleges, but after independence its teaching received increased attention. As is the case in other parts of West Pakistan, Urdu has become a compulsory subject in NWFP up to 12th grade. In the district courts Urdu was already used before Partition, but now the situation is such that everything is done in Urdu, except the verdict."[56] Faced with intensifying Urduization, NWFP's writers and intellectuals mobilized to promote Pashto. Fazal ur-Rahim Marwat divides them into three tendencies: (1) active nationalists, political followers of Abdul Ghaffar Khan like his son Abdul Ghani Khan, Ajmal Khattak, Abdul Akbar Khan Akbar, and Nasrullah Khan Nasr; (2) "passive" nationalists (merely "literary" followers of Abdul Ghaffar Khan) like Rahat Zakheli and Hamza Shinwari; and (3) Marxists like *Kakaji* Sanober Hussain.[57] These Pashtun writers founded some organizations, such as the *Olsī Adabī Jirgā* (Association for Popular Literature) in 1950 and the *Abasin Arts Council* in 1955, to promote Pashto and its literature.[58] Both organizations organized literary meetings and poetic symposiums. Each year the *Olsī Adabī Jirgā* celebrated Rahman Baba's annual *Urs* with great devotion, and this celebration became a symbol of the struggle for Pashto.[59] Pashto-speaking intellectuals and writers also launched literary journals such as *Lāṛah*, *Rahbar*, and *Nangyālai*, journals that, according to Fazal ur-Rahim Marwat, carried highly subversive articles, arguing for the creation of *Pashtunistan*.[60] While only one journal in Pashto was active at the time of independence (Abdul Ghaffar Khan's *Paxtūn*), seven Pashto journals were active in 1955.[61]

To counter this rise of Pashtun nationalism in literature, the government created the Pashto Academy in 1955 and entrusted its management to Maulana Abdul Qadir, a Pakistani nationalist who had been Pakistan's ambassador to Kabul in the early 1950s. The academy's stated purpose was "to develop the Pashto language in the field of literature, technical and pedagogical knowledge and to bring it to the same level as other modern languages of the world," but it appears that its real aim was to provide an alternative to Pashtun nationalist discourse by producing Pashto books promoting the state ideology, stressing the unifying role of Islam, the links between Urdu and Pashto, and so on.[62] The academy also organized Pakistan's first Pashto conference in Peshawar in March 1957, to which several Afghan scholars were invited. Pashto corpus planning was one of the subjects of discussion during the conference, in particular the modernization of Pashto vocabulary. Participants were divided on this issue: Supporters of an Islamic or Pakistani identity wanted new Pashto words to be coined from Perso-Arabic morphemes; others advocated the use of Pashto morphemes, thus giving primacy to Pashtun identity over Islamic identity.[63]

The Balochi Movement

Balochistan came under British control in 1877, and Urdu was chosen as its official language by the colonial authorities. Thus, Urdu was used all over the province in schools and the lower levels of administration and justice.

A new national consciousness emerged among the Balochs in the 1930s, prompting writers and activists to promote their mother tongue. One of these writers, Muhammad Hussain Anqa, launched *Bolān*, a weekly in Balochi, which was published in Quetta during the 1930s.[64] The *Anjuman-e Itteḥād-e Balocān* (Organization for the Unity of the Balochs), which had been established in Mastung in 1927, started publishing in the early 1930s in Karachi *Al-Baluch*, a weekly in Balochi and Urdu, which claimed an independent state comprising the principality of Kalat, British Balochistan, Dera Ghazi Khan, parts of Sindh, and Iranian Balochistan.[65] Activities in favor of Balochi intensified after independence as language activists living in Karachi and Quetta actively promoted their language. In 1949, in Karachi, Maulana Khair Mohammad Nadvi aired the first radio program in Balochi (a daily program of forty-five minutes).[66] It was during this program that Muhammad Ishaq Shamim's *Hall Šāh Murīd* was broadcast, the first radio play in Balochi.[67] In 1951, also in Karachi, Maulana Khair Mohammad Nadvi launched *Oman*, a Balochi monthly that expressed nationalist aspirations and served as a platform for Baloch nationalists in the region.[68]

In Quetta, Abdullah Jan Jamaldini, a young writer influenced by the Marxist *Anjuman-e Taraqqī-pasand Muṣannifīn* (Progressive Writers' Association), which had opened a branch in the city in 1951, founded, with the help of Gul Khan Nasir (Balochistan's most revered poet, who had started writing in Balochi in the early 1940s), the *Balocī Zubān-o Adab Dīwān*, an organization for the promotion of Balochi literature and language.[69] In 1952, it published *Gulbāng* (Call of the Flower), the first poetry collection in Balochi of Gul Khan Nasir, and the first modern poetry collection in Balochi. It became very popular among educated Balochs, and its publication contributed to the promotion of Balochi.[70] In 1953 in Quetta, Azat Jamaldini, brother of Abdullah Jan Jamaldini, published his collection *Mastīṁ Tawār* (The Challenge), which also became very popular.

Thanks to the efforts of the *Balocī Zubān-o Adab Dīwān*, local politicians included the promotion of Balochi in their program. In 1955, when Prince

Abdul Karim (brother of the Khan of Kalat) and the poet Muhammad Hussain Anqa founded the *Ustaman Gall* (Party of the People), a nationalist party aiming at establishing a "linguistically and culturally Baloch province," they specified that Balochi would be its official language.[71]

In 1955, the Jamaldini brothers relocated to Karachi, and in 1956, Azat Jamaldini launched *Balocī*, a monthly journal publishing texts in all kinds of literary genres (poetry, fiction, plays, essays) and promoting a literature strongly influenced by the progressive writers. It ceased publication in 1958.[72]

In August 1958, the first Balochi conference took place in Mastung. A large number of writers, poets, political leaders, and tribal chiefs participated, their main purpose being to discuss a project of establishment of a Balochi Academy. The Balochi Academy's first draft charter was presented and discussed on this occasion, but the government of the time vetoed the project. The Balochi Academy was finally founded in Quetta 1961.[73]

Typology of Language Movements

The language movements that emerged in Pakistan after 1947 can be classified into two groups. The first group comprises the Bengali and Sindhi movements; their aim was to reclaim for these languages—which had been used until independence in literature, press, administration, and education—a space that was now shrinking as a result of Urdu's promotion by the state. Both movements enjoyed popular support. The second group comprises the Pashto and Balochi movements; their aim was to create space for languages whose scope was limited because Urdu was used in the press, administration, and education in the provinces where they are majority languages. These movements did not enjoy much popular support. They were initiated by different groups of intellectuals who—believing that the progress of a language is conditioned by the progress of its literature—focused on the production of a modern literature in their vernacular and launched journals to feature these new productions. However, their literary productions did not fit into any preexisting market and had an extremely limited readership. They belonged to what Pierre Bourdieu calls the "sub-field of producers for producers" because the readers were above all men of letters.[74]

We can notice similarities between these two groups of linguistic movements. First, all these movements were politicized, supported by major nationalist figures such as Abdul Ghaffar Khan and G. M. Syed or political parties like the *Ustaman Gall* in Balochistan and the *Awami League* in East Bengal. Second, all movements demanded the creation of academies, sponsored by the Pakistani state, to give official legitimacy to these vernaculars. The foundation of an academy dedicated to the promotion, protection, or standardization of a vernacular was not only a symbolic gain for language activists, it was also a gain for the state. Academies were often headed by intellectuals close to the ruling establishment, who would strive to ensure that their activities and publications were in line with the state ideology or promoted it. Some of these academies tried to bridge the gap between the vernacular they promoted and the official language, Urdu, by publishing vernacular-to-Urdu and Urdu-to-vernacular translations and dictionaries. Third, none of these movement was monolithic. Language activists were often divided among anti-government nationalists, pro-government elements, and Marxists (associated with the All Pakistan Progressive Writers' Association, or APPWA). Marxist intellectuals participated in these language movements because the APPWA had since its 1949 conference been encouraging the development of vernaculars as well as the production of literature in these languages.[75] Even if Marxist activists were outnumbered by nationalists and pro-government elements in these movements, their style of literature had an undeniable influence on the literature produced in vernaculars during this period.

The Punjabi movements, discussed in the following chapters, clearly belong to the second group of language movements. They aimed not at reclaiming a lost space for a previously established vernacular but at creating a new space, as Punjabi had never been previously used in the administrative sphere and its scope in the educational sphere had been somewhat limited (used mainly in nonstate education). Punjabi activists focused above all on developing modern Punjabi literature and launched journals to feature modern literary productions. They also lobbied for the establishment of a Punjabi Academy. But a big difference remained: none of these movements became politicized, and none of them promoted any form of Punjabi nationalism.

TWO

The Linguistic Situation in Punjab

IN THE PREVIOUS chapter, we analyzed Pakistan's overall linguistic situation during the period under study, examining the official state policy of Urduization and the movements born in reaction to this process in the provinces of East Bengal, Sindh, NWFP, and Balochistan. This chapter looks specifically at the linguistic situation in Punjab.

Two trends have dominated Punjab since the beginning of the colonial period: the gradual development and spread of Urdu—a language introduced by the British shortly after the annexation of Punjab in 1849—and the progressive marginalization of Punjabi. We first discuss Punjab's linguistic situation during the colonial era (1849–1947), depicting the process through which the British imposed Urdu in the newly annexed province and how opinion was divided regarding Punjabi, with British officials and upper-class Muslims expressing disdain for the language and Sikhs promoting it. We also discuss pro-Punjabi movements during the colonial period, as well as efforts by philologists to document and analyze the Punjabi language, literature, and folklore. Then we turn to the linguistic situation of Pakistan's Punjab province after 1947, a situation marked on one hand by an intensification of Urduization—a result of the provincial authorities' official policy as well as of a vigorous Urdu movement aiming at turning Punjab into an Urdu-speaking province—and on the other, by a further marginalization of Punjabi. We discuss Punjabi's status in the province after independence, its place in the public sphere, the survival of the colonial triglossic situation, and the popular perception of Punjabi.

The Linguistic Situation in Punjab During the Colonial Period

Urduization of Punjab

The first literary Punjabi texts date from the thirteenth century, penned by the Sufi saint Fariduddin Masood Ganjshakar, commonly known as Baba Farid or Sheikh Farid (1173–1265). With him started a long poetic tradition of Sufi writers, of which Shah Hussain (1538–1599), Sultan Bahu (1630–1691), Baba Bulleh Shah (1680–1757), Waris Shah (1722–1798), Hashim Shah (1735–1843), Mian Muhammad Bakhsh (1830–1907), and Khwaja Ghulam Farid (1845–1901) are the most important representatives. In the fifteenth century, after the arrival of Guru Nanak (1469–1539), Punjabi became one of the main components of *Sant Bhasha*, the liturgical language of the Sikhs, but at no time in the history of Punjab was Punjabi used as an official language.[1] Beginning in the eleventh century, Persian was the language of administration of the province. Persian was introduced by the Ghaznavids when they took control of Punjab during Mahmud's reign (997–1030) and retained this status under the various dynasties and governments that succeeded one another until the annexation of Punjab by the British in 1849. For generations, the Punjabi elites were educated in Persian, and Persian was widely adopted as a language of literary expression.[2] Its use in the literary field continued even after the British established their rule in Punjab, as evidenced by the production in Persian of Allama Iqbal (1877–1938).[3]

As soon as they annexed Punjab in 1849, the British established a commission, which, after consultation with locally based British officials, decided to use Urdu as the official language of the province. Why did the British authorities give preference to Urdu over Punjabi? Tariq Rahman mentions three reasons:

1. British officials had already been using Urdu since 1837, when Urdu replaced Persian as the administrative language in North India, and "they found it more convenient to carry on administration with their existing skills."[4]

2. British officials were prejudiced against Punjabi: "Letter after letter reveals that most British officers assumed that Punjabi was a rural patois of which Urdu was the refined form."[5] (We will examine some of these prejudices later.)
3. British officials equated Punjabi (in the Gurumukhi alphabet) with the Sikh Empire, which had given them a hard time; they therefore deemed it dangerous to promote it.[6] In a letter dated June 16, 1862, the British commissioner in Delhi wrote to the government of Punjab: "Any measure which would revive the Goormukhee which is the written Punjabee tongue, would be a political error."[7]

Urdu was therefore used, from the years following the annexation of Punjab, at the lower and middle levels of the colonial administration and of the colonial judiciary. It also became the main medium for government schools (vernacular schools).[8] Traditional ("indigenous") schools continued to operate alongside government schools, as before the British annexation: Muslim *Maktabs* and *Madarsas*, where Persian and Arabic were taught; Hindu *Pathshalas* of Hindus, teaching Sanskrit; and *Gurumukhi* schools, which taught the sacred scriptures of the Sikh Gurus in *Gurumukhi* script.[9] They outnumbered government schools in the years following annexation, but after two decades of British rule, government schools were outnumbering them: government schools enrolled 33,368 pupils in 1860, but 132,993 in 1885.[10] The job market that gradually emerged during British colonial rule favored students educated in government schools; without knowledge of Urdu, one could not be recruited into the local civil service.

The demand for Urdu books and periodicals increased dramatically with the emergence in Punjab of a class literate in Urdu: in 1868, 65 percent of the 183 books and pamphlets printed in the province were in Urdu (the remaining 18 percent were in Hindi and 17 percent in Punjabi *Gurumukhi*); by 1912, 91 percent of publications were in Urdu.[11] Urdu also became the predominant language of the Punjabi press: in 1883, Urdu was the language of eleven of the thirteen vernacular newspapers published in Lahore; in 1901, 137 of the 186 vernacular newspapers and periodicals published in the province were in Urdu.[12] Some of these Urdu newspapers had a very large circulation: in 1903, the weekly edition of *Paisā Axbār* (a newspaper launched in Lahore in 1887) reached 13,500 copies, an astonishing figure for the time, given that the 1901 census recorded the literacy rate of Lahore district (with a population of around 1.62 million) at only 4.4 percent.[13]

Given the systematic use of Urdu at school, in the press, and in the administration, as well as its promotion in the job market, a large number of Hindus and Sikhs became more conversant with Urdu than with Hindi or Punjabi written in *Gurumukhi*. Newspapers aimed at the Hindu and Sikh communities therefore began to publish in Urdu. According to the journalist and newspaper editor-in-chief Shorish Kashmiri, four "Hindu newspapers" in Urdu were published in Punjab before Partition (Kashmiri added ironically that these Urdu newspapers were staunch advocates of Hindi): Mahashay Krishan's *Pratāp*, Khushhal Chand Khursand's *Milāp*, Lala Lajpat Rai's *Vande Mātaram*, and Mela Ram Wafa's *Vīr Pratāp*.[14] The journalist and newspaper editor-in-chief Majeed Nizami mentioned in a report two "Sikh newspapers" in Urdu: *Ajīt* and *Ranjit*.[15] The contribution to Urdu of Punjab's Hindus and Sikhs was not only journalistic. They produced an impressive body of literature in this language too: Hindu writers such as Upendranath Ashk, Krishan Chander, Fikr Taunsvi, Kanhaiya Lal Kapoor, and Devendra Satyarthi and Sikh writers such as Rajinder Singh Bedi and Balwant Singh established themselves as important figures in twentieth-century Urdu literature.

As for English, after Punjab's annexation it became the language of the higher judiciary and upper administration. It also became the medium of instruction of the educational institutions attended by children of the Punjabi upper class (such as Aitchison College and Kinnaird College in Lahore), as well as the language of higher studies: most subjects were taught in English in colleges and universities.

The diglossic situation that prevailed before Punjab's annexation, with Persian being considered high and Punjabi low, was transformed by the British into an English/Urdu/Punjabi triglossia, which survives today in Pakistani Punjab.

Punjabi's Status During the Colonial Period

Punjabi's status was very controversial during the colonial period: it had a large number of opponents and a few defenders. These defenders gradually mobilized and initiated some movements to promote Punjabi, whose impact nevertheless remained limited. We examine first the discourse of Punjabi's opponents and then the initiatives undertaken by its defenders.

PUNJABI'S OPPONENTS

ENGLISH CIVIL SERVANTS

As early as 1849, English officials stationed in the Punjab overwhelmingly opposed the use of Punjabi as an administrative language and as a language of instruction. This opposition had a political origin (for them, Punjabi in *Gurumukhi* was a symbol of Sikh identity), but it was also based on linguistic prejudices. These prejudices are visible in the official correspondence between British civil servants and their superiors. Ayesha Jalal provides very telling examples of them in *Self and Sovereignty*: A British official declared in 1862 that Punjabi is "merely a dialect of Urdu with 'no literature of its own,' and one of his colleagues described the different dialects of Punjabi as a barbarian mixtures of Hindi and Persian of which Oordoo . . . is the pure type."[16] According to another official, Punjabi was "inflexible and barren and wholly incapable of expressing nice shades of meaning, and exact logical ideas so necessary for legal proceedings."[17] The same official, in order to illustrate his argument, wrote that giving Punjabi the status of the language of the courts in place of Urdu would be like using "the broad Scotch in the Courts North of the Tweed, or the barbarous patois of Summersetshire in the Courts."[18] Here we see an English civil servant projecting onto Punjabi the prejudices that prevailed at the time among the British educated classes against England's local vernaculars. He sees in Urdu the equivalent of English—a pure and sophisticated language—and in Punjabi the equivalent of one of those vernacular languages, therefore considering it a mere patois.

Some civil servants harbored such strong prejudices toward Punjabi that they declared themselves favorable to its extinction and replacement with Urdu. A. W. Stogdon, a magistrate stationed at Jalandhar, declared in a letter dated August 3, 1895: "As for the encouragement of Punjabi, I am of the opinion that it is an uncouth dialect, not fit to be a permanent language, and the sooner it is driven out by Urdu the better."[19]

It would be an exaggeration to say that all English officials were opponents of Punjabi and supporters of Urdu. Ayesha Jalal also quoted a pro-Punjabi statement by J. Wilson, deputy commissioner of Shahpur, who proposed in an 1894 note to his superiors that Punjabi be used as a medium of instruction in Punjab's primary schools, arguing that a Punjabi schoolboy receiving instruction in Urdu "is not taught to read the language he speaks, but a language many of the words in which he does not understand until they are translated for him into his own Punjabi."[20] But this proposal was ignored, as the consensus in favor of Urdu among British civil servants was overwhelming.

MUSLIM RULING CLASS OF PUNJAB

Upper-class Punjabi Muslims, too, opposed the use of Punjabi as an administrative language and as a language of instruction. Over time they had absorbed the prejudices of the British officials and, in this period of growing communal polarization, were seeking to distinguish their community from that of the Sikhs, whose sacred language was Punjabi. Thus, when Dr. PC Chatterjee, vice-chancellor of Punjab University, suggested in a convocation speech in 1908 that Punjabi be used instead of Urdu as a medium of instruction in the province, the *Paisā Axbār*—which had gradually established itself as the voice of the Muslim ruling class in Punjab—mounted an opposition campaign, publishing articles and editorials slamming this suggestion.[21] The statements of the authors of these editorials and articles echoed those of the British civil servants quoted by Ayesha Jalal. They argued that Punjabi did not deserve to be used as a medium of instruction, even at the primary level, because it was a mere dialect/patois, whereas Urdu was a fully fledged language: "Urdu and Punjabi come from the same source, their constituent parts are much the same, but one has progressed and become a sophisticated and civilized language while the other has remained a mere dialect (*meḥẓ bolī*)."[22] A *Paisā Axbār* editorialist, after listing Punjabi's weaknesses and limitations, went so far as to compare it to the babbling of toddlers and the "grunts" of those who were deaf or mute:

> Punjabi, at the time when the lights of knowledge are spreading, and the printing press and culture are advancing, is so limited that its literature consists of nothing else than a few versified love stories. And no scholarly essay can be written or even translated into this language. Previously Punjabi did not even have these few love stories, and it was already—it still is now—a tool for expressing basic needs. Punjabi is from its beginnings just a basic form of speech and a simple means of communication like that of children or mute people who convey a meaning by gesturing or grunting.[23]

Another *Paisā Axbār* editorialist argued that Punjabi was unfit to become a medium of instruction because it had no standard variety. He argued that Punjabi was basically a dialect continuum, and dialects that change every few miles are not mutually intelligible. "Punjabi—a dialect which varies in each district and which, because of its poverty is unable to express scientific ideas, how can it become a medium of instruction in schools? And then there are such variations from one district to another that an inhabitant of a certain district cannot even understand an inhabitant of another."[24] This controversy also had a political dimension. According to Tariq Rahman, many of the *Paisā Axbār* editorialists believed that "the promotion of Punjabi was a conspiracy to weaken Urdu and, by implication, Muslims."[25] *Urdu*, *Muslim*, and *Islam* were already, for members of the Muslim ruling class of Punjab, synonymous.

MOVEMENTS TO DEFEND AND PROMOTE PUNJABI

THE SIKHS' MOVEMENT

Punjabi was rejected by the Muslim elites of the province and ignored by its Hindu community, whose representatives and leaders had been focusing since 1882 on the promotion of Hindi, demanding its introduction into the provincial education system (their movement was successful, as Hindi was included in 1917 in the provincial primary school curriculum).[26] As a result, it was mainly Sikh intellectuals who defended and promoted Punjabi, through a newly founded organization, the *Singh Sabhā* (Society of Singhs), which established a branch in Amritsar in 1873 and another in Lahore in 1879.[27] The *Singh Sabhā* lobbied—unsuccessfully—to make Punjabi in *Gurumukhi* the medium of instruction in primary schools for Sikh children.[28] They also promoted journalism in Punjabi (in *Gurumukhi*), launching newspapers in Lahore and Amritsar, including *Xalsā Axbār*, *Xalsā Gazette*, *Singh Sabhā Gazette*, and *Xalsā Samācār*.[29] The *Singh Sabhā* gave an impetus not only to Punjabi journalism but also to modern Punjabi literature in *Gurumukhi*. It was in the *Xalsā Samācār* that Bhai Vir Singh, the founder of Punjabi modern novel, published in serialized form three historical novels: *Sundarī* (1898), *Bijay Singh* (1899), and *Satwant Kaur* (1900).[30] Soon a new generation of writers emerged, who, under the influence of modern Indian authors (Premchand and the Bengali realists) as well as

Russian authors (Chekhov, Gorky), produced a new type of fiction, no longer historical but realistic, depicting contemporary Punjabi society. The novelist Nanak Singh (whose novel *Ciṭṭā lahū*—The White Blood—was published in 1932) as well as short story writers Charan Singh Shahid (whose collection *Hāsde hāṁjhū*—Tears of Laughter—was published in 1933) and Sant Singh Sekhon (whose collection *Samācār*—The News—was published in 1943) belong to this generation.[31] This inclination toward realism became part of a sociopolitical agenda in the mid-1930s after the foundation of the All India Progressive Writers' Association, whose Marxist ideas influenced writers such as Kartar Singh Duggal and Prof. Mohan Singh.[32]

Modern Punjabi poetry emerged in the 1920s. Puran Singh's 1923 collection *Khule maidān* (The Open Meadows) and Bhai Vir Singh's 1927 collection *Bijlyāṃ de hār* (Thunderbolt Necklaces) included the very first specimens of modern poems in Punjabi.[33] Prof. Mohan Singh and Amrita Pritam (whose collections *Sāve pattar*—The Green Leaves—and *Amrit lehrāṃ*—The Waves of Nectar—were both published in 1936) followed in their footsteps, establishing themselves as the two most important proponents of modern Punjabi poetry of their generation.[34] Some modern poets, such as Darshan Singh Awara (whose book *Bijlī dī kaṛak*—Thunderbolt—published in 1923 was considered seditious and subsequently banned by the British authorities), devoted themselves to producing political poetry, glorifying the Indian freedom struggle.[35] Literary journals like Gyani Hira Singh Dard's *Phulvāṛī* (founded in 1925), Charan Singh Shahid's *Maujī* (founded in 1926), and Gurbaksh Singh's *Prītlaṛī* (founded in 1933) played an important role in the emergence of modern Punjabi literature, publishing texts by contemporary writers.[36]

Sikh intellectuals undoubtedly realized that Punjabi's place in the very rigid colonial administrative and educational system was to remain limited. Therefore, they decided to focus on an area in which the colonial power would not be able to interfere: literature. They strove to promote the Punjabi language and to give it legitimacy by developing its literature, modernizing the Punjabi literary subfield, which until the end of the nineteenth century had been dominated by tradition and didacticism.

INITIATIVES BY MUSLIMS AND CHRISTIANS

Some Muslim and Christian writers—who wrote Punjabi in Persian script (*Shahmukhi*)—took up the task of modernizing Punjabi literature in the beginning of the twentieth century. The pioneers of this movement were the poets Maula Bakhsh Kushta (1876–1955), whose *Dīwān* (collection of *ġazals*) was published in 1903 in Amritsar, and Sir Shahabuddin (1865–1949), whose first poem (*naẕm*) *Ābādkārāṃ de hāṛe* (Supplications of the New Cultivators) was published in 1907.[37] Khwaja Ghulam Farid (1845–1901) and Mian Muhammed Bakhsh (1830–1907)—the last great representatives of the tradition of Sufi poetry started by Baba Farid in the thirteenth century—were still alive at the turn of the century, but instead of carrying on the Sufi tradition, Kushta and Shahabuddin chose to turn away from the genres and contents that characterized it. Instead, they adopted genres popular in Urdu literature of the time, such as the *ġazal* and the *naẕm* (long poem on patriotic, social, or pan-Islamic themes popularized by Altaf Husain Hali and Allama Iqbal), thus bridging the gap between Punjabi poetry and modern Urdu poetry. This new legacy was carried forward by Peer Fazal Gujrati (1897–1972), who devoted himself to Punjabi *ġazal* in the early 1920s, and Faqeer Mohammad Faqeer (1900–1974), who composed poems in the vein of Sir Shahabuddin and published his first collection *Ṣadā-e Faqīr* (Faqeer's Call) in 1924.[38]

In the 1920s, a group of popular poets was formed in Lahore: the *baitbāz* (verse improvisers).[39] This group included Firoz Din Sharaf (1901–1955), Ustad Hamdam (1877–1954), Ustad Ishq Lehr (1869–1948), and Ustad Daman (1907–1984). These *baitbāz* came from a modest background and were poorly educated (Ustad Ishq Lehr was even illiterate).[40] They met in the city's numerous parks and engaged in improvisation contests.[41] Their poetry was primarily oral, and was not published.

Muslim and Christian writers' efforts to modernize Punjabi literature were not confined to poetry. Miran Bakhsh Minhas (1884–1957) and the Christian writer Joshua Fazal Din (1903–1976) produced modern Punjabi fiction in *Shahmukhi*. In the 1920s and 1930s, Miran Bakhsh Minhas published eleven short novels, of which *Jaṭṭ dī kartūt* (The Misdeed of the Farmer) is the most famous. This novel, published in 1929, is often considered the first modern story written in Punjabi by a Muslim author. It carries a rather clear reformist message, warning readers against backward traditions, extravagant expenses occasioned by marriages, accumulation of debt to Hindu moneylenders, and the like.[42] Joshua Fazal Din also produced some reformist fiction in Punjabi, but added to it a sentimental/romantic dimension reminiscent of the Urdu fiction popular at the time. He published two collections of short stories—*Adabī afsāne* (Literary Stories, 1933) and *Axlāqī kahānyāṃ*

(Moralist Stories, 1935)—as well as two short novels: *Muṇḍe dā mull* (The Price of the Boy, 1938) and *Prabhā* (1945).[43]

In order to promote and circulate this modern Punjabi literature, Joshua Fazal Din and another Christian writer, Bhola Nath Waris (1867–1936), launched two Punjabi literary journals in *Shahmukhi*: *Panjābī Darbār* and *Sārang*. Joshua Fazal Din's *Panjābī Darbār*, published between 1928 and 1935, was apolitical and intercommunal: Muslims contributed to it (Sir Shahabuddin, Qazi Fazl-e Haq, Miran Bakhsh Minhas, Maula Bakhsh Kushta, Firoz Din Sharaf, Abdul Majeed Salik), as well as Sikhs (Teja Singh, Bhai Sher Singh, Bawa Budh Singh, Prof. Mohan Singh), Hindus (I. C. Nanda, Dhani Ram Chatrik, Banarsi Das Jain), and Christians (Bhola Nath Waris, Rehmat Masih, and Joshua Fazal Din himself).[44] Apart from poems, fiction, and dramas, *Panjābī Darbār* featured essays. The ambition to enrich Punjabi and make it a scientific language is testified to by the wide range of subjects and disciplines covered by these essays: logic, medicine, pedagogy, history, and of course Punjabi language and literature.[45] Qazi Fazl-e Haq (1889–1939), a renowned professor at Lahore's Oriental College and committed Punjabi activist, published in *Panjābī Darbār* forty-six biographical and critical essays discussing classical authors such as Maulvi Ghulam Rasool Alampuri, Hafiz Barkhurdar, and Peelu.[46]

Bhola Nath Waris's journal *Sārang*, published between 1930 and 1936, presented content that was similar to that of *Panjābī Darbār*, featuring poems, fiction, dramas, and essays by writers who were also contributing on a regular basis to Joshua Fazal Din's journal (Qazi Fazl-e Haq published several articles in *Sārang*).[47]

Sārang and *Panjābī Darbār* both published some essays in which authors presented suggestions regarding Punjabi's corpus planning or status planning. The most notable of these essays is Miran Bakhsh Minhas's *Panjābī nūṃ vādhā kiveṃ hove?* (How to Develop Punjabi?), published in *Panjābī Darbār* in November 1928. It is an important document because it shows that not only Sikh activists but also some Muslim activists advocated for Punjabi to be used in the public sphere, at school, and in administration. Many of Minhas's suggestions anticipate those made in the 1950s by members of the conservative Punjabi movement, such as Faqeer Mohammad Faqeer, Sardar Khan, and Mohammad Baqir.

Minhas starts his essay by emphasizing the need to standardize Punjabi, arguing that one of its dialects should be selected to become the foundation of standard Punjabi; otherwise the language would remain forever divided into geographical and religious varieties:

> In Punjab the dialects of Pothohar, of the Dhani-speaking Gujjars, of the Dogras, of the Jatts, of the Thal desert, of Malwa and of Doaba are different and the language of the towns is different from that of the villages. On the other hand, the Punjabi spoken in the homes of Sikhs and the Punjabi spoken in Muslim homes differ. Now we will have to choose from all these types of Punjabi a dialect that will serve as a common language.[48]

On which dialect should this standard Punjabi be based? Miran Bakhsh Minhas suggests it should be the dialect spoken between Lahore and Gujrat, because this area is the geographical and cultural heart of Punjab (Punjab's greatest Sufi poets, including Waris Shah, were born in this region). "We should consider as the norm the language spoken between Lahore and Gujrat, and Sialkot and Lyallpur by educated and literate people, taking into account above all the one spoken by Muslims."[49] Minhas thus proposes adopting the Muslim variety of this dialect (a variety full of Arabic and Persian words), because Muslims represent the majority of the population of Punjab. He also argues that Punjabi's standard script should be the *Shahmukhi* script:

> We propose that Punjabi be read and written in Persian characters so that it is easier for a school child to learn Urdu, Persian and Arabic. We will thus kill two birds with one stone: as a result, Muslims will not turn away from Punjabi, and on the other hand, we can benefit from the gems offered by Urdu and Persian and make precious necklaces out of them. It is unrealistic to say that Punjabi cannot be written in the Urdu alphabet when thousands of books written by Muslims as well as the stories and epics which people read with passion are written in the Persian alphabet.[50]

After discussing Punjabi's corpus planning, Minhas discusses its status planning. He suggests that Punjabi be used as a medium of instruction in schools: "Girls should receive their education in Punjabi. and it would be appreciated if the boys also receive it in this language for the first three years of school."[51] It should also be taught in colleges, alongside Urdu, English, and Persian: "Punjabi must have in colleges a place comparable to that of other languages."[52] He further proposes that Punjabi be partially used in the administrative field. Individuals should be allowed to write applications in Punjabi: "The government must be prepared to receive applications written in Punjabi in Persian characters."[53]

Minhas's suggestions in terms of corpus planning are quite radical: that all communities living in Punjab, regardless of their religion or geographic location, should write their mother tongue in the *Shahmukhi* script and that the Muslim dialect of Central Punjab should be the basis of standard Punjabi. His suggestions in terms of status planning aim less at "developing" Punjabi than at reconnecting the Muslim community with a language it has neglected for a long time in favor of Urdu, thus giving it a privileged place in the linguistic market, a place adapted to the profile, needs, and identity of this community. It is not known to what extent these suggestions were debated among Punjabi activists, but some of them (such as the adoption of the Lahore-Gujrat dialect as a standard dialect, the adoption of the Urdu alphabet, the use of Punjabi as a medium of instruction in schools, and the teaching of Punjabi in colleges) were included in conservative Punjabi activists' program in the 1950s (discussed in chapter 5).

THE CONTRIBUTION OF PHILOLOGISTS

Without actively campaigning for Punjabi to be used for education or in the administrative field, some European philologists—who were personally convinced of the importance and value of this language—began at the beginning of the nineteenth century to translate texts from/into Punjabi, to compile dictionaries and grammars of Punjabi, to analyze its dialect continuum, and to study its history and its links with neighboring languages. Their work, even if it did not change the perception of Punjabi in the colonial society of the province, nevertheless provided arguments for the defenders of Punjabi, because it highlighted the richness, complexity, importance, and archaic origins of a language that its opponents considered a mere "patois" and likened to the "grunts" of the deaf and mutes.

The first European philologist to take an interest in Punjabi was William Carey (1761–1834), a missionary who settled in Serampore (West Bengal) in 1800. He published partial translations of the Bible in Punjabi (in the *Gurumukhi* script) between 1811 and 1826, as well as a grammar of Punjabi in 1812.[54] Carey died in 1834, but his legacy was carried on by missionaries of the American Presbyterian Mission, which had established a center in

Ludhiana in 1836. They published a large number of Punjabi translations of biblical works in *Gurumukhi* or *Shahmukhi* script and wrote grammars and dictionaries to teach Punjabi to newly arrived civil servants and missionaries. John Newton published a grammar of the Punjabi language in 1851 and a dictionary in 1854. This work was continued in the twentieth century by another missionary, Reverend Grahame Bailey, who published *A Brief Grammar of Panjabi as Spoken in the Wazirabad District* in 1904 and a *Panjabi Manual and Grammar* (written in collaboration with Thomas F. Cummings) in 1912.[55] The contribution of army officers is also worth mentioning. Captain Starkey published in 1849 a dictionary and grammar of Punjabi (written with the collaboration of Basawa Singh), and Richard Carnac Temple published between 1884 and 1900 *The Legends of the Punjab* in three volumes, which included a total of fifty-nine stories. Temple hired local bards (*mirāśī*) to sing these stories and subsequently transcribed and translated them.

Besides missionaries and army officers, two philologists, G. Grierson (1851–1941) and Hafiz Mehmood Shirani (1880–1946), did groundbreaking work in the field of Punjabi philology. Grierson published an eleven-volume *Linguistic Survey of India* between 1898 and 1928; the eighth and ninth volumes analyze the linguistic situation of the Punjabi-speaking regions.[56] He divided Punjab into two linguistic areas, identifying the area extending to the east as the Punjabi-speaking area and the area extending to the west as the Lahnda-speaking area, which he further divided into northern Lahnda (which includes Hindko and Pothohari) and southern Lahnda (which includes Siraiki and its dialects). Grierson argued that Lahnda was a language distinct from Punjabi. His analysis was criticized by several linguists but nevertheless remained popular for decades among Punjabi activists and scholars.[57]

Panjāb meṃ Urdu (Urdu in Punjab), a book in Urdu by Hafiz Mehmood Shirani (professor at the Oriental College of Lahore), was published in 1928 and was widely discussed in intellectual circles.[58] Shirani contended that Punjabi and Urdu share much of their core vocabulary, pointing out the presence of Punjabi words in Old Urdu, in Dakhini, as well as in modern Urdu expressions.[59] From these examples, Shirani concluded that Urdu is a developed form of Punjabi. He thus argued that Urdu was born in Punjab after it was conquered by the Ghaznavids in the late tenth century and that the Muslims brought this language to Delhi when they seized the city in 1193. This theory gained a lot of popularity among scholars in Punjab, both among those who supported Urdu (enabling them to argue that Urdu is not a foreign language in Punjab, imposed from outside) and among those who promoted Punjabi (enabling them to assert the anteriority and therefore the "seniority" of Punjabi over Urdu).

The Linguistic Situation in Punjab After 1947

The Official Urduization of Punjab

Urdu was already a well-established language in the Punjab province, but after independence it gained so much popularity in Pakistani Punjab that soon Lahore became a center of Urdu, surpassing Karachi in terms of institutions and organizations promoting Urdu and of journals and newspapers in Urdu.[60] On January 5, 1948, the authorities of Pakistani Punjab took their first step toward making Urdu the official language of the province in place of English. On that day, the Regional Legislative Assembly decided to use Urdu instead of English as the language of the proceedings (deputies would be authorized to speak in English only by special permission). Minister of Education Sheikh Karamat Ali promised during this session: "The medium of instruction in all public educational institutions and colleges will be Urdu. And the government will even try to ensure that Urdu becomes the language of the administrations."[61]

The field in which the replacement of English by Urdu was considered the most urgent was education, where it was considered the first concrete step toward decolonization. Deputy Raja Syed Akbar declared during the January 6, 1948 session of the Regional Legislative Assembly: "Our educational system is a legacy of the British authorities, and as you know Lord Macaulay said when imposing the English educational system here that his aim was to make these slave people Indian by look but totally English intellectually."[62]

To facilitate the replacement of English by Urdu, the government of Pakistani Punjab took the following steps:

1. Creation in October 1948 of an Urdu department at Punjab University (headed by Dr. Syed Abdullah, Dr. Ibadat Barelvi, and Waqar Azeem), responsible for training teachers capable of teaching and promoting Urdu, as well as some experts in translation and terminology. An MA Urdu degree was introduced the same year.[63]

2. Creation of a *Majlis-e Zubān-e Daftarī* (Administration Language Committee) in December 1949. This *Majlis* tackled the herculean task of translating into Urdu all the English terms and all the English forms used until then in government offices. By 1951, it had translated two thousand forms and by 1955, 19,165 terms. These terms were included in specialized glossaries that were distributed to all government offices. (The *Majlis-e Zubān-e Daftarī* translated a total of 35,000 terms between 1949 and 1976.)[64]
3. Creation of a *Majlis-e Tarjuma* (Translation Committee) in May 1950, with an initial budget of 100,000 rupees. Its aim was the translation into Urdu of scientific books to be used in schools and universities.[65]

Subsequently, the Punjab government ordered, by decree, the use of Urdu instead of English in all administrations. A government circular issued on August 10, 1950 stipulated that all district government offices should submit their reports only in Urdu. In February 1951, a second circular stipulated that they should use Urdu in all their official correspondence. On July 14, 1951, a third circular stipulated that the forms translated by the *Majlis-e Zubān-e Daftarī* should be used in all government offices. On February 29, 1952, the chief minister of Punjab, Mian Mumtaz Daultana, announced to the Provincial Assembly that Urdu would be the working language of all courts (including the Supreme Court).[66]

The use of Urdu increased in Punjab's government offices, but government circulars were not implemented everywhere. The highest officials of the province, posted at the Punjab Secretariat, ignored all circulars regarding Urdu and continued to use English in their reports and correspondence. Hamid Nizami explained why in an article published in November 1951: "The question of using Urdu in government offices has recently arisen. The government has decided that Urdu will be the language of the administrations. But this decision has not been followed, because the senior officials do not know how to write Urdu at all. As long as they can, they will stick to English."[67]

The Urdu Movement in Punjab

In order to take adequate steps ensuring the switch from English to Urdu, the Punjab government decided to seek advice from some experts and activists, organizing between March 26 and 28, 1948, the first Urdu Conference ever held in Pakistan. The venue of this conference was Punjab University in Lahore; participants included political personalities such as Abdur Rabb Nishtar and Zafar Ali Khan, education experts such as M. D. Taseer, and Urdu activists such as Sir Sheikh Abdul Qadir, Maulvi Abdul Haq, and Maulana Salahuddin Ahmad. This conference coincided with the visit of Muhammad Ali Jinnah to Dhaka, during which he made a historic speech in favor of Urdu as the national language of Pakistan.[68] During his inaugural speech on March 26, 1948, Dr. Umar Hayat, vice-chancellor of Punjab University, addressed the participants and introduced the purpose of the conference: "You are all experts in Urdu language and literature, and we have brought you together because our university would like to know what means we must use to make Urdu a medium of instruction, to transfer to this language all the treasures of the sciences and the arts, and also to make it a truly international language."[69] Since the Urdu/Bengali controversy was raging in East Bengal and demands were being made to grant Bengali the status of national language (*Qaumī zubān*), Maulvi Abdul Haq started his speech with a statement in favor of Urdu, explaining why "provincial and local" languages (including Bengali) should be sacrificed in its favor. In his speech, he declared that all vernacular languages of Pakistan were "undeveloped" when compared to Urdu:

> Provincial and local languages (*Ṣūbā'ī aur maqāmī zubāne<u>n</u>*) have neither the popularity nor the breadth of a language like Urdu, and if we favored provincial and local languages over Urdu, people would be deprived of the sophistication, open-mindedness, and national conscience which are the prerogatives of Urdu speakers. Thanks to its varied qualities, Urdu has made astonishing progress. No provincial language (*Ṣūbā'ī zubān*) possesses such an abundance of books on religion, history, literature and other sciences and arts. For this reason, we should completely accept the superiority of Urdu over the provincial languages.[70]

Then he presented his own definition of a national language and explained why only Urdu could fulfil this role: "A local language (*Maqāmī bolī*) is only the language of a specific place (*Maqām*). A National Language (*Qaumī zubān*) is the language of an entire Nation (*Qaum*). It gives the opportunity to each individual to be heard by the Nation. It reflects the peculiarities and traditions of this Nation. A National Language is what keeps the Nation together and prevents it from falling apart."[71] He added: "Nowadays to support Urdu is to support the Nation, the progress of Urdu is the progress of the Nation, and the existence of Urdu is the existence of the Nation."[72] Urdu was placed at the center of a language ideology that merged language and nation. Challenging the higher place of Urdu would thus be considered an attack on the nation.

In his speech, M. D. Taseer presented another argument to justify why Urdu (and not Bengali) should become Pakistan's national language. He argued that Urdu should become the country's national language because it is entirely Islamic: "Of all the languages of the world, only Urdu is born from Islam. Arabic existed before the advent of Islam. But Urdu developed and flourished only after Islam spread here. It is for this reason that it would not be incorrect to say that it is an Islamic language."[73]

It was during this conference that a specific aspect of the language ideology of the supporters of Urdu in Punjab emerged: Pakistani Punjab was designated as a shelter for Urdu, a language threatened in India after the mass migration of Muslims and the adoption of Hindi. This idea had been first presented by Dr. Umar Hayat during his inaugural speech: "We should not forget that Urdu spent most of his life in Punjab, and in these times when the existence of Urdu is threatened in different parts of India it seems to us that it will only have hope for a future in Punjab."[74] The allusion to the theory of Hafiz Mehmood Shirani, according to which Urdu was born in Punjab, is notable. Urdu supporters would continue using it to prove that Urdu was not an alien language but a vernacular of Punjab that had relocated outside the province and the Urdu-speaking migrants from India were bringing back home. Maulvi Abdul Haq—who had himself recently migrated from Delhi—requested hospitality in Pakistan for Urdu, a language he compared to a refugee expelled from his country:

> Gentlemen! Hundreds of thousands of refugees have come to your country. People of all classes, of all status and of all ages. You have warmly welcomed them, you have dried their tears, you have commiserated with them, you have given homes to those who did not have any, and food to those who were hungry. Another refugee, very honorable and respectable has joined these unfortunate ones, it is our National Language. It is as miserable as these refugees; it was exiled from its country. And it came to seek refuge at your home. Respect and appreciate it! It will do many things for you; it will render many services to you. It will destroy Sectarianism, Regionalism, and jealousy, it will extinguish the fire of

> discord, bring hearts together and turn the People of Pakistan one entity, with one heart and one body.[75]

In Maulvi Abdul Haq's opinion, of all the provinces of Pakistan, Punjab was the most likely to become the new sanctuary of Urdu: "The province of Punjab has always been at the forefront in terms of the spread and popularization of Urdu, and I hope that, like the hundreds of thousands of refugees who have had the opportunity to settle in this province, this refugee language will receive there the treatment which is due to it."[76] He reckoned that the resettlement of Urdu in Punjab would result in the long-term replacement of Punjabi with Urdu. To those who were likely to object to this, Maulvi Abdul Haq replied:

> Those who say that the language of the Punjabi people is not Urdu are not entirely wrong. But I would ask them: before the arrival of the Arabs was Arabic the language of the inhabitants of Egypt? Did the people of Iraq, Syria, Morocco, and North Africa speak Arabic before that? Now the mother tongue of the inhabitants of all these countries is Arabic. In the same way, a day will come when the language of the people of Punjab will be Urdu, yes, it will really be the case! Myself and many of us will not be there to see this day. But the generations that will follow us will prove by their actions that I was right![77]

According to Maulvi Abdul Haq, the replacement of Punjabi by Urdu would be a natural development. It was an inevitable part of a process of "linguistic conversion" (from a "non-Islamic" to an "Islamic" language), similar to Arabic replacing the vernacular languages in the regions that were conquered by the Arabs.

As soon as the Urdu Conference ended, Maulvi Abdul Haq headed toward Karachi, where he got involved in various activities tied to the promotion of Urdu in the capital (the establishment of an Urdu college, the reorganization of *Anjuman-e Taraqqī-e Urdu*, and the launch of *Urdu* journal, among others). It was mainly Maulana Salahuddin Ahmad, an intellectual from Lahore, who led the Urdu movement in Punjab. In 1946 Maulana Salahuddin Ahmad had launched the *Urdu Bolo Teḥrīk* ("Speak Urdu!" movement) through his journal *Adabī Dunyā* in reaction to the activities of local pro-Hindi organizations and in opposition to the growing use of English in administration and in public life.[78] In his *Adabī Dunyā* editorials, time and again he urged his readers to use Urdu (instead of their own vernacular) in daily interactions, in order to make the language more prominent. He also urged parents to speak Urdu to their children, to facilitate their education (in government schools, where the majority of the children of the province studied, the primary medium of instruction was Urdu): "If a child's language of instruction is also the language that he speaks daily, he will progress much faster than the child who receives instruction in a language other than his own."[79]

Maulana Salahuddin Ahmad focused his efforts on Punjab because it was in this province that he encountered the greatest number of people willing to give up their own vernacular and switch to Urdu: "The 'Speak Urdu!' movement has flourished in places where one could not even imagine that it would meet with any success. And now the sweet words of Urdu resonate in the remote rural areas of Mianwali and Shahpur, as well as in the small backward cities of the regions of Rawalpindi and Multan."[80] The creation of Pakistan in 1947 and the adoption of Urdu by the provincial and central governments in the months following independence seemed to lead directly to the fulfilment of his dream. But the situation had changed: English and Hindi no longer presented a threat to Urdu. Rather, threats were now posed by vernaculars like Bengali and Sindhi, whose activists were determined to gain official status for them. Maulana Salahuddin Ahmad castigated those who defended and promoted these vernaculars: "As soon as our national language tries to replace English our old regionalist and tribal feelings awaken and we bring our local languages into the arena to fight against the National Language. We are ready to be reduced to slavery by foreigners but we do not accept to be guided by people of our own breed."[81] He summarized the language ideology of the new Urdu movement a few months after the Urdu Conference in his essay *Taqsīm-e mulk kā aṡar urdu zubān aur adab par* (The Impact of Partition on the Urdu Language and Literature). In this essay, he repeated some of the ideas he had formulated earlier during the *Urdu Bolo Teḥrīk* and developed further some of the ideas expressed by Maulvi Abdul Haq in his conference speech, including the idea that Punjab was going to be a new sanctuary for Urdu. Ahmad read this essay at the annual meeting of the *Ḥalqa-e Arbāb-e Żauq* in Lahore and published it in December 1948 in his journal, *Adabī Dunyā*, and it soon became a manifesto for the Punjabi supporters of Urdu.[82] For historian K. K. Aziz, this essay showed "how cowardly and calmly the Punjabi literati and intelligentsia submitted to the strictures of the Urdas against the Punjabi language."[83]

Maulana Salahuddin Ahmad begins his essay by stating bitterly that Urdu has no future in India, where Hindi is being promoted by the central government. He continues with an emotional plea similar to the one by Maulvi Abdul Haq a few months earlier during the Urdu Conference.

> There is no longer any space for Urdu in India. The city of Delhi has been destroyed, Lucknow is rapidly changing, Hyderabad has only a few days left to live. Urdu has not found even after an intense search any place where it could take shelter. It was born in Punjab, grew up in Delhi, spent its youth in Lucknow, was widowed there, and now is back to its parents' house. Has it lost its spouse? Is its heart broken? Let's see how the inhabitants of its parental home will treat it. Their traditions are not that bad. They are known for their hospitality. They say they have huge hearts, so let's see how they will accept this unhappy girl.[84]

He then states the reasons why Punjab is an ideal sanctuary for Urdu. First, its main competitor, Punjabi, has stopped being promoted since the exodus of the Sikhs and of the British (whose government was backing them). Their departure has thus cleared the way for Urdu:

> The future of Urdu in Western Punjab is not so bad. Punjabi ceased to be taught after the departure of Sikhs. . . . The previous regime considered the diploma of *Gyānī* of Punjabi equivalent to the diploma of *Urdu Fāẓil*,[85] and Punjabi, this language of which all the literature would only fill a cupboard, competed with Urdu and was quite successful. The ignorance and indifference of our leaders had a lot to do with it and would have continued to perpetuate this situation. But our independence has solved this problem and we are grateful to it.[86]

Second, Punjab is devoid of the strong regional and ethnic sentiments that prevail in NWFP and Sindh, which do not allow Urdu to take roots in these provinces: "In my humble opinion, NWFP will not be able to implement programs like those that we are setting up here to promote Urdu. Local and racial prejudices in NWFP will prevent it from giving to Urdu the place of Pashto, and it will be more or less the same story in Sindh. Whatever Maulvi Abdul Haq may say, it is almost impossible for the tree of Urdu to produce fruits when planted in the sands of Sindh or in the arid soil of NWFP." Third, the arrival of Urdu-speaking migrants will greatly facilitate the spread of Urdu in Punjab. Urdu will soon become a vernacular language, and Punjabi children, who used to hear Urdu only at school, will now hear it in the streets and houses of their villages, thanks to the presence of these native speakers, and will absorb it:

> You have guessed by listening to my statements that in my humble opinion the future homeland of Urdu will be Western Punjab and that Lahore will be its center. The exodus of Muslims from India provides us daily with thousands of Urdu speakers who are spreading in all corners of the province. It has been two years since I launched the *Urdu Bolo Teḥrīk*. I was extremely surprised when I received oaths of allegiance to Urdu from remote rural areas of Punjab and thought it was certainly the result of some divine intervention.
>
> Now this dream has come true: if Allah continues to support this exodus, then in just a few days we will begin to hear pure *Kārxāndarī* Urdu in Dera Ghazi Khan's countryside.[87]
>
> Earlier on, children would study Urdu at school, but as soon as they would come home they would forget everything and start speaking their Punjabi again, and it is clear that despite the considerable time they spent writing and reading Urdu, the language did not enter their veins, and they did not adopt it in the truest sense of the word. But the situation has just taken a revolutionary turn. The Muslims of Karnal have just entered the 16 districts of Western Punjab, and besides them 500,000 Muslims from Delhi have also arrived (and each week a new group of 5,000 or 6,000 people is arriving from UP). It is not certain that food will remain available in large quantities in Punjab, but Urdu will certainly be available in large quantities.[88]

The replacement of Punjabi by Urdu, to which Maulvi Abdul Haq had alluded in his conference speech, describing it as a slow process whose outcome people of his generation would probably not see, Maulana Salahuddin Ahmad expected to occur in the very near future.

Punjabi's Place and Its Perception in Pakistani Punjab

Partition led to a radical change in the religious composition of Lahore's population, as it led to the exodus of the Hindu and Sikh communities that had constituted 30 percent and 5 percent, respectively, of the total population of the city (429,747 inhabitants) in 1931.[89] Among them was a huge number of Punjabi writers belonging to these two communities: the poets Amrita Pritam, Prof. Mohan Singh, Pritam Singh Safir, Prabhjot Kaur, and Mohan Singh Mahir; the playwrights I. C. Nanda, Balwant Gargi, and G. S. Khosla; the fiction writer Kartar Singh Duggal; and the folklorist Devendra Satyarthi. After their departure, several Punjabi journals in *Gurumukhi*, including Mohan Singh Mahir's *Panjdaryā* and Pritam Singh Safir's *Prītam*, ceased publication. Punjabi in *Gurumukhi* had been taught until 1947 in schools and colleges run by Sikhs, such as the Sardar Bahadur Bhagat Singh Khalsa High School and the Sikh National College (founded in 1938), as well as Oriental College (since 1877). After the Sikh exodus, Punjabi was not taught anywhere: the Sardar Bahadur Bhagat Singh Khalsa High School became Islamia High School, the Sikh National College became Maclagan Engineering College, and the Oriental College's Punjabi department closed down.[90] While all signs of the former presence of Hindus and Sikhs were being erased, books and journals in Hindi and Punjabi (in *Gurumukhi* script) also disappeared from private homes and libraries. They were sold to ragpickers, thrown into the streets, or burned. Raja Risalu, who witnessed these scenes, wrote:

> After the creation of Pakistan, all the knowledge which had materialized in the form of journals, newspapers and books ended up on the footpaths. People with high taste sifted through the houses of the Hindus and Sikhs who had left Lahore and took everything that was of use to them . . . If they found books or journals in a house, they sold them to the ragpickers as trash, and this way books and journals ended up on the footpaths. The libraries of the schools and colleges of Sikhs and Hindus were indiscriminately looted and their books too ended up on the footpaths. The Sanatan Dharma School library was emptied, and a mountain of books was sold to the ragpickers, and many of them were thrown into the street and burnt.[91]

Many people in Pakistani Punjab believed that the Punjabi language was a vestige of the Sikh presence and no longer had any reason to survive. Ain ul-Haq Faridkoti, wrote: "In August 1947, when the sun of independence rose, the people of Pakistan started a new journey and tried to progress in all areas of life, but it was Punjabi language's ill-luck that whenever someone would talk about promoting it his suggestion would be dismissed and he would be told: 'Let it be, Punjabi is just the language of the Sikhs!' "[92] Rashid Jebi wrote: "When the largest Muslim country on the planet—Pakistan—appeared on the world map nobody was giving a damn about Punjabi. Everyone would call it a coarse and wild language . . . Some people would even say that Punjabi was merely the language of the Sikhs, and the Sikhs have moved to India."[93] Prejudices against Punjabi were common not only among the Punjabi Muslims, who had always wanted to distinguish themselves linguistically from the Sikhs, but also among the Urdu-speaking *Mohajirs* who had newly migrated to Punjab. *Mohajirs* settled in Punjab were imbued with a cultural arrogance similar to that of the Karachi *Mohajirs* (described by Tariq Rahman as well as Rashid Abbas and Farida Shahid), who were proud of having as their mother tongue a prestigious language that was also the national language of the country.[94] A student, Qamar uz-Zaman, gave a few examples of this cultural arrogance in a letter published in 1952 in *Monthly Panjābī*: "Our brothers who have come from UP suddenly ask us: 'Is Punjabi a language? One cannot consider a language something which is neither written nor read.' And they add that only two or three old books have been written in Punjabi, and no Punjabi journal is published."[95] As a result, most *Mohajirs* refused to learn Punjabi, which they considered an inferior language. The poet Noor Bijnauri, himself a *Mohajir*, criticized this attitude in a letter published in *Daily Imroz* on October 6, 1951:

> I felt very sad when I saw that among our non-Punjabi poets and writers at least 90% don't even try to understand Punjabi. It is really a pity if an individual cannot understand or speak well the language of the place where he lives. When one carefully looks at them, one can see narrow-mindedness and ignorance. I therefore address all writers and poets who have come from UP and ask them to get acquainted as much as possible with the Punjabi language. This way we will get closer culturally and a number of issues will be resolved.[96]

Triglossia in Pakistani Punjab

An English/Urdu/Punjabi triglossia developed soon after Punjab was annexed by the British and continued to prevail in Pakistani Punjab after independence. English remained the "high" language, the one that gave access to higher education, to the senior civil service, to the judiciary, and to the army schools for officers. It continued to be taught in prestigious schools based on the British model. Urdu remained the language of primary and secondary education, of lower administrations and lower courts. Urdu's prestige, due to its introduction in the university and its use in the Provincial Assembly, had increased, but it was not the main tool for high social mobility. Punjabi remained the "low" language. It was used neither in school nor in the administration and was not endowed with any symbolic value.

Cartoonist Anwar Ali's short story "*Wāriṡ Šāh dī zubān kauṇ samjhe?*" (Who Would Understand Waris Shah's Language?) is a lively illustration of Pakistani Punjab's triglossic situation after independence.[97] This story presents the inner monologue of an English-speaking Punjabi civil servant, proud of his proficiency, who never hesitates to display it in order to impress his interlocutors and get priority over everyone, such as at the post office:

> *Maiṃ paṛhyā likhyā angrezī na bolāṃ te lokāṃ te rʿob kiveṃ pove? Aih hor gall ai pa'ī baṛe baṛe velyāṃ ais firangī dī zubān ne maiṃnūṃ dhokhā dittā ai . . . Āxir maiṃ bhī lokāṃ te rʿob pāṇā hoyā nān? Phīr aih bhī gall ai pa'ī bohutī vārī rʿob pai bhī jāndā ai. Ḍāk-xāne dī tākī te jadoṃ maiṃ bābū nūṃ akhdā āṃ* "Two mini order forms, six acknowledgment letters" *te bābū sab nūṃ chaḍke merā kamm pehle kardā. Maiṃnūṃ bʿad bārī ohdī āndī ai jihne kahyā sī "Do lifāfe aur ek jawābī karḍ dijiye." Sāryāṃ toṃ bʿad bābū os tehmad wāle nūṃ puchdā ai "Hāṃ oe tūṃ kī kahiyā sī?" Tehmad wālā phir akhdā "Bābū jī maiṃnūṃ tin panj panj rūpe wāle ṭikeṭ te ikk hawā'ī jahāz wālā lifāfā cāhīdā" te bābū jawāb dendā ai: "Oe tainūṃ dikhdā na'īṃ? Maiṃ ḥisāb kitāb kardā piyā. Żara tākī toṃ pare hoke khaṛā ho lo!" Vāre nyāre jā'ie firangī dī zubān toṃ kiḍḍe kamm dī cīz ai!*
>
> If I, an educated person, don't speak English, then how am I going to command respect? It is nevertheless a fact that this language of white people has deceived me on many occasions . . . Because I have to impress my people, don't I? And often it works. When, at the post office counter, I say [in English] *Two mini order forms six acknowledgment letters*, the employee dumps everyone and serves me first. Next comes the turn of the person who says [in Urdu]: "Please give me two envelopes and a card." And once he has served us, the employee asks a *dhoti*-clad man: "Yes, what were you telling me?" The *dhoti*-clad man replies [in Punjabi]: "Sir, I need three five-rupee stamps and an airmail envelope." And the employee replies: "Can't you see that I'm doing the accounts. Move away from the counter and wait!" It's a real miracle. The White language is really a useful thing!

This scene illustrates the value placed on each of the three languages used in Pakistani Punjab's linguistic market. English enjoys the highest value (the narrator is served before everyone after addressing the post office employee in English), followed by Urdu, which has a value lower than English (the Urdu-speaking customer is served after the English-speaking one) but higher than that of Punjabi, a language that inspires only contempt. The Punjabi-speaking customer is served last, and the employee behaves rudely toward him and makes him wait.

During the years that followed Partition, Punjabi, in spite of its lack of value in the linguistic market, remained the language of intragroup communication for Punjabis from all strata of society. Faqeer Mohammad Faqeer noticed that it came to them so spontaneously that they ended up using it even in formal settings when they were expected to use English or Urdu:

> I saw in schools and colleges teachers and professors teach English, Persian and Urdu, yet provide explanations to students in Punjabi. In the courts, magistrates and lawyers would begin to plead in English and switch to Punjabi. The boys and girls studying in colleges and universities, who wrote, read, and spoke Urdu, as soon as they would be out of the classroom, would clean off with Punjabi the moisture that the humidity of other languages had deposited on their tongues.[98]

The triglossia prevalent in Pakistani Punjab created paradoxical situations, described by K. K. Aziz in "The Coffee House of Lahore" (2007). He noticed that the intellectuals who hung out in the Lahore coffeehouse conversed in an anglicized form of Punjabi (which K. K. Aziz named ironically *Punjlish*), but in formal settings used Urdu with the same people with whom they usually spoke in Punjabi. Moreover, although their daily oral interaction was in Punjabi, they produced literature only in Urdu:

> The coffee house talked for 14 hours a day, in what we may call Punjlish, a unique mixture of two tongues which gave everyone the ability to express his thoughts and feelings with enviable precision. Beyond that there were exasperating contradictions and fallacies. The Punjabi spoke Punjlish with his family and friends and teachers. But the arrival or presence of a single Urda made him and his circle switch immediately to Urdu. He also wrote his literature in Urdu, and discussed its finer points also in Urdu, but only in the halqa or other formal

causeries. The post-halqa meetings in the Coffee house and Tea House were conducted in Punjlish.[99]

Though Punjabis stuck to their language during intragroup interaction, the Punjabi activist Raja Risalu noticed a growing tendency among upper-class Punjabis to speak Urdu with their children: "We have seen in wealthy families that when a father and a mother would converse, an old father would address his young son or friends would meet outside the house they all would use Punjabi, but when the same people would talk to young children at home, they would use Urdu."[100] This practice is a clear manifestation of the biases upper-class Punjabis held against their own language: they habitually spoke it with people of their generation (or older people), but did not deem it worthy of being passed on to their children.

Punjabi in Radio and Cinema

After the exodus of the Sikh community, the scope of Punjabi narrowed. It vanished from schools, colleges, libraries, and bookshops, but it continued to be used in radio and cinema, as it was the only medium through which one could reach the Punjabi masses.

A branch of All India Radio opened in Lahore on December 16, 1937. From its inception, this station broadcast a daily thirty-minute program in Punjabi titled *Dehātī bhāyoṃ ke liye* (For Our Rural Brothers), in which two radio hosts exchanged remarks meant to instill moral values and civic sense among rural listeners.[101] A short Punjabi drama was performed and broadcast live once a week during this program. One of these weekly dramas, Rafi Peerzada's *Akhyāṃ* (The Eyes), which aired for the first time in 1938, became such a hit that it had to be broadcast several times.[102] This daily Punjabi program continued after independence; the writer Sajjad Hyder, who joined the Lahore branch of All India Radio in 1944, was in charge of it. The program was renamed *Jamhūr dī āwāz* (The Voice of the People), and its duration was extended to between forty-five minutes and an hour, but its content remained the same. *Jamhūr dī āwāz* became extremely popular thanks to the radio host Mirza Sultan Baig, who performed the role of farmer Nizam Deen, conversing with the other host, Rashid Jebi, in the role of farmer Qaym Deen.[103] The Nizam Deen character was an embodiment of rural common sense, and Mirza Sultan Baig was so popular that in May 1955 the very serious newspaper *Daily Imroz* invited him to contribute to its weekly Punjabi page, publishing his humorous remarks under the title *Xabrāṃ dyāṃ gallāṃ* (Few Words About the News) and *Hafte dyāṃ xabrāṃ* (The News of the Week). After independence, Radio Lahore broadcast a thirty-minute Punjabi drama every month.[104] Many of these dramas, which generally revolved around rural themes or moral dilemmas, have been preserved through Faqeer Mohammad Faqeer and Abdul Majeed Salik's Punjabi journal *Montly Panjābī*, which, in 1952 published in each issue the Punjabi drama broadcast the previous month.

The Lahore cinema industry started in 1929, when A. R. Kardar opened a film studio and set up a production company, United Players Corporation, in the city. The industry grew rapidly, producing several films a year.[105] The majority of these films were in Urdu, but Punjabi films were shot at regular intervals. The first Punjabi film shot in Lahore was *Hīr Rāṃjhā* (directed in 1932 by A. R. Kardar); it was followed by *Rājā Gopī Cānd* in 1933, *Sohṇī Mahīṃvāl* in 1937, and *Sassī Punnūṃ* in 1938. In total, thirty-one Punjabi films were shot in Lahore between 1932 and 1947. The Partition and the exodus of Hindu and Sikh artists, as well as A. R. Kardar's departure for Bombay, badly affected Lahore's film industry. The first Punjabi films to be shot in Lahore's studios after independence were *Phere* (Sacred Steps) and *Mundrī* (The Ring), both in 1949. Three Punjabi films were shot in Lahore's studios in 1950—*Lāṛe* (Grooms), *Gabhrū* (The Youngster), and *Šammī*—and another three in 1951: *Cānve* (O my Moon), *Dilbar* (Beloved), and *Billo* (Darling). In total, forty-four Punjabi films were shot in Lahore between 1949 and 1960, most of them narrating conventional romantic intrigues against a backdrop of village rivalries.[106] Several did very well at the box office. Lahore's Punjabi film industry was successful and profitable. A number of well-known poets, including Firoz Din Sharaf, Baba Alam Syahposh, Tanvir Naqvi, Saghar Siddiqui, and Ahmed Rahi, wrote song lyrics for Punjabi films.

THREE

Lahore's Intellectual Landscape

HAVING ANALYZED THE linguistic landscape of Pakistan, and particularly of Punjab, in the years following independence, we turn to our analysis of the different movements in favor of Punjabi that were initiated after independence. Because these movements originated mostly in the city of Lahore, in order to better contextualize and understand them, we begin by examining Lahore's intellectual landscape in these years. This landscape was polarized, divided in two camps: a Marxist camp and a conservative camp. The journalists, academics, poets, and fiction writers who were involved in promoting Punjabi language in Pakistan after 1947 were affiliated with one of these two camps. Marxist writers such as Ahmad Nadeem Qasmi and Ahmad Rahi and conservative intellectuals such as Abdul Majeed Salik and Hamid Nizami, all staunch supporters of Punjabi, operated through the platforms (journals, organizations, meetings, conferences) specifically used by the camp to which they belonged and in accordance with its ideology. This polarized landscape has been depicted by Intizar Hussain, K. K. Aziz, Anis Nagi, and Hameed Akhtar in their literary memoirs and analyzed by Kamran Asdar Ali and Sadia Toor in their histories.[1]

Despite their ideological differences, Marxists and conservatives promoted a similarly heteronomous conception of literature: for both groups, literature was the vehicle of a political and social message. This prevalent heteronomous conception of literature was later challenged by a group of young modernists gathered around Safdar Mir, professor of English at the

Government College of Lahore, who thus constituted a third camp: the modernist camp.

The Marxist Camp

The Marxist camp was composed of three groups, which collaborated closely: the progressives, the communists, and Mian Iftikharuddin's group.

The Progressives

The progressives were affiliated to the All Pakistan Progressive Writers' Association (APPWA), founded in December 1947 in Lahore, whose general secretary was the writer Ahmad Nadeem Qasmi. APPWA emerged from the split of the All India Progressive Writers' Association (AIPWA) that occurred in the wake of Partition. The AIPWA, founded in the 1930s in England by a group of Indian students, including Mulk Raj Anand, M. D. Taseer, and Sajjad Zaheer, promoted a new literature highlighting the poverty, deprivation, and servitude of the Indian masses and aimed at fighting against the reactionary forces that dominated society. From its beginnings, AIPWA had a Marxist orientation, and it quickly became close to the Communist Party. The association attracted writers and intellectuals from all parts of India, and its first conference was held in Lucknow in 1936.[2]

In Punjab, a group of committed intellectuals (Faiz Ahmad Faiz, Mahmud uz-Zafar, Rashid Jahan, Bari Alig) established a branch of the organization in Amritsar in 1936. Another branch was established in Lahore the same year. Its secretary was Sufi Ghulam Mustafa Tabassum, and later Abdullah Malik, but it was inactive at the time of Partition.[3]

The exodus of progressive intellectuals from East Punjab and Urdu-speaking areas gave new impetus to the progressives' activities in newly created Pakistan. The All Pakistan Progressive Writers' Association (APPWA) soon established itself as the country's most influential intellectual and literary organization. By the early 1950s, it counted 217 members and had established seven branches in the country (including Peshawar, Rawalpindi, Quetta, and Karachi). Its largest branch was the Lahore branch, with

60 members.[4] Of all the events organized by APPWA, its second All Pakistan Literary Conference, held on November 11–13, 1949 at the open-air theater of Lawrence Garden in Lahore, was the most memorable. It was a large-scale event, attended by 100 local delegates, and was supposed to include a delegation of Soviet writers specially dispatched from the USSR, but unfortunately they arrived in Lahore right after it ended.[5]

The APPWA's Lahore branch organized weekly meetings during which young writers read their recent works before members of the association, who then critiqued them. This provided an opportunity for progressive writers to reemphasize the principles of social realism promoted by the association.[6] The works read and critiqued during these meetings were subsequently published in *Saverā*, *Adab-e Laṯīf*, or *Nuqūš*, the three literary journals associated with the progressives.[7] Chaudhry Nazir Ahmad, the owner of *Saverā*, also ran *Nayā Idāra*, a publishing house that published mostly books by progressive writers.

One can count among the progressives young emerging writers (in their twenties or early thirties) such as Zaheer Kashmiri, Ahmad Rahi, Hajira Masroor, Khadija Mastoor, Sahir Ludhianvi, Arif Abdul Mateen, Abdullah Malik, Hameed Akhtar, Safdar Mir, Zaheer Babur, and Qateel Shifai, and also a few well-established writers whose careers had begun long before Partition: Ahmad Nadeem Qasmi, Faiz Ahmad Faiz, and Abdul Majeed Bhatti.

The Communists

The Communist Party of Pakistan (CPP) was founded during a congress in Calcutta in February–March 1948, when the leaders of the Communist Party of India (CPI) decided to split the party. Sajjad Zaheer was appointed as general-secretary of the CPP. The CPP's leadership team (the Politburo and the Central Secretariat) included Sibte Hasan, Ishfaq Beg, and Shaukat Ali.[8] The veteran trade unionists Mirza Ibrahim (president of the Pakistan Trade Union Federation), Dada Amir Haider, and Firozuddin Mansoor also collaborated with this team.[9]

The CPP operated in a semi-clandestine manner, as arrest warrants had been issued against Sajjad Zaheer and Sibte Hasan (both lived in hiding in

Lahore for several years). The CPP owned the People's Publishing House (PPH), which was managed by Abdul Rauf Malik.[10] The CPP also clandestinely published a magazine named *Nayā Zamāna*.[11] The CPP fielded eleven candidates in the 1951 Punjab parliamentary elections, but none were elected.[12]

Mian Iftikharuddin's Group

Hailing from an old family of landowners from Lahore, Mian Iftikharuddin, previously affiliated with the Muslim League, founded his own political party, the Azad Pakistan Party (APP), in 1950. This party was openly Marxist; it demanded democracy and social justice, rejected Pakistan's inclusion in the Commonwealth, and criticized the British presence in the country and Anglo-American interference in national and international politics.[13] Mian Iftikharuddin launched two newspapers in 1948: *Daily Imroz*, an Urdu daily edited by Chiragh Hasan Hasrat (1948–1951) and Ahmad Nadeem Qasmi (1951–1959), and *Pakistan Times*, an English daily edited by Faiz Ahmad Faiz (1948–1951) and Mazhar Ali Khan (1951–1959). These two dailies soon established themselves as mouthpieces of the Marxist camp.[14]

The Marxist camp dominated the intellectual scene in Pakistan during the early 1950s, but it gradually disappeared as a result of constant government persecution. Marxist journals and organizations were considered suspicious by the Pakistani government, which was close to the British and American governments. Marxists were accused of being financed and supported by the USSR and faced constant government persecution, culminating in the so-called Rawalpindi Conspiracy. In March and April 1951, Faiz Ahmad Faiz and Sajjad Zaheer were arrested along with some senior army officers (including General Akbar Khan) on charges of planning a coup d'état. Twenty Marxist intellectuals were arrested along with them, on charges of sedition: the communists Sibte Hasan, Firozuddin Mansoor, and Shaukat Ali; the progressives Ahmad Nadeem Qasmi, Zaheer Kashmiri, and Hameed Akhtar; and four journalists working for *Daily Imroz* (including Zaheer Babur).[15] As a result, the activities of the All Pakistan Progressive Writers' Association were suspended for nearly a year. On July 24, 1954, the Communist Party of Pakistan, the People's Publishing House, and the All Pakistan

Progressive Writers' Association were banned by the government, and eleven Marxist intellectuals were arrested.[16]

Mian Iftikharuddin's newspapers *Daily Imroz* and *Pakistan Times* continued to be published even after the 1954 ban, but both were nationalized in 1959 by Ayub Khan's government. Ahmad Nadeem Qasmi, editor-in-chief of *Daily Imroz*, and Mazhar Ali Khan, editor-in-chief of *Pakistan Times*, resigned in protest. This nationalization put an end to the last two bastions of the Marxist camp that had survived bans and censorship.[17]

The writers of the Marxist camp produced an abundant literature in Urdu: fiction (Ahmad Nadeem Qasmi, Hajra Masroor, Khadija Mastoor), poetry (Faiz Ahmad Faiz, Zaheer Kashmiri, Ahmad Rahi, Sahir Ludhianvi, Arif Abdul Mateen, Qateel Shifai, Syed Mutalibi Faridabadi), and essays (Sibte Hasan, Sajjad Zaheer, Abdullah Malik, Hameed Akhtar, Abid Hassan Minto).[18]

The Conservative Camp

A heterogeneous group of intellectuals was engaged in a battle of ideas against the Marxist camp, which was gradually crumbling under the attacks of the state. These intellectuals hailed from different backgrounds, but what brought them together was their strong nationalism, their unwavering commitment to Islam, and their deep anti-Marxist sentiment. These intellectuals constituted the conservative camp, within which one can distinguish six distinct groups.

The Nationalist Veterans

The nationalist veterans were direct disciples of Allama Iqbal. They included Zafar Ali Khan and his son Akhtar Ali Khan, editors-in-chief of *Zamīndār*, an anti-British newspaper founded in 1903 and edited by Zafar Ali Khan since 1911; Abdul Majeed Salik and his associate Ghulam Rasool Mehr, editors-in-chief of *Inqilāb*, a newspaper founded in 1927; and Waqar Ambalvi, a senior journalist who had worked during his career for nearly twenty newspapers.

The Nawā-e Waqt *Group*

The *Nawā-e Waqt* group was composed of intellectuals close to Hamid Nizami, editor-in-chief of *Nawā-e Waqt*, a newspaper founded in 1940. Nizami had initially supported the Muslim League, but after Partition he joined the opposition, supporting Nawab Iftikhar Hussain Khan Mamdot (a former Muslim League politician who formed his own party, the Jinnah Muslim League, in 1950) against his rival, the Muslim League politician Mumtaz Daultana. As a result, when Daultana became Punjab's chief minister in 1951, he banned *Nawā-e Waqt* for a year.[19] Chiragh Hasan Hasrat, the first editor-in-chief of *Daily Imroz*, joined *Nawā-e Waqt* in 1952 after leaving *Daily Imroz*.

The Caṭṭān *Group*

The *Caṭṭān* group consisted of Shorish Kashmiri, editor-in-chief of the Urdu political magazine *Caṭṭān* and secretary-general of the *Majlis*-e *Eḥrār-e Islām* (Society of Free Muslims), and his followers.[20]

The Jamā'at-e Islāmī *Group*

The *Jamā'at-e Islāmī* is an Islamist political party founded in 1941 in Lahore by Syed Abu Ala Maududi (1903–1979), a journalist and theologian who was the first to demand that Pakistan become a true Islamic country by fully applying the *Shariah*. The leading figure of this group was the journalist and novelist Naseem Hijazi, who worked as an editorialist for *Tasnīm*, the party's official newspaper.

The Ḥalqa-e Arbāb-e Żauq *Group*

The literary organization *Ḥalqa-e Arbāb-e Żauq* (Circle of the Men of Good Taste), founded in 1939, organized weekly literary meetings. Its most prominent members were the poets Qayyum Nazar and Yusuf Zafar and the Urdu activist Maulana Salahuddin Ahmad. This organization advocated art for art's sake, strongly opposing the politicization of literature advocated by the Marxist camp.[21] Maulana Salahuddin Ahmad published a literary journal, *Adabī Dunyā*, that featured texts read during the weekly meetings of the *Ḥalqa-e Arbāb-e Żauq* or penned by its members.[22]

The Taseer and Askari Duo

M. D. Taseer was one of the founders of the All India Progressive Writers' Association but changed sides in 1947; Mohammad Hasan Askari had been an independent since the beginning of his writing career. The two united to counter the Marxist intellectuals, using all available conservative platforms (*Caṭṭān, Nawā-e Waqt*) to launch attacks on Marxist intellectuals.[23]

* * *

While the Marxist camp was composed of young intellectuals who emerged right before or soon after Partition, the conservative camp included a large number of very senior intellectuals. Zafar Ali Khan began his career at the turn of the century; Abdul Majeed Salik, Ghulam Rasool Mehr, Waqar Ambalvi, and Akhtar Ali Khan in the early 1920s; and Naseem Hijazi, Shorish Kashmiri, and M. D. Taseer in the early 1930s. Hamid Nizami and Mohammad Hasan Askari, whose careers began in the 1940s, were the youngest members of this camp.

On the other hand, while the Marxist intellectuals were united and followed a similar agenda, the conservatives were divided on several matters. One of them was the Ahmadi issue, which gained importance in 1953 after the launch of an anti-Ahmadi movement in Lahore that resulted in deadly riots.[24] While Abdul Majeed Salik supported the Ahmadi faith and Hamid Nizami adopted a tolerant attitude, Zafar Ali Khan, Akhtar Ali Khan, Shorish Kashmiri, and the *Jamāʿat-e Islāmī* members strongly opposed it.

Conservative intellectuals, like their Marxist rivals, faced imprisonment, censorship, and harassment by the Pakistani state. Akhtar Ali Khan and Shorish Kashmiri were imprisoned in 1953 during the anti-Ahmadi movement. The *Zamīndār* and *Tasnīm* newspapers were banned the same year.[25] In the 1950s, three of the leading conservative intellectuals passed away (Zafar Ali Khan in 1956, his son Akhtar Ali Khan and Abdul Majeed Salik in 1959); nevertheless, their demise did not weaken the conservative camp. Its influence, on the contrary, was increasing, as it was gradually filling the vacuum created by the disappearance of the Marxist camp.

The literature in Urdu produced by conservative writers reflected their ideology. The conservative poets (M. D. Taseer, Asar Sehbai, Hafeez Jalandhari, Yusuf Zafar, Waqar Ambalvi) celebrated Islam and composed patriotic poems (*Qaumī Šāʿirī*).[26] The conservative fiction writers wrote either short stories and novels in the romantic style condemned by the progressives (Mirza Adeeb, Shafiq ur-Rahman, A Hameed) or historical novels celebrating the heroes of Islam (Naseem Hijazi, M. Aslam).[27] Some of them wrote Partition novels, narrating the events of 1947 from a Muslim nationalist point of view. Thus, in M. Aslam's novel *Raqṣ-e Iblīs* (Dance of Iblis), all Muslim characters behave heroically while all Sikh and Hindu characters are hell-bent on committing horrors.[28] Literary critics from the conservative camp created and promoted two concepts in order to counter some of the trends that the Marxist intellectuals had popularized. Mohammad Hasan Askari created the concept of *Pakistānī Adab* (Pakistani literature); the poet Mahir ul-Qadri and the scholar Naeem Siddiqui created the concept of *Adab-e Islāmī* (Islamic literature).[29] For them, literature was meant to be above all a vehicle for the expression of purely Pakistani or Islamic values. These two concepts—as well as the idea of "art for art's sake" advocated by the *Ḥalqa-e Arbāb-e Żauq*—were strongly criticized by Marxist intellectuals during the All Pakistan Literary Conference held in November 1949 in Lahore.[30]

The Modernist Camp

An analysis of the intellectual landscape of Lahore would be incomplete without mention of the modernists, a group that formed in the mid-1950s around the critic, playwright, and poet Safdar Mir, a professor of English at the Government College of Lahore, previously an eminent member of the Progressive Writers' Association.[31] This apolitical group had a purely literary vocation and was consequently not connected to any of the preexisting camps. It claimed autonomy for literature, attempting to free it from external, ideological, or moral constraints. This group consisted of two teachers at Lahore Government College (Safdar Mir and Jilani Kamran), some students at different colleges (Zahid Dar, Anis Nagi, Iftikhar Jalib, Shehzad Ahmad, Zafar Iqbal, Abdul Haq Khammi), and two medical students (Anver Sajjad and

Salim ur-Rahman). Three other writers joined the group later: Abbas Athar, Munir Niazi, and Akhtar Ahsan.[32] The modernists distanced themselves from the type of literature being promoted by the Marxists and conservatives, focusing instead on the production of an experimental literature inspired by Anglo-American Imagism, nineteenth-century French poetry, Existentialism, and stream of consciousness. The influence of this emerging group on the intellectual life of Lahore remained limited during this period, but its contribution to Punjabi literature was important.

* * *

Marxists, conservatives, and modernists all took an interest in Punjabi language and tried to promote it. Using the resources and platforms at their disposal, they produced texts that reflected their ideology and their aesthetics. Thus, Punjabi became (along with Urdu) the medium of a Marxist, conservative, or modernist literature.

As the individuals involved in pro-Punjabi activities after independence in Lahore belonged to different camps, used distinct platforms, and followed (and expressed in their literary works in Punjabi) antagonistic ideologies, it would be inaccurate to argue that a unified Punjabi movement emerged in the post-Partition years. Rather, three small-scale Punjabi movements emerged, initiated by intellectuals from three different camps. The chapters that follow are devoted to analyzing the movements for the promotion of Punjabi initiated in each of these three camps—Marxist, conservative, and modernist—in the period from 1947 to 1960.

FOUR

The Marxist Punjabi Movement (1947–1959)

MARXIST INTELLECTUALS HAD been active in Punjabi-speaking cities such as Amritsar, Lahore, and Rawalpindi since the 1920s, but until 1947 it was mainly Sikh Marxists (such as Kartar Singh Duggal and Amrita Pritam) who produced literature in Punjabi. Urdu was the preferred medium of expression of Muslim Marxists. The Marxist poet Sharif Kunjahi, who had been writing poems in Punjabi since 1938, was an exception. Thus, after the exodus of the Sikh community in 1947, Pakistani Marxist writers counted only one writer of Punjabi in their ranks. This vacuum was quickly filled: In 1948–49, Afzal Parvez, Ahmad Rahi, and Abdul Majeed Bhatti started writing in Punjabi, and Marxist publishing houses such as PPH and *Nayā Idāra* helped promote literature in this language, as did the literary journal *Saverā*, the official organ of the progressives. Mian Iftikharuddin also devoted space to Punjabi in his prestigious newspaper *Daily Imroz*, which increased the visibility of the language, boosted its readership, and encouraged Marxist writers to write in this language.

A discourse in defense of Punjabi emerged and developed in those years. Marxist Punjabi activists Sharif Kunjahi, Ahmad Rahi, Shaukat Ali, and Zaheer Babur wrote essays in defense of Punjabi, thus challenging the extensive Urduization initiated by the central government (as well as the provincial governments) at the cost of regional languages. Thus, between 1948 and 1959, Pakistani Marxists produced a large corpus of essays, poems, and short stories in Punjabi that bear their hallmark and express their ideology. Of all the regional languages of West Pakistan, Punjabi is the one that received the most attention from them, the one in which they produced the most literature, and the one that they championed the most consistently.

Initiatives of Progressives and Communists in Favor of Punjabi, 1947–1954

The Progressive Writers' Conference (1947)

The issue of regional languages in Pakistan (and Punjabi in particular) was raised for the first time in a public forum postindependence during a conference organized by the Progressive Writers' Association at the YMCA of Lahore on December 5–6, 1947. It was presided over by Abdul Majeed Salik, and all writers, poets, artists, and musicians present in Lahore were invited to attend, whether or not they were sympathizers of the progressive movement. As a result, conservatives such as Hafeez Jalandhari, M. D. Taseer, Maulana Salahuddin Ahmad, and Shorish Kashmiri participated alongside Marxists such as Faiz Ahmad Faiz, Zaheer Kashmiri, Qateel Shifai, Ibrahim Jalees, Sahir Ludhianvi, and Arif Abdul Mateen.[1] Six resolutions were adopted at the end of this conference; one of them, adopted after a heated debate, recommended the use of Urdu as a language of instruction all over Pakistan.[2] The progressive organizers of the conference had first proposed a resolution recommending Pakistan's regional languages (Bengali, Pashto, Punjabi, Sindhi, and others) as means of instruction. This proposal infuriated M. D. Taseer, who violently opposed it. Thus, it was withdrawn and replaced with a resolution in favor of Urdu.[3]

A few months later, M. D. Taseer clarified his position in an article published in the *Daily Imroz* of August 15, 1948:

> Punjabi is only a dialect of Urdu, and since Punjabi is different in each district, Urdu has been used throughout the province. . . . During the first conference of the progressives a resolution was proposed, recommending that a large place be given to the languages of the provinces in the educational system. I insisted that Punjabi should not be among these languages, because Punjabi is not as advanced in regards to Urdu as Bengali is. Consequently, this resolution concerning the languages of the provinces was not adopted.[4]

Ten months later, on June 27, 1949, Shorish Kashmiri's magazine *Caṭṭān* featured an article by M. D. Taseer in which he again discussed the resolution. This time he adopted a harsher tone, denouncing the progressives who wanted to replace Urdu with Punjabi, thus blindly implementing the concept of nation and the language policy that Stalin had introduced in one of his pamphlets: "According to them, Pakistan is an aberration. Making Urdu a medium of instruction is an aberration. According to Stalin's definition of the nation, religion cannot be the basis of unity, and instruction must be given in the mother tongue, and since Urdu is not our mother tongue, during their first meeting . . . they objected to Urdu becoming a medium of instruction in Punjab. They support Punjabi literature from this perspective."[5] It is clear that M. D. Taseer's position had become more radical. In his August 1948 article, he opposed the use of Punjabi as a medium of instruction for practical and linguistic reasons; in his June 1949 article, he opposed it for ideological reasons. Since according to him supporting Punjabi was tantamount to promoting a regional identity against a unifying religious identity, supporting Punjabi ultimately meant opposing the very idea of Pakistan. This article echoed one published in October 1948 by Mohammad Hasan Askari who, reacting to the withdrawn resolution of the December 1947 conference, wrote: "Urdu is not the vernacular of any part of Pakistan, but Muslims intend to make it their instrument of unity. The Communist Party does not want the Muslims to be able to strengthen their unity, and the communist Muslims are manipulated."[6]

The progressives had lost a battle but not the war. After withdrawing under pressure their resolution regarding regional languages as means of instruction, and facing violent attacks from M. D. Taseer and Mohammad Hasan Askari, they reiterated during their next conference their support for regional languages, and in particular Punjabi.

The All Pakistan Literary Conference (1949)

M. D. Taseer's objections and Mohammad Hasan Askari's attacks did not deter progressives from expressing support for regional languages and from asserting the need to make them a vehicle for their own ideas. The conference they organized in Lahore's Lawrence Garden open-air theatre on

November 11–13, 1949 gave them the occasion to express their position.[7] The manifesto (*manšūr*) of the All Pakistan Progressive Writers' Association (APPWA), was read and adopted on the second day of the conference.[8] It stated:

> Until now we have largely neglected the literatures of the peoples of Pakistan, the literatures of Sindhi, Pashto, Bengali, Punjabi. Our duty is to carefully read the ancient and modern literature of these languages, and make use of it. We declare that we will invite writers of these languages to join our movement, and adopt these languages as means of expression. Thus, not only will we contribute to the preservation and progress of these languages, but we will better understand the feelings and ideas of ordinary people and the problems they face in their daily lives, and will better portray them in our writings.[9]

This program was implemented during the conference itself. Since it was organized in Lahore, on Punjabi-speaking land, the progressives invited some working-class Punjabi poets to present their texts on the stage. On the first day of the conference, the peasant poet Allah Rakha Sajid read the following Punjabi poem on the stage:

Āzādī vāṃḍ la'ī amīrāṃ
Ḥiṣṣa pāke nāl wazīrāṃ
Gall tere hor zanjīrāṃ
Uṭh eke dā nʿara lāke

The rich have shared Independence among themselves
They have reserved a share of it for the ministers
More chains are binding your neck now
Get up and tell them that you want Equality.[10]

On the second day of the conference, the progressive poet Ahmad Rahi came to the stage and recited his first poem in Punjabi. Addressing the peasants and workers present in the audience, he assured them:

Mil mazdūro ate kisāno dukhlaḍe mere vīro . . .
Maiṃ vī ikk mazdūr hāṃ, sāthi maiṃ rāje ghar jamyā na'īṃ

Kāl te bhukh dā jhagṛā mere la'ī vī hūṇe thamyā na'īṃ
Sāḍḍyāṃ naẕmāṃ sāḍḍyāṃ faṣlāṃ sāḍḍī meḥnat kakhoṃ sastī
Sāḍḍe xūn de bālke dīve meḥlāṃ vic hove xarmastī

Workers and peasants, my unhappy brothers . . .
I too am a worker I was not born in a palace
I am still struggling with starvation and hunger
Our poems and our harvests are cheaper than a handful of dust
The palace dwellers light candles made of our solidified blood and make merry[11]

This poem was well received by the audience.[12] Punjabi had become not only a medium of expression for revolutionary and Marxist ideology but also the vehicle for a dialogue between the working class and progressive poets.

But the progressives did not only recite poems in Punjabi during their conference. On the last day of the conference, they devoted a full session to Punjabi, during which they discussed the status of the language, the obstacles to its development, and its future. The session started with Sharif Kunjahi's reading of his Punjabi essay *Ūṃṭ te baddū* (The Camel and the Bedouin), in which he discussed some of the recent statements made by Urdu supporters, responded to the criticism frequently made by opponents of Punjabi, and analyzed the historical reasons that had led Punjabi Muslims to perceive their own language negatively.[13] Some of the argumentative strategies used in this essay to defend Punjabi (such as dissociating it from the Sikh community or asserting that it was an older language than Urdu) were often used subsequently by Punjabi activists.

Sharif Kunjahi started his essay with a parable:[14]

Once upon a time there was a Bedouin and his camel on a cold winter night. The Bedouin was sleeping in his tent and in the middle of the night the camel stuck his head in the tent and said, "It's cold, can I tuck my neck in your tent?" The Bedouin took pity on him and the camel thrust its long neck into the tent. A little later the camel shook the Bedouin's feet and said to him "Could you move a bit? My feet are cold." The Bedouin accepted, and finally, the camel completely entered the tent and the Bedouin ended up outside.

The same story is being repeated in Punjab at the moment. Soon the camel will be inside the tent and the Bedouin will be waiting outside. It is strange that

> no one is opposing the use of Pashto in NWFP, of Bengali in Bengal, or of Sindhi in Sindh. If the children of the schools of these regions study, learn to read and write in their own languages, that does not harm Urdu, but if somebody says that Punjabi must be taught in Punjab's schools then it triggers a public outcry. . . . We have nothing against Urdu, but we find it difficult to understand why, among all provinces and regions of Pakistan, it is only Punjab which is expected to pay tribute to Urdu. Urdu is the official language of Pakistan and its status should be the same throughout the country.

The parable of the Bedouin and the camel, which stretches over the first paragraph of Sharif Kunjahi's essay, is a humorous response to the activists Maulvi Abdul Haq and Maulana Salahuddin Ahmad, who were calling for Punjab to become a haven for Urdu. Sharif Kunjahi predicts that Urdu (the camel) will abuse the hospitality granted by Punjabi language (the Bedouin), and Punjabi will soon find itself ostracized and dispossessed of its own territory (its tent). In the second paragraph, Sharif Kunjahi responds to M. D. Taseer's objection to Punjabi being used as a medium of instruction in Punjab by exposing his double standard, once again expressing reservations regarding the notion that Punjab must be a sanctuary of Urdu.

In the next paragraph of the essay, Sharif Kunjahi answers two arguments often put forward by the adversaries of Punjabi to discredit the language: (1) Punjabi is not a "real" language (its lexicon—its "wings"—comes from other languages); (2) Punjabi is the language of the Sikhs.

> Some people say that Punjabi cannot be considered a language in its own right. . . . Its wings are borrowed. Some even consider it to be the language of the Sikhs. They use these hollow arguments to prove that Punjabi deserves the fate reserved for it in our time. Those who know about languages, and those who have studied them know that just like no individual, country or ethnic community can flourish without the help of others, no language can pride itself on not having borrowed its wings from others. Only a tree that is not meant to grow and flourish will take nothing from the ground and air. Thus, languages are not fundamentally linked with religions but with places and regions. Religions use them to convey their message to people. A language is born in a region as naturally as anything else. . . . Punjabi has been spoken here since a time when Urdu did not yet exist. And at that time the Sikhs did not exist either. People spoke Punjabi before Guru Nanak was born. It sometimes occurs to me that the English have

used languages to pit people against each other. . . . They pitted Sikhs against Muslims and Muslims against Sikhs. As a result, the Punjabi Muslims do not consider Punjabi their own language.

By asserting the anteriority of Punjabi, Sharif Kunjahi manages to refute the position of those who consider Punjabi a mere dialect of Urdu (since Punjabi existed before Urdu) and those who consider it as the language of the Sikhs (since it existed before Guru Nanak). And by highlighting the colonial origin of the Punjabi Muslims' prejudices against their own language (they are a mere outcome of the British game of "divide and rule") he intends to shame those who harbor them.

In the concluding section of his essay, Sharif Kunjahi tackles a third argument often put forward by the opponents of Punjabi: that not many literary works have been written in Punjabi (Maulana Salahuddin Ahmad had claimed that all its literature "would only fill a cupboard").[15] Sharif Kunjahi admits this, thus making a concession, but on the basis of this admission he calls for "nurturing" this "hungry language":

One can say that a lot was not written in Punjabi. But the reason for this is that Punjabi did not get many opportunities (the Sikhs though have written a lot in Gurumukhi); and deciding that a language should disappear because little has been written in it is as aberrant as wringing a starving man's neck instead of giving him food. This is what happens with hungry languages. Their bellies are begging for food. But you prepare a rope that you will slip around their neck.

While Sharif Kunjahi's essay is mainly devoted to providing an answer to the opponents of Punjabi, it also indirectly suggests two concrete steps for the promotion and development of Punjabi: Punjabi should be used as a means of instruction at school, as other regional languages are in the provinces where they are prevalent, and the new generation should nurture Punjabi by enriching its literature.

It does not seem that this essay won unanimity among progressives. It was not published in the issue 7–8 (1950) of *Saverā* alongside other authors' essays read and "approved" during the conference, and Abdullah Malik only mentioned it in a few lines—and with certain reservations—in his report:

> Sharif Kunjahi read an essay in Punjabi written in support of Punjabi. It had been a long time since we had heard a good essay in Punjabi. . . . It is clear that when our rulers impose Urdu by force and the languages of different peoples are crushed in this way, one sees a kind of hatred for Urdu develop in some people, and unfortunately this hatred is apparent in Sharif Kunjahi's essay. Progressive intellectuals should adopt a democratic approach to languages, and give to all languages the opportunity to flourish. Giving to one language an official status doesn't justify attacking other languages. For us all languages are equal. We recognize that some languages are more advanced (*taraqqī-yāfta*) and some less, but that is no reason to continue to crush languages that are themselves already crushed.[16]

This last sentence—which paraphrases the last sentences of Sharif Kunjahi's essay—clearly shows that for the author Punjabi is a "less advanced" language. It is obvious from this section of Abdullah Malik's report that Sharif Kunjahi's condemnation of the systematic Urduization of Punjab did not please some of the Marxists. Sajjad Zaheer's remarks regarding Punjabi in his book *Rūšnā'ī* (The Light), published in 1956, certainly echoes their objections:

> There is no doubt that when the masses are in power Punjabi will be further promoted. . . . But it would be wrong to say that Urdu is a foreign or alien language in Punjab. Syntaxical and grammatical similarities make Urdu and Punjabi akin to each other, their vocabulary is to a large extent similar, and the Urdu tradition has been part of the cultural life of Punjab for centuries. This is why the promotion of Punjabi in Punjab should not mean the end of Urdu.[17]

Sajjad Zaheer—like several other Marxists—believed Punjabi had to be promoted but that its promotion should not affect Urdu's status in Punjab.

Introduction of Punjabi in the Weekly Meetings of the Progressives and in Saverā *(1950–51)*

The new manifesto and Sharif Kunjahi's *Ūṃṭ te baddū* essay had a strong impact on the Lahori progressives. They decided to promote Punjabi and to devote a session of their literary meetings to it every month. Abid Hassan Minto recounted the introduction of Punjabi in these meetings:

> I remember that at our weekly meeting of progressive writers . . . well we decided that every month we would have someone read his work in Punjabi. But I don't remember how long this practice lasted. There were not so many writers who wrote in Punjabi and who were progressive . . . Ahmad Rahi came regularly to our weekly meeting of the Progressive Writers' Association, and read his poems in Urdu and Punjabi. I remember one occasion when he had to read a poem in Punjabi . . . it was the first time I met him in person, he read his poem, I listened and the discussion that followed took place in Punjabi.[18]

The progressives had been holding weekly meetings since 1948, sometimes in the hall of the YMCA, sometimes at Dyal Singh College, and sometimes at the residence of Tahira Mazhar Ali Khan.[19] During these meetings, some texts would be read by their authors before an audience and critiqued by members of the audience. A senior writer (or any senior intellectual, such as a journalist or an academic) chaired these meetings.[20] Reading a text in Punjabi and discussing it in this language during a literary meeting was a revolutionary step in Lahore's literary milieu. Other literary organizations, such as the *Ḥalqa-e Arbāb-e Żauq* (Circle of the Men of Good Taste), did not allow Punjabi texts to be read during their sessions, and the critical discussions always took place in Urdu, even if the people who took part in the discussion were Punjabi speakers and, outside of the sessions, spoke to one another in Punjabi.[21] But unlike the *Ḥalqa-e Arbāb-e Żauq*, whose sessions were recorded in writing by its secretary, progressives did not keep any record of their sessions.[22] We therefore don't know which Punjabi texts were read during these sessions (nor what were the comments of the participants). However, as Rauf Malik stated during an interview, many of these texts were later published in *Saverā*, which in 1951 created a special Punjabi section titled *Panjāb Rang* (Color of Punjab).[23]

The progressives thus used for the promotion of Punjabi not only their organization but also their literary journal. Issue number 9 (1951) of *Saverā* featured in its Punjabi section five poems by Amrita Pritam, Sharif Kunjahi, Tanvir Naqvi, Afzal Parvez, and Ahmad Rahi; issue number 10–11 (1951) had four poems by Amrita Pritam, Abdul Majeed Bhatti, Sharif Kunjahi, and

Ahmad Rahi; and issue number 12 (1952) had five Punjabi poems by Amrita Pritam, Abdul Majeed Bhatti, Sharif Kunjahi, Tanvir Naqvi, and Ahmad Rahi.[24] The publication of Punjabi texts in *Saverā* ceased after issue number 12. A total of eleven poems by progressive Pakistani authors (along with three by the Indian author Amrita Pritam) were published in *Saverā* between 1951 and 1952. It can therefore be assumed that a large part of the texts read during the monthly Punjabi session of the progressives between 1951 and 1952 were published in *Saverā*.

Abid Hassan Minto's Program (1951)

In October 1951, CCP's first program regarding the linguistic policy of Pakistan was published in Lahore in the journal *Adab-e Laṭīf*, under the title *Pakistān meṃ zubān kā masla* (The Language Issue in Pakistan). It was penned by Abid Hassan Minto at the request of the communist leader Dada Amir Haider in order to clarify the CCPs position on the language issue in Pakistan.[25] This essay does not discuss only Punjabi's status, but it outlines a general policy that, if implemented, would have a major impact on it. The program was read by Abid Hassan Minto in November 1949 at an informal session during the Progressive Writers' Association's conference before being published in the journal *Adab-e Laṭīf*.[26] The essay begins: "The government of Pakistan announces that Urdu will be the Official Language of the country because, by doing so it gets the sympathy of educated middle-class people, and also because it can use Urdu the same way the English imperialist government was using English: to keep 90% of the population illiterate and ignorant."[27] After this rather abrupt introduction, Minto explains that opposing Urdu would be a bad move for the CCP, as it would attract the wrath of the government and of the middle class. He adds that while Urdu is necessary at the national level, it is not always so at the regional level, because its sphere of use varies according to the province and the degree of advancement of the vernacular languages spoken there:

> In Bengal and Sindh, in my opinion, Urdu is not really needed, and the people of these provinces have already protested against Urdu. Bengali is much more advanced than Urdu, and in Sindh all the writing on walls, the advertisements

> and the street signs are in English or Sindhi. Some daily newspapers are also published in Sindhi. Therefore in Sindh and Bengal the movement which has developed against the imposition of Urdu is justified. In Punjab, Balochistan and NWFP, the local languages are not very advanced, and the educated class knows only Urdu (whereas the same class in Bengal is mostly proficient in Bengali). In these provinces, until now, we have not seen the beginning of a popular movement, and there are few chances that there will be any. Therefore, in my opinion, there should be no objection to Urdu being adopted in these provinces as an official language. And our demand should be that Urdu be used instead of English and that primary education be imparted in local languages. . . . We should not fight against the adoption of Urdu as an official language in other provinces than Sindh and Bengal, but fight for the development of the local languages of these provinces. . . . After our revolution, in Punjab, Balochistan and NWFP local languages will immediately progress, but Urdu will still have to be used there for some time, as it will take time for local languages to become as advanced as it. This is one more reason why we must not oppose Urdu.[28]

Abid Hassan Minto's position echoes that of Abdullah Malik (expressed in his commentary on Sharif Kunjahi's essay), in that he does not consider Punjabi to be a developed language (*taraqqī-yāfta*); he places it—alongside Balochi and Pashto—in a category of languages less developed than Urdu.[29] Because of these reservations regarding the state of advancement of these languages, Minto presents a minimum action program for Punjabi, which can be summed up in two points: (1) Primary instruction should be imparted in Punjabi in Punjab, and (2) Punjabi should be further "developed" (the modalities of this development are not specified).

One can wonder if the notion of Punjabi as a "nonadvanced" or "undeveloped" language, which we encounter in the writings of Abdullah Malik and Abid Hassan Minto, is not itself the result of a diglossic complex. These two intellectuals, whose mother tongue was Punjabi but who belonged to the educated class and therefore knew perfect English and Urdu, despite their adherence to Marxism had, in terms of language, internalized the dominant sociolinguistic patterns and therefore regarded Punjabi as an "inferior" language. But since they had to use sophisticated and diplomatic language, they used terms like *nonadvanced* and *undeveloped*.

Ahmad Rahi's Intervention at the Waris Shah Seminar (1953)

Three years after their Lahore conference, progressives reiterated at a public event their support for Punjabi. It was on the occasion of a seminar, held on February 26, 1953 in the hall of the YMCA, organized by the *Pak Punjabi* League of Abdul Majeed Salik to celebrate the legacy of the poet Waris Shah (1722–1798). Ahmad Rahi, representing the progressives at this seminar, read a paper (in Urdu) that was published in *Daily Imroz* on February 28, 1953 under the title *Panjāb ke 'awāmī adab aur śaqāfat kā ṣaḥīḥ tarjumān Wāriś Śāh* (A True Spokesperson for Punjab's Popular Literature and Culture: Waris Shah). This was the last time a prominent member of the All Pakistan Progressive Writers' Association spoke in a public forum on the issue of Punjabi, as the association was banned a year later.

In his paper, Ahmad Rahi discussed Waris Shah's poetry and Heer Waris Shah's social relevance, but he also discussed the current status of the Punjabi language in Pakistan. He complained about the utter disregard Punjabi Muslims had shown for their language, explaining it by the popularity of the sociolinguistic cliché associating Punjabi with the Sikhs:

> No region of the subcontinent has been more indifferent to the promotion of its language than Punjab. The basic reason for this is that the English masters have continuously oppressed the people of this region and used them as mere cannon fodder. But another reason is that our people themselves have ignored their language. Punjab has always been neglecting its language, this Punjabi language in which the young girls and boys express their love and the elderly people discuss their daily issues during the panchayats, Punjabis have never considered it as their own. Manipulative politicians further complicated the matter, and eventually planted in the minds of Punjab's Muslims the idea that Punjabi is not the language of the Muslims but of the Sikhs.
>
> Punjabi is the language of the Punjabi people, regardless of the fact that they are Muslim, Hindu, Sikh, Christian or untouchable (*bhangī*). It is the language of every Punjabi, but it is also true that Sikhs have paid a lot of attention to it and made it their exclusive language. Regarding the connection between Punjabi and the Sikhs, let me remind you that the religious traditions of the Sikhs are linked to Punjab. This sect was born and raised here. Sikh shrines are all here. From this point of view, therefore, they have no connection with the other

> regions of India. This is the reason why they made the language of their region their religious language. And we shouldn't condemn them for that. If the other inhabitants of Punjab who tried to adopt Urdu and Hindi are not blamed for it why should Sikhs be blamed for serving the Punjabi language? I will therefore say once again that Punjabi is the language of Punjab, not of the Sikhs. And if in spite of this some of our friends insist on calling it the language of the Sikhs then I will remind them that Punjabi is the language of Sulṭan Bahu, Khwaja Farid, Bulleh Shah and Maulvi Ghulam Rasool.[30]

Ahmad Rahi's paper was not as controversial as the essay Sharif Kunjahi had read during the 1949 conference, as the author did not discuss the negative impact Urdu's promotion could have on Punjabi. Rahi intended only to fight against certain received ideas regarding Punjabi. What constitutes the originality of his intervention is the strategy he adopted to defend Punjabi: instead of denying the special bond that unites Sikhs to Punjabi or dissociating these two entities (a strategy that prevailed among the Pakistani defenders of the Punjabi of the time), Rahi acknowledged it and paid tribute to the services rendered by the Sikhs to the language. In a way, in this paper Ahmad Rahi defended the Sikhs—sons of the soil—as much as Punjabi.

The Editorial Activities of PPH (1953)

Before being banned, PPH (the official publishing house of CCP) published two Punjabi books in 1953: *Tirinjan* (The Assembly of Women), a poetry collection by Ahmad Rahi, and *Navī rut* (A New Season), a selection of poems by Amrita Pritam.

Founded by the Communist Party of India (CPI) a few years before Partition to publish Marxist-Leninist literature, the Lahore branch of the PPH was managed by Rauf Malik.[31] After independence, the PPH published essays such as Zafarullah Poshni's *Marxī falsafa* (Marxist Philosophy) and Shaukat Ali's *Daulat-e muštarika aur Pākistān* (The Commonwealth and Pakistan), as well as Urdu translations of Marx, Engels, Lenin, Stalin, Mao Tse-Tung, and Gorky.[32] Then, at the end of 1952, PPH for the first time published a poetry collection: *Dast-e ṣabā* (Hand of Breeze) by Faiz Ahmad Faiz, who was then in prison.[33] In 1951, Rauf Malik was impressed by a poem read by Ahmad Rahi during one of the weekly meetings of the Progressive Writers' Association and encouraged him to continue writing in Punjabi, promising that he would publish his poems: "Rahi recited a poem in Punjabi during a meeting of the progressive writers. This poem fascinated me and I told him 'Keep writing in Punjabi.' He then asked me: 'if I write poems in Punjabi, will you publish them?' I said 'Of course, I will publish them!' He needed some money, and he told me a few days later, 'I've written a whole book.' "[34] Ahmad Rahi's Punjabi poetry collection was published under the title *Tirinjan* (The Assembly of Women) in February–March 1953. It was dedicated to Amrita Pritam and consisted of forty-three poems; 1,100 copies were printed. Rauf Malik did whatever he could to ensure *Tirinjan*'s success. To make the book attractive, he entrusted its calligraphy to Mohammad Hussain, one of the greatest calligraphers of Lahore, and requested Abdur Rahman Chughtai, one of Pakistan's most famous painters, to design its cover.[35] In order to make *Tirinjan* more "marketable," Rauf Malik included two texts written directly in Punjabi by two illustrious Urdu writers: a preface by Ahmad Nadeem Qasmi, and a blurb by Saadat Hasan Manto (this is Manto's only known text in Punjabi).[36] Once the book was ready, a function was organized at Dyal Singh College to launch it. The event was chaired by Abdul Majeed Salik; Z. A. Bukhari, director of the Lahore radio station, and Faqeer Mohammad Faqeer spoke. This event even attracted Urdu supporters, such as Ibadat Barelvi, head of the Urdu department at Punjab University.[37]

Tirinjan was a success. Its 1,100 copies were sold in one year, and the book was included in the syllabus of *Panjābī Fāẓil*.[38] Only a few months after its publication, *Tirinjan* had already become a classic.

Encouraged by this success, PPH published *Navī rut* (A New Season), a selection of poems by Amrita Pritam, which also met with great success (but was not included in the *Panjābī Fāẓil* syllabus because it was written by an Indian author).[39] But the arrest of Rauf Malik, along with ten other members of the Communist Party, on July 24, 1954, as well as the banning of the PPH, put an end to these Punjabi editorial activities.

Firozuddin Mansoor and Sibte Hasan's Program (1953)

The political situation changed in the years following the publication of Abid Hassan Minto's program. The language movement of East Bengal brought the debate on the official language to the forefront, and the CPP leadership was compelled to clarify its position in relation to the demands of the Bengalis and on the question of the official language. Firozuddin Mansoor and Sibte Hasan, two important members of the CPP, were detained together in 1951–52.[40] During their detention, they had numerous discussions regarding the Bengali language issue and the issue of the official language. The outcome of these discussions was the pamphlet *Pākistān meṃ qaumī zubān kā masla* (The Issue of the Official Language in Pakistan), published by PPH in 1953. Only Firozuddin Mansoor's name appears on the cover, but according to Rauf Malik most of the pamphlet was written by Sibte Hasan. Since Mansoor was released from prison before Hasan, he brought the manuscript with him and published it under his own name (Hasan was disappointed with Mansoor for doing so).[41] The major part of this pamphlet consists of an analysis of the Bengali movement (the authors express their support for the movement and condemn the attacks of Urdu supporters like Maulvi Abdul Haq against the Bengali language), but the last pages outline a program regarding Pakistan's vernacular languages that is much more radical than Abid Hassan Minto's cautious program. Like Minto's program, this text is not specifically about Punjabi, but it is still highly relevant for Punjabi as it presents a general program whose implementation could have radically modified the status of the language. The program was as follows:

> We will not face a disaster if we adopt all the national languages of Pakistan like Sindhi, Bengali, Balochi and Pashto alongside Urdu as Official Languages. After all, why not use Pashto—which is the native language of Pashtuns—in all governmental and administrative affairs and as a medium of instruction in NWFP? Why not do the same with Sindhi in Sindh, Balochi in Balochistan, Bengali in Bengal and Punjabi in Punjab?
>
> The main reason why our masses have remained backward in all fields is that they are forced to read, write, think and work in a language which is not their mother tongue. For centuries knowledge has been the monopoly of the higher classes and the masses have been kept ignorant.
>
> Depriving vernacular languages of the possibility of conveying knowledge, and not allowing them to become a medium of instruction or an administrative language is an old tactic used to keep people ignorant.
>
> In order to endow our people with the treasures of knowledge, English should cease to be used either as a medium of instruction or as an administrative language, the mother tongues of the masses should be used in the fields of

instruction and administration in the provinces, Punjabi, Sindhi, Bengali, Pashto and Balochi should become languages of instruction and administrative languages in Punjab, Sindh, Bengal, NWFP and Balochistan. Provincial governments must also promote the languages of their provinces.

Urdu is the language which different communities living in Pakistan use to communicate with each other. And it is the mother tongue of the refugees who have come from UP, Bihar, Ambala division and Rajasthan. It should be taught as a second language in schools and colleges, and promoted as a second language. It should, for practical reasons, be made a medium of instruction for the *Mohajirs*.

Provincial governments should carry out their administrative tasks in the language of their province; jobs in governmental and semi-governmental bodies should be given to individuals who can write, read and speak the language of their province; finally, schools and colleges must be set up to teach the languages of the provinces to state officials.

This is the real solution to the Official Language issue in Pakistan.[42]

This maximum program is undoubtedly the most radical of those presented during the period we are considering. But it could not stir up controversy in intellectual circles because the circulation of *Pākistān meṃ qaumī zubān kā masla* remained confidential and limited, and its copies quickly disappeared, as all the stock of the PPH was seized when it was banned. Was this program unanimously approved by the Marxist intellectuals who had access to it? We doubt it. Since there is no reference to it in the Marxists' writings of the time, we can only conclude that they simply chose to ignore a program that was too radical even for them.

Pākistān meṃ qaumī zubān kā masla was one of the last official statements of the CPP, which was banned the following year, and one of the last publications of PPH.

The Publication of Dil Darya *(1955)*

The Marxist camp vanished over the years. The All Pakistan Progressive Writers' Association was banned in 1954, its members were sent to prison or kept under strict surveillance, and the journal *Saverā*, which had been its official organ, had no connection with it anymore.[43] The publishing house

Nayā Idāra, headed by Chaudhry Nazir Ahmed, was one of the last vestiges of the Marxist camp. *Nayā Idāra* had published a large number of books by progressive authors in previous years, including the poetry collections of Ahmad Nadeem Qasmi, *Jalāl-o jamāl* (Beauty and Grandeur), and Zaheer Kashmiri, *'Az̤mat-e ādam* (Grandeur of Man). In October 1955, *Nayā Idāra* for the first time published a book in Punjabi, *Dil daryā* (Rivers of the Heart), a collection of sixty-two poems by Abdul Majeed Bhatti, a former member of the progressive group and a regular contributor to *Saverā* and to *Daily Imroz*.[44] A total of 1,200 copies were printed, but the book did not match the phenomenal success of Ahmad Rahi's collection *Tirinjan*, published two years earlier. It was not advertised, no book launch was organized, and it was not reviewed in any journal or newspaper. Its unsold copies are still available today at the book market (*Urdu Bazar*) of Lahore. This failure deterred *Nayā Idāra* from publishing other books in Punjabi.

The Initiatives of Mian Iftikharuddin and His Newspaper *Daily Imroz*

Mian Iftikharuddin

From 1951, Mian Iftikharuddin's newspaper *Daily Imroz* became an important tool for promoting Punjabi.[45] Mian Iftikharuddin was a supporter of regional languages; his position on language rights was similar to that of progressives and communists. He articulated this position in a speech titled "A Democratic Constitution for Pakistan," delivered to the Constituent Assembly of Pakistan on October 22, 1953:

> We the people of West Pakistan want to speak Punjabi, Sindhi, Kashmiri, Balochi, Pushto in our provinces, and when we meet each other across the provincial borders, and in the central government where we have to say something, there is a mixture of our languages. We are pleased to learn and speak Urdu simply because we want to have Urdu as our inter-provincial language in the west, and our main language which had been developing so beautifully for the last two hundred years. Shah Abdul Latif, Syed Waris Shah, Khushhal Khan Khattak were the poets, writers and philosophers before the British colonization whose languages would be equal to any other of their time. But after that,

> knowing it because it was not in their interest and knowing that there was no need to have more than one working language in India, the British wanted to have Hindustani as our language, which is being developed. Let our language in each Province be developed. Let us have inter-provincial language as Urdu in the west and if Bengal wants to have Bengali as their provincial language, let them stick to it. After all Pakistan has been created for the progress and the prosperity of the people of these areas. It is not a modern language institute in which Urdu must be taught.[46]

Iftikharuddin initially used *Daily Imroz*'s editorials to propagate his egalitarian view of regional languages. Then he went a step further: As he was extremely fond of Punjabi, his mother tongue, he granted it a special space in *Daily Imroz*.[47] The newspaper that had initially been simply supporting regional languages thus became an active agent promoting one of them.

Profile of the Daily Imroz *and Its Position on the Official Language Issue*

The daily newspaper *Imroz* was launched on March 4, 1948, in Lahore, alongside the *Pakistan Times*. Faiz Ahmad Faiz wrote its first editorial, and Chiragh Hasan Hasrat was its first editor-in-chief. Its circulation was initially quite limited (8,000 copies in 1949), but it increased over the years, reaching between 25,000 and 30,000 copies in 1958 and exceeding the circulation of its conservative competitor, the daily *Nawā-e Waqt* (whose print run never exceeded 19,000 copies).[48] It was thus the most widely read newspaper in the province of Punjab. Chiragh Hasan Hasrat—who was close to Marxist intellectuals but was not one of them—left *Daily Imroz* in July 1951 along with eight other journalists.[49] The new team that came to replace him and his colleagues was essentially Marxist—including Ahmad Nadeem Qasmi (who would remain editor-in-chief until 1959), Abdullah Malik, Hameed Akhtar, Hamid Hashmi, and Zaheer Babur—and the newspaper quickly established itself as a bastion of Marxist journalism.[50]

Regarding Pakistan's language issue, *Daily Imroz's* position evolved according to Mian Iftikharuddin's political affiliation. As long as Muhammad Ali Jinnah was alive, *Daily Imroz* supported his decision to grant the status of official language only to Urdu.[51] This support was the outcome of the newspaper's anticolonial stance: The adoption of Urdu seemed desirable because it meant the end of English, a vestige of the colonial period that no longer had any place in an independent country like Pakistan. An editorial published on April 15, 1948 states:

> In this era which is ours, when each people is freeing itself from the slavery in which foreign powers have kept it, the first initiative is always to annihilate the domination and supremacy of the languages of these foreign peoples. This is what the Turks and Iranians did after 1924. These peoples previously considered that knowing how to speak and count in this foreign language was a sign of distinction. But their new rulers forbade them this practice, and compelled them to see in the knowledge of their national language a mark of distinction. It is a pity that this has not happened in Pakistan, and that English still enjoys in governmental and non-governmental circles the same superiority it was enjoying in the days of the English, and that the departure of the English has changed nothing to it.

During that initial period, Punjabi and other regional languages were not discussed in *Daily Imroz's* editorials. For *Daily Imroz*, the priority was not to promote these languages but to replace English as soon as possible, and Urdu was the best choice available. The events of February 21, 1952 in Dhaka (*Ekushey*) led to a change in this position. The government's attitude was condemned in the strongest terms in the editorial of February 25, 1952, followed on March 1, 1952 by an editorial titled *Zubān kā masla* (The Language Issue) clarifying the newspaper's stance on the status of Bengali and other regional languages:

> Urdu is not the vernacular of any province in Pakistan, but it enjoys the status of a lingua franca in our country.
>
> On the other hand, we have many provincial languages of Pakistan, among which Bengali is the most advanced, and even, from a certain point of view, it can be said that Bengali literature is more advanced than Urdu literature. If we look at things from a realistic point of view, then we cannot deny that Urdu is not as widely read, written and understood in Bengal as in West Pakistan. In reality, Urdu is as important in East Bengal as Bengali in West Pakistan. . . . People who refuse to grant to Bengali the status of Official language alongside Urdu,

> and regard those who make such a request as fifth-columnists, should realise that if Bengali was granted this status alongside Urdu a climate of harmony would develop between the two parts of the country. Wouldn't the idea of a cultural unity come out of it reinforced?
>
> Would this also mean that the Punjabi, Pashto, Sindhi, Balochi and Kashmiri languages would also be entitled to official status? Can we give official status to seven languages at the same time? We have to take into account here the completely unique situation of Bengali.

But if *Daily Imroz* did not support the right of Pakistan's vernacular languages to become official languages of the country, it still wanted them to be granted administrative status or be used as languages of instruction in the provinces where they were spoken. An editorial published on January 31, 1953 presented the following recommendations:

> If we do not give the opportunity to progress to the vernacular languages of the various provinces and regions that co-exist with Urdu, which is our Official language and the language of communication between provinces, then we cannot imagine that Pakistan can progress on a cultural level. . . . Even if, as we have already said, Urdu is not competing with any provincial or regional language, it is a fact that Urdu and all provincial languages endanger the domination of English, the mother tongue of the commonwealth, and the government should therefore adopt a policy whereby it drives English out of government offices and uses languages which can easily become mediums of expression. It should therefore see to it that the provincial and regional languages develop, so that they can in future be used in the administrations. Thus, it is advisable to promote Urdu all over the country, but also to give inside each province, a good place to its vernacular language.

But the same recommendations did not apply to Punjabi. This editorial ended with the following clarification: "Let one thing be clear: we are not asking here that Punjabi be used as an administrative language or as a language of instruction, because this language has not yet reached the stage of its development where it could be given this status." The distinction between developed and undeveloped languages that we have encountered in Abdullah Malik and Abid Hassan Minto's texts was once again used against Punjabi.

Daily Imroz did not want to grant any status to Punjabi, either as an official language or as a language of instruction, because it was not sufficiently developed. We are here once again faced with a discriminatory discourse that reproduces the same prejudices of backwardness of Punjabi that are widespread in society.

This editorial nevertheless shows the limits that *Daily Imroz* had set for itself in terms of support for Punjabi: it will not demand that it be used in government offices or in schools. *Daily Imroz* deviated only once from its strict stance, asking in its issue of January 31, 1953 for the reopening of optional Punjabi classes at Lahore's Oriental College.[52]

> We were saddened to learn that Punjabi is not taught at Oriental College in Lahore, while every year a good number of students take Punjabi language and literature exams. . . . Since some students are keen on taking the Punjabi exams, it is the duty of the university to organize for them courses and provide them teachers. . . . It is surprising that Russian and French are taught at the university, but that the Punjabi language and literature do not have this privilege.

Punjabi Language in the Daily Imroz

The Punjabi language initially made its appearance in the form of Punjabi poems in the literary pages of *Daily Imroz* around the same time as the journal *Saverā* started its Punjabi section. One of the progressive authors published in *Saverā*—Ahmad Rahi—was the first published in *Daily Imroz*: his poem *Na ro aṛiye* (Don't Cry my Darling) on October 8, 1951 and his poem *Maiṃnūṃ yād rakhī* (Remember Me!) on October 22, 1951. Then *Daily Imroz* published other poets: Hassan Shah's poem *Vicoṛe* (Separations) on November 19, 1951 and the trade unionist Qamar Yurish's *Dʿuā* (A Prayer), a poem for children, on November 24, 1951. Some poems that seem purely sentimental take on political significance when the circumstances in which they were written are highlighted: thus, on November 17, 1951, *Daily Imroz* published *Terī yād* (Your Memory) a poem by Communist Party member Shaukat Ali.

Terī yād, šehd toṃ miṭhṛī, rešm toṃ kaulī, man mohnī yād
Kuwāre bullāṃ vicoṃ nikle pyāre pehle bol toṃ sohṇī yād
Haneryāṃ rātāṃ de xamoš sannāṭe vic

Soc de prāṇ nāl ūḍārī lāndī
Qilʿe dyāṃ uccyāṃ dīwārāṃ nūṃ pār kardī
Cup capetī mere dil vic dāxil ho jāndī

Your memory sweeter than honey, softer than silk, your lovely memory
More beautiful than the first words of love from virgin lips
In the empty silence of dark nights
Flies away with the power of thought
Crosses the high walls of the fort
And enters my heart silently[53]

The content of this poem seems harmless, but the following note, which accompanies it, gives it a new dimension: "You have certainly read in the newspapers about the arrest and release of Shaukat Ali B.A. L.L.B. Mr. Shaukat is not only a political leader but also a good Punjabi poet. The following poem is written in remembrance of the days he spent in Lahore Fort." This way *Daily Imroz* managed to circumvent censorship while drawing the readers' attention to the wave of arrests of communists and progressives that had followed the "unearthing" of the Rawalpindi conspiracy. Alongside these poems of seemingly purely literary content, *Daily Imroz* also published purposive Punjabi poems that depicted the conditions of the poor and the working class, which were ignored by the government. On September 15, 1951, a few months after the Punjab provincial elections (won by the Muslim League) and the appointment as chief minister of the wealthy landowner Nawab Mumtaz Daultana, *Daily Imroz* published a poem by Rahat Gujrati that was a commentary on the social divide that had widened in the province:

Wāh wāh terī šān dātā
Wāh wāh terī šān
Ikk pāse bijlī dyāṃ lāṭāṃ
Dūjī ṭaraf andherā
Ikk ḍare rāt ajjai hai bāqī
Ikk ḍare hoyā saverā
Ikk pāse na'e meḥl māṛyāṃ
Jaham jaham kardā ḍerā
Iknāṃ nūṃ dar dar de dhakke
Koi na'īṃ raiṇ baserā

Look at the miracles you have produced, O Almighty!
Look at these miracles!
On one side there are electric lamps
On the other side there is darkness
On one side people are scared of the night
On the other side people are scared of the morning
On one side there are palaces
And a brightly lit abode
On the other side a handful of beings who go from door to door
And have no shelter to take refuge

This practice distinguished *Daily Imroz* from other newspapers of the time. While ordinary newspapers, in order to comment on current events, published satirical quatrains (*qateʿi*) in Persianized Urdu, *Daily Imroz* preferred to comment on them through Punjabi poems written in a simple and familiar language, giving readers the feeling that the masses themselves were speaking through them.

The Punjabi Column Gall-bāt

The presence of Punjabi in *Daily Imroz* was not limited to poems. Between 1951 and 1953, *Daily Imroz* published a weekly Punjabi column titled *Gall-bāt* (Chit-chat), thus initiating Punjabi journalism in Pakistan. Initially, Mian Iftikharuddin—who had ever-increasing ambitions for Punjabi—wanted to launch a newspaper in Punjabi, but Rauf Malik advised him to devote a page to Punjabi in *Daily Imroz* instead (probably because it was difficult to find writers able to write Punjabi prose). Malik recounted how the *Gall-bāt* column started:

> One day we were all sitting at the office of *Daily Imroz* and having some informal chat. Ahmad Nadeem Qasmi was sitting with us, and Mian Iftikharuddin suddenly said, "We should publish a newspaper in Punjabi." I said, "Sir, publishing a Punjabi newspaper will take time, let's first publish a Punjabi page in *Daily Imroz*." He replied: "You are right!" and addressing Ahmad Nadeem Qasmi told him: "Qasmi *ṣāḥab*, start publishing this page." Ahmad Nadeem

Qasmi started this page, he entrusted Zaheer Babur, his nephew, with this task.[54]

In the beginning, it was not a Punjabi page that was published but a column, spread over half a page and titled *Gall-bāt*. Zaheer Babur took charge of it.[55] This column was published every Friday until July 1953. It was penned initially by Zaheer Babur, and later by various contributors such as Abdullah Malik, Faqeer Mohammad Faqeer, and Ahmad Rahi. *Gall-bāt* was published for the last time on July 3, 1953. *Daily Imroz* was the only Pakistani newspaper of its time that was publishing a column in Punjabi. *Gall-bāt* was published for the first time on August 18, 1951, and was signed *Šerā* (a popular abbreviation of the name *Sher Dil*), a pseudonym behind which was hiding an author whose identity has not been revealed. The column begins with the description of a Sunday:

> *Itvār dā din sī. Āsmān te cāroṃ pāse badlyāṃ murġābyāṃ vāṃgoṃ tairdyāṃ payāṃ san te din de bārah vaje inj lagdā pyā si ki bas rāt paike pa'ī te meṃh vasyā ki vasyā. Aiho jihe vele mauj melā karaṇ de utte kisdā jī na'īṃ cāhvegā? Aise la'ī te maiṃ vī uṭhke ikk dost de ghar vall ṭur pyā*

> It was Sunday. Clouds were swimming in the sky like drakes and it was only noon and it looked like it would soon be dark and it would soon rain. At times like these, who wouldn't want to have some fun? So I got up and went to see a friend.

Then follows a discussion between the narrator and his friend. This discussion revolves around recent tensions between India and Pakistan. The narrator says to his friend:

> *Aih Nehrū jī vī vaḍḍe bhole bādšāh haṇ. Yā fir oh sāri dunyā nūṃ bholā samajhde ne. Ikk pāse tāṃ oh 'aman aman' dyāṃ duhā'ī dende ne. Te dūje pāse Pākistān dī sarḥadāṃ utte apṇī sārī fauj jamʿa kar la'ī ai. Ohnāṃ toṃ koī puche: 'Bholyo, jai tusīṃ apṇe nūṃ aman dā nišān kehnde o tāṃ fir bhalā ai. Faujāṃ dī kī loṛ sī? Siddhī gall tāṃ ai ve ki aman de cakkar vikhāṇ nāl yā aman dī gall karaṇ nāl kujh na'īṃ bandā. Apnyāṃ faujāṃ sarḥadāṃ toṃ haṭā lo tad tuhānūṃ aman dā nāṃ leṇā bhī sajdā ai'.*

> This Nehru is really a great naive king. Or he thinks the whole world is naive. On the one hand he speaks of peace, and on the other he deploys his entire army at

> the borders of Pakistan. If only someone could ask him: "You simpleton, if you are really—as you claim—a beacon of peace, then why did you need to deploy your troops? The truth is that there is no point in pretending to maintain peace or in just talking about it. If you withdraw your troops from the border then you will be worthy of talking about peace."

The use of this oralized style, which contrasts with the high, formal style used in the other articles of *Daily Imroz*, produces an effect comparable to that of Rahat Gujrati's poem quoted above: it feels like a common man armed with strong common sense is expressing his views.

The next installments of *Gall-bāt*, signed by Zaheer Babur, were written in a more formal tone. Babur commented on international news, reflecting the anti-imperialist political orientation of the newspaper. For instance, on August 25, 1951 he wrote:

> This week, if we speak in the style of the national meteorological office, we will say that the weather has not been mild at all. Clouds continued to blanket India and Pakistan. And it was the same in other Asian countries. There is no longer any hope that the clouds will leave Korea. The Iran issue is still not solved. The war continues in Vietnam. The imperialist Anglo-American coalition seems to be winning in Egypt. The other Arab countries are victims of plots hatched by these imperialists.

On September 1, 1951, in accordance with the ideological line of the newspaper, he sharply criticized the Muslim League:

> The Muslim League is really a strange party. Before the establishment of Pakistan it was a political party in the true sense of the word. But since the country has been created it has only been bothered with placing its members in ministries and in the presidency. . . . Seeing what has become of the Muslim League, a certain number of genuine senior members of this party have abandoned it.[56] And those who have stayed are not in good shape.

Zaheer Babur engaged directly with readers in *Gall-bāt*. He quoted letters from readers who protested or welcomed the introduction of a Punjabi column in a prestigious newspaper like *Daily Imroz*. An Urdu-Punjabi controversy started in the column and went on for several weeks. It began with a letter by Asghar Ali, a supporter of Urdu from Gujrat, which was quoted by Zaheer Babur on September 8, 1951: "There is nothing about Punjabi that justifies that a whole column should be devoted to it. Our duty is to promote Urdu in place of Punjabi. And to make our children forget Punjabi and consider Urdu as their own language." Amanullah, a resident of Rawalpindi, wrote a letter expressing his support for Asghar Ali. Babur quoted it on September 22, 1951:

> Mr. Asghar Ali's suggestion that our children should adopt a sophisticated language like Urdu is quite commendable. . . . Punjabi's alphabet has not yet been standardized. Muslims write it in the Persian alphabet, Hindus in Devanagari, and Sikhs in *Gurumukhi*. And this language has no significant grammar, it is totally devoid of it. And as far as a work like Waris Shah's Heer is concerned, it's a simple love story, written in a corrupted language full of old-fashioned words derived from Sanskrit.

These letters show how popular the discourse of Urdu supporters like Maulana Salahuddin Ahmad had become among the educated classes of Punjab. The idea formulated by Asghar Ali that children should speak Urdu instead of Punjabi seems to have been borrowed directly from Maulana Salahuddin Ahmad's essays.

To respond to these controversial statements, Zaheer Babur quoted letters from pro-Punjabi readers, like this letter from Muhammad Tufail, a resident of Lahore, included in *Gall-bāt* on September 8, 1951:[57]

> The greatest service one can render to a language is to raise it. And we can only raise it by promoting the great poets and writers of this language, and by reflecting on their writings. We will then know how far they have progressed in their task, and what their goal was. In general, when one takes a broad look at Punjabi literature, one realizes that the great poets and writers of Punjabi tried to reform the society of their time and took literature as far as it could go. For example, the writings of poets like Madho Lal Hussain, Bulleh Shah and Baba Farid make us climb to the top of a mountain so high that once we have climbed it it is difficult to come down, and their temperament exerts such an influence on our material and social life that we feel for them an attraction to which we cannot resist. . . . I have studied in detail Punjabi, Urdu, English and Persian literatures, and I have found in Punjabi literature a quality which is specific to it, and which

> is rare in the others. For example, Punjabi poets wrote verse dramas with great mastery and wisdom. And we find in them a quality that one cannot find in Shakespeare. . . . We must first of all share the work of the best writers and poets who write in our language, highlight their qualities, and once we have their work in front of us, follow the path they are showing us.

Muhammad Tufail's letter reads less like an essay in defense of the Punjabi language and more like an essay in defense of the Punjabi poets, arguing that they were social reformers (progressives before their time) and that their works exceeded in quality those of the best English playwright. Tufail's argumentative strategies present astonishing similarities with those of the sixteenth-century apologists of French analyzed in two seminal articles by Jean François Courouau.[58] Tufail uses what Courouau calls "le droit de chef d'oeuvre" (the masterpiece argument), which consists in highlighting a literary heritage that grants authority to the language and allows it to be compared to other languages with a literary heritage such as English, Urdu, or Persian.[59] Moreover, Tufail equates language with literature: "The greatest service one can render to a language is to raise it. And we can only raise it by promoting the great poets and writers of this language." He believes that Punjabi writers are the best representatives of the Punjabi language and that promoting their literature is equivalent to promoting the language itself. As a result of this confusion between language and literature, the program for the promotion of Punjabi proposed by Muhammad Tufail is above all a program for the promotion of its literature.[60] He does not suggest any practical steps for language planning.

Zaheer Babur responded himself on several occasions to the anti-Punjabi readers, using a "popular argument," stressing that Punjabi deserves attention because it is above all the daily language of the common people (*'Awām*) of the province. This argument appears in *Gall-bāt* on September 29, 1951: "Twenty million Punjabis use this language everywhere, whether at home or in the market, on their farm, or in the mosque, with their friends or with their enemies. A Punjabi will converse with another Punjabi only in Punjabi. This means that to express their personal feelings people always prefer their mother tongue. So why not develop this language?" This argument appears again in *Gall-bāt* on December 1, 1951: "It is a fact that a nation cannot progress until it develops its official language as well as its local languages. So we shouldn't ignore our local languages because of Urdu. The place of a language should not be judged by the number of educated people who use it but by the number of common people (*'Awām*) who speak it in the whole country." The term *'Awām* (the people/the masses) on which Zaheer Babur puts special emphasis here, is the touchstone of the Pakistani Marxist discourse of the 1950s.[61] It remains, however, that although Babur underlines the need to "develop" Punjabi, he never specifies how this process can be achieved. His only concrete proposal for the development of Punjabi is the foundation of an organization with multiple branches, a project reminiscent of the *Anjuman-e Taraqqī-e Urdu*. This proposal was presented in *Gall-bāt* on December 8, 1951:

> The popularity of our Punjabi column has made us realize that Punjabi lovers have a strong desire to develop this language, but this task is not easy and a column would not succeed in accomplishing it. It is therefore necessary for all Punjabi lovers to unite and set up a society (*Majlis*) or an association (*Anjuman*). This association should have branches in all big and small cities as well as in villages. Efforts are now underway to establish such an association in the city of Lahore. I think people in other cities will think of doing the same thing and will try to set up similar associations. The purpose of this association will not be to fight against Urdu but to develop Punjabi alongside Urdu.

How will this organization attain this goal? Will it attempt to standardize the language? Extend its uses? Or only promote its literature? Babur does not specify. He remains within the limits that *Daily Imroz* set for itself in the editorial of January 31, 1953 quoted earlier: he does not demand that Punjabi be granted an official status or be made a medium of education.

On February 2, 1952, the last *Gall-bāt* column signed by Zaheer Babur was published; from February 9, this column was written by different contributors. It no longer appeared weekly but several weeks (sometimes even several months) apart. Letters from readers were no longer quoted, and contributors did not discuss the status of Punjabi language and literature, preferring to address social issues. The February 9, 1952 column, penned by Abdullah Malik, discussed the economic crisis the Punjab province was facing. The January 17, 1953 column, penned by Faqeer Mohammad Faqeer, discussed the same topic. The *Gall-bāt* columns of June 5, 12, and 19 and

July 3, 1953 were penned by Ahmad Rahi, whose favorite theme was the corruption widespread in society. Each of his column highlighted a different aspect of this corruption.[62] After July 3, 1953, *Gall-bāt* disappeared.

Daily Imroz's *Punjabi Page*

Gall-bāt reappeared in *Daily Imroz* on March 13, 1955, not as a column but as a weekly page. Known as the Punjabi page (*Panjābī ṣafḥa*), it was directly edited by Ahmad Nadeem Qasmi.[63] To reiterate the initial commitment of the Marxists to Punjabi, the first installment of the Punjabi page included the essay *Ūṃṭ te baddū* that Sharif Kunjahi had read during the Progressive Writers' Association's conference of 1949.

The Punjabi page was a sort of mini literary journal, mirroring the literary production in Punjabi of the Marxists. It usually featured four texts: an essay (serious or humorous), two poetic pieces (usually a song and a poem), and a column by Mirza Sultan Baig (star presenter of the radio show *Dehātī bhāyoṃ ke liye*), titled *Hafte dyāṃ xabrāṃ* (This Week's News).[64]

Poetry occupied an important place in the Punjabi page, which featured approximately four hundred poems between 1955 and 1959 (an average of two poems each week). Some of these poems were written by poets who belonged to the literary generation that had established itself in the 1940s (such as Amrita Pritam) and some by poets who belonged to the post-1947 generation (Qateel Shifai and Afzal Parvez), but many were written by poets from the new generation of progressives like Munnu Bhai, Ahmad Zafar, Mohammad Azam Bhatti, Jameel Malik, Ahmad Riaz, and Saleem Kashir. The Punjabi page also featured poems by working-class poets like Firoz Sain or Ismail Matwala, as well as Hindko and Pothohari poems by Muzmir Tatari and Salim Rafiqi. Their publication testifies to a growing interest among the Punjabi page's editorial team in the peripheral dialects of Punjabi. The Punjabi page also contributed to the development of progressive Punjabi fiction. In 1958, it featured the first Punjabi short stories of Nawaz, a prominent progressive short story writer.[65] The Punjabi page also featured some full-fledged essays on literature or folklore, essays that could not have been published a few years earlier when *Daily Imroz* granted to Punjabi only the half page of the *Gall-bāt* column. Thanks to this new page, the corpus of

Punjabi critical prose expanded in a remarkable way. Between 1955 and 1959, the Punjabi page featured thirty-seven essays in Punjabi: eight essays on the Punjabi language, twenty-one essays on Punjabi literature (nine on Waris Shah, six on various aspects of classical literature, and six on contemporary poets like Firoz Din Sharaf, Firoz Sain, and Maula Bakhsh Kushta), and eight essays on folk songs from the Punjab province.[66] It should also be noted that out of those eight essays, two discussed folk songs from the central regions of Punjab and six folk songs from Pothohar.[67] This shows the growing interest of folklorists in areas other than the central area of Majha-Doaba, as well as the wish of the editor of the Punjabi page, Ahmad Nadeem Qasmi, to highlight the cultural specificities of his native area (he was from Angah, a village on the edge of the Pothohar plateau).

It would be impossible to analyze all the essays published in the Punjabi page between 1955 and 1959. Here we will discuss two important essays: Shaukat Ali's essay on Punjabi and Sharif Kunjahi's essay on the poetry of Punjabi sufis.

SHAUKAT ALI'S ESSAY ON PUNJABI

Sāḍḍī Panjābī zubān (Our Punjabi Language), an essay by Shaukat Ali published on the Punjabi page on May 29, 1955, is of special importance as the culmination of a series of Marxist programs and manifestos that began in 1949 with the presentation of Sharif Kunjahi's essay *Ūṃt te baddū* at the Progressive Writers' Association's conference. In *Sāḍḍī Panjābī zubān*, Shaukat Ali, a prominent member of the Communist Party, analyzes the general perception of Punjabi, summarizes the initiatives taken by various activists since independence to develop it, and proposes a program in seven points to promote it.

OUR PUNJABI LANGUAGE

Punjabi is the language of the land of five rivers. But propaganda and rumors have made it the language of the Sikhs, a language with which Muslims have nothing to do, and which no longer has purpose since the departure of the Sikhs. Some have even said that Punjabi language is not a language. Those who have attacked Punjabi the most are the educated Punjabis. It is always amazing to see that these people are allergic to their mother tongue and hate it. When languages are discussed, and some free spirit (*mancalā*) makes the mistake of saying that Punjabi is a language then we see educated people both frowning and smirking, and the free spirit feels he has committed a sin. . . . Different languages are spoken in the various regions of Pakistan, and in all these regions instruction is given at school in the local language, but Punjab is the only region where the local language has never been used as a medium of instruction. The saddest thing is that 8 years after the creation of Pakistan our education experts and people's representatives still do not want to give any importance to Punjabi and still don't have the intention of making Punjabi a medium of instruction. On the contrary, it looks like Punjabi has been exiled from Punjab.

But our leaders' attempts have not been successful. The Punjabi language cannot be eliminated from this land of songs. . . . For some time Punjabi was on the verge of dying and wandered through the towns like a beggar, and it was the illiterate peasants who gave shelter to it. And after that it won the heart of its Ranjha, and began to be discussed by a few educated people in West Punjab.

In order to develop Punjabi a magazine—*Panjābī*—was published, a weekly column in Punjabi was published for some time in the *Daily Imroz*, a beautiful collection of songs titled *Tirinjan* was published in Urdu script.[68] Some traditional Punjabi songs were also collected and published, and now every week *Daily Imroz* publishes texts in Punjabi. And some friends of Punjabi, despite their financial limitations, intend to publish new journals and new books to develop Punjabi. A small association (*majlis*) made up of Punjabi enthusiasts has been founded in Lahore which organizes meetings from time to time.[69] But this is not enough. . . . First of all we would have to bring together the lovers of Punjabi and establish a solid association which would perform the following tasks:

—Publish attractive editions of Punjabi classical literature
—Publish a monthly journal in Punjabi
—Collect contemporary writings in Punjabi and publish them in book form
—Translate into Punjabi from other languages
—Publish a Punjabi Grammar and Dictionary
—Attempt to make Punjabi a medium of instruction at primary level
—Support Punjabi poets

I hope that the poets and writers of Punjabi will consider these proposals and come together in an association, and this way we will be able to develop together our language, and thus ensure that our people, who are immersed in the darkness of ignorance, will benefit from the light of knowledge and embrace life.

Shaukat Ali's essay initially presents three obstacles facing Punjabi: It is identified with the Sikhs, despised by the educated class, and not used in schools. But for the author, a staunch Marxist, the Punjabi issue is above all a class issue: Educated Punjabis reject Punjabi because of their prejudices, whereas the common people of the countryside identify with it and have become its custodian. Only an intervention of the intellectuals will allow Punjabi to develop and finds its place in society. Its development will allow the common people to have access to education and knowledge. The enrichment of its written corpus (the publication of books and translations) and the use of Punjabi at school are the two measures recommended by the author to facilitate this development.

This program completely ignores Firozuddin Mansoor and Sibte Hasan's maximum program; it reads as a continuation of Abid Hassan Minto's minimum program. Like Minto, Shaukat Ali suggests making Punjabi only a medium of primary instruction. His insistence on enriching the literary corpus of Punjabi probably results from a feeling (shared with Minto) that Punjabi is an "undeveloped" language, lacking a literary corpus to ensure its legitimacy as well as the written/printed material to facilitate its promotion. Once its literary corpus expands and the required material is available, Punjabi will play a greater role in society. The publication of classical and contemporary literature and the compilation of a grammar and a dictionary will help fill this vacuum. Finally, the suggestion to create an organization seems to have been inspired by Zaheer Babur's December 8, 1951 *Gall-bāt* column.

A LITERARY ESSAY: ṢŪFYĀṂ DĪ ŠĀ'IRĪ (POETRY OF THE SUFIS) BY SHARIF KUNJAHI

Sharif Kunjahi stands out among Punjabi essayist as one of the most innovative and most imbued with Marxist ideals; his essay *Ṣūfyāṃ dī šāʿirī* (Poetry of the Sufis), published on the Punjabi page on May 1, 1955, is a manifestation of his originality and outspokenness. This essay was the first to apply to classical Punjabi literature the new approach of Marxist critics who considered each text as the product of political and social conditions and a reflection of the mentalities of its time.[70]

THE POETRY OF THE SUFIS

Nānak dukhyā sab sansār (Nanak, the whole world is unhappy): This great guru, Sufi and poet from Punjab summarized in this verse all Sufi poetry, because the poetry of Sufis is based on the notion that the world is the abode of sorrows. This notion seemed to be accepted by all, and even those who were not Sufis did not dare to question it.

In the presence of the arbitrary laws of self-declared kings and emperors, who would have the courage to transform this unhappy world into a happy one? People didn't know that it was even possible for happiness to spread in this world. Good and bad systems are certainly the cause of people's happiness and unhappiness, but in those ancient times people were not inclined to accept it. They considered kings as the shadow of God and accepted and obeyed them. But that was not all. They considered that happiness belonged to the landowner (*caudhrī*) and misfortune to his serf (*kammī*), and that nothing could be changed, that was a legacy from God. It was His decision whether to bring an individual into a family of kings or into a family of serfs. Thus, someone will sleep on a bed of flowers and someone else on a bed of thorns. The individual must at all times accept the will of God. This could be called fatalism (*taqdīr-parastī*), and we find signs of it in the poetry of the Sufis.

To justify their fatalism, the Sufis often gave as example the lives of our elders: Ibrahim was thrown into a stake, Imam Hussain was trampled in Karbala, Zacharias was cut into pieces. And since the Sufis were all good and pious men they came to the conclusion that God was testing his creatures by exposing them to misfortunes. This notion contradicted the approach which consisted in trying to identify the reason for these misfortunes and remedy them. In this way each unfortunate person began to consider himself chosen by God and tried to pass the test that he had imposed on him. For the fatalists the world is a simple caravanserai where one comes to live, and one should not expect anything from it. . . . After having lost all interest in the world, the path generally taken by individuals was that of introspection and celebration of divine love. And once arrived at this divine love the paths of the Sufis separated. Some wanted to live their lives in accordance with Shariah. . . . And others went beyond it. Some avoided engaging in acts which are prohibited by the Shariah or any other Law: Sultan Bahu,

> Shah Inayat and Bulleh Shah were part of this tradition, and they are the propagators of the poison of religious divisions which has gradually entered the veins of the inhabitants of Punjab. . . . Among the Sufis there were some who could be described as drunkards (*rind*). They liked to live in intoxication. Shah Hussain is their leader.
>
> But even though these Sufis differed from each other in manners and practices, they were similar in one respect: they all regarded this world as the abode of sorrows. And all of them were fatalists. And when you read them, these two notions strike you. This is why Allama Iqbal had at a certain period of his life written verses against Hafez Shirazi. After reading the poetry of the Sufis an individual is no longer able to reform the world. Their poetry is the manifestation of a hidden disease that has affected human society for a long time: pessimism (*bezārī dā rog*). We should—on the contrary—try to turn this unhappy world into a happy one. And to organize our existence in such a way that individuals, instead of running away from the world, are interested in it.

Starting from an analysis of the sociopolitical system and the mentality that prevailed at the time the Sufi poets were active, Sharif Kunjahi comes to condemn their harmful role in society and to criticize their literature, and ends up completely demystifying their role and their writings. Kunjahi makes his criticism in the name of a conception prevalent in the Marxist camp of the writer and of literature as agents for the reform of society.[71] His criticism of Sufis' pessimism was also in tune with Marxist literary ideology. Abid Hassan Minto, in an essay published soon after *Ṣūfyāṃ dī šāʿirī*, described pessimism as one of the decadent and archaic tendencies in literature.[72]

The iconoclastic approach of Sharif Kunjahi, who considers the texts of the Sufis not from a religious but from a social angle, and therefore removes their sacred dimension, remained at the time quite marginal.

Urdu Essays on Punjabi Language and Literature Published in the Daily Imroz

Between 1951 and 1959, alongside essays in Punjabi, *Daily Imroz* also published forty-five essays in Urdu on Punjabi's classical and folk literature. These essays were written by Marxist Punjabi activists such as Ahmad Rahi, Abdul

Majeed Bhatti, Afzal Parvez, Rauf Malik, and Jameel Malik, and in some way complemented their activism, as their goal was to revalorize Punjabi literature and folklore. This series began with *Ḍholak gīt* (*Dholak* Songs), an essay by Abdul Qadir Rashk, published on July 2, 1951.

ESSAYS ON LITERATURE

Twenty-seven of these essays discuss Punjabi literature: nineteen on classical literature and eight on contemporary literature (of which four discuss contemporary Pakistani literature in Punjabi and four discuss contemporary Indian literature in Punjabi).[73] The classical poet most discussed is Waris Shah, the subject of ten essays.[74] The other poets discussed are Ghulam Rasool Alampuri, Mian Muhammad Bakhsh, Hashim Shah, Sultan Bahu, Khwaja Ghulam Farid, Bulleh Shah, and Ali Haidar.[75] These essays are purely informative. They follow more or less the same format, beginning with a biographical outline and then listing the themes and figures of speech recurrent in the poet's work. The tone is often one of celebration or panegyric. In his essay *Wāriṡ kī Hīr* (Waris Shah's Heer), published on February 28, 1953, Sufi Ghulam Mustafa Tabassum, through comparisons with Firdausi, Nizami, and Shakespeare, attempts to revalorize a literature often depreciated and disowned by Punjabis themselves.[76]

> So imagine that some two hundred years after this event took place a poet brings this forgotten story to life again, and breathes new life into it, the same way Firdausi breathed new life into the Persian court's ancient history—or the way Nizami breathed new life into the archaic characters of Khusrau and Shririn and Layla and Majnun. . . . In the same way, the characters of Heer Ranjha are now evolving before our eyes, alive, and move on the vast horizon of the world of literature. And they walk in the company of Romeo and Juliet, Shirin Farhad and Wamiq Azra. The character of Kaido reminds us of those of Mukhtar and Yago, and Sehti looks like one of the women of Egypt. Waris Shah has therefore, by the grace of his talent, extracted these characters from the limited space in which they evolved and given them a universal dimension. They are no longer mere elements of Punjabi poetry or Punjabi romantic literature, but universal symbols.

Some other essayists, in order to improve the popular perception of classical Punjabi literature, attempt to show that classical poets conveyed in their works a social message that is still relevant in contemporary society. Ahmad Rahi in his essay *Panjāb ke 'awāmī adab aur śaqāfat kā ṣaḥīḥ tarjumān Wāriś Šāh* (A True Spokesperson for Punjab's Popular Literature and Culture: Waris Shah), also published on February 28, 1953, explains that Waris Shah was an early progressive writer, concerned with the problems of the people, who demonstrated in his *Heer* the impact of social inequalities on individuals:

> Waris Shah observed the people of Punjab very closely, and he tried to solve their problems. Friends may say that he was primarily a romantic poet, and had no connection with the masses, that he just put into poetry the love story of Heer and Ranjha and that's it! It is true that *Heer Ranjha* is a love story, but the style Waris Shah adopted to tell this story, and the details he provided, make it more than just a love story. Waris Shah has—in a very artistic way—shown that a rich man's daughter cannot marry a poor man.

ESSAYS ON PUNJABI FOLKLORE

Between 1951 and 1959, *Daily Imroz* published eighteen Urdu essays on Punjabi folklore. Six of them discuss the folklore of the central regions of Majha and Doab, seven discuss Siraiki folk songs, and five focus on Pothohar's folk songs.[77] As the 1949 conference manifesto shows, Marxists' priority was to "better understand the feelings and ideas of ordinary people and the problems they face in their lives." This approach quite naturally led them toward the study of Punjab's folk literature, a literature that emanates directly from the masses and describes their daily lives. Some works were already available in Urdu on the folk songs of Punjab: two collections by Devendra Satyarthi and two essays by Saadat Hasan Manto titled *Dehātī bolyāṃ* (Countryside Lyrics).[78] While Satyarthi adopted an ethnographic approach, highlighting the context in which folk songs are performed and analyzing their social discourse, Manto adopted a romantic approach. For him, Punjab's folk songs were above all vehicles for the expression of amorous feelings; he imagined the sentimental life of the people who sang them, praising their freshness and inventiveness. Abdul Qadir Rashk, Abdul Majeed Bhatti, and Rahat Gujrati's essays relate to this romantic trend. These authors have a penchant for idealization; they propagate the stereotype (which dominates Manto's writings on folklore) of a cheerful Punjabi countryside, where feelings and emotions are pure and expression is natural and spontaneous. Abdul Qadir Rashk's essay *Dholak gīt* (Tambourine Songs), published on July 2, 1951, begins this way: "Our songs present a picture of the feelings and accidents of life in which the brilliant colors of sensuality keep on appearing. This is the sensuality of the proud and generous youth, of glances full of desire, of lively atmospheres, thanks to which existence becomes a beautiful coquette, whose charm never ceases to enthrall you." By presenting such a romantic picture of Punjabi folk songs, these writers challenged the common prejudices of the educated classes, who viewed them as vulgar and unsophisticated sets of lyrics. For them, these songs fall in the category of literature, and they do not miss an opportunity to praise them, attributing to them qualities that critics usually attribute to texts whose literary value is undisputed (such as Urdu *ġazals*). A good example is Rahat Gujrati's essay on the genre of *Māhyā*, published on October 22, 1951, which starts this way: "Among Punjabi folk songs the *māhyā* enjoys immense popularity. . . . In Punjabi literature its language and ideas have not been surpassed. The lyrics of *māhye* are dense, full of meaning, effect, imagination and nuances. And it is a genre in which one can express all the facets of human feelings in an extremely delicate way."[79] One can sense in the essays on Siraiki and Pothohari folk songs by Dr. Mehr Abdul Haq and Afzal Parvez a gradual shift toward a more methodical and scientific analysis of folklore, devoid of the sentimentalism and romanticism that dominate Abdul Qadir Rashk and Rahat Gujrati's writings. Dr. Mehr Abdul Haq and Afzal Parvez's approach is similar to that of Devendra Satyarthi. They present in a neutral tone specimens of folk songs sorted by themes, introducing their context of performance and emphasizing their connection to the economic and social structure of the area from which they originate.[80]

End of an Era and the Contribution of Daily Imroz

After the Communist Party of Pakistan and the Progressive Writers' Association were banned in 1954, *Daily Imroz* and *Pakistan Times* remained the primary platforms of the Marxist intellectuals for expressing and spreading their ideas. But their survival was short-lived. In April 1959, *Daily Imroz*, *Pakistan Times*, and *Lail-o nahār* (a magazine founded in 1957 and edited by Sibte Hasan)—all three owned by Mian Iftikharuddin—were nationalized by the Ayub Khan government.[81] *Daily Imroz*'s editor-in-chief, Ahmad Nadeem

Qasmi, and the *Pakistan Times* editor-in-chief, Mazhar Ali Khan, both resigned in protest. From then on, these newspapers, now directly under the control of the government, ceased to be the mouthpieces of the Marxist camp.[82] As a result, not only the first phase of the Marxist movement in Pakistan but also the first phase of the Marxist Punjabi movement came to an end. The Punjabi page continued to be published in *Daily Imroz* even after its nationalization (thanks to the efforts of Zaheer Babur), but its content changed. The polemical essays and poems with a sociopolitical message that were the hallmark of the Punjabi page were no longer published, and the Punjabi page ceased to be the mirror of Marxist Punjabi literature.

Daily Imroz played an important role in the development of Punjabi prose and poetry in Pakistan. It also played an important role in the elaboration of a discourse of defense and revalorization of Punjabi language and literature, as well as in the development of Punjabi folklore studies. But most importantly, *Daily Imroz* considerably increased the reach of literature in Punjabi. Each Punjabi text published in *Daily Imroz*—whose circulation varied between eight thousand and thirty thousand copies—reached a readership eight to thirty times bigger than that of a book or a journal (which generally had a print run of about a thousand copies).

The Punjabi Marxist Group

In 1949–50, some members of the Lahori Marxist camp mobilized for the promotion of Punjabi: Ahmad Nadeem Qasmi, Rauf Malik, Ahmad Rahi, Abdul Majeed Bhatti, Qateel Shifai, Tanvir Naqvi, Zaheer Babur, Qamar Yurish, Chaudhry Nazir Ahmed, and Ustad Daman. Mian Iftikharuddin joined them too, as well as Punjabi activists from other cities such as Sharif Kunjahi (based in Gujrat) and Afzal Parvez (based in Rawalpindi). These early activists motivated some young writers (Munnu Bhai, Shafqat Tanvir Mirza, Saleem Kashir, Ahmad Zafar, Jameel Malik, Azim Bhatti, Ahmad Riaz, and Nawaz), who joined their movement in 1953–54. We can distinguish in this Punjabi Marxist group three subgroups:

1. *Mentors*: Mian Iftikharuddin, Ahmad Nadeem Qasmi, and Zaheer Babur can be considered the group's mentors. They provided the group with platforms and frameworks.

2. *Publishers*: This subgroup is composed of Rauf Malik (responsible for PPH) and Chaudhry Nazir Ahmed (owner of *Nayā Idāra* publishing house). They facilitated the circulation of Punjabi writings by publishing them in book form.
3. *Creators*: This subgroup includes Ahmad Rahi, Abdul Majeed Bhatti, Qateel Shifai, Tanvir Naqvi, Qamar Yurish, Sharif Kunjahi, Munnu Bhai, Shafqat Tanvir Mirza, Saleem Kashir, Ahmad Zafar, Jameel Malik, Azim Bhatti, Ahmad Riaz, Ustad Daman, and Nawaz. These writers enriched Punjabi's literary capital through the production of poetry and prose.[83] A distinction can be made within this subgroup between dominant and dominated writers.[84] Ahmad Rahi, Abdul Majeed Bhatti, Sharif Kunjahi, and Afzal Parvez can be considered dominant writers, as they had acquired the recognition of their peers as well as some symbolic profits (their writings were published in the best journals and newspapers of the country, they were invited to poetic symposia and conferences). Munnu Bhai, Saleem Kashir, Ahmad Zafar, Shafqat Tanvir Mirza, Jameel Malik, Azim Bhatti, Ahmad Riaz, Qamar Yurish, and Nawaz can be considered dominated writers; these young writers were slowly moving toward the same peer recognition and the same symbolic profits that the dominants were enjoying. One can also include among these dominated writers Qateel Shifai and Tanvir Naqvi—two lyricists of film songs who were trying to gain recognition in the field of "serious" (noncommercial) literature—as well as the proletarian poet Ustad Daman, who was facing a highly paradoxical situation: he enjoyed greater notoriety than Ahmad Rahi, Abdul Majeed Bhatti, Sharif Kunjahi, and Afzal Parvez but remained excluded from the system of literary consecration.

DOMINANT WRITERS

AHMAD RAHI (1923–2002)

Born in Amritsar as Ghulam Ahmad into a family of shawl traders, he began writing Urdu poetry at a very young age, under the tutelage of his maternal uncle Sadiq Amritsari.[85] After passing his matriculation, he enrolled at Amritsar's Mayo College but was expelled for political activities, as he had come into contact with the Marxist ideologue Bari Alig and developed sympathies for communism and the progressives' ideas.[86] Under the influence of progressive authors like Krishan Chander, Ismat Chughtai, and Saadat

Hasan Manto (who was then still close to the Progressive Writers' Association), he started writing short stories in Urdu.[87] He soon became secretary of the Amritsar branch of the Progressive Writers' Association and in 1946 joined the Communist Party of India.[88] He witnessed the horrors of Partition and worked as a volunteer in refugee camps.[89] In September 1947, he settled in Lahore, where he continued to be associated with the Communist Party, receiving a salary from the party and managing the publication of its magazines, *Nayā Zamāna* and *Apnā Waṭan*.[90] At about the same time, he became coeditor (with Zaheer Kashmiri) of the progressive journal *Saverā*.[91] After migrating to Lahore, he joined the ranks of Marxist bohemians, assiduously frequenting literary cafes with them.[92]

Soon after independence, Ahmad Rahi started writing poetry in Punjabi. His first Punjabi poems were occasional pieces written in Punjabi primarily to be understood by the popular audiences that attended the meetings and events organized by Marxists. "I wrote four or five poems for conferences . . . it was mere sloganeering, but the listeners would still applaud, it would make them happy. They couldn't understand lines like *Yeh dāġ dāġ ujālā* (These tarnished rays). Of course, myself I was writing in Urdu. But when I saw such response I told myself that I should write in Punjabi."[93] It is mostly his feminine poetry in Punjabi, published in his collection *Tirinjan* (he chose not to include his occasional poems in this collection), that made Rahi famous. He told Ahmad Salim that he had tried to exorcise in poetry the trauma of his encounter with "disgraced" (abducted) women in the refugee camps.[94] "Then when I went to the refugee camps, what I saw there, these girls who didn't want to go back home, it all haunted me. When I came here this grief made me write my poem *Tirinjan*. A few months earlier, while going through these horrible things, I had written my poem *Farhād* and some other poems in Urdu, but what I wanted to express could not be expressed in Urdu."[95] Urdu proved inadequate probably because Rahi had chosen to let the victims—young Punjabi-speaking girls from villages—express themselves directly in the first person in his poems. As a consequence, *Tirinjan's* publication in 1953 made Ahmad Rahi famous as a writer of "feminine poetry." Movie producers then asked him to write lyrics for film songs, and he began a successful career as a lyricist in 1953.[96] He remained involved in the Punjabi movement, becoming the secretary-general of the *Punjabī Adabī Sangat* when it was founded in 1963.[97]

SHARIF KUNJAHI (1914-2007)

Born into a family of scholars in Kunjah (near Gujrat city), the son of a schoolmaster, Sharif Kunjahi passed his matriculation in 1930 and his intermediate exam in 1933, but had to discontinue his studies for financial reasons. He then worked as a clerk in the British army.[98] He began to write poems in Urdu, and his first poems were published in the Urdu section of Gurbaksh Singh's journal *Prītlaṛī*.[99] He started gaining fame in literary circles and, in 1941, gained further recognition when his pacifist poem *Paspā'ī* (A Withdrawal) was included by the poet Miraji in his anthology of the best poems of the year.[100] Kunjahi decided to enter the teaching profession. He passed a BA at the Punjab University in 1943, trained as a schoolteacher, and taught in various schools. After obtaining two MAs (one in Urdu in 1954 and another in Persian in 1956), he was appointed professor of Persian at Attock College in 1959. He was then transferred to Government College, Jhelum, from where he retired in 1973. From 1973 to 1980, he taught at the newly opened Punjabi department of the Punjab University in Lahore.

Sharif Kunjahi described himself in his interviews with Khalid Humayun as an outsider, a small-town dweller who was never connected with influential literary circles.[101] This is not entirely true, as the same interviews reveal that he was in close contact with several important literary circles during his career: Gurbaksh Singh's *Prītlaṛī* circle, Miraji's *Ḥalqa-e Arbāb-e Żauq*, and the Progressive Writers' Association.[102] It was Ahmad Nadeem Qasmi—with whom he maintained close ties until the end of his life—who invited him to participate in events organized by the progressives.[103] Kunjahi's poems and essays were published in the best journals of his time, but his first book was published in Pakistan only in 1960: a collection of Punjabi essays entitled *Jhātyāṃ* (Overviews). *Jagrāte* (Night Vigils), his first Punjabi poetry collection, originally published in *Gurumukhi* script in Ludhiana in 1958, was published in Urdu script in Pakistan in 1965.[104]

Sharif Kunjahi had been writing in Punjabi since 1938 (fifteen of the poems in his collection *Jagrāte* were written between 1938 and 1947). Since he could read the *Gurumukhi* script, he read Prof. Mohan Singh's seminal poetry collection *Sāve pattar* (Green Leaves) when it was published and tried his hand at writing in free verse under his influence.[105] Kunjahi explained to Intizar Hussain the reasons why he chose to write in Punjabi:

> I progressively felt that the characteristic fragrance of the area where I come from, and which was inside me, I could not bring it out in my Urdu poetry. And this feeling made me distance myself from Urdu and brought me closer to Punjabi. Each language has a certain intellectual and emotional temperament. It influences a writer and shapes him. The intellectual and emotional temperament of Punjabi is different from that of Urdu. And the temperament of Punjabi is not only different from that of Urdu but also from that of Persian.[106]

Sharif Kunjahi, like Ahmad Rahi, had reached the point where Urdu had become a kind of foreign language, a sort of screen filtering and limiting his expression. It proved to be inadequate for him also because, like Ahmad Rahi, he had chosen to write in a rural feminine voice. One can hear in poems like *Lamyāṃ syālī rātāṃ* (These Long Winter Nights), *Uḍīk* (The Wait), and *Vīr tūṃ Kunjāh dā ai?* (Hey Brother, Are You from Kunjah?) the voice of a countryside girl who speaks in the first person and recounts her misfortunes.[107]

ABDUL MAJEED BHATTI (1902–1974)

Born in a village near Wazirabad, the son of a *Patwari* (village accountant), he abandoned his studies at the age of seventeen and worked as a schoolteacher in Wazirabad, Sheikhupura, Kohat, and Lahore.[108] He then gave up teaching, and worked for some time as a calligrapher for the prestigious literary magazine *Maxzan*, and met the nationalist poet Hafeez Jalandhari, who became his mentor.[109] In 1930, Bhatti started publishing a children's magazine in Urdu entitled *Hūnhār*. After it went bankrupt in the mid-1940s, he edited small magazines such as *Kisān* and *Rehbar* and wrote scripts and songs for radio and cinema.[110] In 1946, he published his first collection of Urdu poetry, *Nām-o nang* (Honor and Repute), which was prefaced by Hafeez Jalandhari.

Abdul Majeed Bhatti's position in the literary landscape was ambivalent. He was close to the nationalist poet Hafeez Jalandhari, but he nevertheless joined the progressives (and was mentioned by Sajjad Zaheer in his book *Rūšnā'ī* as one of the regular participants in the meetings of the Progressive Writers' Association in Lahore in the 1940s).[111] He distanced himself from them after independence and did not participate in their 1949 conference, but his Punjabi poems were published in *Saverā*, and his first Punjabi collection—*Dil daryā*—was published by the progressive publishing house

Nayā Idāra. Poet and essayist, he gradually turned to fiction. His Punjabi short stories were published in *Monthly Panjābī* in 1951, 1955, and 1958, and he wrote a long Punjabi novel—*Ṭheḍḍā* (A Blow)—that was published in 1960.

Abdul Majeed Bhatti explained in the preface of *Ṭheḍḍā* why he chose to write in Punjabi at the age of forty-five, after writing all his life in Urdu. He explained that in Pakistan after independence:

> Nobody was even mentioning the Punjabi language. Moreover, Sikhs had given a different shape to it. That's why the Muslims had abandoned it. . . . When Pakistan was created I said to myself: "Now our official language is Urdu. Thanks to Urdu I will not be a stranger in any corner of the country. Without Urdu I am half of myself. And Punjabi is my substance. If it dies I will die. And if I die who will speak Urdu?" I decided not to let it die at any cost. And I started to write in Punjabi alongside with Urdu.[112]

Abdul Majeed Bhatti had therefore started writing in Punjabi for "ethical" reasons, to safeguard his language.

AFZAL PARVEZ (1917–2001)

Afzal Parvez was born into a scholarly family in Rawalpindi. His brother, Anjum Rizwani, was a well-connected Urdu poet, and through him Afzal Parvez met renowned Urdu poets of his time, such as Abdul Hameed Adam.[113] Throughout his youth, he tried his hand at several jobs and activities (he worked as a painter, ran a restaurant, was an active member of the Khaksar movement).[114] After being drafted into the British army in 1940, he was stationed in Calcutta, Pune, and Delhi and fought on the Burmese front. Once demobilized, he secured a job at Rawalpindi's ration office and finally found his path.[115] He joined the circle of progressive writers of Rawalpindi and, like them, composed Urdu poems with a sociopolitical message. Sajjad Zaheer, who attended a meeting of the Rawalpindi branch during the 1940s, heard him recite his poems and, although he appreciated Parvez's commitment to the principles of the Progressive Writers' Association, passed a harsh judgment on his poetry.[116] It was the ideology of the progressives that prompted Afzal Parvez to write in Punjabi, and he motivated other progressive writers to imitate him: "When I joined the Progressive Writers' Association and realized that literature's aim was to change lives, I thought that if literature was for the common people it should be written in the language of the people. Thus I launched a movement in Rawalpindi's literary circle to encourage writers who knew and spoke Punjabi to produce in Punjabi a literature of the people (*'Awāmī adab*)."[117] As a result, he wrote his first poem in Punjabi *Ulāhmāṃ* (Complaints) in 1948 and went on writing poetry in Punjabi.[118]

After being fired from his job because of his close association with the progressives, in 1952 Afzal Parvez found a new job at Rawalpindi's radio station, where he hosted Pothohari programs *Pindī des* (Rawalpindi Region) and *Jamhūr nā program* (The People's Broadcast) until 1970.[119] During a major part of his life, he collected folk songs from the Pothohar plateau, an activity that led him to be associated with *Lok Virsa* after its creation in 1974.[120]

The four dominant writers were of different ages, hailed from different areas of Punjab, had different trajectories. and their degree of involvement with the Progressive Writers' Association varied. Ahmad Rahi and Afzal Parvez were formally affiliated with it, Sharif Kunjahi was an unaffiliated sympathizer, and Abdul Majeed Bhatti was a free electron, at times close to it and at times distancing himself. The motivations that led them to write in Punjabi differed, too, but writing in Punjabi did not mean giving up on Urdu. For example, Ahmad Rahi published in the same issue of *Saverā* in 1951 one poem in Urdu—*Yehī woh sarzamīn hai?* (Is This Really the Same Country?) and another in Punjabi—*Canāṃ ve terī cannī* (My Beloved, Look at the Full Moon!).[121] Nevertheless, when we look at the place of these four writers in the Urdu literary subfield of their time, we find them among the dominated writers. Even though their Urdu works were noticed and published in well-known journals and anthologized, they remained in the shadow of the "gatekeepers," the transmitters of symbolic capital who launched them: Miraji for Sharif Kunjahi, Hafeez Jalandhari for Abdul Majeed Bhatti, Ahmad Nadeem Qasmi for Ahmad Rahi, and his own brother Anjum Rizwani for Afzal Parvez.[122] They remained minor Urdu poets, whose fame could not be compared to that of Faiz Ahmad Faiz, N. M. Rashid, Hafeez Jalandhari, or Ahmad Nadeem Qasmi. Writing in Punjabi gave them the opportunity to exchange a dominated position for a dominant position.

DOMINATED WRITERS

Inspired by these four dominant writers, some young Marxist writers took to writing in Punjabi between 1952 and 1955: Qamar Yurish, Shafqat Tanvir

Mirza, and Jameel Malik adopted Punjabi in 1952, Ahmad Zafar in 1954, and Munnu Bhai, Saleem Kashir, and Nawaz in 1955. They were still at the beginning of their literary careers and seeking recognition from their peers. Their social and academic capital was generally high: Qamar Yurish and Nawaz were self-taught, but Jameel Malik, Ahmad Zafar, and Shafqat Tanvir Mirza held an MA degree. Jameel Malik and Ahmad Zafar were teachers, and Shafqat Tanvir Mirza was a journalist. Munnu Bhai and Saleem Kashir both held a BA, and both were journalists. This shows that Punjabi had begun to attract intellectuals from the privileged classes. We also note that these writers maintained a bilingual literary activity (Urdu and Punjabi), with the exception of Saleem Kashir, who devoted himself entirely—on the advice of Ahmad Nadeem Qasmi—to Punjabi.[123]

Ustad Daman (1911–1984) occupied a special place among the dominated writers. A tailor by profession, and a disciple of the proletarian Punjabi poet Hamdam, he started his poetic career before Partition, regularly participating in public meetings of the Congress Party (sometimes in the presence of Jawaharlal Nehru himself) and galvanizing the crowds with anti-British poems in Punjabi. After independence, he joined the ranks of the Marxists. His association with them began on May, 1, 1949, when the progressives organized a poetic symposium, chaired by Faiz Ahmad Faiz, in which Daman participated. On this occasion, he came out of the silence in which he had remained since Partition (which had brought its share of traumas: his house had been burned and his wife kidnapped) and recited a poem—*Inqilāb* (Revolution)—in which one can sense the influence of the progressives' poetic language.[124] Daman quickly became a regular participant at the public meetings organized by the Marxists and ended up accompanying Abid Hassan Minto and Mazhar Ali Khan during the electoral campaign of the trade union leader Mirza Ibrahim in 1950–51.[125] Minto recalls that "Daman would also take part in our public meetings. In fact, people came above all to listen to him. So we would write his name in big letters on our posters."[126]

Marxist intellectuals benefited from Ustad Daman's popularity, but certain social prejudices prevented them from giving him his due recognition. It was Sharif Kunjahi, for example, and not Ustad Daman who was chosen at the conference of November 1949 to talk about the status of Punjabi (undoubtedly because Kunjahi was considered more educated/sophisticated than Daman). Daman's poems were not considered sophisticated enough to be published in *Saverā* or *Daily Imroz*, or in book form by PPH or *Nayā Idāra*. It was generally believed that Daman's poems lost their appeal once they appeared as written texts. Amrita Pritam summed up the opinion that prevailed in literary circles: "It is true that Daman's texts lose quite a bit of their brilliance and luster once they are on paper."[127]

Therefore, Ustad Daman continued to occupy a dominated position among Punjabi Marxist writers, as he did not receive the recognition of his peers.

Urdu Writers and Punjabi: The Divergent Attitudes of Faiz Ahmad Faiz and Saadat Hasan Manto

The famous Urdu poet Faiz Ahmad Faiz soon became aware of the growing popularity of Punjabi as a literary medium among Marxist writers. Rauf Malik visited him in jail in 1952 in order to prepare the publication of his collection *Dast-e ṣabā* (Hand of Breeze) and told him about the Punjabi movement initiated by some Marxist writers, and for a while Faiz considered adopting Punjabi like them.[128] He wrote to his wife on July 9, 1952 from Hyderabad prison: "I have been thinking for several days that I should maybe write in Punjabi and see how I write in my language. Urdu is a language so ornate, I find it hard to understand how I should write it so that it can reach people."[129]

But Faiz Ahmad Faiz ultimately did not write anything in Punjabi. It was only in 1971 that he wrote his first poem in Punjabi (followed by six others). I. A. Rehman, in an interview published in *Herald* in March 1984, asked him why:

Q: Why have you not written poetry—except for a few poems—in the language of your folk tradition—Punjabi?

A: Partly because the classical Punjabi poets—Baba Farid, Waris Shah, Bulleh Shah, Sultan Bahu, set up such high standards that one finds the task of picking up where they left extremely difficult. Then, knowledge of a language is not enough to be able to write poetry in it. It demands command over nuances of expression, which require a great deal of apprenticeship to craft. We did not have any academic training in Punjabi, no opportunity of developing a discipline to express in Punjabi verse.

This answer did not convince Shafqat Tanvir Mirza. He reckoned that Faiz's decision not to write in Punjabi was rather prompted by the fear of "declassing" oneself linguistically—that is, abandoning a position of superiority conferred by the knowledge and use of Urdu, a fear common among Urdu literati: "If you want to talk about the literature and the language of the common people you will have to declass yourself linguistically. But their [Urdu literati's], position in Urdu literature was such that they could not abandon the path on which they had embarked."[130]

Safdar Mir too believed that Urdu literati did not adopt Punjabi for fear of losing a position of cultural superiority they had worked hard to acquire: "If one were to examine the mentality of writers, intellectuals and scholars who are afraid to write in Punjabi . . . one would find that what bothers them is not the Punjabi words but the culture they left behind, and which is now only the culture of the common people."[131]

The case of Saadat Hasan Manto is very different from that of Faiz Ahmad Faiz. An anti-conformist figure in literature, sensitive to the fate of people who live on the margins of society, and himself ostracized by the literary establishment of his time, he was certainly not afraid to declass himself. Manto had been interested in Punjabi since the early 1940s (as the publication of two laudatory essays on the Punjabi *Boliyaṁ* in his collection of essays in 1942 shows).[132] This interest increased after his meeting with Ahmad Rahi, to the extent that he wrote a blurb for *Tirinjan* directly in Punjabi, and soon after penned a Punjabi short story, which he wanted Ahmad Nadeem Qasmi to publish on *Daily Imroz's* Punjabi page.[133] Qasmi narrated this special episode in details:

> One day Manto came to the *Daily Imroz* office and said: "I have written a short story in Punjabi for the first time in my life. You publish a Punjabi page in your newspaper, publish it in it!" I expressed great happiness, and took his manuscript. When I read this short story, which was written with a pencil, I found Manto to be at the level he had reached a few years earlier. I asked the office administration to give him an advance and I was planning to advertise the story by announcing "Manto's first short story in Punjabi" in the newspaper before publishing it, but a few days later the police came and raided my office, and handled the manuscripts with such brutality that Manto's story disappeared somewhere. As long as I worked at *Daily Imroz* I kept looking for it in my old files but it is possible that the police had seized it and transferred it "to the other side."[134]

Saadat Hasan Manto did not write any other short story in Punjabi, as he died in 1955. His death represented a missed opportunity for the Punjabi movement, as the regular involvement of a writer of Manto's stature and notoriety would have greatly increased its impact.

The Marxists' Literary Output in Punjabi

Poetic Output

In examining the overall poetic production in Punjabi of the Marxists, one can notice the absence of the genre of *ġazal*, a classical form usually rejected by them, as they considered it a vestige of a bygone feudal era.[135] Marxist poets preferred writings modern poems with a sociopolitical message or songs inspired by Punjabi folklore.[136] Marxist poetic production in Punjabi can be divided into three corpuses: poetic cycles (Ahmad Rahi's *Tirinjan* and Abdul Majeed Bhatti's *Dil daryā*), poems published in *Saverā*, and poems published in *Daily Imroz*.

THE POETIC CYCLES: *TIRINJAN* AND *DIL DARYĀ*

Tirinjan (1953), the first original Punjabi poetry collection published in Pakistan after independence, is a poetic cycle comprising of forty-two poems. One can hear in each poem the voice of an anonymous rural female character who tells her own story in the first person. This stylistic unity was achieved through a strict selection: Rahi excluded all "non-feminine" poems from his collection. Rahi explained this approach in an interview with Ahmad Salim: "In *Tirinjan* you can hear the same character talking constantly. I have never written poetry with a specific project, but when I was compiling this book I had to make a choice. I thought I should make this book just a feminine book, a book of the Earth, and that there should be only one style in it. The poems I had written for conferences were of a different style, so I excluded them during the compilation . . . then this book became a kind of story."[137] *Tirinjan* was thus conceived as a poetic cycle, and the poems included in it, joined end to end, form a plot. Critics who have analyzed *Tirinjan* agree in dividing this cycle into two distinct sections.[138] The first section comprises thirty-one poems, and its plot is summarized by Sharif

Kunjahi as follows: "In these poems a woman, who was once a little girl, expresses her feelings. She gradually becomes a young girl, falls in love, and laments after being unlucky in love."[139]

The progression that Sharif Kunjahi describes is perfectly observable: the first poem of this first section—*Nave nave bor* (New Buds)—describes the heroine's transition to adulthood.[140] The next poems—*Kiklī*, *Naram kāljā ḍol gayā* (My Tender Heart Has Swayed), and *Vanjārā* (The Nomad)—describe her first emotions.[141] Then the heroine's tone becomes bitter, and she expresses her first sorrows in the poem *Vanj karaṇ vanjāre* (The Nomads Do Their Trade).[142] The poem *Jāṇ wālyā* (O You Who Depart) describes the departure of the beloved.[143] Then, in *Kallī* (Alone), the heroine remains alone, and in *Terī yād* (Your Memory), her beloved becomes a mere memory.[144] In the next poems, the heroine adopts an aggressive tone, cursing her beloved for having cheated on her in *Farebyā* (You Cheater!), or repents for having loved him in *Pyār na karṇā* (You Must Not Love).[145]

The second section of the cycle (eleven poems) begins with *Tirinjan* (The Assembly of Women).[146] This poem marks a transition from personal to collective concerns. It denounces the oppression of which women are generally victims, caught between the Sikh and Muslim factions in *Kaido* and *Kheṛe*, coveted by landowners in *Jāgīrāṃ wāle* and by men of power in *Meḥl māṛyāṃ wāle* (Castle and Palace Dwellers). Each of the poems that follow the poem *Tirinjan* thematizes in its own way the violence women have been subjected to during Partition: *Behnāṃ dyo vīro* (Brothers of Your Sisters) is a complaint to brothers who have failed to protect their sisters; in *Būhe khulī rakhī!* (Keep the Door Open!), *Tere būhe āyāṃ* (I Have Come to Your Door), and *Būhe ho ga'e bheṛe* (The Doors are Closed), an abducted girl who has come back home addresses her family members and begs them to accept her again.[147] *Merā koī na dardī* (No One Sympathizes with Me) also thematizes the rejection suffered by abducted women upon their return.[148] The last poem of the cycle—*Jai tūṃ Mirzā hundeo* (If You Were Mirza)—denounces the cowardice of men.[149]

Ahmad Rahi, in these poems, sought to draw public attention to the plight of women abducted at the time of Partition: "At that time I had the impression that this was the fate that awaited these girls. Some disappeared. When they were found they didn't return to their parents' house. Those who returned were rejected. Some became prostitutes."[150]

Tirinjan influenced a whole generation of Pakistani poets. Deeply influenced by Amrita Pritam, Ahmad Rahi borrowed from her poetic language to create his own. Like her, he used forms common in folklore (*ṭappe* and *bolyāṃ*) and, like her, multiplied references to characters from the Punjabi epics (*Hīr, Mirzā, Ṣāḥibāṁ*).[151] He also took up some of Amrita Pritam's recurrent themes, such as the tragedy of the female condition or the violence of Partition. This is the reason *Tirinjan* is dedicated to her.

Dil daryā (Rivers of the Heart), a collection of sixty-two poems by Abdul Majeed Bhatti published in October 1955, shares a number of similarities with *Tirinjan*. These poems also borrow from the folk songs of Punjab and are replete with references to characters of Punjabi epics. We can also hear in each poem an anonymous female voice narrate her misfortunes in the first person, but—and this represents a notable innovation—a second voice sometimes comes to answer her: the voice of her mother in *Kaṇkāṃ te chaṇkāṃ* (Wheat and Tinkles), of her sister-in-law in *Vag vag ni chaitr diye vā'e* (Breath, April Wind!), or of her lover in *Dogānā* (Duet).[152] Like *Tirinjan*, *Dil daryā* is a poetic cycle in which a woman, in poem after poem, recounts her ordeals. In *Kaṇkāṃ te chaṇkāṃ*, she enters adult life and comes into marriageable age, which makes her apprehensive.[153] She becomes aware of her beauty and realizes that she can be an object of male desire in *Maiṃ kallī hondī jāṇī āṃ* (I am More and More Alone).[154] She experiences love for the first time and has her first affairs: *Kamlī maiṃnūṃ ākho na* (Don't Say that I Am Mad!); *Rāhe rāhe jā* (Continue Your Way!); *Koī takdā rahve koī jhakdā rahve* (Someone Is Watching and Someone Is Hesitating).[155] In *Mere hath pīle* (My Hands Are Yellow), she gets married and her new life brings a new set of hardships, because her husband leaves for the army and gives no more news: *Das kāṃvāṃ karmāṃwālyā* (Tell me, O Kind Crow!).[156] She gives birth to a child, but in the absence of her husband, she has to support herself and her child: *Maiṃ kisdā khaṭyā khāṃ* (On Whom Could I Depend?).[157] From this point on, the cycle's poems alternate between reminiscence of her husband gone to the front—*Ve sipāhyā ḍhol māhyā* (O My Beloved Soldier)—and poems lamenting separation: *Pa'ī kūnj vāṃgoṃ kurlāvāṃ* (Should I Howl Like a Crane?); *Bol mere man dyā panchyā* (Tell Me, O Bird of My Mind).[158]

Dil daryā is in many respects a watered-down version of *Tirinjan*, borrowing its language and style without its tragic resonance: the only tragedy evoked in the cycle is the departure of the husband for the army. The violence of Partition, the exploitation of women, and the cowardice of men, recurring motifs in *Tirinjan*, are completely absent from *Dil daryā*. *Dil daryā* presents an image of an immutable and innocent rural world that ignores inequality and exploitation and is immune from sociopolitical upheaval.

POEMS PUBLISHED IN *SAVERĀ*

Most of the poems published in the journal *Saverā* between 1950 and 1952 were penned by poets who had read their Punjabi texts in the meetings of the progressives (Ahmad Rahi, Abdul Majeed Bhatti, Sharif Kunjahi, Tanvir Naqvi, and Afzal Parvez). Their themes generally reflect the sociopolitical concerns of the Marxist group. Each poem denounces and condemns a form of oppression: Tanvir Naqvi's *Idhar odhar* (Here and There) denounces the cynicism of capitalist leaders; Afzal Parvez's *Jaṭṭā pagṛī sambhāl* (O Farmer, Don't Drop Your Turban) condemns the feudal system (*Caudhrāhaṭ*) that prevails in the countryside; Sharif Kunjahi's *Maheṭ* condemns the indifference of the bourgeois class to the fate of the undernourished destitutes, and his *Lammyāṃ syālī rātāṃ* (These Long Winter Nights) denounces the pathetic condition of soldiers' wives.[159] These poems can be classified into two subgenres: feminine poems and revolutionary poems. Feminine poems are not very different from the ones in *Tirinjan* and *Dil daryā*. The revolutionary poems could also be called "challenging poems," as the poet challenges the powerful of this world. Thus, in Tanvir Naqvi's *Idhar odhar* (Here and There), the poet—who has become a spokesperson for the Punjabi peasants— directly addresses the rich and powerful:

Diḍḍhāṃ wālyoṃ sāḍḍī tuhāḍḍī vakhrī vakhrī rāh
Tuhāḍḍe dil vic nafrat kīnā sāḍḍe dil vic cāh
Asīṃ aman de āṃ rākhwāle tusīṃ laṛāyāṃ pāl
Asīṃ vasāyie khet zamīnāṃ tusīṃ puwānde kāl

O you paunchy ones, our paths are very different
Your hearts are full of hatred and resentment, our hearts full of longings
We are the custodians of peace, you are the custodians of war
We spread our fields on the soil and you create famines

POEMS PUBLISHED ON *DAILY IMROZ*'S PUNJABI PAGE

In 1955, the Punjabi page of *Daily Imroz* started featuring poems by emerging Punjabi Marxist writers like Munnu Bhai, Ahmad Zafar, Jameel Malik, Saleem Kashir, and Shafqat Tanvir Mirza. Their poetry presents strong elements of continuity with that of their predecessors whose texts were published some years earlier in *Saverā*. They use the same genres (poems with a sociopolitical message, feminine poems inspired by folk songs), and they share the same social and political concerns. Their poems can be divided into three genres: revolutionary poems, social poems, and feminine poems.

Munnu Bhai's *Sāḍḍe gīt fajr dyāṃ bāngāṃ* (Our Songs Are Like Morning Prayer Calls) is an example of revolutionary poem.[160] The entire progressive group seems to speak in this poem, a united group that challenges the powerful, reiterating its determination to continue the struggle despite persecutions and incarcerations:

Asīṃ mohnyāṃ koloṃ na'īṃ ḍarde asīṃ ṯʿane sunke na'īṃ saṛde
Aih mohne sāḍḍyāṃ khaṭyāṃ ne aih ṯʿane 'umar kamāyāṃ ne
Kujh ās ummīd dittyāṃ ne asāṃ āvaṇ wālyāṃ rāhyāṃ nūṃ
Kujh navyāṃ rāhvāṃ disyāṃ ne sānūṃ jāṇ wālyāṃ rāhyāṃ nūṃ . . .
Tū rākhā kacciāṃ kandhāṃ dā asīṃ dil vagde daryāvāṃ de
ka'ī kandhāṃ asāṃ išāre vic muṃh bharne ḍeg vikhāyāṃ ne

We are not afraid of reprimands, reproaches never anger us
These reprimands we have earned them, these reproaches are our life savings
We gave hope to the travelers of tomorrow
And some young travelers have shown us new paths . . .
You are protecting your walls of mud, and we are the hearts of flowing rivers
And with a single move we have knocked down some of these walls

Some revolutionary poems challenge not the powerful but the masses, calling on them to mobilize and protest. Ahmad Riaz, in his poem *Succā gīt* (A Frank Song), addresses the masses, calling on them to protest against the

Atoms for Peace program announced at the United Nations by U.S. President Dwight Eisenhower in December 1953.[161]

Ā aman de bol sunāye nī
Ā dasye manṣabdārāṃ nūṃ
Aihnāṃ rāhbarāṃ muxtārāṃ nūṃ
Aih jang usāḍḍī rīt na'īṃ
Sānūṃ aṭom nāl prīt na'īṃ

Come, let's talk about peace
Come, let's say to these high officials
To these leaders and caretakers
That war is not in our tradition
We don't like atomic weapons

Daily Imroz's Punjabi page often features social poems depicting the condition of vulnerable people in society. Thus, in his poem *Šāʕir te laṛkā* (The Poet and the Wood Gatherer), Mohammad Azim Bhatti describes the life of the unfortunate people who carry wood on their backs for miles for just a few pennies.[162]

Aṭhāṃ annyāṃ c gaḍḍā šehr vec ānde ne
Aihnāṃ pairāṃ dī kamā'ī ka'ī lok khānde ne
Kadī kadī harjāne vī tāṃ bhare jānde ne
Sāre sāl dī kamā'ī vaḍḍe cāṭ jānde ne

They sell their pile of wood in the city for eight annas
A few people make money from their feet
People who sometimes fine them
And usurp a whole year's income from them

The poem ends with the wood gatherer's desperate complaint:

Kadoṃ phuṭegā ujālā kadoṃ sukh pāvāṃge?
Aihnāṃ paisāṃ dī kamā'ī asīṃ āp khāvāṃge?

When will we see the light of day? When will we be happy?
And enjoy ourselves the money we have earned?

Emerging Punjabi Marxist writers continued to write feminine poems. One can hear in their poems a desperate female voice similar to those heard in the earlier poems of Ahmad Rahi, Abdul Majeed Bhatti, and Sharif Kunjahi. Both Saleem Kashir's *Maiṃ ḍārāṃ de vic kalyāṃ* (I am Alone in This Herd) and Ahmad Zafar's *Buk buk hānjhū kerāṃ* (I Shed Bitter Tears) continue the trend of feminine poems.[163]

Fictional Output

Punjabi fiction appeared to be a budding genre among Marxists who were focusing above all on poetry. Nevertheless, some of them penned Punjabi short stories that followed the progressive canon. The first progressive short story in Punjabi to be published in Pakistan was Abdul Majeed Bhatti's *Bholī* (An Innocent).[164] Published in 1951, it dealt with a theme often addressed by Marxists in poetry, the condition of women in the countryside. *Bholī* tells the story of a young widow coveted by a powerful man from her village. The trade unionist Qamar Yurish also wrote a progressive short story, in 1952: *Āṭe dā sair* (A Kilo of Flour).[165] This story depicts an episode in the daily life of a worker: Rahim arrives late at the factory, is reprimanded and insulted by his foreman, but is compelled to tolerate the humiliation because he cannot lose his job. He has to feed his family.

At the end of the 1950s, Nawaz emerged as the most promising progressive writer of Punjabi fiction. His first Punjabi stories were featured on *Daily Imroz*'s Punjabi page: *Šeryā ve šeryā* (Lion, O Lion!) and *Pinḍ dā bāo* (The "Sir" of the Village).[166] These two short stories are thematically close to *Tirinjan* and *Dil daryā*, as they deal with single women in a rural context. *Šeryā ve šeryā* tells the story of Taji, a woman whose husband has gone to the city to work and disappeared. She raises her daughter alone, but the villagers try to drive her out of the village because they believe she is a "bad woman." The village chief defends her against all odds, but one night he breaks into her home and, under the influence of alcohol, tries to rape her. She resists, falls to the ground, and dies. The village chief runs away. The next day, he gives the villagers permission to expel Taji from the village, but when they enter her house, they find only her corpse, which they consider impure and do not dare to touch. The village's sweeper (*Jamādār*) drags Taji's corpse to the cemetery, and he ends up raising her daughter. *Pinḍ dā bāo* tells the story of an orphan who, by dint of hard work, becomes a schoolteacher—an extremely rare phenomenon in the countryside, where such positions are generally held by men—but is constantly mocked by the villagers, who call her *Bāo* ("Sir"). These two short stories address the same themes: the vulnerability of women in rural communities and the social hypocrisy that prevails there.

Conclusion

The Marxists launched their Punjabi movement in unfavorable circumstances. Their organizations were banned in 1954 and their newspapers nationalized in 1959. Thus, their Punjabi movement was stifled without having been able to give its full measure, and Punjabi was deprived of the Marxists' continued support. The Marxists' precarious position was a significant disadvantage for their Punjabi movement, but it was not the only one. Another was the lack of a clear and unified position among them regarding Punjabi. The statements of Sharif Kunjahi (made during the 1949 conference) and the maximum program of Firozuddin Mansoor and Sibte Hasan were not approved by all Marxists. Marxists did not agree on the place to be given to Punjabi in the Punjab province; for some of them, no doubt, there was no question of Punjabi assuming the role that had been assigned to Urdu for a century. There was nevertheless a consensus on the need to "develop" Punjabi and to enrich its literary capital. The latter goal was achieved: Marxists wrote poetry, essays, and fiction in Punjabi, substantially enriching these three genres. Their literary production followed their specific aesthetics and clearly disseminated their values. A third disadvantage for the Marxists' Punjabi movement was that they adopted from the beginning a cautious strategy, one that differed enormously from the strategies adopted in other language movements such as the Bengali or Sindhi movements. The Marxists did not attempt to mobilize either the masses or the politicians in favor of Punjabi. They did not organize any public meetings or demonstrations, circulate any petitions, or propose any bill in the assembly. The Marxist leader Mian Iftikharuddin, who was a passionate defender of Punjabi, sat in the Punjab assembly during the first half of the 1950s, but he did not play the role of defender of the local vernacular that G. M. Syed exercised in the Sindh assembly during those years.

Why did the Marxists choose such a cautious strategy? One hypothesis would be that, on one hand, since the Bengali movement had been criticized by a large part of the intelligentsia, and individuals involved in initiatives in support of regional languages were often accused of spreading hatred against Urdu (*Urdu-dušmanī*), Marxists deliberately adopted a certain caution and limited their pro-Punjabi initiatives to promoting the language in their newspapers and enriching its literature. On the other hand, it appears also that the diglossic hierarchy prevailing in Punjab (with Urdu as high and Punjabi as low) had been internalized to such an extent by the majority of Punjabi Marxists that they did not find the Punjabi language "developed enough" to assume the role of administrative language and language of instruction. Therefore, they did not consider that this language deserved to have a full-fledged movement (involving mass mobilization) devoted to it.

FIVE

The Conservative Punjabi Movement (1950–1960)

IN 1950, FAQEER Mohammed Faqeer, a senior Punjabi writer associated with the conservative literary camp, secured the support of the province's most senior Punjabi poet (Karam Amritsari), of some Urdu journalists who had sympathy for the cause of Punjabi (Abdul Majeed Salik, Waqar Ambalvi), and of some academics (Mohammad Baqir, Abid Ali Abid) and initiated a specifically conservative movement in favor of Punjabi. This group held a meeting and decided to launch a Punjabi literary journal. This journal was named *Monthly Panjābī* and was positively received by all prominent conservative intellectuals. The group later expanded, welcoming dozens of new members, and founded two organizations for the promotion of Punjabi: the Pak Punjabi League and the Punjabi Cultural Society. It participated in Pakistan's first Punjabi conference in Lyallpur in 1956 and, after receiving financial support from the government, set up a Punjabi Academy on the model of the Bengali and Pashto academies in 1957. The death of Abdul Majeed Salik, one of the group's mentors, in 1959, followed by the shutdown of *Monthly Panjābī* in 1960, put an end to the conservative Punjabi movement.[1]

This chapter discusses the activities of the conservative group between 1950 and 1960. First, it presents in chronological order the initiatives of the conservatives and examines their programs and their language ideology. Next it discusses various aspects of the contribution of *Monthly Panjābī*, the mouthpiece of the conservative group for nine years. Then it analyzes the structure of the conservative group, as well as the trajectories of some of its members, and finally, assesses the literary production of the group.

Activities, Programs, and Ideology of the Conservatives Between 1950 and 1960

The Beginning of Activities and the 1950 Meeting

> Punjabi, my mother tongue, what will become of her? Her sons have turned their backs on her. The places that used to welcome her have abandoned her. Until now Punjabi was taught at Oriental College but it is no longer studied or taught there and the university's benefactors laugh and scoff at it and belittle it. There seems to be no cure for the stupidity of these educated people. What shall we do and how shall we do it? . . . These are the thoughts that used to cross my mind. The refugees continued to arrive from all sorts of places, but Punjabi seemed to me to be more shelterless than them.[2]

These were Faqeer Mohammad Faqeer's thoughts a few months after independence. He reacted with emotion to the disappearance of Punjabi from the public space, its absence from the university syllabus (Oriental College's Punjabi department had been closed) being one of the manifestations of the neglect it was suffering. Notably, the words Faqeer uses to describe Punjabi's present situation—it is a shelterless language—are similar to those that Maulvi Abdul Haq used in those years to describe the fate of Urdu. Nevertheless, for Faqeer, the main victim of the reconfiguration of the linguistic landscape that occurred during Partition was not Urdu but Punjabi.

Confronted with this situation, Faqeer Mohammad Faqeer decided to launch some initiatives to promote Punjabi and, first of all, sought to secure the support of the seniormost and most powerful defender of Punjabi: Sir Shahabuddin (former speaker of the Punjab Legislative Assembly). But the latter discouraged him from initiating anything, declaring: "Doctor, your intention is laudable but doing anything at this time would be dangerous. People's hearts are filled with anger. Some ill-intentioned people could misinterpret you and start riots. So I'm not advising you to start anything, and I don't want to get involved in anything either."[3] Sir Shahabuddin surely meant that popular perception still equated the Punjabi language with Sikhs, and he therefore feared that people's anger would be directed against those who sought to promote it.

This conversation between Faqeer Mohammad Faqeer and Sir Shahabuddin took place in 1948 or 1949. It took a year for a demoralized Faqeer to "recover" from it and find the strength to seek new allies. He then decided to gather some prominent intellectuals of the city to talk about the status of Punjabi and about possible initiatives to promote it, and he obtained from Abid Ali Abid, the principal of Dyal Singh College, permission to use the premises of this institution to organize a meeting. The meeting was held in the library of Dyal Singh College in the first week of July 1950, attended by Faqeer Mohammad Faqeer, Abdul Majeed Salik (who chaired it), Abid Ali Abid, Mohammad Baqir, Professor Firozuddin, M. D. Taseer, Ustad Karam Amritsari, Sufi Ghulam Mustafa Tabassum, and Abdul Majeed Bhatti.[4] How can one explain the absence of pro-Punjabi progressives such as Ahmad Nadeem Qasmi, Ahmad Rahi, or Sharif Kunjahi? It is possible that the presence of M. D. Taseer—the sworn enemy of progressives—discouraged them from participating. However, it is more likely that they were not invited, because this meeting was called with the goal of setting out the main lines of a nationalist and conservative Punjabi movement to perpetuate the monopoly of the conservative group in the Punjabi literary landscape. This is how the Marxist Punjabi activist Abdul Rauf Malik described Faqeer Mohammad Faqeer and his group during an interview by author on July 27, 2018: "These were selfish people. They wanted to continue to dominate the Punjabi landscape and keep everything in their hands."

Abdul Majeed Salik summarizes the deliberations that took place during the Dyal Singh College meeting as follows:

> Everyone thought that circumstances were different before the creation of Pakistan, and that these days we were facing a different type of situation. Hindus and Sikhs had "communalised" the language issue, and supported Hindi as well as Punjabi in *Gurumukhi* script against Urdu. They wanted to weaken Urdu. Muslims could not accept that, because Urdu had already imposed itself as the official language of all India. Punjab was considered the greatest stronghold of Urdu. This is why the Muslims of Punjab did not want Hindi and Punjabi in *Gurumukhi* to spread. But now that Pakistan had been created, Urdu and Punjabi were no longer adversaries. One was the official language and the other was the

> language of our province, and our mother tongue. Both could flourish at the same time and support each other.[5]

This discourse—in which one can sense strong anti-Sikh and anti-Hindu prejudices—contrasts with the discourse of the progressives, who defended Punjabi as part of a general defense of regional languages (the languages of the masses). It contrasts strongly with Sharif Kunjahi or Ahmad Rahi's discourse in defense of Punjabi. Both underlined the positive role of the Sikhs in the development of Punjabi and found unjustified the Sikh-Muslim conflict, which had taken a linguistic turn, because it was orchestrated by the British colonial administration to keep people divided.

Two important resolutions were adopted at the end of the Dyal Singh College meeting:

1. An organization for the defense and development of Punjabi will be established, the Pak Punjabi League, of which Abdul Majeed Salik will be the president and Faqeer Mohammad Faqeer the secretary.
2. A monthly Punjabi journal will be launched. This journal will be named *Monthly Panjābī*, and Abdul Majeed Salik will be its editor-in-chief.

The first issue of *Monthly Panjābī* was published a year after this meeting, in September 1951. Before analyzing the inaugural issue of *Monthly Panjābī* and how it was received, we examine the trajectories of the three leaders of the movement that had just been launched: Faqeer Mohammad Faqeer, Abdul Majeed Salik, and Mohammad Baqir.

The Leaders of the Conservative Movement

FAQEER MOHAMMAD FAQEER (1900–1974)

The moving spirit behind the conservative Punjabi movement was Faqeer Mohammad Faqeer. He was born in Gujranwala into a family that had emigrated from Kashmir in the mid-nineteenth century. His family's ancestral profession was *Ḥikmat* (traditional Arabic medicine). Faqeer received a traditional education, memorizing the Quran and learning Arabic in addition to acquiring the ancestral science of *Ḥikmat*. He was also introduced to Sufism at a very young age and initiated into the *Qadiriyya* brotherhood, taking an oath to Khwaja Mohammad Karimullah, a famous Sufi from Gujranwala and himself a poet in Urdu, Punjabi, and Persian, who died in 1942.[6] Faqeer prefaced Khwaja Mohammad Karīmullah's *Diwān*.This early connection with Sufism had a lasting influence on him: he wrote most of his critical essays on Sufi poets and compiled and published their writings for the Punjabi Academy.

Faqeer interrupted his studies in 1915 and began training as a laboratory technician at Lahore Medical College. Upon completing his training, he went back to Gujranwala, where he practiced traditional medicine and opened his own clinic (this is why the title *Doctor* usually precedes his name). He returned a few years later to Lahore and started working as a government supplier (in iron items, cupboards, and trunks).[7] He earned so much that he was in a position to buy a car, which he donated to Muhammad Ali Jinnah when he visited Lahore. Faqeer had enthusiastically welcomed the Lahore Resolution in 1940 and joined the Muslim League.[8] However, after the creation of Pakistan, his business declined, and by 1950 he was bankrupt and surviving on small literary assignments such as translations and articles.[9]

Alongside his professional career, Faqeer Mohammad Faqeer pursued a literary career. In 1914, he became a pupil of the Punjabi poet Ibrahim Adil and soon wrote his first poems (in Punjabi), which he recited in poetic symposia in Gujranwala. He then began to recite poems in Punjabi influenced by Pan-Islamism at the meetings of the prestigious *Anjuman-e Ḥimāyat-e Islām* (Association for the Support of Islam) in Lahore.[10] These poems were included in his first poetic collection, published in 1924 under the title *Ṣadā-e Faqīr* (Faqeer's Call). Through the *Anjuman-e Ḥimāyat-e Islām*, he met Allama Iqbal, Zafar Ali Khan, Sir Shahabuddin, and Hafeez Jalandhari, and he started visiting Allama Iqbal who allegedly appreciated his poetry.[11] Faqeer Mohammad Faqeer even tried to convince him to write in Punjabi.[12] Faqeer Mohammad Faqeer also participated in popular poetic symposia held in the parks of Lahore.[13] On these occasions, he met the great popular Punjabi poets of his time: Maula Bakhsh Kushta, Lal Din Qaisar, Babu Firoz Din Sharaf, Karam Amritsari. His second collection of Punjabi poems, *Nīle tāre* (Blue Stars), was published in 1939. He gained special recognition thanks to *Sangī* (Companion), a long collection of moral poems he completed in 1939. He presented the manuscript to the Maharaja of Patiala, who was so impressed that he ordered its immediate publication and rewarded him with a large sum of money.[14] Throughout his literary career, Faqeer showed a remarkable consistency in his writing practice: he wrote poetry only in Punjabi.

Traumatized by Partition, Faqeer Mohammad Faqeer held a negative view of the Sikh community. During the Ayub Khan regime, when the central government asked him to translate a history of the Sikhs, he refused, invoking the threats made by Tara Singh outside the Punjab assembly in 1947, which still haunted him.[15]

ABDUL MAJEED SALIK (1895–1959)

Faqeer Mohammad Faqeer would not have been able to launch a conservative Punjabi movement without the support of Abdul Majeed Salik, who went on to play a key role in all activities promoting the language.

Abdul Majeed Salik was born in Batala (Gurdaspur district). He embarked on a journalistic career very early, founding the journal *Fānūs* in Pathankot in 1914. In 1920, he moved to Lahore and became a member of the editorial board of *Zamīndār*, Zafar Ali Khan's anticolonial newspaper, and in 1921 served a one-year prison sentence for publishing an article considered seditious by the English authorities.[16] During his early years in Lahore, he met Ghulam Rasool Mehr, another journalist from *Zamīndār*, with whom he began a lifelong collaboration. A dispute arose between the two companions and Zafar Ali Khan; they resigned from the editorial board of *Zamīndār* in March 1927 and, in April 1927, launched a rival newspaper, *Inqilāb*.[17] *Inqilāb* supported the Unionist Party, which funded it.[18] As early as 1931, *Inqilāb* supported the idea of a separate state for India's Muslims: the Urdu translation of Allama Iqbal's Allahabad Address was published in it in 1930 and commented on with enthusiasm.[19] Abdul Majeed Salik and his alter ego Ghulam Rasool Mehr became in those years disciples and regular visitors of Allama Iqbal.

After independence, the Unionist Party was dissolved, and its official organ, the *Inqilāb* newspaper, went bankrupt, ceasing publication in December 1949. Abdul Majeed Salik then moved to Karachi, where he worked for the central government (writing propaganda articles under a pen name and penning speeches for Khawaja Nazimuddin, governor-general and then prime minister of Pakistan).[20]

Abdul Majeed Salik was respected by writers and journalists from all over the political spectrum. He was close to ultranationalist elements such as

Shorish Kashmiri and radical defenders of Urdu such as Maulvi Abdul Haq, but he also mentored some progressive intellectuals (Ahmad Nadeem Qasmi was one of his disciples) and participated in some of their activities (he chaired their first Pakistani conference in 1947).[21] He supported their social project but did not approve of their secular position, as he remained deeply religious.[22]

Abdul Majeed Salik's involvement with the cause of Punjabi began in 1930 with the publication of an essay titled *Panjābī zubān dā ṣaḥīḥ mʿeyār* (The Right Standard of the Punjabi Language) in the journal *Panjābī Darbār*. In this essay, he presented views on the relationship between Urdu and Punjabi that were clearly influenced by those of Hafiz Mehmood Shirani: "In my opinion 'Urdu' is the name which was given to an evolved form of Punjabi. The reality is that initially there was only one original language. A few branches grew out of it, and one branch has outgrown others. It's like today's locomotive engine that evolved from George Stefanson's *Rocket*. Punjabi is a tree and Urdu one of its branches."[23] Salik soon stopped expressing his support for the cause of Punjabi, as he was disgruntled with what he believed to be the linguistic hegemony of the Sikhs, who were promoting their own brand of the language. He describes this phase of disassociation from the cause of Punjabi in his essay *Sānūṃ Panjābī bolī te faxr ai* (We are Proud of Our Punjabi Language), published in the October 1951 issue of *Monthly Panjābī*:

> Before Pakistan was created, Hindus and Sikhs had pitted Punjabi against Urdu. That's why we didn't even refer to Punjabi, and worked night and day for the promotion of Urdu. The Sikhs had made Punjabi Muslims feel even more frustrated with Punjabi by writing poetry and prose in their purely Sikh style and by insisting on using the *Gurumukhi* alphabet. But now Pakistan has been created. Punjabi and Urdu are no longer adversaries. Both have become friends and supporters.[24]

After the exodus of the Sikh community from Pakistan, Abdul Majeed Salik resumed his promotion of Punjabi, as it was no longer a symbol of Sikh identity. One can also see this renewed involvement as an act of resistance: Because the Urdu speakers newly immigrated to Lahore regarded Punjabi with contempt, Salik decided to embrace its cause. Punjabi was for him the symbol of the independence and cultural autonomy of the Punjabi people.[25] His son, Abdus Salam Khurshid, also joined the conservative Punjabi group.

MOHAMMAD BAQIR (1910–1993)

The third leader of the conservative group was Professor Mohammad Baqir, who was a "new convert." Faqeer Mohammad Faqeer and Abdul Majeed Salik had been working for the promotion of Punjabi for decades, but Mohammad Baqir joined the cause of Punjabi a couple of years after independence. He nevertheless ended up playing an increasingly important role in the conservative Punjabi movement.

Mohammad Baqir was born in Bangla village near Lyallpur into a family originating from Gujranwala. The son of an engineer, he first studied at the Mission School in Wazirabad, where the Reverend Grahame Bailey (who would later become a Reader in Hindi and Urdu at the University of London) taught. He obtained an MA in Persian from Oriental College, Lahore (he was a student of Hafiz Mehmood Shirani) and, after teaching at Dehradun's prestigious Doon School, left India in 1937 to do a PhD in London under the supervision of Grahame Bailey. He returned to India in 1939 and taught at Punjab University, Lahore. He joined the British Royal Air Force during World War II and came back to India in 1946, where he passed and cleared the civil service exams. After becoming a civil servant, he was posted in Delhi. His functions involved overseeing the education of Muslims in Delhi, Ajmer, Marwar, Madhya Pradesh, Bengal, NWFP and Balochistan.[26] He migrated to Pakistan at the time of Partition and became a professor of Persian at Oriental College, Lahore.

Mohammad Baqir initially became interested in Punjabi as an educationist. The linguistic practices of teachers at the Mission School of Wazirabad, who taught English and the Bible directly in Punjabi, had a deep influence on him, convincing him that Punjabi could be used in school.[27] He believed that the use of Punjabi as a medium of instruction was a cure for illiteracy and wrote some essays for *Monthly Panjābī* to clarify this position.[28]

The Publication of Monthly Panjābī *and Its Successful Reception (1951)*

A year passed between the Dayal Singh College meeting and the publication of the inaugural issue of *Monthly Panjābī*. During that year, Faqeer Mohammad Faqeer and Abdul Majeed Salik applied for a Declaration (official authorization to start a magazine or newspaper) and collected the necessary funds to launch the journal. They traveled to Karachi and, through the journalist Majeed Lahori (editor-in-chief of the fortnightly magazine *Namakdān* and a disciple of Abdul Majeed Salik), met several Punjabi businessmen and asked them for contributions.[29] The collection proved satisfactory, and *Monthly Panjābī* began publication in September 1951 with a print run of one thousand copies.[30]

The inaugural issue of *Monthly Panjābī* was very patriotic. It featured three long essays—*Kašmīr dī mālikī* (Kashmir's Ownership) by Faqeer Mohammad Faqeer, *Jaṭkyāṃ gallāṃ* (Farmers' Words) by Sain Sachyar, and *Qaumī quwwat* (The National Power) by Ibrahim Adil; three patriotic poems—*Pāk faujāṃ* (The Pakistani Armies) by Mir Mohammad Ali Shamim and *Jihād* and *Bālāṃ la'ī* (For the Children) by Faqeer Mohammad Faqeer; a patriotic short story—*Daulat zindabād* (Long Live Wealth!) by Waqar Ambalvi; and a message for the women of the province, in which Faqeer Mohammad Faqeer made the following appeal: "We expect from virtuous Punjabi women that they defend their honour, as well as the honour of their parents and of their nation, and that they do not hesitate to sacrifice their lives, their possessions, and their own sons."[31]

This exaggerated patriotism was undoubtedly aimed at avoiding any accusation of support for the Sikh community (and therefore for the Indian neighbor) that could be levied against a journal promoting the Punjabi language, and at showing that Punjabi can be the vehicle of a nationalist ideology: it was indeed a response to the Marxists who were using Punjabi to spread their own ideology. *Monthly Panjābī* thus placed itself in the league of conservative-nationalist publications (of which the magazine *Caṭṭān* and the newspaper *Nawā-e Waqt* are the most famous representatives). Alongside essays by the three leaders of the conservative Punjabi movement (Faqeer Mohammad Faqeer, Abdul Majeed Salik, and Mohammad Baqir) this inaugural issue featured texts by some senior Punjabi writers like Maula Bakhsh Kushta, Joshua Fazal Din, Lal Din Qaisar, and Peer Fazal Gujrati, and also the very first Punjabi texts of well-known Urdu authors such as Abid Ali Abid, Sufi Ghulam Mustafa Tabassum, and Waqar Ambalvi.[32] The editor-in-chief of the journal undoubtedly used these famous names, which were synonymous with high literary standard, to gain the respect and attention of literary circles. This strategy worked: Three prominent newspapers (*Nawā-e Waqt*, *Eḥsān*, and *Daily Imroz*) published reviews of the inaugural issue of

Monthly Panjābī, welcoming its publication and praising its content. *Nawā-e Waqt*'s review (September 28, 1951) stated: "*Panjābī* has been published by Abdul Majeed Salik and Doctor Faqeer Mohammad Faqeer. And prominent Urdu writers and poets have contributed to it. From the point of view of its standard, it can be compared to the best Urdu journals."[33] *Eḥsān*'s review (September 23, 1951) stated:

> It may be the first journal in Punjabi that was published after the creation of Pakistan, and to tell the truth the publication of this journal has truly honored this language. From the delicate designs of its cover until the last page everything is a delight. Among the contributors one can spot the names of some writers who are probably writing for the first time in Punjabi, and one can think that it is thanks to the solicitations of Doctor Faqeer. We also note among them well-known masters of the Punjabi language like Lal Din Qaisar, Kushta, Peer Fazal Gujrati.[34]

Newspapers from all across the political spectrum were unanimous in praising *Monthly Panjābī*. This was a very encouraging start.

In order to raise additional funds, Faqeer Mohammad Faqeer and Abdul Majeed Salik visited Karachi once again in mid-January 1952 to convince the Punjabi businessmen settled in the city to fund *Monthly Panjābī*.[35] The Sialkoti businessman Malik Bagh organized a meeting that was attended by 124 Punjabi businessmen and influential people. Salik chaired the meeting and began with a speech encouraging the attendees to support the newly founded journal. Later, Majeed Lahori recited a bilingual (Punjabi-Urdu) *ġazal*, Salik read one of his Punjabi essays, and Faqeer recited some of his poems.[36]

The attendees were impressed by the standard of the texts that were read during the meeting and made generous donations, thanks to which *Monthly Panjābī* could be published every month until 1954. Then, after a long gap for lack of funds, its publication resumed in October 1955 and continued until March 1960. The donations by Karachi's Punjabi businessmen and influential people also helped Faqeer publish in 1953 *Lehrāṃ* (Waves), an anthology of the best prose pieces published in *Monthly Panjābī* between 1951 and 1953. The book contained forty-one essays, twenty-five short stories, and two plays written in Punjabi by famous Urdu writers like Abdul Majeed Salik, Ghulam Rasool Mehr, Waqar Ambalvi, Zafar Ali Khan, and Abid Ali Abid, as well as emerging writers like Sajjad Hyder, Shafi Aqeel, and Akbar Lahori. It was the first book of Punjabi prose published in Pakistan after independence, and soon after its publication, it was included (alongside Ahmad Rahi's *Tirinjan*) in the syllabus of the *Panjābī Fāẓil* of the Punjab University.[37]

The Expansion of the Conservative Punjabi Group: 1951–1953

The publication of the inaugural issue of *Monthly Panjābī* marked the successful entry of the conservative Punjabi group into Lahore's literary scene, and soon this group started expanding. Faqeer Mohammad Faqeer, Abdul Majeed Salik, and Mohammad Baqir used their contacts and invited dozens of famous writers, academics, and journalists to support their Punjabi movement. Those who accepted announced their support in declarations published in *Monthly Panjābī*. The editors-in-chief of all the major conservative newspapers and magazines announced their support one after another: Shorish Kashmiri, editor-in-chief of *Caṭṭān*, declared his support in October 1951; Hamid Nizami, editor-in-chief of *Nawā-e Waqt*, in November 1951; Akhtar Ali Khan, editor-in-chief of *Zamīndār*, in November 1951; Zafar Ali Khan, founder of *Zamīndār*, in December 1951; and Ghulam Rasool Mehr, cofounder of *Inqilāb* and alter ego of Abdul Majeed Salik, published his declaration—entitled *Bolī dī taraqqī* (The Development of the Language)—in October 1955.[38] Conservative academics, too, announced their support: Abid Ali Abid, principal of Dyal Singh College, published his statement of support in the September 1951 issue of *Monthly Panjābī*, followed by professor of psychology Taj Mohammad Khayal in August 1952 and Mian Bashir Ahmad, vice-chancellor of the Punjab University, in November–December 1953.[39] Thus, all these personalities agreed to play the role of "symbolic bankers," pledging their reputation for the cause of Punjabi and offering as security the symbolic capital they had accumulated.[40]

In their statements of support, these personalities—known above all for their Urdu writings—expressed themselves for the first time in Punjabi, stressed the importance of the Punjabi language and the need to promote it. In his statement, Shorish Kashmiri explained how much this language meant to him and deplored his poor knowledge of it: "Among educated people an idea has spread: Punjabi is a somewhat limited language. I consider this idea unfounded. We are connected to Punjabi through our History. . . . I consider the development of Punjabi to be an important commitment of my life. Unfortunately, although I am Punjabi, I cannot write and read this language."[41] Other personalities were content with more general and neutral statements. Mian Bashir wrote in December 1953: "I think that as Punjabis our common duty is to develop literature and science together in our mother tongue, and to fill the treasure-trunks of Punjabi with the riches of literature."[42]

The publicly acknowledged support of Punjabi by a number of intellectuals and writers who had made a name in Urdu literature and journalism was not to everyone's taste. It was harshly criticized by Maulana Salahuddin Ahmad, leader of the Urdu supporters in Punjab, who viewed it as a betrayal of the Urdu cause. He expressed his disappointment in an editorial in *Adabī Dunyā* in 1954: "Who could have imagined that this language [Urdu] whose survival and stability was one of the fundamental aims of the creation of Pakistan—would be threatened as soon as this country would be created, and that even those who once were never tired of singing its praises would one day refuse to acknowledge its status and would ignore its benefits?"[43] This phase of expansion of the conservative group culminated with a two-day seminar devoted to Waris Shah. This event, organized by the Pak Punjabi League, was held in the YMCA hall on February 26 and 27, 1953. The literary and artistic elite of Lahore attended.[44] The painter Abdur Rahman Chughtai, Sufi Ghulam Mustafa Tabassum, Dr. Mohammad Baqir, Abdul Majeed Bhatti, and Ahmad Rahi spoke during the seminar, which was chaired by Mian Bashir (vice-chancellor of the Punjab University).[45] This seminar was followed by a Punjabi poetic symposium in which Maula Bakhsh Kushta, Ustad Daman, Firoz Din Sharaf, Ahmad Rahi, Sharif Kunjahi, Abdul Majeed Bhatti, Hafeez Hoshiarpuri, Shad Amritsari, Ghulam Hairat, and Hakim Nasir participated.[46]

A New Discourse and a Program (1951–1953)

A DISCOURSE IN DEFENSE OF PUNJABI

Between 1951 and 1953, members of the conservative group published several essays in *Monthly Panjābī* in which they gradually developed a discourse in defense of the language. This proved to be a delicate task, as they had to show that they did not question the official status of Urdu (or the state's ideological narrative), and they had to dissociate themselves from the Sikh community (traditional defenders of the Punjabi language) as well as activists of other language movements (like Bengali), which were usually accused of being anti-national. Thus, they attempted in their essays to defuse some accusations that they could possibly face on account of promoting Punjabi.

As *Urdu-dušmanī* (Hostility Towards Urdu) was one of the accusations likely to be laid against Punjabi language activists, Faqeer Mohammad Faqeer and Abdul Majeed Salik explained that they did not question Urdu's legitimacy and acknowledged the key role that Urdu played in Pakistan as a lingua franca. Faqeer wrote:

> Some people are writing that we are publishing our journal to oppose Urdu. Friends have gone so far as to write that it is completely wrong to want to raise Punjabi to the status of a scholarly language.
>
> I must therefore remind them of the goal of our work, and I openly declare that *Panjābī* journal has no other goal than to develop the Punjabi language and help it become a scholarly language. Urdu is the common language of all of Pakistan. Much of our intellectual, literary and religious capital is already present in Urdu. And transferring it to our own language will not be an easy task.[47]

Abdul Majeed Salik also acknowledged that Urdu was an important part of the Pakistani identity and assured readers that he in no way questioned its legitimacy: "Urdu is our official language. And a big pillar of Pakistan's edifice. When Bengalis, Punjabis, Sindhis, Pashtuns and Balochis speak to each other, they do so in Urdu. Our offices, newspapers, radio stations, films are at the service of Urdu. One can say that just the way an Englishman cannot survive without the English language, a Pakistani cannot remain Pakistani if he abandons Urdu."[48] Faqeer and Salik pointed out that the founders of Pakistan had acknowledged and recognized the importance of regional languages. Faqeer noted: "The Quaid-e-Azam himself went to Bengal and declared—to the satisfaction of the Bengalis—that their official language would remain Bengali, and in each of the speeches of the father of Urdu Maulvi Abdul Haq one finds four or five lines in which he states that he recognizes the rights of regional languages."[49] Salik echoed him: "It is completely wrong to think that the great leaders of Pakistan, or the pillars of the Pakistani government would take a dim view of any initiative aimed at developing the Punjabi language. They themselves have said a hundred times that the development of the languages of the provinces leads to the development of Pakistan's literature and that their development cannot harm the Urdu language."[50] Finally, both authors offered a guarantee: The conservative Punjabi movement would not follow a path similar to that chosen by the Bengali movement, and conservative Punjabi activists would not make any demands to grant Punjabi an official status. Faqeer notably assured readers that their activities in favor of Punjabi would be confined to the "intellectual sphere" and to the Punjab province: "We recognize the natural rights of Punjabi and want to develop this language and expand its use in the intellectual sphere, only within the geographical boundaries of Punjab. And we believe that there is nothing wrong with that."[51] Salik categorically stated: "Punjabi cannot replace Urdu at the federal level."[52]

A RESPONSE TO MAULANA SALAHUDDIN AHMAD

Some of the statements made by members of the conservative group in the essays they wrote for *Monthly Panjābī* appear to be directly responding to Maulana Salahuddin Ahmad's controversial statements on Punjabi. Maulana Salahuddin Ahmad wished that Urdu would replace Punjabi, and Abdul Majeed Salik responded: "The language of our province, our mother tongue that we speak night and day in our homes and with our friends is Punjabi. And it will remain Punjabi until the end of the world. Urdu cannot replace it. To try to replace people's mother tongue is to go against nature."[53] Hamid Nizami echoed him: "Why can't Urdu and Punjabi be used side by side? Urdu has its own place. It is our official language, so there is no doubt that its status is higher than that of Punjabi. But Punjabi has also its place and it cannot be taken away from it."[54]

Maulana Salahuddin Ahmad insisted that parents should speak Urdu to their children, as it would facilitate their acquisition of education in government schools (where the primary medium of instruction was Urdu). Hamid Nizami challenged this practice in his essay *Panjābī dī ibtidā'ī t'alīm* (Primary Education in Punjabi), published in *Monthly Panjābī's* November 1951 issue. He recalled in it an experiment he had conducted with one of his children, with whom he chose to speak Punjabi and not Urdu:

> We speak only Urdu at home. My friends and relatives speak only Urdu with my children. My children speak with us only in Urdu. But since I have made this

> experiment I have observed this strange fact that one of my children would speak Urdu with great speed but would suddenly stop. Because he would suddenly think of a word of which he does not know the equivalent in Urdu. And when I spoke with him in Punjabi he did not stop, and his speech remained fast.[55]

He drew the following conclusion: "Children's primary education must be in their mother tongue, because a second language places a weight on their mind. And if instruction is given in a second language, at some point the child's mind stops progressing."[56]

Hamid Nizami's position was the exact opposite of that of Maulana Salahuddin Ahmad's. For Nizami, it was not necessary to help children adapt to school by speaking to them in Urdu. Rather, it was necessary for schools to adapt to children by using Punjabi as a medium of instruction.

The Program of the Conservative Group

The members of the conservative group presented their program in the essays they wrote for *Monthly Panjābī*. The recognition of Punjabi as an official language is—as expected—absent from this program, but they identified three domains on which they wanted to concentrate their efforts: the literary domain, the educational domain, and corpus planning.

The two objectives the conservative group set for itself in the literary domain were a renewal of Punjabi literature and the development of its prose.

Faqeer Mohammad Faqeer called for a renewal of Punjabi literature, its genres and themes, and advocated a literature devoid of sentimentality and pathos, conveying a positive and dynamic message that the nation could draw inspiration from.[57] His essay *Panjābī adab vic inqilāb dī lor* (Punjabi Literature Needs a Revolution), published in September 1951, was a manifesto in favor of this new literature. In this essay, Faqeer addresses the Punjabi writers, castigating them for producing an overly sentimental literature and urging them to produce a lively literature carrying a positive message:

> Look me in the eyes and answer me: can we make our boat sail on the chest of the murderous storms of the sea with the help of a poetry that moans like a widow, whimpers like a sad woman and swims in false tears? . . . Until when can

> a free nation support a poetry that breaks hearts like ours? When we look at the literature produced around us, why don't we recognize that it is weak and sick . . . artificial and devoid of spirit. . . . Try to make the blood of life flow in the veins of your poetry. Put together for your beloved country words that beat like free hearts and give a lesson in life that your nation will never be able to forget![58]

The initial sentence of this statement clearly hints at Ahmad Rahi and Sharif Kunjahi's poetry, which was written under Amrita Pritam's influence and echoed the voice of female characters and thematized the oppressive conditions under which they lived. Faqeer deemed this trend toxic and believed that Punjabi poetry should instead convey an uplifting message.

In *Bolī dī taraqqī* (The Development of the Language), an essay published in the September–October 1955 issue of *Monthly Panjābī*, Ghulam Rasool Mehr presented a program aimed at enabling Punjabi to become a scholarly language (*'ilmī zubān*) and emphasized the role that prose could play in the development and promotion of Punjabi:

> As far as our Punjabi mother tongue is concerned, we can say that its poetry has been rich in the past but its prose is weak and limited. . . . Now if we focus on the prose of our language and write in Punjabi about religion and history, if we produce good novels and good plays and translate books from foreign languages I am sure that after seven or eight years we will achieve big things, and once our intellectual needs are satisfied by our own language we won't have to go elsewhere to quench our thirst.[59]

In the educational domain, the conservative group presented two objectives: the implementation of Punjabi as a medium of instruction in primary schools in Punjab and the reopening of the Punjabi department of Oriental College, which had been closed since Partition.

The position of the conservatives concerning the use of Punjabi at school was clarified in September 1951 by Mohammad Baqir in his essay *Panjāb te Panjābī* (Punjab and Punjabi):

> It is a known fact that nowadays thousands and hundreds of thousands of Punjabi children complete school, but the children who leave school become again illiterate after a few years since they never encounter Urdu in their daily dealings. And in the end they forget how to read and write. If Punjabi was taught to

> them in primary school they would not forget the language after leaving school, and if newspapers, journals and books were published for them in Punjabi then they would read even more. Even if they don't go to school, they may also learn to read Urdu as adults. I believe that in Punjabi-speaking areas primary school instruction should be in Punjabi. If this step is adopted, people will quickly learn to read and write and will learn them in such a way that they will never forget them.[60]

Faqeer Mohammad Faqeer pleaded with the provincial authorities to reintroduce Punjabi at the Punjab University. This cause was so close to his heart that in order to make his voice heard by as many people as possible, he published, on February 1, 1953, an article in *Daily Imroz* (a newspaper whose ideological line he did not agree with, but which was one of the most widely read newspapers of the time) in which he declared:

> At the time of Partition, Punjabi language was harmed by Punjabis and non-Punjabis, but the greatest injustice was done by the Punjab University, which without warning anyone discontinued the Punjabi courses which were offered by Oriental College, i.e. *Honors*, *High proficiency* and *Proficiency in Punjabi*. It is the greatest injustice of all because an educational institution has murdered knowledge—the very same institution which was established to propagate it. It did not only discontinue the courses, but it dealt such a blow to Punjabi that this language could not recover from it in the past five years. This behavior is discriminatory and our proud Punjabis will not be able to bear it any longer . . . The most shameful thing is that foreign languages such as Spanish and German are taught there while the teaching of the language of our province has been stopped. God knows until when these stigmata of our slavery will remain.

In terms of corpus planning, the conservative group fixed itself two objectives: the selection of a dialect on which the standard written Punjabi of Pakistan would be based and the compilation of a dictionary.

In an editorial published in *Monthly Panjābī* in December 1951, Faqeer Mohammad Faqeer stressed the need to identify a dialect that would become the foundation of standard written Punjabi and suggested using the dialect of the district of Gujranwala, for reasons of prestige and centrality: "We engaged in research, at the end of which we decided to base our standard on this dialect. Gujranwala's long natural relationship with Waris Shah and

Hafiz Barkhurdar, made us take this decision, as well as the central location of this district within the Punjab. It is surrounded by the districts of Lahore, Sialkot, Gujrat, Sargodha, Lyallpur and Sheikhupura."[61] In order to consolidate this process of standardization, Sardar Khan recommended, in his essay *Panjābī luġat* (Punjabi Lexicon), compiling a comprehensive Punjabi dictionary.[62] According to him, such a dictionary would not only contribute to the standardization of the language but would also facilitate mutual understanding among speakers of different Punjabi dialects: "We feel a strong need for a Punjabi Dictionary. Thanks to it, a prestigious language will be created, which will integrate the different dialects and will become the common written standard for Punjabi speakers; because at the present time an individual from one region does not fully understand the dialect of another one."[63] A dictionary would also offer lexical alternatives to Urdu words commonly used in Punjabi. It would therefore enable Punjabi to keep a distinct identity and protect it against assimilation into Urdu: "By overloading Urdu with Arabic and Persian words, a language came into being which can be called *Afardu*, and mixing Urdu vocabulary with Punjabi should not give birth to a language that would be called *Purdu*.[64] What I mean is that Punjabi should remain a separate language and should not end up being seen as a rural and vulgar version of Urdu, as the language spoken by illiterate people."[65] The symbolic importance of the dictionary cannot be denied. At this time, when language movements were gaining momentum in Pakistan, compiling a dictionary was a means of asserting the separate existence and richness of a language. This is no doubt the reason that compilation of a dictionary was also one of the priorities of the newly established *Sindhī Adabī* Board and was to be one of the priorities of the Bengali Academy.

The Punjabi Cultural Society (1954)

THE CONTROVERSY SURROUNDING THE CREATION OF THE PUNJABI CULTURAL SOCIETY

The Pak Punjabi League, established during the Dyal Singh College meeting of 1950, was not very active; its only documented activity was the organization of the Waris Shah seminar in February 1953. In June 1954, Abdul Majeed Salik decided to replace it with a new organization, the Punjabi

Cultural Society. Its president was Abdul Majeed Salik himself, and its general secretary was Mohammad Afzal, the secretary of the board of secondary education on whose intervention *Tirinjan* had been included in the Punjabi syllabus of the Punjab University.[66] The treasurer was the lawyer Chaudhry Mohammad Ismail Bhatti, and its executive committee included Masud Khadarposh (secretary for agriculture with Punjab's provincial government), Sufi Ghulam Mustafa Tabassum, Safdar Mir, Aziz Ahmad Bhatti, the lawyer Khizr Taimiti, Abdul Majeed Bhatti, Faqeer Mohammad Faqeer, Hakim Nasir, Joshua Fazal Din, and Mohammad Afzal Khan (son of the senior poet Maula Bakhsh Kushta).[67] Conservative elements dominated in this group: Of the thirteen members named, Safdar Mir, Sufi Ghulam Mustafa Tabassum, and Abdul Majeed Bhatti were the only individuals associated with the Marxist camp. Sharif Kunjahi, Ahmad Rahi, Afzal Parvez, and Ustad Daman were not members of the Punjabi Cultural Society. It was therefore above all a conservative organization.

On the occasion of the foundation of this organization, Abdul Majeed Salik gave a press conference during which he disclosed its objectives and the list of its members. The presence among them of Safdar Mir—who had the reputation of being a radical communist—aroused a strong reaction in the conservative camp, which resulted in the publication of a polemical article in the *Daily Jang* of June 13, 1954, accusing Abdul Majeed Salik of running his organization with the help of communists and of wanting to promote a form of regionalism (*Ṣūba-parastī*).[68]

Abdul Majeed Salik responded to these allegations in a letter to the editor-in-chief of *Daily Jang*, published in the June 26, 1954 issue. In this letter, he rejected the accusations of collusion with the communists, declaring that the Punjabi Cultural Society was an apolitical organization whose members were from all over the political spectrum:

> *Jang* newspaper has repeated several times that I have initiated this movement with the help of the communists. Although until now there has not been a single communist among the members of the Punjabi Cultural Society.[69] The whole country is aware of my convictions. I am opposed to the creation of camps and sects in the literary sphere. I believe that poets and writers from all parties—whether they are affiliated with Jamāʿat-e Islāmī, Islam League, Awami Muslim League, the Communist Party or the Progressive Association have the right to serve Literature.[70] And they all are in my eyes worthy of respect. . . . Until now

> there has not been a single communist in this organization. It comprises civil servants working for the government and for semi-governmental institutions, lawyers and individuals who cooperate with the government. Any individual whose membership is supported by two other members can join it.[71]

This response was more than necessary. The following month, in July 1954, the Communist Party, the Progressive Writers' Association, and the PPH were banned by the state. In this climate, even a hint of affiliation or support for the Marxist camp was enough to get an organization banned.

As for the accusation of regionalism, Abdul Majeed Salik responded this way:

> I have always been in favor of the development of literature in regional languages. But I am also convinced that no language except Urdu can be declared the official language of Pakistan. Bengali, Pashto, Sindhi, Balochi, Gujarati and Kashmiri are the vernacular languages of our provinces and the mother tongues of some communities, and they possess a fairly extensive literary corpus. This corpus is the treasure of Pakistan. Safeguarding and developing it means serving Pakistan.
>
> If the supporters of one of these languages decide to make their language an official language of the country, or decide to declare it the language of instruction and the official language of their province I will oppose them. On the other hand, if this movement in favor of Punjabi literature remains purely literary and if no type of politics is allowed to interfere in it, I am at its service. . . . Regionalism is something far removed from my concerns. I am in favor of the unity of the country, and from the bottom of my heart for its cultural unity.[72]

To further stress the apolitical nature of the Punjabi Cultural Society and its goals, he recounted the circumstances in which it was born and stated that its main goal was to encourage the production of prose in Punjabi. "What happened is that one day I mentioned to my friends that a lot of poetry has been written in Punjabi but not much prose, and that Punjabis should focus on writing prose in their mother tongue. . . . In my opinion, the desire to write prose in Punjabi is not reprehensible, even though some outstandingly smart people have deemed it a great danger for our nation."[73]

In the final section of his letter, Salik counterattacked, drawing the attention of the editor-in-chief of *Daily Jang* to the discrimination faced by the

Punjabi language. An example of this differential treatment was the fact that the government had started publishing an official journal in each provincial language except Punjabi: "*Jang*'s editor will have noticed that the Publications Department of the Government of Pakistan has started publishing alongside the Urdu journal *Māh-e nau* the Pashto journal *Nanprūn*, the Sindhi journal *Naī zindagī*, and a Bengali journal. But Punjabis complain that an injustice has been done to them, because until now no Punjabi journal has been published by the government of Pakistan."[74]

ACTIVITIES OF THE PUNJABI CULTURAL SOCIETY

To make itself known, the Punjabi Cultural Society organized a huge Punjabi poetic symposium on June 16, 1954 at the open-air theater of Lawrence Garden. The Punjabi poets Ustad Hamdam, Firoz Din Sharaf, Maulana Bakhsh Kushta, Faqeer Mohammad Faqeer, and Joshua Fazal Din, along with the Urdu poets Ahmad Nadeem Qasmi, Sufi Ghulam Mustafa Tabassum, Hafeez Jalandhari, Qayyum Nazar, and Abdul Majeed Salik, recited their poems.[75] Punjab's chief minister Feroz Khan Noon attended this symposium, and Mohammad Afzal Khan reported, "He praised a lot this symposium and pledged the government's support to every initiative aimed at the development of Punjabi literature."[76]

The presence of the province's chief minister in the audience shows that the senior writer and journalist Abdul Majeed Salik was held in high esteem by politicians and government officials. But Feroz Khan Noon's declaration was very cautious: The chief minister talked about the development of Punjabi literature, not about a possible expansion of Punjabi's sphere of use or improvement of its status. His declaration was nevertheless historic: For the first time, a politician at the head of the government of the province expressed some support for a movement promoting Punjabi. Even if no government initiative followed, Feroz Khan Noon's presence and declaration during the June 16, 1954 symposium were an achievement for Abdul Majeed Salik and his group.

Right after its inception, the Punjabi Cultural Society started organizing weekly meetings at the YMCA in Lahore. The format of these meetings was comparable to those of the Progressive Writers' Association or the *Ḥalqa-e Arbāb-e Żauq*: One or two prose pieces and a poetic piece were read and commented on during a session chaired by a literary personality. Two new writers who later played an important role in the Punjabi literary landscape joined the Punjabi Cultural Society: Asif Khan and Raja Risalu. Both of them organized some sessions, as Raja Risalu recalls in his memoirs:

> Chaudhry Mohammad Afzal, Professor Safdar Mir and Joshua Fazal Din were among the senior writers affiliated with the Punjabi Cultural Society. Joshua Fazal Din would always arrive first and say "come on, let's start the session!" There was a time when all these veterans were busy: one was out of town, another one was not available etc and the management of the Punjabi Cultural Society was entrusted to me and Asif Khan. We thus organized weekly meetings for a certain time.[77]

For how long was the Punjabi Cultural Society active? According to Mohammad Afzal Khan, it was six months.[78] According to Safdar Mir, it was a year: "The Punjabi Cultural Society organized for a year meetings during which classical and contemporary literature were discussed. A few emerging educated writers participated in them, who considered that there was nothing wrong with expressing oneself in the language of the masses. Why did this society not remain active? That's another story."[79] Safdar Mir did not explain why the Punjabi Cultural Society ceased activities. The disinterest and lack of support of senior writers (mentioned by Raja Risalu), who were often absent or too "busy" to participate in the meetings, could be one reason. An ideological and generational gap between emerging Punjabi activists (Safdar Mir, Asif Khan, Raja Risalu), and the "old guard" could be another reason. Because of this gap, emerging activists left this organization and created their own, the *Panjābī Majlis* (Punjabi Society, discussed in the next chapter). The lack of support of the senior writers and the dissatisfaction of the newcomers did not give the Punjabi Cultural Society a great chance of survival, even though it had begun on a very encouraging note.

Documenting the meetings of the Punjabi Cultural Society is practically impossible. No member has written minutes of the sessions, and the texts read during them were not published. Its period of activity corresponds to a "slack period" in terms of publication in Punjabi: The *Monthly Panjābī* was not published during that period, and *Daily Imroz's* Punjabi page did not yet exist. Nevertheless, an account is available of a memorable session that took place in the last months of 1954. That session was organized by Raja Risalu and Asif Khan and chaired by Abdul Majeed Salik; Ustad Daman and Saadat Hasan Manto had been invited to present their work. Manto was supposed to read his first Punjabi short story and Ustad Daman to recite his latest poems. This session made such an impression on the audience that one can find three accounts of it (by Amrita Pritam, Raja Risalu, and Akmal Aleemi). We present Akmal Aleemi's account, which gives a fairly accurate idea of the informal and convivial atmosphere of the session:

> When we entered the committee room it was already half past four. The room was filled with people. People's face lit up when they saw Manto. . . . My companions looked at me angrily and the chairman of the session, Abdul Majeed Salik, scolded me: "My friend, members must come on time." . . . Ustad Daman recited his poem *Kāle badal* (Black Clouds) and Manto made Daman recite three or four more poems.
>
> Now it was Manto's turn. He first apologized for not having been able to write his short story, then he announced the title of his intervention: "Punjabi Folk couplets" (*Panjābī boliyāṁ*). The audience listened intently. Manto launched into an extravagant eulogy on Punjabi Folk couplets. He had never before committed this offence in his writings but today he declared his absolute admiration for Punjabi literature. Then he started reciting couplets, couplets about beauty, youth, love, and women, couplets which, according to him, presented a vision of Woman which was so lively that one could not find its equivalent in any other literature in the world. Manto would give a short commentary on each couplet, suggested a title for it, and then recited it.
>
> After reciting a few couplets Manto looked pleadingly at the session's chairman and asked, 'Can I recite a saucy couplet?' Maulana Abdul Majeed looked around, and generously granted him permission. Today, all his sophistication and seriousness had been overcome by Manto's eloquence. Manto recited a couplet. The audience was outraged, but Manto was feeling an almost mystical satisfaction. . . . Hearing the couplets that Manto was reciting, Ustad Daman felt challenged and in an instant the committee room was transformed into Shalimar garden's Festival of Lights (*Melā-e cirāġāṃ*). A competition was raging between Manto and Daman. Manto today demonstrated that he had an extraordinary memory, and Daman, who was himself a poet, proved that he was no exception in this respect. In the end the competition was won by Manto, because he recited couplets that were bolder and even more controversial than Daman's.[80]

The First Punjabi Conference of Lyallpur (1956)

The reputation of Abdul Majeed Salik and Faqeer Mohammad Faqeer as supporters of Punjabi was so high that they were invited by Lyallpur's *Panjābī Bazm-e Adab* (Punjabi Association for Literature) to participate in a Punjabi Conference held on March 9, 1956 at the *Dhobī ghāṭ* stadium in Lyallpur.[81] It was Pakistan's first Punjabi conference.[82] This Punjabi conference ended with a Punjabi poetic symposium during which poets recited poems on the theme of humanity (*Insāniyat*).[83] Some poets from India participated in this symposium alongside Pakistani poets.[84] This conference provided, for the first time since 1947, the opportunity for Pakistani and Indian Punjabi writers to meet. Abdul Majeed Salik (who chaired the conference) and Faqeer Mohammad Faqeer each delivered a speech.[85] Faqeer also read an essay entitled *Panjābī adab* (Punjabi Literature).[86] At the end of the conference, three resolutions were adopted unanimously by the participants (all these texts were published in the April–May 1956 issue of *Monthly Panjābī*).

In his speech, Abdul Majeed Salik explained how the conservative Punjabi movement had begun and how it had evolved over the years, and presented a suggestion directly inspired, it seems, by Mohammad Baqir's essay *Panjāb te Panjābī*: that Punjabi should be used for adult literacy and for the instruction of children in schools, a step that should ultimately facilitate their learning of Urdu.[87] "Try it out yourself: in an adult literacy program, teach adults through one or two Punjabi textbooks and see how quickly they will learn to read Urdu. The same happens with children. You must teach them the curriculum of first and second grade in Punjabi, and then introduce Urdu. Young children will learn to read extremely quickly!"[88] Faqeer Mohammad Faqeer stated in his speech that the production of prose was necessary in order to make Punjabi a "scholarly language," and he encouraged the writers attending the conference to enrich the Punjabi prose corpus with texts in all possible prose genres (fiction, criticism, philosophy, etc.):

> Our language has not progressed as much in prose as in poetry. . . . To excel in poetry is not enough to bring it on the path of progress, and that is the reason why we should now reach in prose a standard comparable to that which we have reached in poetry. Prose, like poetry, is divided into different genres, such as Philosophy, Science, History, Geography, Criticism, Novel and Short

> Stories or Tales. . . . If we don't transfer the knowledge which is relevant for our times into our own language we won't be able to keep it alive and make it last.[89]

Then Faqeer mentions another means of enriching Punjabi's prose corpus: the transliteration in Urdu script of books written in *Gurumukhi* script:

> We have guessed that our Punjabi brothers who live on the other side of the border have done a lot for our language. But as long as their useful and scholarly books will not be available in the Urdu script, how will our fellow-citizens benefit from them? . . . It is therefore necessary that good books written in the *Gurumukhi* script should be available in Urdu script, and that good books written in Urdu script should be published in *Gurumukhi* script. This way we will be able to help our brothers and they will be able to help us, and we will offer a double contribution to our mother tongue.[90]

Thus, for the first time since the inception of the conservative movement, Faqeer Mohammad Faqeer mentioned a possible collaboration with Indian writers; but it was also the last time, for none of his later writings included such a suggestion. Perhaps Faqeer felt compelled to make such statements because he was in the presence of a large number of Indian guests attending the conference.

At the end of this historic conference, the participants adopted the following three resolutions:

1. This conference organized by Lyallpur's *Panjābī Bazm-e Adab* appeals to the Punjab Education Department to make Punjabi the medium of instruction in the primary grades of the school so as to give to 40 or 50 million Punjabis the right they deserve.
2. This conference organized by Lyallpur's *Panjābī Bazm-e Adab* appeals to the Punjab University to resume the Punjabi classes which were taught at the *Oriental College* before the creation of Pakistan.
3. This conference organized by Lyallpur's *Panjābī Bazm-e Adab* appeals to the central government of Pakistan to publish—as it already does for regional languages such as Bengali, Sindhi and Pashto—a journal in Punjabi, which is the language of 40 or 50 million people.[91]

These resolutions were drafted by Abdul Majeed Salik and Faqeer Mohammad Faqeer. The first two stem from the program of the conservative movement in terms of education, while the third reiterates a point made by Abdul Majeed Salik in his June 1954 letter to the editor-in-chief of *Daily Jang*.[92] Notably, Abdul Majeed Salik and Faqeer Mohammad Faqeer did not cross the boundaries set in their first articles: no demand was made in these resolutions for Punjabi to receive any kind of official status.

The Creation of the Punjabi Academy (1957) and the End of the Conservative Movement (1960)

The Punjabi movement initiated by Abdul Majeed Salik and Faqeer Mohammad Faqeer followed a trajectory similar to that of Sindhi and Pashto language movements. Abdul Majeed Salik and Faqeer Mohammad Faqeer mobilized some personalities and activists, presented a program, launched a journal and two organizations, organized a seminar and a poetic symposium, and chaired an important conference. But in order to make this trajectory fully successful, the custodians of the movement were seeking an official recognition that they could acquire only by establishing a state-supported Punjabi Academy.

State-supported academies had been established in different provinces in the previous years: a Sindhī Adabī Board (which fulfilled the role of Sindhi Academy) was founded in Karachi in 1951, a Bengali Academy in Dhaka in 1955, and a Pashto Academy in Peshawar the same year. These institutions were not only responsible for the development and promotion of their relevant language but also aimed at ensuring the production of a literature conforming to the ideology of the state, thus avoiding any drift toward regionalism. The loyalty of the custodians of the Punjabi conservative movement to the state ideology was beyond doubt. The government could safely entrust them with the responsibility to set up a Punjabi Academy. Mohammad Baqir, who had just come back from Karachi, announced in *Monthly Panjābī*'s July 1957 issue that talks were underway with the central government about the establishment of a Punjabi Academy: "In Karachi the *Sindhī Adabī Board* is active, and the members of the Pashto academy also intend to do similar work. We have the duty to create a *Panjābī Adabī Board* so that we can display the elements which contribute to Pakistan's prestige. . . . I have already spoken to some powerful men and they have said: 'Establish an institution, show to people the qualities of this region of Pakistan, and we will help you.' "[93] Government officials were already setting a condition for the establishment of a Punjabi Academy: It would be approved only if it projected a positive (and not critical or political) image of Punjab. The process of creating a Punjabi Academy was thus described by Mohammad Baqir in an interview with Maqsood Saqib:

> My village neighbor Sheikh Mumtaz Hasan, a former finance secretary in the government of Pakistan, was a friend, a sincere friend with an open mind. One day when we were sitting together in the ministry, he said to me, "A Sindhi Academy has been established, and a Pashto Academy too. It will therefore not be a problem to establish a Punjabi Academy. If you put it in place I will give you grants like I did for the other academies."
>
> Education Secretary Sheikh Sharif was also my neighbor in Gujranwala. I wrote an application the next day, and received a cheque of one thousand rupees. The name *Panjābī Adabī Akādemī* was also chosen by Mumtaz Hasan. And one of the conditions imposed by the central government was that the Academy should not publish books in Punjabi. For only Punjab's provincial government could subsidize publications in Punjabi. But I was told that I could publish books about Punjab, its history, its arts and things of that sort.[94]

A Punjabi Academy was thus established on the condition that it did not publish works in Punjabi. The aim of the government officials who approved and subsidized the academy seems clear: They wanted to maintain maximum control over this institution and avoid a drift toward a regionalist discourse. They wanted to prevent this new academy from following the path of the Sindhī Adabī Board, which soon after its creation had published G. M. Syed's *Paiġām-e Laṭīf* (The Message of Shah Abdul Latif Bhittai), a book glorifying Sindhi culture and criticizing the philosophy of Pakistan's national poet Allama Iqbal that soon became a reference text for Sindhi regionalists.[95] This aspect must have been mentioned during discussions among Mohammad Baqir, Mumtaz Hasan, and Sheikh Sharif, because after Baqir came back from Lahore and faced the anger of Abdul Majeed Salik and Faqeer Mohammad Faqeer, who were unhappy the Punjabi Academy was not to publish books in Punjabi, he explained, "The aim of the Academy is not to enhance separatist feelings but to highlight the commitment of Punjab to strengthen Pakistan's unity. This explanation satisfied Doctor Faqeer Mohammad Faqeer and Abdul Majeed Salik."[96]

The Punjabi Academy was established at the end of 1957. Its office was initially situated near the Lahore museum; then it was moved to 12-G, Model Town. The academy's director was Mohammad Baqir, and Faqeer Mohammad Faqeer and Abdul Majeed Salik were board members.[97] The academy published four books between 1958 and 1960, not in Punjabi (per the wish of government officials) but in Persian.[98] The first books were two volumes titled *Panjābī qiṣṣe farsī meṃ* (Punjabi Stories in Persian), with a preface by Abdul Majeed Salik. They were soon followed by Fakir Syed Nooruddin's *Tārīx-e Koh-e Nūr* (History of the *Kohinoor*) and Ghanimat Kunjahi's *Dīwān*.[99]

In 1958, Punjab's provincial government granted a donation to the academy that enabled it to publish books in Punjabi.[100] It was only in 1960, three years after its creation, that the academy published its first book in Punjabi: a complete edition of *Hīr Wāriṡ Šāh*, compiled by Sheikh Abdul Aziz (father of historian K. K. Aziz). The academy also funded the *Monthly Panjābī*: In a letter addressed to Shafi Aqeel, Faqeer Mohammad Faqeer announced that the academy was now the journal's sponsor and that the September–October 1959 issue would be published with its help.[101] It seems that the academy's help did not extend beyond this issue, however, since *Monthly Panjābī* ceased publication in March 1960 for financial reasons (as stated by Shafi Aqeel and Junaid Akram).[102] The shutdown of *Monthly Panjābī*, combined with the death of Abdul Majeed Salik in 1959, put an end to the initial phase of the conservative Punjabi movement.[103]

The *Monthly Panjābī* (1951–1960)

The most important contribution of the conservative Punjabi movement was undoubtedly the creation of the *Monthly Panjābī*, the first literary Punjabi journal published in Pakistan after independence. Its official editor-in-chief was Abdul Majeed Salik, but its de facto editor-in-chief was Faqeer Mohammad Faqeer. Salik's name was used merely to attract readers and give prestige to the journal.[104] *Monthly Panjābī* began publication in September 1951 and was published until March 1960 (with an interruption between December 1953 and September 1955 for lack of funds). It played for the conservative Punjabi camp a role similar to that of the *Daily Imroz* for the Marxist Punjabi camp: It provided a platform for conservative writers and encouraged them to produce Punjabi texts. Between September 1951 and March 1960, *Monthly Panjābī* published 734 texts written by 284 authors. *Monthly Panjābī* also contributed to the elaboration and popularization of a discourse in defense of Punjabi language and literature and published articles offering suggestions regarding the standardization of Punjabi. It also published numerous political texts, making Punjabi the vehicle of a nationalist and Islamic ideology that had, until then, been promoted mainly in Urdu.

Profile and Objectives

The format of *Monthly Panjābī* was similar to that of Joshua Fazal Din's *Panjābī Darbār* and also to that of Urdu literary journals like *Adab-e Laṯīf, Adabī Dunyā*, or *Saverā*. Each issue was fifty to sixty pages long; it included an editorial and some essays, short stories, plays, and poems. Funded by private donors, Faqeer Mohammad Faqeer himself, and subscribers, *Monthly Panjābī* was printed in runs of one thousand copies; it initially targeted, besides Punjabi readers, Urdu-speaking emigrants from India eager to familiarize themselves with Punjabi. An Urdu-Punjabi glossary entitled *Hindūstān toṃ ā'e paroṇyāṃ dī xāṯir* (For the use of our guests from India), intended to help non-Punjabi readers, was printed on page 56 of the November 1951 issue.

The first issue of *Monthly Panjābī* opened with this statement by Faqeer Mohammad Faqeer:

> The idea of publishing *Panjābī* journal had been in the mind of many friends for a long time. When they would compare our situation to that of the other provinces of Pakistan, they would feel an absence, and would always feel that the basic needs of Punjabi language should be satisfied at all cost. For as long as the shawl of knowledge does not adorn the shoulders of a language, it does not dare to raise its eyes and sit along with others. . . . For this reason, I declare with all my sincerity and all my heart that the purpose of this journal is none other than to promote and serve the Punjabi language and people. And as a writer and poet of Punjabi I have even more than anyone else the duty to serve them . . . I want to say once again—with all my due respect—to the educated Punjabis who care

> about the fate of their province that they must not imagine that by publishing the journal *Panjābī* my aim is to oppose Urdu. Such thoughts do not suit educated people like them. I would rather like to ask them to help *Panjābī* by sharing their reflections in some essays that our journal will publish. They will thus contribute to the enrichment of Punjabi literature, and, automatically contribute to the enrichment of their area's and country's literature. Which is the goal that some Punjabi scholars have already set for themselves.[105]

The main objective of Faqeer Mohammad Faqeer in bringing out his journal was—without questioning the role and importance of Urdu—to develop Punjabi by enriching its written corpus. And the written corpus of Punjabi was indeed enriched: Between September 1951 and March 1960, 145 short stories, 106 essays, 25 short plays (radio dramas), 15 autobiographical pieces (*Haḍvartī*), 318 poems, 77 *ġazals*, and 48 songs were published in *Monthly Panjābī*. Though poetry dominates this production (443 poetic texts), prose is also well represented: 291 prose texts (short stories, essays, etc.). *Monthly Panjābī* helped produce a large body of prose.

Monthly Panjābī regularly published senior writers (already writing in Punjabi before 1947) like the poets Firoz Din Sharaf, Peer Fazal Gujrati, Baba Alam Syahposh, Karam Amritsari, Lal Din Qaisar, and Maula Bakhsh Kushta, and the short-story writer and novelist Joshua Fazal Din, but it also published a large number of new authors who began to write in Punjabi after independence: the poets Bashir Manzar, Ghulam Yaqub Anwar, and Sufi Ghulam Mustafa Tabassum; the short story writers Shafi Aqeel, Qasir Amritsari, Akbar Lahori, Noor Kashmiri, and Waqar Ambalvi; the playwrights Mirza Zafar Ali, Mahfuz ul-Hasan Shah Naqvi, and Nazar Fatima; and the essayists Taj Mohammad Khayal, Abid Ali Abid, and Nizamuddin Tawakkuli.

Faqeer Mohammad Faqeer was not only *Monthly Panjābī's* de facto editor-in-chief but also its biggest contributor. Between 1951 and 1960, he published in it forty-nine essays, forty-two editorials, ninety-two poems, and one short story. It should be noted that Faqeer published not only conservative authors but also Marxist authors like Sharif Kunjahi, Ahmad Rahi, Abdul Majeed Bhatti, Qateel Shifai, Shafqat Tanvir Mirza, Munnu Bhai, Saleem Kashir, and Qamar Yurish. Thus, between 1951 and 1952, eight poems by Sharif Kunjahi, seven poems by Ahmad Rahi, and three poems by Qateel Shifai were published in *Monthly Panjābī*. However, the Marxists' poems published in *Monthly Panjābī* were not political. And though Sharif Kunjahi and Ahmad Rahi's poems were published in *Monthly Panjābī*, none of their essays were published in it, maybe to prevent Marxist views from being openly expressed in the journal. Faqeer Mohammad Faqeer kept absolute control over the ideological line of his journal and did not publish essays that deviated from it.

Faqeer did not neglect Indian authors either. Between 1951 and 1960, *Monthly Panjābī* published forty-four texts (nine essays, six short stories, and twenty-nine poems) by Indian authors such as Dhani Ram Chatrik, Darshan Singh Awara, Amrita Pritam, Gurcharan Singh Tej, Prof. Mohan Singh, and Hira Singh Dard. This shows that, despite their religious and ideological differences, some ties remained between Faqeer Mohammad Faqeer and Indian writers. But if Faqeer was publishing with regularity the writings of non-Muslims, their contribution to Punjabi literature was hardly mentioned in the essays published in *Monthly Panjābī*. Conservative critics attempted to rewrite the history of Punjabi literature from a Muslim point of view, emphasizing the role of the Sufis and the Muslim community in the development of Punjabi poetry and obliterating as much as possible the contributions of non-Muslims. Abdus Salam Khurshid did not mention the contributions of non-Muslims to Punjabi literature in his essay *Panjāb dī tārīx te adab* (History and Literature of the Punjab), and Maula Bakhsh Kushta summed them up in three lines: "Hindus have written the story of Puran Bhagat, Roop Basant, Gopi Chand, King Bhartari and some stories of kings and Maharajas. Christians have transcribed the Bible and some of their religious stories into Punjabi, compiled a Dictionary and composed some poems in order to preach their religion. The Sikhs have composed some religious and spiritual poems."[106]

Monthly Panjābī's contribution was not confined to literature. Between 1951 and 1960, the journal published numerous essays written specifically in defense of Punjabi language and literature, a series of essays by linguist Sardar Khan offering suggestions for a standardization of Pakistani Punjabi, and some pages of his dictionary (the first Punjabi dictionary published in Pakistan after independence). Nevertheless, if one compares them with the essays published during the same decade in *Daily Imroz*, one cannot help noticing two major differences: First, *Monthly Panjābī* almost totally ignored Punjabi folklore; between 1951 and 1960, it featured only one essay on this topic.[107] Conservatives were not as interested in folklore as Marxists, whose interest had ideological roots: Marxists were interested in folklore above all because they considered it a direct manifestation of the core culture of the masses. A second difference is that, unlike *Daily Imroz*, *Monthly Panjābī* almost totally ignored Pothohari and Multani/Siraiki. Between 1951 and 1960, *Monthly Panjābī* published only one essay discussing these dialects. The September–October 1959 issue included an essay by Faqeer Mohammad Faqeer on Pothohari folksongs.[108] In this essay, Faqeer argued that the differences between Pothohari and Majhi/Doabi Punjabi were superficial, because Pothohari's basic structure was similar to that of all the dialects included in the dialect continuum that stretches from Lahore to Peshawar.[109] It seems that Pothohari and Multani/Siraiki were mostly ignored by *Monthly Panjābī* for the sake of presenting a homogeneous picture of Punjabi.

A Conservative Political Journal

Monthly Panjābī was also a political journal whose views were close to those of daily *Nawā-e Waqt* and of the magazine *Caṭṭān*. One of Faqeer Mohammad Faqeer's goals was to promote and propagate through Punjabi a conservative ideology that until then had been conveyed mainly in Urdu, and to offer an alternative to the Marxist views expressed in *Daily Imroz's* Punjabi column and articles. Two types of texts conveyed this ideology in *Monthly Panjābī*: Faqeer Mohammad Faqeer's political editorials and patriotic and Islamic essays penned by various contributors (Mohammad Ibrahim Adil, Ghulam Rasool Mehr, Hamid Nizami).

FAQEER MOHAMMAD FAQEER'S EDITORIALS

Until 1953, Faqeer Mohammad Faqeer's editorials discussed only Punjabi language and literature, but after *Monthly Panjābī's* January–February 1953 issue his editorials became openly political, following a format very similar to that of Zaheer Babur's *Gall-bāt* column: a series of short comments on national and international events reflecting the author's political views.

Islam and the notion of *Qaum* (Muslims' Nation) were fundamental for Faqeer Mohammad Faqeer. He therefore approved of all government initiatives reaffirming Pakistan's Islamic identity, such as the adoption of a constitution proclaiming an Islamic state, a step he praised in his February 1956 editorial.[110] He also supported creation of the One Unit Scheme, which in his opinion was an affirmation of the religious and cultural unity of the peoples that form West Pakistan: "Sindh, Punjab, NWFP, these three provinces share the same type of culture. They have the same religion, the same lifestyle, the same kind of food, and the same kind of literature and traditions. If we are, in regard to our lifestyle, really the same, then why do some of our whimsical brothers see something bad in this unity which the government only wants to validate by a legal measure?"[111] Nevertheless, though he applauded and approved the initiatives of the successive civilian governments in Pakistan, Faqeer grew disillusioned with them and welcomed the coming to power in October 1958 of Ayub Khan, whom he considered to be the architect of a revolution that would purge the country of corruption and exploitation. He wrote in his editorial in the November–December 1958 issue of *Monthly Panjābī*: "People who have true empathy for our homeland have in just one week brought about a historic revolution, and we are surprised to see that these friends of the Nation have lifted it from such a deep swamp of exploitation and put it on the path of love. . . . Thank God we hear people from every corner of the country express their happiness!"[112]

In his editorials, Faqeer Mohammad Faqeer slammed Pakistan's enemies: Jawaharlal Nehru (for his unwillingness to set Kashmir free and for maintaining a "puppet government" in that province), the Pashtun nationalist Abdul Ghaffar Khan (whom Faqeer accuses of being an Indian agent and of wanting to divide Muslims), and the Marxist intellectuals.[113] He showed a deep contempt for the Marxists. In his editorial of August 1959, he reported a discussion with one of them (whom he calls *Lāl dallāl*—a red agent) after a meeting in Lahore of the Writers' Guild (a governmental association of writers established in 1959 by Qudratullah Shahab, Ayub Khan's right-hand man):

> In the previous days, a meeting of the *Writers' Guild* was organized in Lahore, and seeing its success, some left-wing writers who considered themselves great writers strongly protested against it. The man of truth (*sacyār*) asked a red agent: "Why are you against this association?" And the red one said, "because all of its members are government agents." The man of truth retorted: "So what? Your Kaʿaba is in Moscow, where the Russian government supports the writers who are favorable to it, makes them write what it wants and publishes them." The red agent got scared and said: "That's another matter." And the man

of truth said to him: "It may be another matter but you still get your dirty sweets from there."[114]

Faqeer Mohammad Faqeer commented on all types of events, but he did not comment on other ongoing language movements, though one could have expected them to have interested him. He discussed a language movement in one of his editorials only once: the Bengali language movement (in February 1956).[115] He commented on the adoption of Bengali alongside Urdu as an official language in Pakistan's constitution, bitterly complaining that Punjabi did not receive similar recognition from a central government that was behaving as if it were a dead language, now replaced by Urdu:

> Look how Pakistan has done justice! If the Bengalis number 40 millions then how can one not make their language—a language spoken by so many individuals—an official language? But it is another matter if Punjabi is spoken by 30 million people, a different matter in the eyes of the government, because those people actually don't speak it, do they? What they speak is Urdu which is also an official language. Then how do they have the right to speak Punjabi if Urdu is already there? And then, after all, who speaks it? It was spoken during the times of Waris Shah and Baba Bulleh Shah. Now, you see, no one speaks it and understands it.[116]

Faqeer consistently ignored the Bengali, Sindhi, Pashto, and Balochi movements (as did other contributors to *Monthly Panjābī*—they are not mentioned in any essay), either because he did not consider worth mentioning movements that had a separatist dimension of which he disapproved or because he was simply indifferent to the fate of other regional languages.[117] Conservatives focused only on Punjabi, a position radically different from that of the Marxists, who viewed their promotion of Punjabi as part of a general initiative in favor of all regional languages, seen as the people's language.

PATRIOTIC AND ISLAMIC ESSAYS

Over the years, *Monthly Panjābī* published a series of patriotic and Islamic essays that complemented Faqeer Mohammad Faqeer's editorials, articulating the ideology that informed them. The first of these essays was Mohammad Ibrahim Adil's *Qaumī quwwat* (The National Power), published in *Monthly*

Panjābī's inaugural issue. It is a sort of manifesto listing the values that Pakistanis should respect: *Sāda zindagī* (simple life), *Axlāq* (morality), *Qānūnī pābandī* (Obedience to the law), *Waṯan-parastī* (patriotism).[118] This essay ends with the following verses:

Des la'ī jyoṇā ḥayātī ai
Des dī xāṯir ai marṇā zindagī

Real life is living for one's country
To die for one's country is to remain alive.[119]

Patriotic essays continued to be published in *Monthly Panjābī* after the inaugural issue. Some of them, which were trying to inculcate a sense of patriotism in the Punjabis through their own language, clearly fall in the category of propaganda. Hamid Nizami's essay *Jamhūrī mulk* (A Democratic Country), published in August 1952, is in this category. The author sings the praises of Pakistan and defends Muhammad Ali Jinnah against detractors:

> In truth the Pakistan government is the first Muslim government in our continent which can be considered truly Islamic, since it is neither a monarchy nor an autocracy. It is the government of the people, and it follows the following principle: the subjects (*rʿiāyā*) will take all the government's decisions and the real power will lay with them. . . . Muhammad Ali Jinnah seemed to be a tough leader and looked like a dictator from afar, but those who had the opportunity to work closely with him or to observe directly his behavior know that a true democratic spirit inhabited him.[120]

The political discourse of the conservative intellectuals writing for *Monthly Panjābī* differs from that of the Marxists not only in ideology but also in terminology, systematically avoiding the use of terms such as *ʿAwām* (masses/proletariat). Hamid Nizami uses the term *Rʿiāyā* (subjects); Faqeer Mohammad Faqeer uses *Qaum* (nation).

Monthly Panjābī also featured essays on Islamic history, narrating the feats of the first heroes of Islam and praising their spirit of sacrifice and justice. The goal here was to portray the greatness of Islam and introduce role models. Ghulam Jilani Barq's *Futūḥāt-e islām* (Conquests of Islam) belong to this genre, as do Ghulam Rasool Mehr's *Islāmī ḥukūmat dā pehlā naqšā* (First

Incarnation of an Islamic Government) and *Islāmi ḥukūmat dā dūjā naqša* (Second Incarnation of an Islamic Government), essays that glorify the first caliphs of Islam.[121]

Defense and Illustration of the Punjabi Language

Sixteen essays in defense of the Punjabi language were published in *Monthly Panjābī* between 1951 and 1960. These essays were penned by Faqeer Mohammad Faqeer, Abdul Majeed Salik, Mohammad Baqir, Akhtar Ali Khan, Shorish Kashmiri, Sardar Khan, Professor Mohammad Yusuf, Professor Taj Mohammad Khayal, and Dr. Aziz ul-Hassan Abbasi.[122] These Punjabi apologists often used similar standard arguments. To legitimize their promotion of Punjabi, many of them stated that Urdu was born from Punjabi, thus referring to the views of Hafiz Mehmood Shirani expressed in *Panjāb meṃ Urdu* (Urdu in Punjab). Akhtar Ali Khan used this argument in his essay *Urdu dī māṃ Panjābī* (Punjabi Is Urdu's Mother): "The efforts undertaken by the journal *Panjābī* for the enrichment and development of Punjabi must be seen as ultimately aimed at the enrichment of Urdu. Because the Punjabi language is after all the mother of Urdu. That is why its enrichment is that of Urdu."[123]

Many Punjabi apologists used the standard lexical argument in their essays, responding to the objections of some Urdu defenders who argued that Punjabi is a "poor" language because its lexicon is limited and largely borrowed from Arabic and Persian. Faqeer Mohammad Faqeer, in order to show that Punjabi is not lexically poor, listed in one of his essays forty-three common "pure" Punjabi words used for "cow" (*gā'ī, jhūtī, bhabaṇ, pehlaṇ, wikvī dī, sajar sū*, etc.), concluding: "In Punjabi one does not find a handful but an incalculable number of examples of this type. You can deduce from this how rich it is."[124]

Three authors stood out among these apologists, putting forward original and radical arguments in their essays. The linguist Sardar Khan countered the common argument that Punjabi is a mere dialect of Urdu through historical and linguistic arguments; Dr. Aziz ul-Hassan Abbasi argued that the survival of the Punjabi language was vital for the survival of Punjabis as a distinct community; and Abdul Majeed Salik argued that the circumstances following Partition contributed to the development of Punjabi and the weakening of Urdu.[125]

SARDAR KHAN'S ESSAY

Sardar Khan, in his essay *Panjābī luġat* (Punjabi Lexicon), refuted the position of M. D. Taseer and other Urdu supporters who considered Punjabi a mere dialect of Urdu, arguing that Punjabi is a full-fledged language. He compared the trajectories of Punjabi and Urdu, listed their similarities and differences, and, in view of the lexical differences between them, concluded that Punjabi is a language in its own right:

> Punjabi and Urdu should be regarded as two sisters, and therefore it is wrong to consider Punjabi as a dialect of Urdu. If Urdu has evolved from the *Apabhramsha* which gave birth to the *Kharī Bolī* and was formed by mixing with *Braj Bhasha*, Punjabi has evolved from the *Apabhramsha* which gave birth to *Lahnda*, and came into being after passing through different stages. It is a fact that Punjabi never received any patronage, but that does not mean that its status should be lowered and it should be considered a mere dialect of Urdu. The grammar of Punjabi is similar to that of Urdu but its vocabulary distinguishes it from Urdu. This is one of the criteria which can help assess whether it is a language or a dialect.[126]

In his essay *Zubān te bolī* (Language and Dialect), Sardar Khan further developed the demonstration begun in *Panjābī luġat* and reiterated that the grammatical similarities between Punjabi and Urdu should not lead to the conclusion that Punjabi is a dialect of Urdu. Their lexical differences are enough to distinguish them: "Urdu and Punjabi, since they belong to the same family, are practically similar grammatically, but the lexicon of Punjabi is so different from that of Urdu that we must on this basis consider Punjabi as a fully-fledged language. This vocabulary was not borrowed from Urdu. But it derives from the same source from which Urdu derived its own vocabulary."[127]

DR. AZIZ UL-HASSAN ABBASI'S ESSAY

Dr. Aziz ul-Hassan Abbasi stated in his essay *Āsīṃ te sāḍḍī bolī* (We and Our Language) that the Punjabi language is a shield that protects Punjabis against a brutal process of acculturation that would lead them to degenerate and disappear.[128] Adopting English or Urdu would initiate this process; protecting Punjabi would help Punjabis to resist it.

Faqeer Mohammad Faqeer had used this argument in his essay *Nīm firangī* (Half White People), in which he ridiculed Anglicized Punjabis who could no longer speak their language, concluding, "The individual who moves away from his language moves away from his roots, and the individual who moves aways from his roots has no longer any place in this world."[129]

This argument was further developed and expanded by Dr. Aziz ul-Hassan Abbasi. Alongside the dangerous consequences of Anglicization, Abbasi warns of another process that he deems even more harmful: Urduization. He begins his essay with a description of the diglossic complex that affects educated Punjabis to such an extent that they speak Urdu or English and not their mother tongue with their children. Then he presents his main point: The adoption of a foreign language leads to the adoption of a foreign culture and the disappearance of one's own culture.

> In Pakistan our Punjabi brothers and sisters (especially those who have learned English) are the enemies of their own language. And the worst thing is that they have passed on this feeling of hostility to their children. In their homes, Urdu or English are spoken instead of Punjabi. These simpletons do not understand that the language of a people is the vehicle of its culture. The culture of a people is what keeps it alive. A people which has abandoned its language and started to speak other languages is doomed in the short term. No sane person will refuse to recognize that learning a language and speaking it has inevitable implications for an individual.[130]

To illustrate his point, Dr. Aziz ul-Hassan Abbasi depicts the consequences of Anglicization and Urduization. Describing the consequences of Anglicization, he conjures up the stereotypical image of Westernized Pakistanis who no longer have moral values:

> We, slave by birth, have learned English in order to survive and now we have to deal with the consequences of it. The English disease was at first confined to men, but once it reached women the repercussions were terrible for our people: indecency and vulgarity, lipstick and make-up. These women walk around the market with their heads uncovered, dressed in tight-fitting clothes. But before them, the culprits were those men who had started to wear trousers instead of *pajamas* and *shalwars*, English headgear instead of traditional hats

and turbans, and coats instead of dresses. The result is that the men have become some *Sahibs* and their wives some *Memsahibs*.[131]

In depicting the consequences of Urduization, Abbasi—who was convinced that Urdu was the main instrument used by the *Mohajirs* from India to dispossess and acculturate Punjabis—conjures up the ethnic stereotype of a pan-chewing effeminate *Mohajir*. He warns readers that by adopting Urdu, the martial Punjabis ("lions and lionesses") will degenerate and become effeminate.

> The enemies of Punjab have come from across the Yamuna river and are trying to destroy it through temptation and trickery, and their main weapon is their language. They want to kill two birds with one stone: first they will try to erase our language. Because once our language will be erased, our culture will also be erased. And when we will have forgotten and lost our language and our culture, we will be slaves to others. What will become of the lions and lionesses of Punjab under the effect of this slavery? See for yourself: men will not carry a stick on their shoulder but will have in their hand a box full of betel leaves and a small box filled with betel nuts, and instead of wearing a turban will wear a hat with flaps that fold down, and they will wear a silk *kurta* . . . and a narrow *pajama* like those worn by eunuchs. . . . And they will read the poetic collections of the Urdu poets of the East instead of epics like Heer Ranjha, Sassi Punnu and Sohni Mahiwal.[132]

Abbasi then presents an example of a people that has lost its culture and language: the *Camyār* (Untouchables), former Sindhi merchants, former builders of the civilizations of Mohenjodaro and Harappa, who were unable to resist the hegemony of Hindu Aryans and were reduced by them to the role of pariahs:

> There is another people we know as *chūhre* or *camyār*. These poor damned beings are a telling picture of the sad destiny of a great empire and civilization, which failed to save its culture in difficult times. These untouchables (from now on I will call them "Sindhis") are the descendants of those individuals whose greatness is testified by places like Mohenjodaro and Harappa. This Sindhi culture had reached its apogee 2800 years before the birth of Christ. . . . The Hindu savages came later from Central Asia, arrived in India after crossing Afghanistan,

> and spread throughout the country. When they descended to the south they came into contact with the inhabitants of Harappa and Mohenjodaro. The Sindhi merchants, who were accustomed to comforts and pleasures lost against these naked savages. As a result their empire and their culture were destroyed. . . . And now their condition is such that they consider themselves a stain on the face of Humanity. And their mere shadow is enough to pollute a Hindu.[133]

He concludes: "This is what will happen if Punjabis start speaking Urdu instead of their own language. . . . The individual or the people who/which thinks that the language or the ways of others are better than his/its own cannot progress because he/it remains mentally the slave of others."[134]

This essay conveys a stereotypical and prejudiced image of peoples. Its author depicts *Mohajirs* and Sindhis as weak and decadent and Punjabis as a superior people of lions and lionesses, a martial people not yet degenerated. Abbasi considers the migration of some *Mohajirs* to Punjab as an invasion, comparing it to that of the Aryans, against whom the inhabitants of Mohenjodaro and Harappa had to fight. The conflict between Urdu and Punjabi, interpreted by the Marxists as a conflict between the bourgeoisie and the masses, here acquires an ethnic dimension, identifying Urdu with the community of Urdu-speaking migrants. The conflict appears fundamentally linked to an ongoing struggle for hegemony between Urdu-speaking settlers and Punjabi natives. This radical anti-Urdu position is quite atypical, and it is difficult to know to what extent it was shared by other members of the conservative group. The publication of this essay in *Monthly Panjābī* suggests that at least the editorial board of the journal agreed with it.

ABDUL MAJEED SALIK'S ESSAY

Dr. Aziz ul-Hassan Abbasi's anti-*Mohajir* sentiments were shared by a prominent member of the conservative group: Abdul Majeed Salik. He argues in his essay *Urdu dā navāṃ daur* (The New Era of Urdu) that his sentiments were fueled by the arrogance and superiority complex of the *Mohajirs*.[135] Like Abbasi, Salik identifies Urdu with the community of Urdu-speaking migrants and sees the Urdu-Punjabi controversy as the result of an ongoing confrontation between Urdu-speaking settlers and Punjabi natives. *Urdu dā navāṃ daur* depicts this confrontation. Salik appears himself as a character in this essay, praising Punjabi in front of an arrogant *Mohajir* who laughs after hearing the Punjabi word *Pacvinjā* (fifty-five), finding its sound vulgar and comical. When the *Mohajir* asks him, "But you agree that Urdu is a better language than Punjabi, don't you?," Salik replies:

> I cannot prove that Urdu is a better language than Punjabi, nor do I claim that Punjabi is better than Urdu. Each individual regards his own language as the best in the world, and all languages are good. There is nothing bad in any language, and I can prove that Punjabi is a good language by the sole argument that it is my mother tongue. . . . The only thing that justifies your preference for Urdu is that it is your mother tongue. And if you list ten qualities of Urdu, I will list twenty-five qualities of Punjabi.[136]

The superiority of Urdu (as well as, to some extent, the very foundation of diglossic hierarchy, since all languages are "good") is thus questioned by a Punjabi speaker, who will not let Urdu replace his own language. Punjabi becomes here a tool of self-assertion in front of an Urdu-speaking community imbued with cultural arrogance.

Abdul Majeed Salik feels that the fates of Punjabi and Urdu are so inextricably linked that the emergence of Punjabi is only possible if Urdu's status changes, and he believes that the new conditions created by Partition (the exodus of Urdu speakers to Pakistani Punjab and of Punjabi speakers to Delhi) will lead to this change. Addressing the same *Mohajir* who tried to get him to say that Urdu is a better language, Abdul Majeed Salik draws his attention to the fact that Punjabi is a majority language in a city like Delhi, which until Partition was a center of Urdu, and that the Urdu spoken by the *Mohajirs* living in Pakistani Punjab—since the community is no longer exposed to the standard of Lucknow and Delhi—is on the verge of losing the purity of which its speakers are so proud. It will be increasingly influenced by Punjabi, to the extent that soon they will use words like *Pacvinjā*!

> Urdu is undoubtedly your mother tongue, but the mother of Urdu had two mammaries: Lucknow and Delhi. After Partition the milk of these two mammaries has dried up. How can we consider the language of Delhi as our standard now that out of 2,500,000 inhabitants of Delhi 1,500,000 are Punjabi? At present in the schools of Delhi out of 100 pupils only 30 speak Urdu. And then

in the schools of our Punjab 90% of schoolchildren are Punjabi and 10% Urdu speakers. So tell me, is Punjabi going to be influenced by Urdu or Urdu by Punjabi? Today, the word *Pacvinjā* makes you laugh, but tomorrow—God Willing—you will hear your children use this same *Pacvinjā* and you will tear your hair out in desperation![137]

A Defense of Punjabi Literature

The conflation of language and literature is common among apologists of Punjabi; the Punjabi language is generally equated with its literature. This confusion is the basis of the popular "masterpiece argument," which explains why, alongside the essays in defense of the Punjabi language, one also finds a certain number of essays in defense of its literature.[138] In the minds of apologists, revalorizing Punjabi literature is revalorizing the Punjabi language itself. Three strategies of revalorization dominate the discourse of apologists of Punjabi literature: comparing it with Urdu literature, comparing it with Western masterpieces, and asserting the anteriority of Punjabi literature.

Comparing Punjabi and Urdu literature is the main strategy used by Taj Mohammad Khayal in his essay *Panjābī dī benaṣībī* (Punjabi's Misfortune).[139] He writes:

> I dare to declare here that Punjabi literature is no less chaste than that of Urdu. And in fact, if considered honestly, it is even chaster than Urdu literature. Individuals who have studied the poetry of both languages cannot deny that this cursed practice of Persian poetry which consists in not specifying whether a declaration of love is addressed to a man or a woman was common in Urdu from the end of the 19th century until the beginning of the 20th century.[140] The result of this peculiar practice is that hundreds or even thousands of Urdu verses can not be read by a respectable man aloud and in public. On the contrary, if you read all the classic books of Punjabi you will notice that, apart from a few, the majority of the verses are impregnated with Sufism. In many books the love for Allah and his prophet is visible on every page. . . . Punjabi literature and poetry are full of moral values and spirituality. And to say that this literature is inferior and clumsy compared to the literature of other languages is like slapping your own face.[141]

Obscenity and pederasty in Urdu poetry, purity and chastity in a Punjabi literature dominated by spirituality and religiosity—for Taj Mohammad Khayal, Punjabi literature is superior to Urdu literature from a moral point of view.

Another revalorizing strategy consists in comparing a Punjabi text to a classic of Western literature. This strategy was adopted by Nawabzada Mehdi Ali Khan in his essay *Shakespeare dī angrezī te sāḍḍī Panjābī* (Shakespeare's English and Our Punjabi), in which he compared two verses of Shakespeare taken from *Romeo and Juliet* with some verses of a popular Punjabi poet and showed that both poets used the same image, thus proving that even popular Punjabi poetry is of a very high standard.[142]

> Romeo, standing under the window, began to sigh. And this sight of Juliet's face leaning on her hand, Shakespeare depicted it in these words, from Romeo's mouth: *Had I been the gloves of your hands I would have touched your cheeks.*[143] It is noteworthy that this great English poet has expressed a desire to caress a cheek in these words, and that our illiterate, simple-minded poet who is not worthy to associate with educated people while improvising a *māhyā* has said: *Sāḍḍe naloṃ button cange jiṛe sīne nāl lāe ho'e nī* (These buttons are better off than me, because they can touch your chest). Just think about it, is there a difference between the content of the verse of the great English poet and that of this illiterate man whom we meet every day in our lane?[144]

A third strategy for revalorizing Punjabi literature consists in asserting that Punjabi literature is older than Urdu literature. Abdus Salam Khurshid, in his essay *Panjāb dī tārīx te adab* (History and Literature of Punjab), traces the beginnings of Punjabi literature to pre-Islamic Punjab, as the legends later narrated by Punjab's epic poets were circulating long before the spread of Islam in the province.[145] In his essay on Mirza Sauda's Punjabi poetry, published in July 1956, Faqeer Mohammad Faqeer reminds readers that Punjabi literature was fully developed and setting an example of literary standard in the eighteenth century when Urdu literature was still in its infancy: "The poor Urdu at that time had just started her journey . . . but she didn't have a good companion, and didn't know her way. From Peshawar to Hyderabad it was the Queen Punjabi who reigned, and only her standard was considered."[146]

Khurshid's and Faqeer's version of the history of Punjabi literature have one thing in common: For the sake of giving Punjabi a new, completely Islamic identity, both authors emphasize the role of Sufis and of the Muslim community in the development of Punjabi literature and ignore the contribution of non-Muslims. Although Faqeer, in the essay he read during the 1956 Punjabi conference, paid tribute to the contribution of Amrita Pritam, Darshan Singh Awara, and Prof. Mohan Singh to the Punjabi literature of the twentieth century, he mentioned only one pre-twentieth-century non-Muslim author: the Hindu Damodar Das, author of the first known version of the story of *Heer Ranjha*.[147]

An Attempt at Standardizing Pakistani Punjabi: Sardar Khan

The standardization of Pakistani Punjabi was far from complete in 1951 when the first issue of *Monthly Panjābī* was published. Sardar Khan, in a series of essays published in *Monthly Panjābī* under his own name and under various pseudonyms (Kardar, S. Khanum) presented suggestions for a standardization and even a kind of Pakistanization of Punjabi.[148] He also published in *Monthly Panjābī* a few pages of a Punjabi dictionary he was in the process of compiling (the first volume of which was published in 1964).[149] Some of Sardar Khan's suggestions appear to have been ideologically motivated, responding to what he perceived as the linguistic hegemony of the Sikh community over Punjabi. The brand of Punjabi he advocated was therefore a Punjabi purified of elements considered specific to the Sikh community, including the *Gurumukhi* script and lexicon borrowed from Sanskrit/Hindi.

THE SCRIPT ISSUE

There were still writers in Pakistan after Partition who believed that the *Gurumukhi* script was best suited to Punjabi. P. D. Raphael, in his essay *Panjābī 'ilm* (Punjabi Science), presented two reasons for adopting the *Gurumukhi* script: It was more phonetic than the Urdu alphabet and its use would help maintain interaction with Punjabi speakers living in India.[150] "Why not use the *Gurumukhi* script to write Punjabi? In terms of reading and writing, the *Gurumukhi* letters don't give us the opportunity to hesitate for even a second. Which makes us think that a Punjabi scholar invented this science. And if we adopt *Gurumukhi* we will be able to maintain intellectual exchanges with our brothers who live on the other side of the border."[151] Sardar Khan responded to this suggestion in his essay *Panjābī luġat*, his first article published in *Monthly Panjābī*, listing the weaknesses of the *Gurumukhi* script.[152] It is indeed phonetic, but this phoneticism is an obstacle to fixing a unified orthographic norm: Everyone writes a word as he pronounces it, thus resulting in spellings that differ according to the area, and in the end, the spellings used by the largest number (i.e. "illiterates") will be consensually adopted. Khan also regarded as a major weakness the absence of specific letters in *Gurumukhi* to transcribe some specific sounds of Arabic and Persian (like [tˤ], [ʕ] and [ɣ̞]):

> The *Gurumukhi* script was invented to write Punjabi, but using this script gives you the feeling of writing Urdu in Latin alphabet. . . . You write exactly what you hear. . . . Because of this specificity of *Gurumukhi* any word, if pronounced slightly differently in one region, will be written with a slightly different spelling. . . . Writing a language in a phonetic manner means that you are letting illiterates decide how you will spell words, therefore adopting *Gurumukhi* means defining Punjabi as the language of the illiterate people.
>
> When words from foreign languages are introduced in a given language they usually affect its spelling system. But the sounds represented by the letters ط ع and غ disappear altogether in *Gurumukhi*, because it does not have specific letters for these sounds.[153]

Khan then presented his arguments in favor of using the Urdu alphabet: "If it is true that the place of origin of Urdu is Punjab or Sindh, then we will have to write Punjabi in the Urdu alphabet, like Sindhi which is written in Arabic letters, and this way Punjabi will remain close to our official language, Urdu."[154]

In 1956, Sardar Khan published an essay titled *Panjābī de ḥurūf* (Punjabi Letters) in which he further developed the argument used in his 1953 essay, advocating the use of the Urdu alphabet and alleging its anteriority—that it was used to write Punjabi before the *Gurumukhi* alphabet was invented, while Urdu was still in its nascent stage.[155]

> If we ask Urdu where it found its alphabet, it will not know because it no longer remembers which womb it came out from. It forgot the days when it was being

> raised by Punjabi on the soil of Punjab.[156] After that it travelled to Delhi and refined itself, called itself Urdu and the Punjabis promoted more than their own this new language which they had raised themselves. . . . What I mean is that it is in Punjab that the Punjabis had created a new alphabet, by adding the letters: ٹ, ڈ ڑ to the Persian alphabet. And nowadays this alphabet is called Urdu alphabet. It is very strange that it is Punjab which created this alphabet and that now the same Punjab is looking for an alphabet for its Punjabi language. . . . This alphabet, which is commonly known as "Urdu alphabet," is in fact the Punjabi alphabet. The fact that Urdu made it its own is another story.[157]

THE SELECTION OF A STANDARD VARIETY

Another important issue that Sardar Khan discussed in his essays was the choice of which variety should become the basis of Pakistani standard Punjabi. As we have seen, Faqeer Mohammad Faqeer argued in December 1951 that standard Pakistani Punjabi should be based on the dialect of the Gujranwala district because of its central geographic location and the presence of a literary corpus in this dialect. Sardar Khan agreed with this suggestion and presented arguments justifying it in his essay "Standard Panjābī."

Sardar Khan begins his essay with a long description of the linguistic situation of Punjab, distinguishing two branches of Punjabi: a western branch (called *Lahnda* by the linguist George Grierson), which includes Multani/Siraiki, Pothohari, and Hindko, and an Eastern branch, whose main dialect is the *Sant Bhasha* (or *Sikhī*), which includes the *Majhi* (Middle Language) dialect spoken in Lahore and Amritsar. Sardar Khan explains that the Chenab River marks the boundary between these two branches, with a buffer zone where *Punjabi Lahnda*—a mixture of *Majhi* and *Lahnda*—is spoken. This area stretches from Sialkot district upto the north of the princely state of Bahawalpur, crossing Wazirabad, Gujranwala, Sheikhupura, Okara, and Pak Pattan. The variety that should serve as the basis for standard Punjabi can therefore potentially belong to one of these three groups: *Lahnda*, *Majhi*, or *Punjabi Lahnda*. Sardar Khan automatically disqualifies *Majhi*, as it happens to be the favorite language both of the Sikhs (connected to their *Sant Bhasha*) and of the Ludhiana-based missionaries, who have used it as the basis of their dictionary and their writings, intending to make it written Punjabi's standard variety. Sardar Khan notes: "In reality Punjabi's soul could not tolerate the preaching of the Englishmen and after some time this standard was eliminated."[158]

After disqualifying *Majhi*, Sardar Khan has to choose between *Lahnda* and *Punjabi Lahnda*. He writes:

> Until now it can be observed that every Punjabi writer has used *Lahnda* extensively in his writings, and why shouldn't he have done so?[159] The language of Lahore has not yet gotten rid of the soul of *Lahnda*, so how could a writer get rid of it? Punjabi is not a language distinct from *Lahnda*. And all the sweetness of its flavor can only be retained if we decide to make it a literary standard. From this point of view, an expert like Grahame Bailey was right to say that under the present situation if a language can claim to become a literary norm, it is *Lahnda*, in particular the one spoken in Wazirabad area.[160]

Sardar Khan therefore suggests Wazirabad's *Lahnda* as the basis of Pakistani standard Punjabi. Wazirabad's *Lahnda*, according to the classification presented at the beginning of his essay, falls in the category of *Punjabi Lahnda*. And since Wazirabad is part of the Gujranwala district, Sardar Khan's reasoning naturally leads him to back Faqeer Mohammad Faqeer's suggestion in favor of the dialect of the Gujranwala district.

THE ISSUE OF NEOLOGISMS AND THE PUNJABI DICTIONARY

The process of standardization of a language also involves the introduction of neologisms. Sardar Khan conveyed his views regarding this process in his essay "Standard Panjābī," expressing his strong disapproval of Sikh lexicographers' way of forming neologisms by borrowing Hindi words.

> Nowadays the literary Punjabi of the Hindus and Sikhs living in East Punjab is slipping dangerously into the mold of modern Hindi. Mohan Singh, at a session of the *Punjabi Society* of Government College in Lahore in 1930 had declared that Muslims, by mixing Arabic and Persian with Urdu had created a language that should be named *'afārdū*.[161] . . . But if we look at the present situation in East Punjab it does not seem that Hindi is influenced by Punjabi to the point that one can call it *p'hindī*.[162] On the contrary we are witnessing the gradual transformation of Punjabi into *hanumān Panjābī*.[163]

Sardar Khan disapproved of Punjabi's Hindiization in Indian Punjab, but he was equally unhappy with Punjabi's Urduization in Pakistani Punjab. The latter trend was championed by Waqar Ambalvi, who, in his essay *Pāk Panjābī*, after listing some Urduisms in some Punjabi essays published in *Monthly Panjābī*, wrote: "These examples show how a new form of Punjabi is gradually developing, and how Urdu expressions are making their way into it. Whether it is done consciously, or as a result of the habit of writing in Urdu, it is a beautiful and delightful practice. Because of its beauty and flavour, I have named this new form *Pāk Panjābī* (Pure/Pakistani Punjabi)."[164] This *Pāk Panjābī* did not meet with Sardar Khan's approval, and he always refrained from using the term to designate the Pakistani standard of Punjabi he was promoting. Thus, in *Panjābī dī gatayyā* (The Braiding of Punjabi), another essay discussing neologisms, he declared that Punjabi's Urduization was as artificial and harmful as Punjabi's Hindiization, concluding: "Punjabi should not be built by introducing Hindi words into it as is the practice in East Punjab, nor by introducing Urdu words into it as it is customary to do in Pakistan. Otherwise it will become *Purdū*."[165]

Faced with the two opposing trends of Hindiization and Urduization, Sardar Khan recommended following the natural tendency: introducing foreign words into Punjabi, but after Punjabiizing them. "Arabic, Persian and English words have already gone through Punjabi's whetstone. And other words will go through it. Because it will not borrow words directly from a source as modern Hindi does, it will first sharpen them. This is why writers should try to make all the words they import into Punjabi wear Punjabi clothes."[166] The compilation of a dictionary was necessary to the process of standardization of Pakistani Punjabi. Sardar Khan underlined, in his 1953 essay *Panjābī luġat*, that Punjabi's systematic corruption through Urduization and Hindiization rendered the compilation and publication of a dictionary (in Urdu characters, of course) absolutely necessary: "We should compile this Dictionary to guide people and prevent the language from becoming corrupt."[167]

Sardar Khan himself took the first step in that direction, publishing in the June–July 1956 issue of *Monthly Panjābī* three pages of a dictionary he had begun working on.[168] These pages were published with a short introductory remark by Faqeer Mohammad Faqeer in which he expressed the desire to publish a few pages of this dictionary in each issue of *Monthly Panjābī*. This first instalment contained sixty-six entries, from *ṭopā* (a unit of measure) to *ṭomb-ṭākī* (rags), with definitions in Urdu. After certain definitions, the dialectal origin of the word is mentioned (*Multānī, Poṭhohārī*), which shows an ambition to write a dictionary covering all the dialects, as well as a desire to facilitate intercomprehension among them (a goal already announced by Sardar Khan in his article *Panjābī luġat*).

Faqeer Mohammad Faqeer's desire, unfortunately, remained unfulfilled. Pages from Sardar Khan's dictionary did not appear with regularity in *Monthly Panjābī*. Only one more installment of Sardar Khan's dictionary was published (in the September 1957 issue).[169] This installment consisted of 103 entries (extending over five pages), from *khānḍ* (experienced) to *khiṭṭī* (a thorny bush), with definitions in Urdu and indications of the word's dialectal origin (*Jaṭkī, Šāhpurī, Pinḍocī, Multānī, Ludhyānī, Poṭhohārī*). This turned out to be the last installment before *Monthly Panjābī* ceased publication in March 1960.

The Conservative Punjabi Group: Structure and Trajectories

Structure of the Conservative Punjabi Group

The conservative Punjabi group, formed in 1950, initially included Faqeer Mohammad Faqeer, Abdul Majeed Salik, Abid Ali Abid, Mohammad Baqir, M. D. Taseer, Ustad Karam Amritsari, Sufi Ghulam Mustafa Tabassum, and Abdul Majeed Bhatti. In the years that followed, some senior Punjabi writers joined it, along with some of the most eminent members of the conservative intellectual camp. The conservative Punjabi group kept on expanding, as the Pak Punjabi League and the Punjabi Cultural Society attracted a lot of writers and poets. Among them we can distinguish three subgroups:

1. *Leaders*: Faqeer Mohammad Faqeer, Abdul Majeed Salik, and Mohammad Baqir stand out as the leaders of the movement. These three influential personalities used their economic and social capital as well as their symbolic capital for the promotion of Punjabi, launching *Monthly Panjābī*, and establishing the Pak Punjabi League, the Punjabi Cultural Society, and the *Panjābī Adabī Akādemī*.

2. *Prestigious supporters*: This subgroup includes personalities endowed with high symbolic and social capital such as Zafar Ali Khan, Akhtar Ali Khan, Hamid Nizami, Shorish Kashmiri, Ghulam Rasool Mehr, Abid Ali Abid, Taj Mohammad Khayal, and Mian Bashir Ahmad. Between 1951 and 1953, they published in *Monthly Panjābī* declarations of support for the conservative Punjabi movement, along with some articles.
3. *Creators*: This subgroup includes the fifty writers who regularly contributed to *Monthly Panjābī* with the aim of enriching the literary capital of Punjabi through the production of poetry and prose.[170]

The conservative Punjabi group was multigenerational, unlike the Marxist Punjabi group, which was dominated by young writers who began their writing career right after independence or in the early 1950s. Maula Bakhsh Kushta and Karam Amritsari belonged to the literary generation that had established itself at the beginning of the twentieth century and participated in the emergence of modern secular Punjabi poetry; the last representatives of this generation died in the 1950s (Maula Bakhsh Kushta in 1955 and Karam Amritsari in 1959). Authors born at the end of the nineteenth century or the beginning of the twentieth, like Abdul Majeed Salik (b. 1895), Peer Fazal Gujrati (b. 1897), Lal Din Qaisar (b. 1899), Faqeer Mohammad Faqeer (b. 1900), Firoz Din Sharaf (b. 1901), and Joshua Fazal Din (b. 1903), belonged to the literary generation that established itself in the 1920s. Some of them were associated with the Punjabi literary journals *Panjābī Darbār* and *Sārang*. Authors like Sajjad Hyder and Agha Ashraf, who began to write in Punjabi in the years preceding Partition, belonged to the literary generation that established itself in the 1940s. Others, like Noor Kashmiri, Shafi Aqeel, Tayeb Rizvi, Saqib Zairvi, Maratib Ali, Nazr-e Fatima, Akbar Lahori, Ghulam Yaqub Anwar, Sardar Khan, Aslam Rahi, Asi Rizvi, Rashida Rashid Simeen, and Shahbaz Malik, belonged to the new literary generation. These authors started writing in Punjabi in the 1950s, and their first texts were published in *Monthly Panjābī*.

A distinction can be made in this multigenerational group between a dominant (endowed with high symbolic capital) and a dominated (in the process of accumulating capital and struggling to acquire peer recognition) pole. One can divide individuals at the dominant pole into three groups, according to the type of capital they were endowed with. The first group comprises individuals with important social capital: editors-in-chief of newspapers and leading columnists like Abdul Majeed Salik, Ghulam Rasool Mehr, Majeed Lahori, and Waqar Ambalvi; senior civil servants like Nawabzada Mehdi Ali Khan; and politicians like Joshua Fazal Din. The second group are those with important educational capital: university professors and college principals like Mohammad Baqir, Sufi Ghulam Mustafa Tabassum, Abdus Salam Khurshid, Qayyum Nazar, and Abid Ali Abid. The third are individuals with a symbolic type of notoriety: senior Punjabi poets like Faqeer Mohammad Faqeer, Peer Fazal Gujrati, Maula Bakhsh Kushta, Mohammad Ibrahim Adil, and Lal Din Qaisar. Of these sixteen individuals at the dominant pole, only seven had written texts in Punjabi before the inception of the movement (Faqeer Mohammad Faqeer, Abdul Majeed Salik, Joshua Fazal Din, Peer Fazal Gujrati, Maula Bakhsh Kushta, Mohammad Ibrahim Adil, and Lal Din Qaisar). The others (Mohammad Baqir, Majeed Lahori, Waqar Ambalvi, Nawabzada Mehdi Ali Khan, Sufi Ghulam Mustafa Tabassum, Abdus Salam Khurshid, Qayyum Nazar, Ghulam Rasool Mehr, and Abid Ali Abid) had not written anything in Punjabi before being requested by Faqeer Mohammad Faqeer to do so. Their main medium of expression was Urdu, and most of them returned to Urdu after writing and publishing a few texts in Punjabi. However, Mohammad Baqir's, Abdus Salam Khurshid's, and Sufi Ghulam Mustafa Tabassum's commitment to Punjabi was lasting.[171]

Opposite this dominant pole, one can distinguish a dominated pole comprising of thirty-six writers more or less advanced in the cycle of consecration, some having barely entered this cycle and others already in the ascending phase. None of them reached a notoriety comparable to that of the writers at the dominant pole. One can divide them into subgroups according to their social positions.[172] Ten of them belong to journalistic circles (Noor Kashmiri, Shafi Aqeel, Hanif Chaudhry, Bashir Manzar, Saqib Zeervi, Mahfuz ul-Hasan Shah Naqvi, Nizamuddin Tawakkuli, Malik Mohammad al Din, Fida Hussain Fida, Wafa Jafri); nine are civil servants (Khalil Atish, Rashida Rashid Simeen, Abdul Karim Samar, Ahmad Bashir, Mumtaz Ali Muztar, Syed Ali Shah, Sardar Khan, Aslam Rahi, Chaudhry Ahmad Din); five are commercial writers, working for radio or cinema (Agha Ashraf, Sajjad Hyder, Nazar Fatima, Saghar Siddiqui, Talib Jalandhari); two are landowners (Zohair Bigi, Suhail Yazdani); two are teachers (Hanif Bawa, Ahmad Hussain Qaladari); and two are lawyers (Akbar Lahori, Ghulam Yaqub Anwar). The remaining writers are traders (Asi Rizvi), accountants (Shahbaz Malik), or *ḥakīms* (Tayeb Rizvi), or live in precarious conditions (Sehrai Gurdaspuri is a mason, Talib Chishti an itinerant bookseller, and Saeen Naqad a fakir). The vast majority of the writers at this dominated pole belong to the educated petty bourgeoisie, a social class that enjoyed a stability that was lacking for most writers of the Marxist Punjabi group, who, due to their reputation and activities, had an unstable professional situation and lived in near poverty.[173]

Trajectories of Two Representatives of the New Literary Generation

We have previously examined the trajectories of two senior conservative writers (Faqeer Mohammad Faqeer and Abdul Majeed Salik), but in order to present a complete picture of the Punjabi conservative group, we deem it necessary to examine the trajectories of two writers who belonged to the new literary generation: the poet and translator Ghulam Yaqub Anwar and the playwright and short story writer Sajjad Hyder. A close look at their trajectories can help us determine the reasons that led them to write in Punjabi and what role the adoption of this language played in their literary or professional career.

GHULAM YAQUB ANWAR (1915–1974)

Ghulam Yaqub Anwar belonged to the new generation of poets associated with the conservative movement. A native of Gujranwala, the son of a renowned Punjabi poet who also worked as a prison director (Abdul Ghani Wafa), he was born in Mianwali, passed his matric examination in Eminabad in 1930, and completed his BA at Forman College, Lahore in 1934. He began an MA in philosophy at Government College, Lahore, but failed to complete it. He then started working in the colonial administration and was appointed as a tax officer. After postings in Sialkot, Lahore, Sargodha, Gujrat, and Attock, he finally resigned and established himself as a lawyer in Gujranwala.[174]

Ghulam Yaqub Anwar explained, in the preface to his collection *Can dī khārī* (Moon Basket), that in the course of his literary career he had been in close contact with three different literary circles.[175] He initially interacted, thanks to his father, with the Punjabi poets of Gujranwala; among them, he met his *Ustad*, Ghulam Hassan Khan Gamon, then considered a master of the Punjabi *ġazal*.[176] Then, during his posting in Lahore, he came in contact with the modernist poets Miraji, Yusuf Zafar, Qayyum Nazar, and Mukhtar Siddiqui (the three founders of the *Ḥalqa-e Arbāb-e Żauq*). Finally, in the early 1950s, after rediscovering the classical poetry of the Sufis, he joined Faqeer Mohammad Faqeer's group. Three of his Punjabi poems, one of his Punjabi *ġazals*, and one translation from English were published in *Monthly Panjābī* between 1952 and 1958. After *Monthly Panjābī* shut down, his Punjabi poems were published in *Panjdaryā* and *Panjābī Adab*, and a Punjabi collection titled *Can dī khārī* (Moon Basket) was published posthumously in 1976.

As a result of Anwar's interactions with these different circles, his poetic production in Punjabi is very eclectic: He wrote traditional *ġazals* under the influence of his father and of Ghulam Hassan Gamon, as well as free verse poems like Miraji and his modernist followers. Like Miraji, Anwar was an avid reader of foreign literature, and like him he translated foreign poetry into his mother tongue.[177] *Can dī khārī* includes Punjabi translations of English, Arabic, French, Sanskrit, and Bengali poems.[178] To explain his decision to write in Punjabi rather than in Urdu, he stated that he was following the model of Dante, who chose to write *La Divina Commedia* in his mother tongue and not in Latin.[179] However, this decision was also, to a large extent, a consequence of his family background (his father was a Punjabi poet) and his initial literary socialization. By writing in Punjabi, Ghulam Yaqub Anwar was perpetuating a family tradition and the literary tradition of his area.

SAJJAD HYDER (1920–1990)

The trajectory of Sajjad Hyder, a short story writer, playwright, and radio producer, is more peculiar than that of Ghulam Yaqub Anwar. His adoption of Punjabi as a medium of expression was not linked to a family or cultural tradition, but purely coincidental.

Born in Gujrat into an educated family (his father, an alumnus of Aligarh University, was working as a school inspector), Sajjad Hyder was initially interested in Persian and Urdu. He completed an MA in Persian at Government College, Lahore, where he studied under Sufi Ghulam Mustafa Tabassum, and he translated Tagore's "The Gardener" into Urdu. Unable to find a job for two years after completing his MA, he was finally hired in 1944 at the Lahore radio station as a "senior program assistant" in charge of the daily Punjabi program *Dehātī bhāyoṃ ke liye* (For Our Rural Brothers). He started writing Punjabi songs and radio dramas for this program.[180] It was therefore out of professional obligation, not out of sentimental or aesthetic choice, that he switched to Punjabi.[181]

The Lahore radio station was in those years a launching platform for young authors. Famous playwrights like Rafi Peerzada and Imtiaz Ali Taj and emerging writers like Kartar Singh Duggal, Rajinder Singh Bedi, Abdul Majeed Bhatti, and Siraj Nizami were associated with it.[182] Sajjad Hyder also benefited from this platform: His radio drama *Hawā de hūke* (Sighs of the Wind) drew a lot of attention, and Hyder was noticed by Amrita Pritam, with whom he became romantically involved. She encouraged him to write his first Punjabi short story—*Nacnī* (The Dancer)—which she published in *Gurumukhi* script in *Hitkārī*, her father's literary journal. Hyder wrote a few other Punjabi short stories, which were published in the same journal.[183] Amrita Pritam introduced him to the progressive writers of Lahore, and after she migrated to India, he continued interacting with them, maintaining relationships with Abdullah Malik, Sahir Ludhianvi, and Bari Alig.[184] He ended up participating in the "Ghalib day" organized by the progressives on February 14, 1948 at the YMCA in Lahore, during which he read an essay.[185] However, he never formally became a member of the Progressive Writers' Association, probably because he knew that this membership could put his government job in jeopardy, but also because, according to Rauf Malik, he was a purely "literary" person who refused to mix literature and politics.[186]

In the early 1950s, Sajjad Hyder developed ties with conservative Punjabi intellectuals and became a regular contributor to *Monthly Panjābī*; in it, between 1951 and 1952, he published five short stories and a radio drama. He also benefited from the support of Abdul Majeed Salik who, in 1957, prefaced a collection of his radio dramas titled *Hawā de hūke*.[187]

Sajjad Hyder pursued a brilliant career in radio: He wrote around forty radio dramas, was in charge of Radio Pakistan's Dhaka station in the 1960s, and retired as director of the Lahore station. Sajjad Hyder is one of the few (possibly the only) writers of the new literary generation who managed to make a living out of writing in Punjabi.

The Literary Production of the Punjabi Conservatives

Poetic Production

Although Faqeer Mohammad Faqeer and Abdul Majeed Salik made the development of Punjabi prose one of the goals of their movement, poetry dominates the literary output of the conservative Punjabi writers. One can divide their poetic production into two corpuses: first, the 93 poems of Faqeer Mohammad Faqeer included in his collection *Muwāte* (Sparks), published in 1956; and second, the 318 poems, 77 *ġazals*, and 48 songs penned by different poets that were published in *Monthly Panjābī* between 1951 and 1960.

MUWĀTE AND THE POETRY OF FAQEER MOHAMMAD FAQEER

Faqeer Mohammad Faqeer's collection *Muwāte* (1956) is his response to Ahmad Rahi's *Tirinjan* and Abdul Majeed Bhatti's *Dil daryā*. It reflects an aesthetic and an ideology that are completely opposite to those of Marxist Punjabi poetry. While Ahmad Rahi and Abdul Majeed Bhatti used poetic forms inspired by Punjabi folklore, Faqeer attempted to bring Punjabi poetry closer to the Urdu poetry of Allama Iqbal, making his poems a vehicle for a metaphysical and moralizing discourse. While the poems of *Tirinjan* and *Dil daryā* deal with the condition of women, written in their voice, *Muwāte's* poems describe and glorify a male figure reminiscent of Allama Iqbal's *Mard-e Momin* (The Believer), a superman whose faith (*īmān*) makes him invincible and capable of dictating his will to destiny.[188] This superman is depicted in the poem *Momin dī naẕar* (The Gaze of the Believer):

Hai bijlī vāṃg aihdī ākh mārdī lišak
Zubān aihdī dī nok ai dār dī lišak
Aihdī gall aṡar jādū dā ai sagvāṃ
Naẕar momin dī ai talvār dī lišak

The eye of the believer is like a lightning bolt, it flashes
His tongue is like the shine of the tip of the gallows
His word has a magic effect
The gaze of the believer is as bright as the sword[189]

Many of *Muwāte*'s poems spell out the principles that must guide a man so that he rises to the level of a *Mard-e Momin*. He must of course possess an unwavering faith:

Rakhde īmān wāle kund talvārāṃ na'īṃ
Fataḥ hathīṃ karaṇ wāle vekhde hārāṃ na'īṃ

Men who have faith do not possess dull swords
Those who hold victory in their hand do not even see defeat[190]

He must follow his passion (*'Išq*), and not his reason (*'Aqal*):

'Išq kartūtāṃ dā pīr ai 'aqal gallāṃ dī murīd . . .
'Išq Faqīr kare kartūtāṃ 'aqal zubānī gallāṃ

Passion is action's teacher and reason words' pupil . . .
O Faqeer, passion acts, reason only talks[191]

And he should not be afraid of fighting to defend his faith. The *Mard-e Momin* is above all a fighter; his main attribute is the sword.

Dil vic jihde īmān Faqīr nāhīṃ ohde hath vic phaṛī talvār kī ai?

O Faqeer, he who has faith in his heart if he has no sword in his hand, what can he achieve?[192]

Faqeer Mohammad Faqeer also emphasizes the role of women in creating a *Mard-e Momin*. Women must, above all, encourage their husbands and sons to overcome their fear and to sacrifice themselves, because it is this ultimate sacrifice that will make their family proud:

Momin māṃ te āp jihād utte putar lāṛe banāke ṭordī rahī
Jānde putar te sa'īṃ nūṃ ākhdī ai kare pakyāṃ baṛī tākīd dyāṃ
Hāṃ maiṃ māṃ ikk ġāzī dī ākh sakāṃ bīwī maiṃ ikk mard šahīd dī āṃ.

The believing (*momin*) mother herself sent her son to the front, dressing him as a bridegroom

And said with great insistence to her son and her husband at the time of departure
I want to be the mother of a warrior, the wife of a martyr.[193]

Faqeer refers in his poems to heroes from the past, such as the conqueror of the Iberian peninsula Tariq Ibn Ziyad (670–720) and the conqueror of northern India Mahmud of Ghazni (998–1030), who embody the qualities of a *Mard-e Momin*.[194] Their example shows that no armies and no borders can stop a fighter motivated by faith. He refers also to Imam Hussain and his family and to Mansur Hallaj, who embodied the readiness to sacrifice one's life.[195] Faqeer sees the same fighting spirit and spirit of sacrifice in the Punjabi troops who fought on the Kashmir front in 1948, and he salutes their bravery.[196] He contrasts it with the cowardice of the materialistic Westerners (*firangī*), who have conquered the world not by the sword but through money and trade.[197] Faqeer's ideology of *Mard-e Momin* culminates in nationalism and anticolonialism.

A major portion of *Muwāte's* poems exalt the *Mard-e Momin*, but it also includes some poems of a different type: poems celebrating the Punjabi language or the founder of the nation Muhammad Ali Jinnah, and even some romantic poems.[198] These romantic poems, describing sad moonlit landscapes, are a sort of transposition into Punjabi of the moonlight scenes for which the romantic poet Akhtar Shirani was famous.[199]

POEMS PUBLISHED IN *MONTHLY PANJĀBĪ*

Faqeer Mohammad Faqeer was arguably the last proponent of the Iqbalian metaphysical poem in Punjabi. This genre, loaded with heavy rhetoric and hyperboles, was gradually becoming obsolete and was now supplanted by the sociopolitical poem that the progressives had popularized and that many conservative poets had started adopting.[200] The poems being published in *Monthly Panjābī* addressed the sociopolitical issues that Faqeer had failed to address in his metaphysical poems. These poems often addressed the issue of social injustice (the favorite issue of the progressives), whether in a melodramatic way as in Ashfaq Naqvi's *Dʿuā* (A Prayer), in which the poet begs God to make men compassionate toward one another, or in a sarcastic way as in Asi Rizvi's *Nakheṛā* (Distinction), which praises ironically the "qualities" of a powerful man.[201] Some conservative poets expressed anger over social injustice, like Aslam Rahi, who in *xāṣ vairī* (Special Enemies) denounced the rich and wealthy, these "special enemies" of the country who suck people's blood; others, like Suhail Yazdani in *Dosto* (O My Friends), proclaimed their desire to run away from a society plagued with inequalities.[202] Some poets expressed optimism about the future, like Talib Jalandhari who, in *Raušan savere* (Shining Mornings), imagined a better tomorrow for the country.[203]

Another theme frequently addressed by conservative poets in their socio-political poems was the decadence of the current political system. Saqib Zeervi openly criticized this system in *Ithoṃ uḍḍ!* (Fly Away from Here!), but other poets preferred to express their criticism through metaphors.[204] Asi Rizvi, in *Rākhe* (Protectors), used the metaphor of the garden for the country and of the gardener for its ruler, drawing inspiration from the metaphorical language of progressives like Faiz Ahmad Faiz.[205]

Another genre very much in vogue among conservative poets was the romantic poem (*rūmānī naẓm*), a genre that Akhtar Shirani had made popular in Urdu in the 1930s and was now being imported into Punjabi.[206] Moonlight scenes abound in these romantic poems. Abdul Hamid Amar's *Rāt* (Night), Suhail Yazdani's *Naqš-e naẓar* (Trace of a Gaze) and *Meḥrām yār* (My Friend My Confidant), and Talib Chishti's *Dīp jalāvāṃ* (Let Me Light a Lamp) all depict a lover contemplating a nocturnal landscape while waiting for his beloved.[207] The landscape, described in all its beauty, is clearly a substitute (or a metaphor) for the absent beloved. In Suhail Yazdāni's *Canāṃ can tainūṃ ghūr ghūr vekhe* (My Beloved the Moon Stares at You) and Asi Rizvi's *Mīṃh dī mutyār* (Beloved of the Rain), a poet whose beloved has finally managed to join him seduces her, praising her beauty in a *Sarāpā*.[208] In Alim's *Farār* (Escape), the beloved has succumbed to the poet's advances, and now he convinces her to run away with him.[209] Romantic poems thus describe the different stages of a romance: waiting, meeting, seduction, and escape.

The genre of the *ġazal*, condemned by Marxists, was very popular among conservatives.[210] Peer Fazal Gujrati was, in the 1950s, the most famous proponent of the Punjabi *ġazal* in Pakistan. A prolific poet, he published a *ġazal* in almost every issue of *Monthly Panjābī*. But his *ġazals* were mere transpositions of their Urdu models, borrowing their themes, metaphors, comparisons, meters, and vocabulary. Reacting to this hyper-Urduization, the poet and critic Abid Ali Abid expressed in his essay *Panjābī ġazal* the wish that poets adapt the *ġazal* to Punjabi by using traditional Punjabi meters, vocabulary, and expressions.[211] Some conservative *ġazal* poets ignored this recommendation: Sufi Ghulam Mustafa Tabassum's and Talib Chishti's Punjabi *ġazals* (published respectively in the December 1951 and March–April 1959 issues of *Monthly Panjābī*) were still very close to their Urdu models. But a few poets did follow it: Tariq Suhdarvi published in the February–March 1952 issue of *Monthly Panjābī* an "indigenized" *ġazal* in Hindi (not Persian) meter that contains a minimal number of Urdu words:

Ḍubyā can te chup ga'e tāre
Hijr de sāthi rus ga'e sāre
Jyoṃ na'īṃ sakde ġam de māre
Chaḍ de sajṇāṃ nit de tāre

The moon has disappeared, the stars have hidden
The companions of the days of separation are angry
Their grief does not allow them to live
Abandon your beloved! The stars will always be there!

Ghulam Yaqub Anwar also followed Abid Ali Abid's recommendations: His *ġazal*, published in February–March 1960 issue of *Monthly Panjābī*, used a Hindi meter and *Tadbhav* words (directly borrowed from Sanskrit). But these attempts at "indigenizing" *ġazal* still appear marginal. The Punjabi *ġazal* was struggling hard to free itself from its Urdu model.

Fictional Production

The fictional output of conservative writers consists of 145 Punjabi short stories published in *Monthly Panjābī* between 1951 and 1960, twenty of which were included in the anthology *Lehrāṃ* in 1953.[212] They all deal with contemporary subjects, but two distinct corpuses can be identified: rural/urban stories and post-Partition stories.

RURAL/URBAN STORIES

Many rural stories narrate a love story with a tragic ending and convey a moral message. Rigid rural traditions and customs, together with the large number of ongoing feuds, generally lead to tragic consequences for lovers if their union is not approved by families and clans. The lovers in Waqar Ambalvi's story *Kūhjā* (The Deformed) are forced to run away from their village and sever ties with their families; when they return to their native village ten years later, they can no longer find their homes because during their absence their families have clashed and destroyed each other.[213] The lovers in Shafi Aqeel's *Jhanāṃ dyāṃ rohṛyāṃ* (Eddies of the Chenab) also escape from their village, but the Chenab, which flows nearby, is in flood, and they are swept away by the river as they try to cross it.[214] Nevertheless, some love stories have a happy ending, like Sadiq Qureishi's *Jalālpur dā caudhrī* (The Chief of Jalalpur), which narrates the romance between the son of a poor farmer and the daughter of a rich village chief (*caudhrī*).[215] The farmer's son initially meets with strong opposition from the village chief but, by dint of hard work, rises through the ranks of society and ends up marrying his beloved. These stories include a moral message based on traditional conservative values. The escape of Waqar Ambalvi's selfish lovers precipitates the downfall of their families; Shafi Aqeel's lovers are punished by nature for running away from their community; and the social success and love marriage of the hero of Sadiq Qureishi's story prove that virtue and work are always rewarded.

Some rural short stories depict the specific issues of village women. Sajjad Hyder's *Kāng* (The Flood) begins with the discovery of a decomposed body in a river near a village.[216] The body is identified as that of Bano, a once very beautiful woman. In her youth, she rejected Salabat, a young landowner, who later committed suicide; she then aged prematurely after marrying a man who turned out to be physically abusive. Noor Kashmiri's *Moḥabbat* (A Love) portrays the tragic life of Rabia, a woman whose husband has gone to work in Karachi and has not been heard from since.[217] Shafi Aqeel's *Kaṇak de siṭṭe* (Ears of Wheat) narrates the story of Naziran, the sole daughter of an elderly couple so attached to her that they are reluctant to let her marry.[218] She ends up being seduced by a handsome boy and runs away with him. These stories too carry a moral message based on traditionalist values. Sajjad Hyder suggests that the marital violence suffered by Bano is a punishment for rejecting a sincere lover and being the cause of his death. The moral of Shafi Aqeel's *Kaṇak de siṭṭe* is that girls should be married young, otherwise they get corrupted.

A significant number of rural stories relate feuds between rival clans. This gives the writer the opportunity to describe the customary justice mechanisms at work in rural areas. In Suhail Yazdani's *Muhāṇe dī dhī* (Imran's

Daughter), a young girl is kidnapped by the son of a landowner.[219] This kidnapping gives a right of revenge to the girl's brothers, even if their social position is lower than that of the landowner's son. Waqar Ambalvi's *Sāvā līrā* (A Green Piece of Cloth) describes a session of a village council (*Pancāyat*) before which a man is brought because he stole some sugarcane.[220] The anonymous hero of Akbar Lahori's *O kauṇ sī?* (Who Was He?) is a respectable old man whose three sons have become criminals.[221] Villagers burn his house per customary practice in spite of the fact that they hold him in high esteem.

Urban short stories usually have the same melodramatic ending and include the same kind of moral message as rural short stories, emphasizing that sinners and criminals always get punished for their wrongdoings. Ahmad Bashir's *Gujhyā rog* (A Hidden Illness) is a good example.[222] Nasir is unable to marry his sweetheart Kulsum because his mother wants him to marry his cousin, and he ends up poisoning his mother. Before dying, she tells him once again that he should marry his cousin and not Kulsum. He is overwhelmed with regret and dies as he tells his story to the narrator.

Among the urban stories are also several working-class stories, recounting the trials and tribulations that workers face in their daily lives. Chaudhry Mohammad Asghar Khan's *Ġarīb de bhāg* (The Fate of the Poor) narrates the story of a worker who, failing to pay his rent, is threatened with eviction by his landlord.[223] He nevertheless manages to avoid expulsion and to have his son educated. The son manages to complete his studies and is promised a decent job, but before starting his job he is run over by a car in the street and dies on the spot.

POST-PARTITION STORIES

Surprisingly, none of the short stories published in *Monthly Panjābī* depicts the violence that occurred during Partition. They deal instead with the immediate consequences of Partition. One consequence is the separation of families and the subsequent conversion of siblings and other relatives left behind. This is the topic of Faqeer Mohammad Faqeer's *O milke na mil sake* (They Met Without Meeting), which narrates the story of an elderly Pakistani couple who go to the Pakistan-India border after receiving a mysterious letter signed by two Sikhs.[224] Once at the border, the couple realize that these two Sikhs are in fact the husband's brother and sister, who stayed on the other side of the border and have changed their name and religion. They try to get closer to them physically, but are prevented from doing so by the border guards. The siblings are thus twice separated: by religion and by border. Nazr-e Fatima's *Jannat de meḥl* (Palaces in Paradise) discusses another consequence of Partition: the redistribution of evacuee property (the property abandoned by departing Hindus and Sikhs during the mass migrations after Partition).[225] It highlights the corrupt behavior of the officials in charge of this redistribution. Mansoor and his mother, who reside in Lahore, see their house reduced to ashes accidentally when the Muslim mob burns down an adjoining Sikh house. Having become a refugee in his own town, Mansoor goes to the evacuee property office, talks about the services he rendered to the Muslim League before independence, mentions his burnt house, and requests a new house. The civil servant praises his commitment to the ruling party, saying *Tusāṃ apṇe wāsṯe jannat vic meḥl banvā liye ne* (You have built for yourself palaces in paradise), but declares that he will not be allotted any property because he is a local resident and not a refugee. Later, Mansoor shows his mother the house that the same official got himself allotted, in spite of the fact that he is not a refugee, and his mother tells him they should not expect anything from the administration and be content with whatever they have because *Āsāṃ apṇe wāsṯe jannat vic meḥl banvā liye ne* (We have built for ourselves palaces in paradise).

The Punjabi fiction produced by conservative authors strongly contrasts with that produced by Marxists. A large number of the conservatives' short stories belong to the romantic (*rūmānī*) genre that was very popular in earlier decades, for which the Marxists manifested their aversion.[226] Another aspect that distinguishes conservative fictional production in Punjabi from Marxist fictional production is the absence of denunciation of the social system. Thus, for example, the condition of women—a subject dear to Marxists—is addressed in a certain number of conservative short stories, but the patriarchal system prevalent in society is never exposed or denounced. The theme of poverty is also addressed by conservatives, but the causes of poverty are never mentioned. Fate is generally evoked as the main cause of misfortunes and inequalities. This fatalistic ideology strongly contrasts with the Marxists' outlook: Marxists refuse to believe in the existence of a transcendent force and acknowledge only social dynamics.

Radio Dramas

Another genre that conservative writers have particularly promoted is the radio drama. They published thirty-three radio dramas between 1951 and 1960: twenty-five in *Monthly Panjābī* and eight in Sajjad Hyder's collection *Hawā de hūke.*[227] Most of them dealt with contemporary subjects. As they were to be broadcast on the radio, they were short (not more than half an hour) and included a clear moral message, as they were meant to sensitize listeners about specific issues. For instance, Sajjad Hyder wrote his radio drama *Dilāṃ de rogī* (The Heart Patients) to sensitize the public to the plight of abducted women brought back to Pakistan.[228]

These short radio dramas include all the standard components of melodrama: pathetic and often unlikely situations, misunderstandings and tragic endings, a Manichean confrontation between good and evil, and the omnipotence of Fate. This melodramatic aspect makes them similar to the movies of the same period, in both Urdu and Punjabi. Their plots usually revolve around a crime: a love crime, as in Nazr-e Fatima's *Rāh dā ghaṭṭā* (The Dust of the Path); a vendetta, as in Sajjad Hyder's *Dil daryā*; or an accidental murder, as in Sajjad Hyder's *Jhanjharāṃ de magar magar* (Behind the Anklets) or Nazr-e Fatima's *Ṭakkar* (The Collision).[229] In some cases, the crime was committed long before the drama begins, and the perpetrator is identified in the course of it, as in Agha Ashraf's *Sa'īṃ Dino* (The Fakir Dino).[230] But it is not necessary for one of the protagonists to be murdered to produce a melodramatic situation; the person can also die under natural circumstances. Thus, the drama begins when a protagonist is about to die and ends with the person's death. Sultan Masud Mirza's *Ranḍī* (The Prostitute) portrays the tragic last moments in the life of Anwar, a man who was ostracized by his family after he married a prostitute.[231] Sajjad Hyder's *Dilāṃ de rogī* also depicts the last moments of a protagonist.[232] Of all the radio dramas penned by conservative writers in the 1950s, it is probably the only one that engages with Partition and one of its consequences: the return of the abducted women. The drama begins where Saadat Hasan Manto's famous short story *Khol do!* (Open That!) ends—in a hospital, where a kidnapped girl brought back to Pakistan is examined by doctors. She worries that she will not be accepted by her family after being "dishonored" by her captors, but her fears turn out to be unfounded: Her parents are happy to have found her and run to her bedside, but too late, as their daughter dies in front of them.

Autobiographical Production

A rather new genre to which conservative writers have given special attention is that of autobiographical texts, or *Haḍvartī*. Fifteen short autobiographical texts were published in *Monthly Panjābī* between 1951 and 1960. These texts fall into three categories: travelogues, reminiscences of childhood, and reminiscences of Partition.

Travelogues narrate a trip abroad—Ghulam Rasool Mehr in *Merā safarnāma* (My Travelogue) recounts a journey by plane to Cairo—or a local trip to a rural area—Sadiq Ali Ajiz in *Pūraṇ dā khūh* (Puran's Well) recounts a journey to Sialkot to see a mythical well.[233] Some travelogues recount a short and apparently ordinary trip that special circumstances make particularly memorable and difficult: Waqar Ambalvi, in his *Pāṇī vic panj din* (Five Days in the Water), recounts a forty-kilometer-long journey from Sharaqpur to Lahore in a time of flood, describing the drowned fields and houses along the road and paying tribute to the resilience of the area's inhabitants.[234]

One of the most notable examples of childhood reminiscences is Zafar Ali Khan's *Merā cuṭpanā* (My Childhood), the author's only known text in Punjabi.[235] In this text, Zafar Ali Khan looks back on his education in a missionary school, his discovery of Sir Syed Ahmad Khan's philosophy, and his long political career, and concludes with a patriotic profession of faith: "I thank God a thousand times for giving me the opportunity to witness since the days when I was a student the bad influence which the sinister English slavery has exerted on the hearts of people, and for allowing me to combat it. Now I am a free citizen of a free Pakistan. And now I feel myself coming back to life and I feel my nation coming back to life and I am convinced that the fight I have waged all my life has been fruitful."[236]

Some writers have chosen to recount in their autobiographical texts the events they witnessed during Partition, in order to spread a message that is both patriotic and anti-Sikh. Noor Kashmiri, in his *Haḍbītī* (Autobiography), recalls the circumstances under which he had to migrate from his predominantly Sikh village in 1947.[237] Sikh rioters were shouting slogans all night long (*Sāddā xalṣa kadī na ḍole dhartī bešak ḍol jā'e*—"Our *Khalsa* will not shake even if the whole earth should shake"), and their attack on Muslim villagers was imminent.[238] Noor Kashmiri left the village with a friend at night to go to the railway station. They were intercepted by some enraged Sikhs, to whom Noor Kashmiri declared: *Jad tuhāḍḍā xalṣa kadī na'īṃ ḍoldā te asīṃ Moḥammad 'arabī dī ummat hoke kyoṃ ḍoliye?* (If your *Khalsa* does not shake, then we, who belong to the community of Mohammad the Arab, why should we shake?) Impressed by his courage and determination, the Sikhs spared both travelers and let them continue their journey. Similarly, Saqib Zeervi, in *Rabb jāne* (Only God Knows), recounts the circumstances that led him to flee his village.[239] He highlights the negative role of Baba Amarnath, the Sikh leader of his village, who had been wrongly informed by another Sikh, an alcoholic and a drug addict, that a Sikh boy of the area named Devinder had been murdered by Muslims. Without verifying the information, he ordered his men to attack the Muslim community of the village to avenge the alleged murder of the boy.

Conclusion

The Punjabi conservative movement was undoubtedly more successful than the Marxist Punjabi movement. Between 1950 and 1960, Faqeer Mohammed Faqeer, Abdul Majeed Salik, and Mohammad Baqir launched a monthly journal, established two cultural organizations, took part in the first Punjabi conference held after the creation of Pakistan, and convinced the central government to set up an academy on the model of the Pashto and Bengali academies. They also managed to secure the support of some of the most famous and popular conservative writers of the time, as well as of all senior Punjabi writers active in Pakistan, and they motivated and promoted a new generation of Punjabi writers who produced a huge body of literature (in all genres). They also launched initiatives aimed at the standardization of Punjabi.

This success can be attributed to several factors. Faqeer Mohammad Faqeer, Abdul Majeed Salik, and Mohammad Baqir, the three leaders of the movement, were extremely well connected. Faqeer Mohammad Faqeer, being a senior Punjabi poet, knew all the prominent Punjabi poets of his time. Abdul Majeed Salik, as a senior journalist and Urdu writer, was well acquainted with the literary and journalistic elite of the province, and Mohammad Baqir had strong ties with academic circles and with top bureaucrats. A certain unity existed among these three leaders. While some Marxists supported a minimum action program for Punjabi and others a maximum program, all three leaders of the Punjabi conservative movement endorsed and supported the same agenda and presented it on many occasions in various forums. Another factor that contributed to the success of their movement was the ideology it promoted: a Pakistani nationalism perfectly in line with the ideology of the state. The activities of the conservative group were therefore not deemed suspicious by the state. The presence of the chief minister of Punjab (Feroz Khan Noon) at the poetic symposium organized by the Punjabi Cultural Society in 1954 and the allocation of government funds to establish a Punjabi Academy proves that those activities appeared acceptable and rather innocuous to the state.

However, one should also acknowledge that the scope of the conservative Punjabi movement remained limited. Its field of intervention was above all literary, and none of its nonliterary initiatives—such as the campaign to reopen the Punjabi department and the demand for primary instruction in Punjabi—met with success. These demands were not taken into account by the government. Moreover, while Faqeer Mohammed Faqeer, Abdul Majeed Salik, and Mohammad Baqir rather successfully mobilized writers and journalists in favor of Punjabi, they did not attempt to mobilize the masses, probably because they knew that the cause of Punjabi language had no appeal for them or might even be met with hostility, as the Punjabi language was generally equated with the Sikh community. In fact, the likelihood was so high that the debate around Punjabi could be communalized or politicized that a senior conservative Punjabi activist like Joshua Fazal Din, who was (like the Marxist Mian Iftikharuddin) an elected member of the Punjab provincial assembly during the 1950s, avoided raising the issue of Punjabi during his tenure.

SIX

The Punjabi Modernist Movement (1957–1959)

AFTER THE PROGRESSIVE Writers' Association was banned in 1954 and its Punjabi sessions were discontinued, and after Abdul Majeed Salik's Punjabi Cultural Society became inactive in 1955, some intellectuals felt the need to establish an organization to promote Punjabi literature and organize sessions during which Punjabi texts would be read and discussed. Writers with various political leanings, some previously associated with the conservative group and some with the Marxist group, joined hands with a handful of young writers studying in different colleges in Lahore and, in December 1957, formed an organization aimed at the promotion and modernization of Punjabi literature: the *Panjābī Majlis* (Punjabi Society). This literary association attempted to go beyond the Marxist-conservative polarization and introduce modernist trends in Punjabi literature. The modernist Punjabi movement was born.

The movement lasted only a year and a half, as the *Panjābī Majlis* was banned in 1959. In this chapter, we retrace the history and contribution of this movement: first presenting, in chronological order, the initiatives of the modernists and discussing their program and language ideology; then analyzing the structure of this group of writers, as well as the trajectories of some of them; and finally examining their literary production.

The history of the *Panjābī Majlis* was recounted by one of its members, Raja Risalu, in his memoirs, which were published in 2008.[1] On the basis of his account, we can distinguish two periods in the history of the Punjabi modernist movement: The first period stretches from the creation of the *Panjābī Majlis*, in December 1957, until the promulgation of martial law by Ayub Khan, in October 1958; the second runs from the promulgation of martial law until the prohibition of the *Panjābī Majlis*, between April and June 1959.

The Initial Year of the *Panjābī Majlis*: From December 1957 to October 1958

The Foundation of the Panjābī Majlis

The *Panjābī Majlis* was founded in December 1957. Raja Risalu describes the circumstances of its creation:

> In December 1957 some friends gathered at Chaudhry Mohammad Afzal's *Anglo-Punjabi College* on Temple road. During this meeting, we all agreed that it was necessary to launch some concrete initiatives for the development and promotion of the Punjabi language. After a long discussion, a *Panjābī Majlis* (Punjabi Society) was founded and it was decided that it would hold a critical session every Friday. It was also decided that a monthly journal would be published which would feature a detailed report of each session, and that the essays, poems, *ġazals*, songs and plays that will be presented in these sessions will be published in this journal, in order to preserve them and to encourage new writers.
>
> The first secretary was the poet and columnist Zafar Iqbal from Okara, a man with a unique style. He was studying law at that time at the Law College. The first meeting was attended by professor Safdar Mir, Akmal Aleemi, Mohammad Asif Khan, Raja Risalu, Chaudhry Akbar Lahori, Hakim Nasir, Baba Alam Syahposh, Asa Wasifi, Anis Nagi, Abdul Haq Khammi, Salim ur-Rahman, Syed Sajjad, Anver Sajjad, Siddiq Salimi, Iqbal Geoffrey and Iftikhar Jalib.[2]

The first weekly "critical session" of the *Panjābī Majlis*, during which recently written Punjabi texts were read and commented on, took place on December 27, 1957 at the Anglo-Punjabi College. *Nīle dā aswār* (The Rider of the Blue Horse), a play by Safdar Mir, was among the texts read during one of the first sessions of the *Panjābī Majlis*. Then the sessions ceased to take place at the Anglo-Punjabi College—its owner, Mohammad Afzal Khan, dissociated himself from the *Panjābī Majlis*, of which he was a founding member—and moved to the Lahore Corporation library, located in the middle of a park outside Mori Gate.[3] Akmal Aleemi, a member of the *Panjābī Majlis*, enthusiastically described (and publicized) these sessions in the *Daily Imroz*: "The sessions of the *Panjābī Majlis* are successfully held in the park adjoining Mori Gate. During these sessions, Waris Shah, Shah Hussain and Baba Bulleh Shah are discussed, but also Ezra Pound and Jean-Paul Sartre."[4]

During the year that followed its inception, the *Panjābī Majlis* organized fifty-one critical sessions, in which 110 texts in prose and poetry, written by forty writers, were read and discussed.[5] One can only speculate about the texts read during the sessions, and only imagine the discussions that followed, since, like the Progressive Writers' Association and the Punjabi Cultural Society, the *Panjābī Majlis* left behind no written report of its activities. No list of texts read during the sessions is available; no discussions were recorded in writing. Only a few indications can be found in Raja Risalu's memoirs, including the figures cited above.

In June 1958, the *Panjābī Majlis* went through a phase of reorganization. Zafar Iqbal wanted to return to his hometown of Okara as his studies were coming to an end, and a new secretary had to be chosen to replace him. On June 6, 1958, the members met to elect a new secretary. Professor Safdar Mir stood for the post, but the young writers voted in the majority for another youngster, electing Abdul Haq Khammi as secretary, with Anis Nagi as assistant secretary.[6] Both were students at Lahore's Government College. The members also elected a central committee, which included Mohammad Safdar Mir, Akbar Lahori, Salim ur-Rahman, Mohammad Afzal Khan, Sadiq Ali Ajiz, and Akmal Aleemi.[7]

The Launch of Monthly Panjdaryā

In accordance with the program adopted during its founding meeting in December 1957, the *Panjābī Majlis* launched a monthly journal. It was named *Panjdaryā* (The Five Rivers), and its first issue was published in January 1958. Raja Risalu describes the circumstances that led to its publication:

> In order to start a monthly journal, we asked the late Chaudhry Mohammad Afzal Khan to file a request for official authorization to publish. It was decided that

> the journal would be called *Panjdaryā*. Chaudhry Mohammad Afzal Khan did not have to face any special obstacles. He soon got permission, and *Panjdaryā* was launched. The late Hakim Nasir contributed financially to its publication, but as he was a very independent man he quickly dissociated himself from it. . . . The essays, poems, *ġazals*, songs and plays included in its first issue had been penned by more or less all our friends.[8]

Panjdaryā's format was inspired by that of *Montly Panjābī*. The sessions of the *Panjābī Majlis* were initially a reservoir of texts for *Panjdaryā*, as the essays, poems, short stories, and plays written by its members were published regularly in this journal.[9] But its owner, Mohammad Afzal Khan, did not intend to make his journal a mere mouthpiece of the *Panjābī Majlis*. He also published texts by writers associated with Faqeer Mohammad Faqeer and Abdul Majeed Salik's conservative Punjabi group, and soon he completely severed ties with the *Panjābī Majlis*.[10] In his September 1960 article *Pākistān te Bhārat vic Panjābī* (Punjabi in Pakistan and India), recounting the circumstances under which *Panjdaryā* was launched, Mohammad Afzal Khan deliberately omitted to mention the *Panjābī Majlis*, stating that the journal was launched with the sole aim of facilitating literary collaboration between Pakistani and Indian Punjabi authors. He wrote: "In January 1958 the journal *Panjdaryā* was launched. Its aim was to establish a literary collaboration between the two Punjabs, and to ensure that the writers and poets of the two Punjabs, leaving aside all political and religious considerations but maintaining their respect and love for their respective countries, would be united though their language."[11]

Panjāb Rang *and the Language Ideology of the Modernists*

The publication of the monthly *Panjdaryā* was only a partial success for the modernist group, as it gradually escaped from its control, and the group soon felt the need to bring out a bulletin that it would fully own and that would publicize its activities.[12] This bulletin was published in September 1958, under the name *Panjāb Rang* (Color of the Punjab), and was introduced in its editorial as the "First Bulletin" (*Pehlā Bulletin*) of the *Panjābī Majlis*. The members of the *Majlis* intended to bring out more bulletins, but did not manage to do so.

Panjāb Rang is a full-fledged anthology of Punjabi modernism rather than a bulletin. It includes nineteen texts (eleven poems, two essays, two short stories, a short play, a travelogue, a book review, and a presentation of the *Panjābī Majlis*) written by fifteen authors affiliated with *Panjābī Majlis* (Raja Risalu, Jilani Kamran, Safdar Mir, Munir Niazi, Arif Abdul Mateen, Shehzad Ahmad, Salim ur-Rahman, Zafar Iqbal, Saleem Kashir, Habib Jalib, Sher Mohammad Nasir, Hassan Erafi, Akbar Lahori, Anver Sajjad, and Mohammad Siddiq Salimi). These texts are interspersed with quotes by Dostoevsky (p. 10) and Baudelaire (p. 74), translated into Punjabi. The texts were selected and collected by the *Panjābī Majlis's* secretary, Abdul Haq Khammi. The aim of *Panjāb Rang* was to show, through the diversity of the texts featured, that Punjabi modernism not only existed but spawned a variety of genres: short story, play, poetry, travelogue, etc. We will study this eclectic production later in the chapter. Here we focus on the unsigned editorial as well as the essay *Sāḍḍī zubān* (Our Language) by Raja Risalu, as these two texts introduce the goals as well as the language ideology of the modernist group.[13]

Panjāb Rang's anonymous editorialist starts by recounting the progress achieved by different language movements in Pakistan during the previous eleven years, underlining, by contrast, Punjabis' neglect of their own language: "Pakistan was born eleven years ago. But the issue of provincial languages has not yet been resolved. The other provinces have by their constant efforts obtained recognition of their language by the state, but until now the inhabitants of Punjab have not paid due attention to their own language."[14] The main reason for this neglect, he suggests, is the central role played by Punjab in the political history of the country (and in the movement for the creation of Pakistan), so that Punjabis have focused above all on promoting a vehicular language like Urdu that could connect them to the rest of the country's Muslim community. Since the fate of Urdu has been settled once and for all by granting it official status, he argues, it is time now to develop Punjabi:

> The other provinces immediately launched initiatives in favour of the development of their vernaculars, but as Punjab was the heart of all the political movements, the Punjabis always paid special attention to a central language. . . . The issue of Urdu was resolved when it was declared an official language. Now it is time for Punjabis—like the inhabitants of the other provinces—to try and develop their language, and for the government to recognize Punjabi and to undertake

> to develop it as it has done with the other vernaculars of the different provinces.[15]

To highlight Punjabis' neglect of their own language, the editorialist describes the inferiority complex of writers with regard to Punjabi—the idea that writing in Punjabi is tantamount to being declassed. (Shafqat Tanvir Mirza and Safdar Mir also drew attention to this attitude in their writings and interviews.)

> As far as writing in Punjabi is concerned, two groups of writers can be distinguished here. Those who belong to the first group consider the idea of writing in this language as a mere joke. The writers of the second group do not deny the necessity of writing in this language, but they are not ready to write in Punjabi. The first group is composed of individuals who not only oppose Punjabi but also—deep inside—oppose Urdu, because if it were up to them they would write in the language of their former masters. In the second group we find individuals who owe their prestige to the Urdu language and they imagine that if they start writing in Punjabi their prestige will diminish.[16]

Raja Risalu's essay *Sāḍḍī zubān* (Our Language), like the anonymous editorial, begins by stating that Punjabi Muslims have adopted Urdu for political reasons.[17] "Some time ago Punjabis were forced, for political reasons, to support Urdu. And it was necessary at that time.[18] In the past, the province of Punjab had always served Urdu with great dedication."[19] But now that independence has been achieved and Urdu has secured official status, the Punjabi language is still neglected. "I think Urdu now has a higher status since it was declared an official language, and my wish is for it to flourish and have a great destiny. But what is wrong with Punjabi? Why have its speakers run away from it?"[20]

Raja Risalu believes that this neglect results from Punjabi's being perceived as the language of the Sikh community, and he tackles this prejudice with a standard argument (which we have already encountered in Sharif Kunjahi and Ahmad Rahi): Punjabi is not the language of one but of all religious communities living in Punjab. "Some people view Punjabi as the language of a specific religion, whereas it is not the language of any religion but of the land of Punjab. And it is the language of the inhabitant of this land, whatever his religion."[21]

Then, after expressing his appreciation for the role played by Amrita Pritam and Ahmad Rahi in the readers' renewed interest in Punjabi literature (but omitting to mention the contributions of Faqeer Mohammad Faqeer, Abdul Majeed Salik, and their group), Raja Risalu discusses an issue facing all Pakistani Punjabi writers: the issue of the written standard and, more especially, the lexicon. "One question remains, among others: what should Punjabi be like? Should it incorporate words from other languages or not? In reality, each language has two variants: a spoken variant, which educated and illiterate people alike use, and a written variant. The latter will be purer than the former."[22] Taking Urdu as an example—whose strength lies in its ability to adopt words from other languages—Raja Risalu considers that Punjabi should develop a similar flexibility:

> I consider it a quality of a language to have the courage to adopt words from other languages. One reason for Urdu's progress is that it has adopted words from all languages. And look at where it stands now! . . . We should choose words which our tongue can pronounce easily and which are not difficult to assimilate. And if we can manage with a word like *ṣadar* (the president) we don't need to find equivalents like *pardhān* and *khirpīnc.*[23]

This last sentence refers to the recent trend in Indian Punjabi to replace Arabic-Persian words with words considered more "indigenous" (often borrowed from Hindi). Raja Risalu suggests that Pakistani Punjabi should not imitate its Indian neighbor: there is no need to replace frequently used Arabic-Persian words like *ṣadar* that have entered the common vocabulary of Pakistani Punjabi.

The anonymous editorialist of *Panjāb Rang* and Raja Risalu both mentioned several obstacles to the development of Punjabi but did not propose any concrete measures or programs. Another common point of these two texts is that they discussed the attitude toward Punjabi not of the masses but of writers, evoking their role (and responsibilities) with regard to the development and promotion of Punjabi. At this stage, the modernists presented their movement as a purely literary one, thus distinguishing it from the Marxist and conservative Punjabi movements, whose aims were not only to enrich Punjabi's literary capital but also to promote primary education in Punjabi, change the general perception of the language, and contribute to its standardization.

Competing Against the Conservative Movement

At the time *Panjāb Rang* was published, the conservative Punjabi movement was at its apogee. Why did members of the *Panjābī Majlis* ignore the platforms made available by the conservative group (*Monthly Panjābī*, Punjabi Academy, and Punjabi Cultural Society) and establish their own platforms? The editorialist presented some reasons:

> After Pakistan's creation some individuals founded in Punjab some associations to promote Punjabi language and literature, but they vanished without accomplishing any task. The reason for their failure was that the individuals who were involved in these associations, instead of working for the language, were just "patronizing" it. And instead of doing constructive work they turned these associations into platforms from which they could further their own interests, or even settle old scores. Some of them considered themselves gods of the Punjabi language. They imagined that if they were to die, no one would care about the language anymore. And to keep themselves alive they disassociated themselves from any other movement that worked for the promotion of the Punjabi language and literature.[24]

The hint is clear: Two Punjabi organizations had been established so far in Lahore, the Pak Punjabi League and the Punjabi Cultural Society, the former run by Faqeer Mohammad Faqeer and the latter by Abdul Majeed Salik. The editorialist thus suggests that the *Panjābī Majlis* was founded in reaction to the narcissistic and paternalistic attitude of these two personalities and the monopoly exercised by them in the Punjabi literary subfield.[25] He gives some more hints in his final remarks: "At the beginning, when the *Panjābī Majlis* was founded, many individuals assured us of their cooperation, and they were usually members of the *Punjabi Cultural Society*. But after a while as soon as they realized they couldn't use it for their personal benefits they started to walk away from it."[26]

The editorialist thus harshly criticizes senior members of the conservative Punjab group and highlights the fact that competition has arisen in the Punjabi subfield between the *Panjābī Majlis* and the conservative Punjabi group. His sarcastic and acerbic remarks did not go unnoticed in the small world of Punjabi letters, but neither Faqeer Mohammad Faqeer nor Abdul Majeed Salik bothered to respond. It was some young writers from their group who responded, belittling what mattered most to the *Panjābī Majlis* members: their literary production. In February 1959, *Monthly Panjābī* published a letter from a regular contributor to the journal, Suhail Yazdani, in which he castigated the modernists for importing French literature's noxious obscenity into Punjabi. The deputy secretary of the *Panjābī Majlis*, Anis Nagi, was the direct target of his attacks:

> These immature disciples of Baudelaire, Cocteau and Sartre have already gifted to Urdu literature their obscenity and poisonous material, and these "mall-roaders" are now trying to bring their filth into Punjabi literature.[27] The members of the *Panjābī Majlis* have published their first bulletin under the title *Panjāb Rang*, which features Anis Nagi's short story *Lāl haneri* (The Red Darkness). As he was desirous to write in the progressive style and to replicate the obscenity of French authors, *Monsieur* Nagi incorporated in his short story indecent and pornographic phrases and allusions which would perhaps be appreciated in Paris's *Cafés* but that the literary circles of our country which privilege morality and decency can only condemn. Because until now the writers and readers of Punjabi are not as reckless, indecent and immoral as the inhabitants of Europe and France.[28]

In the March–April 1959 issue of *Monthly Panjābī*, another regular contributor, Yaqub Anwar, condemned the obscene literature produced by the *Panjābī Majlis*: "If this *Kama Sutra* kind of stuff is high poetry and great literature, then why should we even mention Waris Shah? The real literary master is the one who drinks and dances on the occasion of the *Vaisakhi* festival and sings obscene verses while spinning around. The *Panjābī Majlis* should look for his poetry and publish it."[29]

The Second Year of the *Panjābī Majlis*: October 1958 to April 1959

A new era in the history of the *Panjābī Majlis* began with Field Marshal Ayub Khan's coup and the promulgation of martial law in October 1958. A climate of oppression and suppression of civil liberties was gradually developing, and the members of the *Panjābī Majlis* started feeling that their organization could be targeted by the new regime. Raja Risalu writes: "As soon as the martial law was imposed, there was general panic. Political parties had of course been banned, but one still did not know whether intellectual and literary organizations would fit in the same category for the new regime."[30] The key members of the *Panjābī Majlis* met in the room occupied by Safdar Mir in a hotel in the Anarkali neighborhood to decide on the strategy to adopt in the face of these new political circumstances. Safdar Mir suggested that the *Majlis* should remain discreet and that its meetings should take place not in public but in his hotel room. Raja Risalu and Akbar Lahori recommended, on the contrary, increasing the visibility of the *Majlis*, to show the authorities they had nothing to reproach themselves for or to hide, and suggested that its next meetings take place not only in public but in a very popular place like the YMCA hall. This decision was approved by all key members. The next meeting of the *Panjābī Majlis* was held in the YMCA hall and went off without a hitch.[31]

The First Anniversary of the Creation of the Panjābī Majlis

Following the adoption of the strategy of public visibility advocated by Raja Risalu and Akbar Lahori, the *Panjābī Majlis* celebrated with pomp and circumstance the first anniversary of its creation on December 26, 1958. A large meeting was organized on this occasion in the hall of the Lahore Law College and was chaired by Sufi Ghulam Mustafa Tabassum.[32] Raja Risalu describes this event:

> The secretary of the *Majlis* Abdul Haq Khammi read the activity report of the year and the chairman of the session Sufi Tabassum delivered his presidential address. . . . In his speech he praised the efforts of the members of the *Panjābī Majlis* and congratulated them. He said: "I pray that you may continue to work with the same ardour and dedication and give to the Punjabi language its true place". . . . During the meeting papers were read about the development and promotion of the Punjabi language. Folk musicians and singers performed poems by Shah Hussain, Bulleh Shah, Waris Shah, Mian Muhammad Bakhsh, Khwaja Ghulam Farid and other Sufi poets.
>
> On this occasion some requests were made to the Punjab government, the most notable of which are the following:
>
> 1. That Punjabi be taught to children from primary school
> 2. That the government should print school books and textbooks (in Punjabi)
> 3. That Punjabi teachers be recruited for the schools[33]

During this meeting, the *Panjābī Majlis* for the first time addressed demands to the Punjab provincial government. These demands were similar to those of the Marxists and the conservatives, who also stressed the use of Punjabi as a medium of primary instruction. The modernists thus, willingly or unwillingly, affirmed their continuity with their predecessors.

The function organized to celebrate the first anniversary of the foundation of the *Panjābī Majlis* was a success, but the atmosphere of paranoia prevailing in Lahore's intellectual circles since the promulgation of martial law—which Intizar Hussain humorously described in his memoirs *Cirāġoṃ kā dhu'āṃ* (The Smoke of the Lamps)—soon started affecting some members of the *Panjābī Majlis*, prompting them to distance themselves from the organization.[34] Abdul Haq Khammi and Anis Nagi, two ambitious students at Government College, left their posts as secretary and assistant secretary of the *Panjābī Majlis*, believing that it would eventually be banned and that being associated with a banned organization could harm their budding careers. They were replaced by Raja Risalu and Asif Khan.[35]

The Publication of Sajre Phull

In April 1959, the *Panjābī Majlis* published its second anthology (thanks to Raja Risalu and Asif Khan's financial assistance). Edited by Anis Nagi and titled *Sajre phull* (Fresh Flowers), it featured sixty-three Punjabi poems penned by twenty-one contemporary Pakistani poets and four Indian poets. It also included a back-cover blurb by Ahmad Nadeem Qasmi and a preface by Anis Nagi.[36] *Sajre phull* is divided into three sections. The first section consists of nineteen poems by poets labeled as "traditionalists" by Anis Nagi, most of them associated with the conservative Punjabi group (Karam Amritsari, Faqeer Mohammad Faqeer, Sufi Ghulam Mustafa Tabassum, Ustad Daman, Abdul Majeed Bhatti, Hakim Nasir, Daim Iqbal Daim, Peer Fazal Gujrati).[37] The second section contains eighteen poems by progressive poets (Ahmad Rahi, Hassan Erafi, Sharif Kunjahi, Arif Abdul Mateen, Habib Jalib, Saleem Kashir), and the third section twenty-six poems by modernist poets (Safdar Mir, Munir Niazi, Salim ur-Rahman, Zafar Iqbal, and Anis Nagi).[38] In his blurb, Ahmad Nadeem Qasmi praises the dedication of the young modernists to their mother tongue and expresses his admiration for their contribution to Punjabi poetry: "See to what heights and depths these new Punjabi poets have taken poetry! And how much they have expanded its themes!"

In his preface, Anis Nagi analyzes, one after another, the poetic production of the traditionalists, the progressives, and the modernists whose poems are included in the anthology. He moderately praises the poetry of the progressives (expressing some reservations about their language and their diction, which he considers outdated) and openly criticizes the traditionalists'/conservatives' poetry as plain and nonpoetic, merely complying with tradition: "When a poet or a writer inherits a tradition, he can either expand it or pass it on as it is to subsequent generations. The poets of this time did not use tradition as they should have, i.e. to understand well an experience or a feeling. They convey to readers ideas and events simply as they are, without observing the rules of poetry."[39] We can safely assume that these harsh remarks were Anis Nagi's response to Yaqub Anwar and Suhail Yazdani's letters, published in *Monthly Panjābī* in the months before *Sajre phull* was published, in which the two authors belittled his literary output as well as that of other Punjabi modernists. After settling a score with his conservative enemies, Anis Nagi discussed the poetic production of his own group—the modernists—which he praised, presenting it as a Punjabi version of Anglo-American Imagism:

> Imagist poetry in Punjabi was initiated by the poets of this era. They have created personal images to express themselves, and these images take their poetry towards abstraction or in some cases towards ambiguity (*ibhām*). . . . They have tried to infuse words with new meanings, and used various similes and phrases in a way which has made us realize how important they are in Punjabi poetry. They not only freed the poem from old ways of expression but also paid attention to the inner rhythm of the poem.[40]

The Ban on the Panjābī Majlis

The *Panjābī Majlis* imposed itself in a very short time on the literary scene and opened new horizons for young writers. Nevertheless, the fears expressed by some of its members after the promulgation of martial law proved to be justified. There was definitely a risk that the *Panjābī Majlis* would be banned, and so was it. In mid-1959, it was declared a political organization and banned by the government of Punjab. The *Majlis* members learned about this ban by reading the newspapers. Anis Nagi later wrote: "One day, we read in the newspaper that the Punjab government has declared the *Panjābī Majlis* a leftist organization and banned it."[41]

Raja Risalu presents a slightly different version of this event. He writes: "The government communiqué about the *Panjābī Majlis* which had been published in the newspapers could be summarized as follows: 'The *Panjābī Majlis* is declared a political organization. It had received help from an enemy foreign country and the intentions of the organizers of the *Panjābī Majlis* were not good.' "[42] What were the official reasons for this decision?[43] Risalu's and Nagi's accounts differ on this point: Raja Risalu wrote that the *Panjābī Majlis* was banned because it was accused of being financed by India ("enemy foreign country"), but Anis Nagi wrote that it was banned because it was considered a Marxist organization.

Anis Nagi's version seems the more plausible. In the last months of 1958 and the first months of 1959, the Ayub Khan government launched a series of attacks on all remaining elements of the Marxist camp, imprisoning Faiz Ahmad Faiz, Sibte Hasan, and Ahmad Nadeem Qasmi, nationalizing *Daily Imroz* and *Pakistan Times*, and banning the *Anjuman- e Āzād-xiyāl Muṣannifīn* (Association of Free-Spirited Writers), an association launched by the Marxist writer Arif Abdul Mateen after the ban on the Progressive Writers' Association.[44] Safdar Mir was expelled from the Government College in Lahore at the same time because of his Marxist leanings.[45] Arif Abdul Mateen and Safdar Mir—who had both recently become persona non grata—were members of the *Panjābī Majlis*, and Ahmad Nadeem Qasmi, who had also recently become persona non grata, had expressed support for the *Panjābī Majlis* by writing the laudatory blurb for *Sajre phull*. The support and involvement of these three controversial personalities were enough to arouse the suspicions of the government officials and prompt them to believe that the *Panjābī Majlis* served as a cover for a left-wing organization.

The date on which the *Panjābī Majlis* was banned also remains to be clarified. Neither Anis Nagi nor Raja Risalu mentioned it in their accounts, and the writer Anver Sajjad, a former member of the *Panjābī Majlis* whom we interviewed in August 2018, did not remember.[46] It can nevertheless be inferred from other sources that the *Panjābī Majlis* was banned between April and June 1959. The editorial in the April 1959 issue of *Panjdaryā* mentions that details of the meetings of the *Panjābī Majlis* will be published in the next issue, but the next issue (May–June 1959) contains no such details. One can therefore assume that the *Majlis* was banned in the interval between the publication of these two issues.

The Panjābī Majlis: Structure and Individual Trajectories

Structure of the Modernist Group

Among the members of the *Panjābī Majlis*, we can distinguish three subgroups. The first was composed of former members of the Punjabi Cultural Society (Mohammad Afzal Khan, Hakim Nasir, Akbar Lahori, Raja Risalu, Asif Khan). A second subgroup was formed of Marxists (Safdar Mir, Hassan Erafi, Arif Abdul Mateen, Habib Jalib, Saleem Kashir), often former members of the Progressive Writers' Association. A third subgroup consisted of young students from Government College (Adul Haq Khammi, Anis Nagi, Iftikhar Jalib, Shehzad Ahmad), King Edward Medical College (Anver Sajjad, Salim ur-Rahman) and Law College (Zafar Iqbal). Jilani Kamran, a young professor at Government College, barely older than these students, and Munir Niazi, a young bohemian poet in his twenties, also fit in this subgroup.

The reasons that led individuals to join the *Panjābī Majlis* were different for each subgroup. The former members of the Punjabi Cultural Society were dissatisfied with that ineffective organization, the Marxists were in need of a free literary platform after the ban on the Progressive Writers' Association and *Anjuman- e Āzād-xiyāl Muṣannifīn*, and the students were motivated by Safdar Mir, who was encouraging students and young writers to write in Punjabi. Anis Nagi writes that "Safdar Mir was obsessive about the promotion of Punjabi language and literature. And he had made some new Urdu poets promise him that they would never again write in Urdu."[47]

One can distinguish within this eclectic group a dominant and a dominated pole. At the dominant pole were writers who had accumulated a certain symbolic and social capital, such as Safdar Mir, professor of English at the Government College; Mohammad Afzal Khan, who had taken over from his father as director of the Anglo-Punjabi College and was editing *Panjdaryā*;

and Arif Abdul Mateen, founder of the *Anjuman- e Āzād-xiyāl Muṣannifīn*. The advocate Akbar Lahori and Hakim Nasir, both established writers and professionals, belong also to this pole. At the dominated pole were two activists without any creative project (Raja Risalu and Asif Khan) who were devoting their time and efforts to the promotion of Punjabi, students from the third subgroup mentioned above, and the emerging poets Jilani Kamran, Munir Niazi, and Habib Jalib. The students and the three emerging poets had just started their literary careers and were still trying to make a name for themselves in the Urdu literary subfield. The students had published a few texts in local literary journals (*Ravi Magazine*, *Saverā*), and the emerging poets were about to publish their first poetry collection: Jilani Kamran's *Istanzā* and Munir Niazi's *Tez hawā aur tanhā phūl* (The Swift Wind and the Lonely Flower) were published in 1959, and Habib Jalib's *Barg-e āwāra* (A Wandering Leaf) in 1960.

The degree of commitment to Punjabi varied among writers from both poles: Some devoted themselves fully to Punjabi (Mohammad Afzal Khan, Raja Risalu, Asif Khan, Hakim Nasir) and did not write in any other language; others wrote in Punjabi and Urdu (Munir Niazi, Akbar Lahori, Safdar Mir, Habib Jalib); and many, after a few attempts at writing in Punjabi, gave priority to Urdu. This was the case with Jilani Kamran and the students, who were known as modernists (*Jiddat-pasand*) or Imagists. All of them, despite their initial enthusiasm, completely stopped writing in Punjabi by the beginning of the 1960s. One reason was the harsh criticism they faced from writers already established in the Punjabi literary subfield. If conservative writers like Suhail Yazdani and Yaqub Anwar rejected them and belittled their output, some radical Marxists, who completely disagreed with their conception of literature, did not spare them either. The communist Rauf Malik, who had attended several sessions of the *Panjābī Majlis*,[48] portrayed them this way in an article on the Punjabi literary landscape:

> A second group is composed of writers and artists who use Punjabi only as a tool for expressing their modernism, and in order to distinguish themselves from other contemporary writers. But the truth is that they know neither Punjabi's classical and folk literature, nor the traditions on which its culture is based. And the result is that they produce sometimes some ridiculous literature which has no connection at all with our real life. These young people do not know anything

> about the different poetic and literary movements which have emerged in Punjabi. They are more familiar with the decadent and regressive ideas which have gained currency in Europe and France. They are more interested in Sartre's Existentialism than in Bulleh Shah's Sufi poetry. And, instead of trying to understand the real problems of the Punjabis, they portray people's sexual frustration and moral dilemmas.[49]

Rauf Malik's criticism is similar to that of the conservatives, even though he belongs to their rival camp. He reproaches the young modernists for being too familiar with decadent French authors and not sufficiently anchored in their own culture, tradition, and society. His criticism of their "psychologizing" approach stems directly from the Progressive Writers' Association's official ideology, expressed in their 1949 conference manifesto, which condemned literature produced under the influence of "Freud and other bourgeois psychologists."[50]

The hostility young modernists generally faced from established Punjabi writers convinced them that there was no room for their modernism in the Punjabi literary subfield. On the other hand, the Urdu literary subfield, accustomed to modernism and experiments (thanks to the poets Miraji and N. M. Rashid) since the 1940s, was more diversified and better able to accommodate them.

Two Trajectories: Safdar Mir and Anis Nagi

The two poles of the *Panjābī Majlis* can be illustrated by examining the trajectories of two writers: the dominant writer Safdar Mir and the dominated writer Anis Nagi.

SAFDAR MIR (1922–1998)

Safdar Mir was born in the city of Gujrat, where he spent his childhood and youth. A brilliant student, he was admitted to Lahore's prestigious Government College, where he took an MA in English. Then, in 1945, he left for Bombay to try his luck in the world of Hindi cinema. His attempts proved unsuccessful, but he came in contact with several progressive writers and started attending the weekly meetings of the Bombay branch of the Progressive Writers' Association. He also participated in theater performances organized by the Indian People's Theater Association (IPTA), a Marxist theater group. After Partition, he migrated to Pakistan and taught English at Gujrat's Zamindar College, then at Lahore's M.A.O. College, and finally at Government College (between 1951 and 1959).[51] By then he had become an active member of Pakistan's Progressive Writers' Association, taking part in its 1949 conference (during which he was given the honor of reading the association's annual report) and attending its weekly meetings.[52]

Safdar Mir's involvement in the promotion of Punjabi began in 1954, when he joined Abdul Majeed Salik's Punjabi Cultural Society. Mir, who until then had only written free verse poems in Urdu (under the influence of Miraji), penned a Punjabi play titled *Nīle dā aswār* (The Rider of the Blue Horse) on a theme borrowed from Punjabi folklore (the legend of Raja Risalu). This play was published in Government College's *Ravi Magazine* in 1957, read during one of the first sessions of the *Panjābī Majlis* in 1958, and became so popular that it was broadcast several times on Lahore's Radio Pakistan.[53] Safdar Mir spent a lot of time in Lahore's literary cafes, where he met students interested in literature and young writers; he mentored them and incited them to write in Punjabi.[54] Some of the arguments he used to motivate students and young writers to write in Punjabi are suggested in an article in which he discusses the reasons that led him to switch to Punjabi:

> I have nothing against Urdu. Until now, I have used this language as a means of expression. As thousands of my fellow Punjabi writers do. But my writing practice has taught me two things: the first is that, whether in verse or in prose, I cannot express everything that is inside me in Urdu. Especially the experiences which are related to the Punjabi milieu. Expressing them in Urdu is totally impossible. This is the reason why our middle class has not been able to depict our family life in its literature. You can use as many Punjabi phrases and words in Urdu as you want; their look distinguishes them from other words and one has the impression when one comes across them in Urdu texts that a street dog has come to sit among domestic dogs of high pedigree. I have also noticed that the life of our workers and peasants has not been well depicted in our literature. Ahmad Nadeem Qasmi has written I don't know how many short stories about peasant life. But as he did it in Urdu one cannot fully grasp the characters who

> appear there. Their irony, their anger or their love, expressed in another language, seems translated. This is the reason why even Qasmi's best stories seem to be about a foreign country and milieu.[55]

In 1959, Safdar Mir was expelled from Lahore's Government College. The reason for his dismissal was, according to him, his promotion of Punjabi, which was not appreciated by the college's new principal, Khwaja Manzoor Hussain, a staunch Urdu supporter. According to the historian K. K. Aziz, who had been his colleague, Mir was dismissed "because he was a communist and president Ayub Khan wanted to cleanse all government institutions of the leftists."[56] Safdar Mir soon found a job at Sahiwal's Government College, where he spent six months. He then left Sahiwal, moved back to Lahore, and turned to journalism in English, writing literary columns under the pen name Zeno for the *Pakistan Times*.

Safdar Mir's commitment to the cause of Punjabi did not end after the *Panjābī Majlis* was banned. He contributed regularly to the Punjabi journal *Panjābī Adab* throughout the 1960s, publishing in it two chapters (titled *Kālī* and *Puṣ̌pā*) of an unfinished novel based on his experiences during his stay in Bombay, as well as some lengthy articles.[57] Nevertheless, his production in Punjabi is not comparable in volume to his production in Urdu and English.[58] He wrote occasionally in Punjabi but consistently in Urdu and English, as these two languages guaranteed a wider reach and audience.

ANIS NAGI (1938–2010)

The son of a very religious judicial magistrate (with strong Wahabi inclinations), Anis Nagi was born in Sheikhupura and spent his childhood in different cities (Rohtak, Jalandhar) where his father was transferred.[59] In 1947, his father decided to emigrate to Pakistan, and the family settled in Dera Ghazi Khan and then in Lahore.[60] He began studying at Lahore's Government College, along with Zahid Dar, Iftikhar Jalib, Shehzad Ahmad, and Zafar Iqbal, but his precocious talent for literature and criticism set him apart from his classmates. He became the editor of the Punjabi section of *Rāvī*, the prestigious literary magazine of the Government College, and the secretary of the *Majlis-e Iqbal* (Iqbalian Society), the literary society of the college.[61] While in college, he met Safdar Mir, who had a tremendous influence on him. He became a regular visitor of Pak Tea House, a literary café where he met prominent writers of his time like Intizar Hussain and Nasir Kazmi, and where Camus's and Sartre's books and ideas were often discussed.[62] He read Dostoevsky and Baudelaire, discovered Rimbaud, and began to translate *A Season in Hell* into Urdu.[63] He gradually became an existentialist/modernist.

While studying at Government College, Anis Nagi launched the Urdu literary movement *Naī šāʿirī* (New Poetry) along with a few classmates and acquaintances (Iftikhar Jalib, Zahid Dar, Tabassum Kashmiri, and Jilani Kamran). These new poets were turning their backs on the Urdu poetic tradition, writing free verse poems (or prose poem) and using personal and unconventional images and symbols. They also rejected Urdu progressive poetry, which aimed at conveying a sociopolitical message; their poems included none and were deliberately obscure.[64] Their poems were published in some literary journals, and they were given an opportunity to read them during a session of the conservative *Ḥalqa-e Arbāb-e Żauq*, where they were severely criticized by the audience.[65] But the *Naī šāʿirī* movement—as controversial as it might be—was launched and influenced the upcoming generation of Urdu poets. It was during the initial years of this movement that Anis Nagi and other modernist poets (Shehzad Ahmad, Salim ur-Rahman, Zafar Iqbal, Munir Niazi) published their Punjabi poems in *Panjāb Rang* and *Sajre phull*. These were Punjabi adaptations (or translations) of their Urdu poems and thus manifested all the characteristics of poems written in the spirit of the new movement. This foray of the modernists outside Urdu proved to be the last. Anis Nagi devoted himself to Urdu after 1959, establishing himself as an Urdu novelist, critic, and poet in the years that followed.

The Literary Production of the Punjabi Modernists

Despite their ideological differences, Marxist and conservative Punjabi writers promoted a similarly heteronomous conception of literature: for both groups, literature was the vehicle of a political and social message. But the young modernists of the *Panjābī Majlis* soon rejected heteronomy and, since they were not connected to any party or ideology, claimed autonomy for literature, focusing on the production of an experimental literature, influenced by Anglo-American Imagism, nineteenth-century French Decadent poetry, Existentialism, and stream of consciousness. While attempting to "modernize" Punjabi literature, they produced texts belonging to three genres: poetry, short stories, and theatre.

Poetic Production

The modernists' poetic production in Punjabi consists of thirty-seven poems, included in two anthologies: nine in *Panjāb Rang* and twenty-eight in *Sajre phull*.[66] This production is characterized by a predilection for free verse. Poets like Miraji, Yusuf Zafar, and Zya Jalandhari had been composing free verse poems in Urdu since the 1940s. Modernists introduced free verse in Punjabi: Safdar Mir's *Nikke nikke sukh* (Small Satisfactions), *Jīve Lāhor šehr* (Long Live the City of Lahore!), and *Ikk nazm* (A Poem); Anis Nagi's *Šehr Lāhor* (The City of Lahore), *Banbās* (The Exile), *Navāṃ sāl* (The New Year), and *Jhūlā* (The Swing); Salim ur-Rahman's *Ikk xwāb* (A Dream) and *Parchāvāṃ* (A Silhouette); Zafar Iqbal's *Ikk nazm* (A Poem); and Munir Niazi's *Patjhaṛ dī šām* (Autumn Evening).[67] These are the first examples of free verse Punjabi poems in Pakistan.

Punjabi modernists often used unusual images at odds with the conventional images that Punjabi poets had been using until then. Many of these images were uncanny personifications. There are many examples of such personifications in the poems of Munir Niazi:

Lammyāṃ sunjyāṃ galyāṃ de vic sūraj hūke bhardā ai.

The sun sighs in the long empty streets[68]

Safdar Mir:

Te ciṭyāṃ ciṭyāṃ yādāṃ khamb khalārke
Phaṛphaṛ kardyāṃ
Nīlī nīlī pavaṇ vic uḍḍ jāndyāṃ ne

And the immaculate memories open their wings
Wave them
And fly away in the blue air[69]

and Zafar Iqbal:

Ambar dī nīlī cādar haiṭhāṃ
Badlāṃ ne pair pasāre.

Under the blue blanket of the sky
The clouds have stretched their legs[70]

Modernists discarded the rural setting that prevailed in the poems of Ahmad Rahi, Sharif Kunjahi, and Abdul Majeed Bhatti. The setting of their poems is predominantly urban. The city appears as a character in its own right; it is, so to speak, the main character in Safdar Mir's *Nikke nikke sukh* and *Jīve šehr Lāhor* and in Munir Niazi's *Ikk ujāṛ šehr* (An Abandoned City).[71] In *Ikk ujāṛ šehr*, the city is described like a frightening and hostile character from a fantastic tale:

Sāre lokī ṭur ga'e le ga'ī nāl qaẓā
Galyāṃ hūke bhardyāṃ rondī phire hawā
Kandhāṃ sunj musanjyāṃ koṭhe vāṃg balā
Kūkāṃ devaṇ hawelyāṃ sāḍḍe vall na ā

All the inhabitants have left, death has taken them away
The alleys sigh, the wind keeps crying
The walls are desolate, the houses are like demons
And the mansions are screaming, 'Don't come close to us!'[72]

Love is totally absent from the cities described by the modernists, and totally absent from their poems. The poet is depicted in poems like Anis Nagi's *Šehr Lāhor* as a lonely, alienated man, looking for affection and human warmth in a hostile and dangerous space where he is trapped:

Ḍaināṃ de is šehr vic
Sabb kujh sunghyā
Sabb kujh phakyā
Sab thāṃ mathāṃ bhanyā
Kujh na labhyā . . .
Kithe jaiye?

Kiṛī ṭhandī chāṃ nūṃ apṇā ḥāl sunāye?
Kisdi sunye?

In this town of witches
I have smelled everything
And tasted everything
I have wandered everywhere
I've found nothing . . .
Where should I go?
Which cool shade should I confide to?
And who should I listen to?[73]

The modernists' poems are above all a depiction of contemporary urban alienation.

Short Stories and Drama

Punjabi modernists focused primarily on poetry. Their fictional output consists of only two short stories: *Lāl hanerī* (The Red Darkness) and *Gujhyāṃ lāṭāṃ* (The Hidden Flames), both by Anis Nagi.[74] These two stories are in a way extensions of the urban poems the modernists had a predilection for. Anis Nagi stages, in a nocturnal urban setting, characters totally alien to society, on the verge of madness, haunted by the idea of suicide, victims of hallucinations who struggle against their traumas and fears. The main character in *Lāl hanerī* has crossed the India-Pakistan border to look for his sister, who remains stranded in India; he is arrested, imprisoned, and molested by the other inmates. The main character in *Gujhyāṃ lāṭāṃ* is married to a sick woman and haunted by the idea of her impending death. These two characters are afraid of the world and withdraw from it: The character in *Gujhyāṃ lāṭāṃ* takes shelter in his bathroom; the one in *Lāl hanerī* smokes hashish to forget the reality around him.

These two stories break with the formats followed by conservatives as well as progressives. In both, Anis Nagi uses stream of consciousness, telling the story in flashbacks (old memories constantly streaming through the mind of the protagonist) rather than through linear narration. Nagi's Punjabi stories share strong similarities with some Urdu short stories of Sajjad Zaheer,

Mohammad Hasan Askari, and Intizar Hussain, in which a similar technique is used.[75]

The modernists' contribution in the field of drama is limited to Safdar Mir's radio drama *Nīle dā aswār* (The Rider of the Blue Horse).[76] The setting is Chandan Nadi, a mythical city whose king has gone mad and whose inhabitants are compelled by their ruler to abandon their daughters in a mysterious basement (*Pātāl*), never to find them again. Raja Risalu—a legendary character of Punjabi folklore who has become a fakir—enters the city and incites its inhabitants to rebel against the mad king and break down the city walls. The inhabitants follow his exhortations and recover their freedom.

Nīle dā aswār is a slow-paced drama, with a tiny plot. Its first part is mainly descriptive, in which the inhabitants of Chandan Nadi evoke very poetically the landscape around them. In the second part, two voices echo each other: the insane voice of the king, who is constantly hallucinating (he sees ghosts and witches), and the wise voice of Raja Risalu, who encourages the inhabitants of the city to overcome their fear and to revolt.[77]

Nīle dā aswār is completely different from other radio dramas of the time (the melodramatic dramas on modern subjects favored by the conservatives). It is devoid of melodrama, it borrows from Punjabi folklore, its action is set in archaic times, and it is written in a Sanskritized language meant to recreate the language of those pre-Islamic times. It belongs to a poetic-mythical subgenre of which it is undoubtedly the only example in Pakistan. (There is another representative of this subgenre among Indian Punjabi dramas: Shiv Kumar Batalvi's poetic drama *Lūṇāṃ*, published in 1965).

Conclusion

Of the three movements in favor of Punjabi that we have analyzed, the modernist movement is the only one that moved beyond the polarization of the Lahori intellectual field of the postindependence period and brought together writers of different camps. The attempt at bringing together different writers on the same apolitical platform continued even after the *Panjābī Majlis* was banned. On July 12, 1961, a Punjabi branch of the Writers' Guild was founded in Lahore, welcoming Punjabi writers from different camps. It was led by two writers from two different camps: the conservative Abdus Salam Khurshid (son of Abdul Majeed Salik) and the Marxist

Shafqat Tanvir Mirza.[78] The *Panjābī Majlis* had therefore set a precedent, which was soon followed.

The modernists did not present any program for the promotion and development of Punjabi, and their first (and only) demands regarding the status of Punjabi were made in 1958 during the function that marked the first anniversary of the *Panjābī Majlis*. Their main field of intervention remained literature, and it is in this field that their contribution has been important. When the *Panjābī Majlis* was established in December 1957, the gap between Urdu and Punjabi literature was immense. Conservative Punjabi writers were still producing the kind of romantic and moralistic literature that had been popular two decades earlier, and the social realism promoted by Punjabi Marxists was also on the way to becoming obsolete. The new approaches and techniques adopted by contemporary Urdu writers were still unknown in the Punjabi subfield. The writers of the *Panjābī Majlis* attempted to bridge the wide gap between contemporary Urdu and Punjabi literatures by producing resolutely modern texts in Punjabi. When they introduced modern trends and techniques in Punjabi, they faced relentless criticism, which discouraged them from continuing their modernization of Punjabi literature. Nevertheless, the writers of the *Panjābī Majlis* broke the mold of convention and forged a path that was subsequently followed by the writers of the *Panjābī Adabī Sangat*: Najm Hosain Syed (a former student of Safdar Mir), Afzal Ahsan Randhawa, Ahmad Salim, Mushtaq Soofi, and Nasreen Anjum Bhatti. The radical literary modernity that emerged with the publication of Najm Hosain Syed's poetry collection *Kāfyāṃ* in 1965 owes a lot to the literary experiments initiated by the Punjabi modernists six or seven years before.[79]

Conclusion

THIS STUDY OF the Punjabi movements between 1947 and 1960 would remain incomplete if we did not mention a few positive developments that occurred soon after these movements disappeared, and were their direct outcome. In 1960, Punjab's secondary board of education allowed Punjabi to be taught in government schools as an optional subject between the sixth and twelfth grades, and the Punjab University announced that it would award a prize to the best book in Punjabi published in the previous year.[1] The same year, a Punjabi program named *Rāvī Rang* (Color of the Ravi River) started on the Lahore radio station.[2] This cultural program, broadcast in addition to the popular program *Dehātī bhāyoṃ ke liye*, played a major role in the promotion of Punjabi literature, as poets, fiction writers, and essayists were regularly invited to read from their work. Also in 1960, Raja Risalu and Asif Khan launched the journal *Panjābī Adab*, which published the first texts of personalities who were to dominate the Punjabi literary scene during the following decades: the activist Shafqat Tanvir Mirza; the critic, poet, and playwright Najm Hosain Syed; and the novelist and poet Afzal Ahsan Randhawa. A number of important Punjabi books were published in Lahore in 1960: Maula Bakhsh Kushta's monumental *Tażkira panjābī šāʿirāṃ dā* (Encyclopedia of Punjabi Poets); Abdul Majeed Bhatti's *Ṭheḍḍā* (A Blow), the first Punjabi novel published in Pakistan after independence; Nawaz's *Dūnghyāṃ šāmāṃ* (Deep Evenings), the first collection of Punjabi short stories published in Pakistan after independence; Sharif Kunjahi's *Jhātyāṃ* (Overviews), the first collection of critical essays in Punjabi published in Pakistan after independence; and Munir Niazi's groundbreaking poetic collection *Safar dī rāt* (The Night of the Journey). That same year, the Punjabi Academy published its first Punjabi book: Sheikh Abdul Aziz's critical edition of *Heer Waris Shah*.[3]

Additional positive developments followed. In 1961, a Punjabi branch of the government-sponsored Writers' Guild was established, chaired by Shafqat Tanvir Mirza and Abdus Salam Khurshid.[4] In 1962, this branch awarded, for the first time, a prize to a literary work in Punjabi.[5] Finally, in July 1963, came the establishment of the *Panjābī Adabī Sangat*, which is still active today.[6]

The biggest success achieved by the Punjabi movements of the 1950s was on the literary front. By 1960–61, Punjabi literature had ceased to be a marginal literature. It enjoyed government sponsorship, and a new generation of Punjabi writers was emerging, who chose to write only in Punjabi. That the impact of these movements was mainly literary is not surprising, given the priorities set by Marxist, conservative, and modernist activists and the strategy they chose to adopt, focusing above all on enriching Punjabi's literary capital. This moderate strategy is specific to the Punjabi movements, setting them apart from other contemporary language movements. While Bengali and Sindhi activists demanded the inclusion of their language in the constitution, Baloch activists lobbied for their language to become the official language of their province, and Pashtun activists campaigned for their language to be used in schools, courts, and administrations, the most common demand formulated by Punjabi activists was that their language be used as a medium of instruction in primary schools (from this perspective, Punjab's secondary board of education's decision to teach Punjabi as an optional subject between the sixth and twelfth grades was only a semi-victory). A second feature specific to the Punjabi movements was that activists never attempted to mobilize the masses, focusing instead on intellectual circles. A third element specific to the Punjabi movements was that the Punjabi politicians who expressed support for them did not include the promotion and recognition of Punjabi in their political agenda. Maulana Bhashani and A. K. Fazlul Huq openly espoused the cause of Bengali, G. M. Syed that of Sindhi, Abdul Ghaffar Khan that of Pashto, and Prince Abdul Karim and Muhammad Hussain Anqa that of Balochi, but Mian Iftikharuddin and Joshua Fazal Dinboth—two prominent members of the provincial assembly known for their sympathy for the Punjabi language—did not launch any initiative on an official level (such as drafting a bill, submitting a memorandum, or posing a question to the government) to promote their language and further its cause.

Why did Punjabi activists adopt such a moderate strategy? Why did they not try to mobilize the masses and instead presented such limited demands? Why did pro-Punjabi politicians abstain from launching any serious initiative? L. V. Khokhlova, in her article "The Role of Punjabi Language in Self-Identification of Punjabi Community," gives an answer:

> There were no serious ethnic movements for widening the social functions of the mother tongue of Punjabis who constitute the majority of the population. One of possible explanations may be that ethnic movements are usually based on grievances of the disadvantaged groups concerning ethnic disparities, but Punjabi-speaking community is anything but a disadvantaged ethnic group. Influential class of rich Punjabi landlords, the largest in absolute numbers educated middle class, which provides most of the personnel for white-collar professions and the pool for recruitment into civil and military service—all that makes both general public as well as political analysts consider Punjabis as a privileged group.[7]

The Punjabis, a numerically large group, played a key role in the movement for Pakistan. A group that occupied a preponderant place in the army and the administration, whose intelligentsia had adopted and championed Urdu, unlike Bengalis and Sindhis, did not consider themselves harmed by the steps taken by the Pakistani government to implement Urdu. It was therefore unlikely that they would mobilize in large numbers for their language or that Punjabi politicians would commit to defending it. This may also explain why the Punjabi movements—unlike other language movements born at the same time—did not take a nationalist turn. Tariq Rahman explains:

> Punjabis already have power which ethnicity would only threaten. This is why the Punjabi movement mobilizes people not for instrumentalist but for sentimental reasons. The pre-modern sentimental attachment to a distinctive way of life, conveniently symbolized by Punjabi, is really what is at stake. The domination of Urdu, no matter how useful for the elite, does take away the language and literature of the Punjab from the Punjabis. The activists feel that this is a price

> which should not be paid; the others do not take it seriously. Hence, the movement is a weak, middle-class phenomenon, concentrated mainly in Lahore. It is unique among all the language movements of Pakistan because it is the only one which is not motivated by rational, goal-directed, instrumentalist reasons.[8]

Even if the Punjabi movements have not had as their goal the acquisition of power, it is reductive to conclude—as Alyssa Ayres does—that their only goal is "the pursuit of symbolic capital accumulation as an end in itself."[9] This ignores the spirit of linguistic resistance that animates and characterizes these movements. Punjabi language activists reclaimed and redefined Punjabi to assert their identities, express dissent, and resist cultural imperialism, highlighting the political and social implications of the language in shaping narratives and identities.

Punjabi movements lacked two key elements that could have ensured their success: a popular base and the support of some political leaders. But these were not the only hurdles they faced. A major hurdle was the lack of unity among the groups that promoted Punjabi: They did not form—unlike Sindhi and Bengali groups—a strong front that could put pressure on the state. The Punjabi groups, as we have shown in the previous chapters, were constantly competing against one another. Marxists began a movement in 1949; in response, conservatives mobilized in 1950, thus competing with them. Conservatives, following the dismantling of the Marxist camp in 1954, subsequently dominated the Punjabi literary landscape. Their dominance was then challenged and threatened by the creation in 1957 of the *Panjābī Majlis*, an organization that rejected conservative literature and conservative initiatives (as well as the Marxist literary canon). Ideological differences and competition prevented these groups from uniting. Another major hurdle was the state's constant interference in the activities of dissenting intellectuals, as a result of which Marxists and modernists could not carry on with their promotion of Punjabi. One can imagine that if the Marxist group had not been targeted by the government in 1954 and 1959, and if the *Panjābī Majlis* had not been banned in 1959, the movements they launched would have had a deeper and wider impact.

But the biggest hurdle facing the Punjabi movements that emerged in Pakistan after independence was the lasting impact of the communalization of Punjabi society during the colonial period, as a result of which Punjabi Hindus supported Hindi, Punjabi Muslims Urdu, and Sikhs Punjabi. Punjabi

Muslims became so strongly biased against Punjabi, which they considered a non-Muslim language, that a decade of activism and of promotion of Punjabi was not enough to dispel their prejudices. This communalization of Punjabi society had an adverse impact on Punjabi's status in Indian Punjab too. Punjabi Hindus identified so closely with Hindi that they objected to Punjabi's being given official status in the state. In the Indian Punjab's censuses of 1951 and 1961, Punjabi Hindus declared Hindi as their mother tongue (even though they were Punjabi speakers), thus skewing the results.[10] Punjabi competed with Hindi for two decades, and it was only after a long struggle, culminating in the dismemberment of the state of Indian Punjab in 1966, that it succeeded in gaining official status.[11]

In Pakistani Punjab, Punjabi has not yet gained official status, as the intelligentsia still identifies with Urdu. Their overall perception of Punjabi is practically unchanged since 1947, as seen in Fateh Mohammad Malik's editorial in the May 2004 special issue of *Axbār-e Urdu*, the official journal of the *Muqtadra qaumī zubān* (National Language Authority). Malik, then chairman of the *Muqtadra qaumī zubān*, harshly criticizes the chief minister of Punjab, Chaudhry Perwaiz Elahi, who, on the occasion of a visit of his Indian counterpart, Captain Amarinder Singh, in January 2004, declared that Pakistani Punjab should follow the model established by Indian Punjab and make Punjabi its medium of instruction in schools. Malik stated that this proposal was the result of a conspiracy aimed at de-Islamizing the province and proudly rejected it, arguing that Urdu could not be replaced by Punjabi in schools because "Urdu is Punjab's mother tongue."[12]

The overall perception of Punjabi by the provincial intelligentsia has not changed, and the policy of the provincial authorities regarding Punjabi has not changed either. The concessions granted over the years by the government of Pakistani Punjab have crystallized into symbolic measures encouraging literature and research but have not affected the status of Punjabi on the ground.[13] At present, Punjabi—the mother tongue of 110 million people in Pakistan—is still used neither in the administration, nor in the courts, nor as a medium of instruction in schools, thus giving rise to the paradoxical situation summed up in one sentence by the novelist and journalist Mohammed Hanif: "Punjabi is a language where you can do an MA in, but you cannot do high school."[14]

Notes

Introduction

1. On the notion of language ideology, see Bambi Schieffelin, Kathryn Woolard, and Paul Kroskrity, *Language Ideologies, Practice and Theory* (New York: Oxford University Press, 1998). Schieffelin defines *language ideology* as the "self-evident ideas and objectives a group holds concerning roles of language in the social experience of members as they contribute to the expression of the group" (4).
2. Anwar Sadid, *Urdu adab kī teḥrīkeṃ* (Karachi: Anjuman-e Taraqqī-e Urdu Pakistan, 1996); Tahir Kamran, "Urdu Migrant Literati and Lahore's Culture," *Journal of Punjab Studies* 19, no. 2 (2012): 173–192; and Farina Mir, *The Social Space of Language: Vernacular Culture in British Colonial Punjab* (Berkeley: University of California Press, 2010).
3. Ahmad Rahi, *Tirinjan* (Lahore: Al-Hamd, [1953] 2005); Abdul Majeed Bhatti, *Theḍḍā* (Lahore: Hūnhār Book Depot, 1960).
4. Christopher Shackle, "Punjabi in Lahore," *Modern Asian Studies* 4, no. 3 (1970): 239–267.
5. Alyssa Ayres, *Speaking Like a State: Language and Nationalism in Pakistan* (Cambridge: Cambridge University Press, 2009), 64–104.
6. Virinder Singh Kalra and Waqas Butt, " 'In One Hand a Pen in the Other a Gun': Punjabi Language Radicalism in Punjab, Pakistan," *South Asian History and Culture* 4, no. 4 (2013): 538–553.
7. Sara Kazmi, "The Marxist Punjabi Movement: Language and Literary Radicalism in Pakistan," *Sudasien chronik-South Asia Chronicle* 7 (2017): 227–250.
8. Tariq Rahman, "The Punjabi Movement," in *Language and Politics in Pakistan* (Karachi: Oxford University Press, 1996), 191–209; Tariq Rahman, "Punjabi,"

in *Language, Ideology and Power* (Karachi: Oxford University Press, 2008), 221–246; Kanwal Mushtaq, "Panjābī dī pehlī conference," *Saver*, August 1997, 12–14; "Panjābī bolcāl te likhnā paṛhnā," *Saver*, September 1997, 13–16; "Panjāb vic 1951 dyāṃ conāṃ te Panjābī zubān," *Saver*, October 1997, 9–12; "Pāk Panjābī League te Punjabi Cultural Society," *Saver*, December 1997, 11–14; "Panjābī lehr te tanẓīmāṃ," *Saver*, March 1998, 14–16; "Sarkārī tanẓīmāṃ te idāre," *Saver*, June 1998, 14–16; Maqsood Saqib, ed., *Puchāṃ dasāṃ* (Lahore: Suchet, 2013).

9. Shafqat Tanvir Mirza, "Interview," in *Puchāṃ dasāṃ*, ed. Maqsood Saqib (Lahore: Suchet, 2013): 189–205.
10. Mirza, "Interview." The presence of nationalists among the first supporters of Punjabi calls into question the idea that Pakistani nationalists always supported Urdu (considered a vector of the unity of the nation), an idea presented by Tariq Rahman: "In Pakistan, on the other hand, identity-conscious Punjabis and their left-leaning sympathizers supported Punjabi much as the Sikhs and Hindus had done earlier, while establishment and right-wing people supported Urdu" (*Language, Ideology and Power*, 230).
11. Khizar Humayun Ansari, *The Emergence of Socialist Thought Among North Indian Muslims, 1917–1947* (Karachi: Oxford University Press, 2015).
12. The Abdullah Malik Collection, at the Government College Library, was pointed out to me by Dr. Ali Usman Qasmi, to whom I am immensely grateful.
13. Poetry collections: Rahi, *Tirinjan*; Faqeer Mohammad Faqeer, *Muwāte* (Lahore: Bazm-e Faqīr Pākistān/Sānjh, [1956] 2015); Abdul Majeed Bhatti, *Dil daryā* (Lahore: Nayā Idāra, 1955). Radio play collections: Sajjad Hyder, *Hawā de hūke* (Lahore: Qaumī Kutub-Xāna, 1957); Safdar Mir, "Nīle dā aswār," in *Ṣafdar Mīr dyāṃ likhatāṃ*, ed. Sheema Majeed (Lahore: Pakistan Punjabi Adabī Board, 2002; first published in *Rāvī Magazine*, Lahore, 1957), 69–99. Literary anthologies: Faqeer Mohammad Faqeer, ed., *Lehrāṃ* (Lahore: Qureishi, 1953); Abdul Haq Khammi, ed., *Panjāb Rang* (Lahore: Panjābī Majlis, 1958); Anis Nagi, ed., *Sajre phull* (Lahore: Panjābī Majlis, 1959). Communist pamphlets: Abdullah Malik, *Mustaqbil hamārā hai* (Lahore: PPH, 1950); Firozuddin Mansoor and Sibte Hasan, *Pākistān meṃ qaumī zubān kā masla* (Lahore: PPH, 1953).
14. Aslam Rana, "Jošua Faẓal Dīn, ḥayātī, fikr te fan," *Khoj* 45–46 (2001); Anwarul Haq, "Pākistān vic panjābī adab dā irtiqā" (master's thesis, Lahore Oriental College, 1974); Lyaqat Hussain, "Allama Ġulām Yaqūb Anwar, ḥayātī fikr te fan" (master's thesis, Lahore Oriental College, 1983); Shahzad Ahmad, "Ḥakīm Tayeb Riẓvī, ḥayātī te šāʿirī" (master's thesis, Lahore Oriental College, 1988); Mohammad Tariq Zafar, "Xalīl Ātiš dī šāʿirī te kalām" (master's thesis, Lahore Oriental College, 1988); Sania Zafar, "Aḥmad Ẓafar dī panjābī šāʿirī" (master's thesis, Lahore Oriental College, 2010); Anwar Ahmad Qazi, "Ṣeḥrā'ī Gurdāspūrī, ḥayātī te kalām" (master's thesis, Lahore Oriental College, 1988); Nasrullah Mughal, "Ismaīl Matwālā ḥayātī fikr te fan" (master's thesis, Lahore Oriental College, 1989); Asya Ehsan, "Teḥrīk-e Pākistān te Ẓahīr Nyāz Bīgī" (master's thesis, Lahore Oriental College, 1999); Arifa Kausar, "Bašir Manẓar dyāṃ panjābī adab la'ī xidmatāṃ" (master's thesis, Lahore Oriental College, 2002); Faiza Zaidi,

"Nizām Dīn Tawakkulī te ohnāṃ dī inšāya-nigārī" (master's thesis, Lahore Oriental College, 2008); Muhibullah Malik, "Ḥanif Caudhrī ḥayātī te fan" (master's thesis, Lahore Oriental College, 2010).

15. Raja Risalu, *Lā prīt ajehī Moḥammad* (Lahore: Pakistan Punjabi Adabī Board, 2008); Anis Nagi, *Ek adhūrī sarguzašt* (Lahore: Jamāliyāt, 2008); Intizar Hussain, *Cirāġoṃ kā dhu'āṃ* (Lahore: Sang-e-meel, 2012); Ahmad Salim, *Aḥmad Rāhī bātāṃ mulāqātāṃ* (Islamabad: Kūnj, 2005); Shorish Kashmiri, *Ḥamīd Nizāmī* (Lahore: Caṭṭān, [1966] 2010); Shorish Kashmiri, *Nau rattan* (Lahore: Caṭṭān, [1967] 2010); Shorish Kashmiri, *Teḥrīk-e Xatam-e Nubuwwat* (Lahore: Caṭṭān, [1974] 2011); Ahmad Nadeem Qasmi, *Mere hamqadam* (Lahore: Sang-e-meel, 2007); K. K. Aziz, *The Coffee House of Lahore: A Memoir 1942–1957* (Lahore: Sang-e-meel, 2007); Akmal Aleemi, *Lāhor ke ahl-e qalam* (Lahore: Sang-e-meel, 2014); Hameed Akhtar, *Pursiš-e aḥwāl* (Lahore: Afra, 1999); *Rūdād-e Anjuman* (Lahore: Book Home, 2011); Ahmad Salim, *Sawāneḥ-e 'umrī Ḥamīd Axtar* (Lahore: Book Home, 2010).

16. Rauf Malik, Lahore, March 16, July 27, August 3, October 16, 2018; Abid Hassan Minto, Lahore, March 14, 2018; Anver Sajjad, Lahore, August 1, 2018; Zahid Dar, Lahore, October 6, 2018; Dr. Kanwal Feroze, Lahore, October 11, 2017; Raza Kazim, Lahore, March 31, 2019; Ahmad Salim, Islamabad, February 23, 2016; and Junaid Akram, Lahore, July 26, July 29, 2018. Junaid Akram held the Dr. Faqeer Research Chair in the Punjabi Department of Oriental College, Lahore, between 2013 and 2018.

17. Zafar Iqbal founded a Punjabi organization in Sahiwal in 1958 with the assistance of Professor Anvar Shabnam (*Panjdaryā*, August 1959, 4); a Punjabi literary society named *Bazm-e Adab*, active in Lyallpur since independence, was founded by Ulfat Warsi, and in 1958, Talib Jalandhari, Chaudhry Ali Mohammad Mahi, and Chaudhry Ali Mohammad Khadim established a second organization in Lyallpur (*Panjdaryā*, August 1959, 4); an organization called Punjabi Cultural Circle was founded in 1959 in Karachi by Shafi Aqeel and Noor Kashmiri (*Panjdaryā*, August 1959, 4).

18. Pierre Bourdieu, *Ce que parler veut dire: L'économie des échanges linguistiques* (Paris: Éditions Fayard, 1982); "Le champ littéraire," *Actes de la recherche en sciences sociales* 89 (1991): 3–46; *Les règles de l'art: genèse et structure du champ littéraire* (Paris: Seuil, 1992).

19. Gisèle Sapiro, "De l'usage des catégories de droite et de gauche dans le champ littéraire," *Sociétés et représentations* 11 (2001): 19–53; "Forms of Politicization in the French Literary Field," *Theory and Society* 32 (2003): 633–652; "Modèles d'intervention politique des intellectuels, le cas français," *Actes de la recherche en sciences sociales* 176–177 (2009): 8–31; "Le champ littéraire français," in *Art et société, savoirs croisés en sciences humaines et sociales Brésil / France*, ed. Alain Quemin and Glaucia Villas Bôas (Marseille: Open Edition, 2016): 69–84.

20. Denis Matringe, "Disguising Political Resistance in the Sufi Idiom: The Kafian of Najm Husain Sayyid of Pakistan," in *The Islamic Path: Sufism, Politics and Society in India*, ed. Saiyid Zahir Husain Jafri and Helmut Reifeld (Ahmedabad: Rainbow, 2006): 110–130.

1. Pakistan's Linguistic Landscape

1. Tariq Rahman, *Language and Politics in Pakistan* (Karachi: Oxford University Press, 1996), 86.
2. Quoted in Alyssa Ayres, *Speaking Like a State: Language and Nationalism in Pakistan* (Cambridge: Cambridge University Press, 2009), 42.
3. Quoted in Ayres, *Speaking Like a State*, 43.
4. Rahman, *Language and Politics in Pakistan*, 90–91.
5. Rahman, *Language and Politics in Pakistan*, 95.
6. Rahman, *Language and Politics in Pakistan*, 85.
7. Rahman, *Language and Politics in Pakistan*, 231.
8. Tariq Rahman, *Language, Ideology and Power* (Karachi: Oxford University Press, 2008), 157.
9. Rahman, *Language, Ideology and Power*, 197–198.
10. Rahman, *Language, Ideology and Power*, 158.
11. See Tariq Rahman, "The Urdu-English Controversy in Pakistan," *Modern Asian studies* 31, no. 1 (1997): 177–207.
12. Kalim Sehsarami, "Mašrīqī Pākistān meṃ Urdu," in *Pākistān meṃ Urdu*, ed. Mohammad Tahir Faruqi and Khatir Ghaznavi (Peshawar: University Book Agency, 1966), 81.
13. Ghulam Hussain Zulfiqar, "Punjab University aur Urdu," in Faruqi and Ghaznavi, *Pākistān meṃ Urdu*, 556; Sharar Nomani, "Ilāqā Sarḥad meṃ Urdu," in Faruqi and Ghaznavi, *Pākistān meṃ Urdu*, 113; Akbar Hussain Qureishi, "Balocistān meṃ Urdu," in Faruqi and Ghaznavi, *Pākistān meṃ Urdu*, 94.
14. Abdul Rashid Fazil, "Urdu College," in Faruqi and Ghaznavi, *Pākistān meṃ Urdu*, 591.
15. Commission on National Education (Sharif Commission), *Report of the National Education Commission* (Karachi: Government of Pakistan, Ministry of Education, 1959), 292.
16. Sharif Commission, *Report of the National Education Commission*, 288.
17. Andrew Amstutz, *Finding a Home for Urdu: The Anjuman-i Taraqqī-yi Urdu, 1903–1971* (AIPS, 2013), 1.
18. Anisa Nargis Azim, "Anjuman-e Taraqqī-e Urdu Pakistan," in Faruqi and Ghaznavi, *Pākistān meṃ Urdu*, 515.
19. Fazil, "Urdu College," 597.
20. Azim, "Anjuman-e Taraqqī-e Urdu Pakistan," 517.
21. Nomani, "Ilāqā Sarḥad meṃ Urdu," 118; Qureishi, "Balocistān meṃ Urdu," 98; Sehsarami, "Mašrīqī Pākistān meṃ Urdu," 84.
22. The *Mohajirs* are Muslims mainly from the Ganges Valley (present-day Uttar Pradesh), Delhi, present-day Madhya Pradesh, Rajasthan, Deccan's Hyderabad, and Bihar who settled in Pakistan during and in the years that followed Partition.
23. Ilyas Ahmad Chattha, "Partition and Its Aftermath: Violence, Migration and the Role of Refugees in the Socio-Economic Development of Gujranwala and Sialkot Cities, 1947–1961" (PhD diss., University of Southampton, 2009), 111.

24. Rahman, *Language and Politics in Pakistan*, 111.
25. Rahman, *Language and Politics in Pakistan*, 117.
26. Rahman, *Language and Politics in Pakistan*, 112.
27. Majid Nizami, *The Press in Pakistan* (Lahore: Department of Political Science, University of the Punjab, 1958), 70–71.
28. Nizami, *The Press in Pakistan*, 71.
29. Rahman, *Language and Politics in Pakistan*, 2, 79.
30. Papiya Ghosh, "The Changing Discourse of the Muhajirs," *India International Center Quarterly* 28, no. 3 (2001): 58; Ian Talbot, *Pakistan: A Modern History* (London: Hurst, 1998), 101.
31. Musarrat Jabeen, Amir Ali Chandio, and Zarina Qasim, "Language Controversy: Impacts on National Politics and Secession of East Pakistan," *South Asian Studies* 25, no. 1 (2010): 105–106.
32. Jabeen, Chandio, and Qasim, "Language Controversy," 107–108.
33. Kabir Choudhry, *Bengali Academy: A Summary of Its Achievements and Aspirations* (Dhaka: Bengali Academy, 1970), 8–9.
34. Rahman, *Language and Politics in Pakistan*, 94–95.
35. Rahman, *Language and Politics in Pakistan*, 79.
36. Rahman, *Language and Politics in Pakistan*, 104–109.
37. Rahman, *Language and Politics in Pakistan*, 114.
38. Kamran Asdar Ali writes in *Surkh Salam: Communist Politics and Class Activism in Pakistan 1947–1972* (Karachi: Oxford University Press, 2015), 263: "The One Unit administration was put in place to ostensibly solve the government's problem of governing parts of Pakistan that were a thousand miles apart. The programme merged the four provinces of West Pakistan to bring it into numerical parity with East Pakistan. West Pakistan's capital was in Lahore and East Pakistan's in Dhaka." General Yahya Khan dissolved the One Unit Scheme in 1970, creating the five provinces of Sindh, Balochistan, Punjab, NWFP, and Bengal.
39. Khadim Hussain Soomro, *The Path Not Taken: G. M. Syed, Vision and Valor in Politics* (Sehwan Sharif: Sain, 2004), 51–52.
40. Soomro, *The Path Not Taken*, 174–175 ; Julien Levesque, *Etre sindhi au Pakistan: Nationalisme, discours identitaire et mobilisation politique 1930–2016* (PhD diss., EHESS, 2016), 116–117.
41. Levesque, *Etre sindhi au Pakistan*, 286.
42. Levesque, *Etre sindhi au Pakistan*, 288–289.
43. Rahman, *Language and Politics in Pakistan*, 115.
44. Subho Gyan Chandani, interview with Mazhar Jamil, Muslim Shamim, and Rahat Saeed, in *Guftagū: Taraqqī-pasand teḥrīk ke naẕrī masā'il, aṡrāt aur muxālifīn ke aʿitrāẓāt par mašāhīrīn-e adab se bātchīt*, ed. Mazhar Jamil (Karachi: Maktaba-e Danyāl, 1986), 216–217.
45. Levesque, *Etre sindhi au Pakistan*, 128.
46. Levesque, *Etre sindhi au Pakistan*, 286; Annemarie Schimmel, "The Activities of the Sindhi Adabi Board, Karachi," *Die Welt des Islams* 6, no. 3 (1961): 226–234.
47. Levesque, *Etre sindhi au Pakistan*, 243–249.
48. Levesque, *Etre sindhi au Pakistan*, 306.

49. Levesque, *Etre sindhi au Pakistan*, 209–210; Schimmel, "The Activities of the Sindhi Adabi Board," 225.
50. Sharif Commission, *Report of the National Education Commission*, 284.
51. Rahman, *Language and Politics in Pakistan*, 137.
52. Rahman, *Language and Politics in Pakistan*, 137. *Paxtunistan* is a Pashtun country that would result from the unification of Afghanistan and the province of NWFP.
53. King Amanullah had established a *Pašto Tolane* (Pashto Academy) in the mid-1920s, and Pashto was declared the national language of Afghanistan, replacing Persian, by royal decree in 1936 (Rahman, *Language and Politics in Pakistan*, 142).
54. Mohammad Sohail, Syed Munir Ahmad, and Hafiz Muhammad Inamullah, "The Educational Services and Philosophy of Bacha Khan," *Journal of Applied Environmental and Biological Sciences* 4 (2014): 161.
55. Rahman, *Language and Politics in Pakistan*, 138–139.
56. Nomani, "Ilāqā Sarḥad meṃ Urdu," 114.
57. Fazal ur-Rahim Marwat, "Pashto Literature: A Quest for Identity in Pakistan," *Faultines* 18 (2007): 2.
58. Rahman, *Language and Politics in Pakistan*, 151
59. This is a celebration at a shrine to mark the death anniversary of a Sufi master.
60. Marwat, "Pashto Literature," 3–4.
61. Nizami, *The Press in Pakistan*, 71.
62. Khatir Ghaznavi, "Dīgar muqtadar idāre," in Faruqi and Ghaznavi, *Pākistān meṃ Urdu*, 553–554.
63. Rahman, *Language and Politics in Pakistan*, 152.
64. Brian Spooner, "Balochi: Towards a Biography of the Language," in *Language Policy and Language Conflict in Afghanistan and Its Neighbors: The Changing Politics of Language Choice*, ed. Harold Schiffman (Leiden: Brill, 2012), 328.
65. Taj Mohammad Breseeg, *Baloch Nationalism: Its Origin and Development* (Karachi: Royal Book Company, 2004), 229.
66. Spooner, "Balochi," 328.
67. Allessandro Bausani, "Recenti notizie dal Pakistan sulle literature bahui e beluci," *Oriente Moderno* 54, no. 4 (1974): 46.
68. Bausani, "Recenti notizie dal Pakistan," 45; Breseeg, *Baloch Nationalism*, 98.
69. Mir Abdullah Jamaldini, *Laṭxāna* (Quetta: Sangat Academy, 2002), 72–73; Jamaldini, *Laṭxāna*, 76–77.
70. Jamaldini, *Laṭxāna*, 103–104.
71. Breseeg, *Baloch Nationalism*, 277–278.
72. Mir Abdullah Jamaldini, interview with Mazhar Jamil and Muslim Shamim, in *Guftagū: Taraqqī-pasand teḥrīk ke naẕrī masā'il, aśrāt aur muxālifīn ke aʿitrāẓāt par mašāhīrīn-e adab se bātchīt*, ed. Mazhar Jamil (Karachi: Maktaba-e Danyāl, 1986), 234–237.
73. Website of the Balochi academy, http://academy.balochiacademy.org/.
74. Pierre Bourdieu, "*La production de la croyance: contribution à une économie des biens symboliques*," *Actes de la recherche en sciences sociales* 13 (1977): 10.

75. Abdullah Malik, *Mustaqbil hamārā hai* (Lahore: PPH, 1950), 82–83. At least one Marxist activist participated in each movement: Shahidullah Kaiser in the Bengali movement, Subho Gyan Chandani in the Sindhi movement, *Kakaji* Sanober Hussain in the Pashto movement, and Gul Khan Nasir in the Balochi movement.

2. The Linguistic Situation in Punjab

1. Christopher Shackle, *An Introduction to the Sacred Language of the Sikhs* (London: School of Oriental and African Studies, University of London, 1983).
2. Farina Mir, *The Social Space of Language: Vernacular Culture in British Colonial Punjab* (Berkeley: University of California Press, 2010), 35–36.
3. A list of Iqbal's works in Persian can be found in Denis Matringe, " 'L'appel de la cloche': spiritualité, écriture poétique et vision politique chez Muhammad Iqbal (1877–1938)," in *Convictions religieuses et engagement en Asie du Sud depuis 1850*, ed. Catherine Clémentin (Paris: École Française d'Extrême-Orient, 2011), 50–51.
4. Tariq Rahman, *Language and Politics in Pakistan* (Karachi: Oxford University Press, 1996), 193.
5. Rahman, *Language and Politics in Pakistan*, 193.
6. It was after fighting two wars against the Sikh Empire (1845–46 and 1848–49) that the British succeeded in annexing Punjab.
7. Rahman, *Language and Politics in Pakistan*, 194.
8. Mir, *The Social Space of Language*, 55.
9. Gottlieb Wilhelm Leitner, *History of Indigenous Education in the Punjab Since Annexation and in 1882* (Lahore: Republican Books, [1882] 1991), 10.
10. Leitner, *History of Indigenous Education in the Punjab*, 5; Mir, *The Social Space of Language*, 55.
11. Tariq Rahman, *From Hindi to Urdu, a Social and Political History* (Karachi: Oxford University Press, 2011), 343–344.
12. Mir, *The Social Space of Language*, 33.
13. Mir, *The Social Space of Language*, 33.
14. Shorish Kashmiri, *Nau rattan* (Lahore: Caṭṭān, [1967] 2010), 72.
15. Majid Nizami, *The Press in Pakistan* (Lahore: Department of Political Science, University of the Punjab, 1958), 5.
16. Quoted in Ayesha Jalal, *Self and Sovereignty: Individual and Community in South Asian Islam Since 1850* (Delhi: Oxford University Press, 2001), 110.
17. Quoted in Jalal, *Self and Sovereignty*, 110.
18. Quoted in Jalal, *Self and Sovereignty*, 55.
19. Quoted in Rahman, *Language and Politics in Pakistan*, 196.
20. Quoted in Jalal, *Self and Sovereignty*, 122.
21. Tariq Rahman, *Language, Ideology and Power* (Karachi: Oxford University Press, 2008), 230.
22. Editorial, *Paisā Axbār*, March 7, 1909, 6.
23. Editorial, *Paisā Axbār*, March 17, 1909, 2.

24. Editorial, *Paisā Axbār*, April 12, 1909, 6.
25. Rahman, *Language, Ideology and Power*, 230.
26. Jalal, *Self and Sovereignty*, 114, 121.
27. Denis Matringe, "L'Apparition de la nouvelle et du roman en panjabi 1930–1947," *Journal Asiatique* cclxxii, no. 3–4 (1985): 427.
28. Rahman, *Language and Politics in Pakistan*, 195. Until then, Punjabi in *Gurumukhi* characters was taught only in a few private schools run by Sikhs as well as in specialized departments of a few colleges (Oriental College, Lahore, and Khalsa College, Amritsar).
29. Matringe, "L'Apparition de la nouvelle et du roman en panjabi," 428; Maula Bakhsh Kushta, *Tażkira panjābī šāʿirāṃ dā* (Lahore: Azeez, [1960] 1988), 14.
30. Matringe, "L'Apparition de la nouvelle et du roman," 429.
31. Igor Serebryakov, *Punjabi Literature* (Moscow: Nauka, 1968), 93–94; Serebryakov, *Punjabi Literature*, 74–76, 95; Matringe "L'Apparition de la nouvelle et du roman," 431, 434–436.
32. Serebryakov, *Punjabi Literature*, 81. In *Rūšnā'ī* (New Delhi: Qaumī Council Barā-e Furūġ-e Urdu, [1956] 2006), 304–305, Sajjad Zaheer recounts meetings before Partition in Lahore at the Progressive Writers' Association, during which the Punjabi writers Kartar Singh Duggal and Prof. Mohan Singh read their texts in Punjabi.
33. Serebryakov, *Punjabi Literature*, 66–69.
34. Serebryakov, *Punjabi Literature*, 105–108.
35. Aslam Rana, "Jošua Faẓal Dīn, ḥayātī, fikr te fan," *Khoj* 45–46 (2001): 278.
36. Kushta, *Tażkira*, 14–15.
37. Kushta, *Tażkira,* unnumbered preface, 307.
38. Mohammad Munir Ahmad Salich, *Pīr Faẓal Gujrāti, ḥayātī te bāqī kalām* (Lahore: Punjab Institute of Language, Art and Culture [PILAC], 2012), 30–31; Kushta, *Tażkira,* 459–460.
39. Safir Rammah, "West Punjabi Poetry: From Ustad Daman to Najm Hosain Syed," *Journal of Punjab Studies* 13 no. 1–2 (2006): 218–219.
40. Rana, "Jošua Faẓal Dīn," 229.
41. Ustad Daman, interview with Munnu Bhai and Nawaz for Radio Pakistan, June 29, 1974, https://www.youtube.com/watch?v=ltIXLeSzQGM, accessed June 12, 2025; Sajjad Hyder, "Interview," in *Puchāṃ dasāṃ*, ed. Maqsood Saqib (Lahore: Suchet, 2013), 231.
42. Kushta, *Tażkira*, 388–389; Rana, "Jošua Faẓal Dīn," 240–242.
43. Rana, "Jošua Faẓal Dīn," 345–349.
44. Rana, "Jošua Faẓal Dīn," 393, 399–402.
45. Rana, "Jošua Faẓal Dīn," 402–403.
46. Qazi Fazl-e Haq's commitment to maintaining a connection between Punjab's Muslim community and the Punjabi language is seen in his advocating for Muslim degree candidates in Punjabi (*gyānī*) to write their exams in *Shahmukhi* instead of *Gurumukhi,* and for a Punjabi section in *Shahmukhi* entitled *Rāvī dyāṃ challāṃ* (Waves of the Ravi River) to be included in Government College's prestigious journal *Rāvī.* Bazl-e Haq Mehmood, *Panjābī maẓmūn* (Lahore:

Sang-e-meel, 2003), 56–57. See also Mehmood, *Panjābī maẓmūn*, 55–56; Rana, "Jošua Faẓal Dīn," 242–245.

47. Iqbal Qaiser, "Sārang, ikk mʿeyārī panjābī risāla," *Saver*, November 1997, 9–11.
48. Miran Bakhsh Minhas, "Panjābī nūṃ vādhā kiveṃ hove?," *Panjābī Darbār* 1, no. 6 (November 1928): 9.
49. Minhas, "Panjābī nūṃ vādhā kiveṃ hove?," 10.
50. Minhas, "Panjābī nūṃ vādhā kiveṃ hove?," 15.
51. Minhas, "Panjābī nūṃ vādhā kiveṃ hove?," 16.
52. Minhas, "Panjābī nūṃ vādhā kiveṃ hove?," 16.
53. Minhas, "Panjābī nūṃ vādhā kiveṃ hove?," 17.
54. Nasir Rana, "Panjābī lisāniyāt," *Saver*, September 2004, 14.
55. Rana, "Panjābī lisāniyāt," 14–15.
56. George A. Grierson, *Linguistic Survey of India*, vol. 8, part 1, *Sindhi and Lahnda* (Delhi: Motilal Banarsidass, [1916] 1968); *Linguistic Survey of India*, vol. 9, part 1, *Western Hindi and Punjabi* (Delhi: Motilal Banarsidass, [1919] 1968).
57. Denis Matringe, "L'Utilisation littéraire des formes dialectales par les poètes musulmans du Panjab de la fin du XVIe au début du XIXe siècle," in *Dialectes dans les littératures indo-aryennes*, ed. Colette Caillat (Paris: Publications de l'Institut de Civilisation Indienne, Collège de France, 1989), 530.
58. Hafiz Mehmood Shirani, *Panjāb meṃ Urdu* (Islamabad: Muqtadra Qaumī Zubān, [1928] 1998); Rana, "Jošua Faẓal Dīn," 395–396.
59. Dakhini is the form of Urdu spoken in the Deccan plain. It retains certain features of the spoken Urdu of the seventeenth and eighteenth centuries and is strongly influenced by neighboring languages (Telugu, Kannada, and others).
60. Maqbul Anwar Daudi, "Išāʿatī idāre," in *Pākistān meṃ Urdu*, ed. Mohammad Tahir Faruqi and Khatir Ghaznavi (Peshawar: University Book Agency, 1966), 635; Khatir Ghaznavi, "Dīgar muqtadar idāre," in Faruqi and Ghaznavi, *Pākistān meṃ Urdu*, 539.
61. Quoted in Mohammad Arshad Owaisi, "Panjāb assembly meṃ Urdu," *Axbār-e Urdu*, March/April 2004, 364.
62. Quoted in Owaisi, "Panjāb assembly meṃ Urdu," 363. Thomas Babington Macaulay (1800–1859) was a British politician and historian who played an important role in introducing English and Western sciences/subjects into the educational curriculum in India. He summarized his views in his *Minute on Indian Education* (1835), in which he advocated the creation of a class of English-speaking Indians who would become "interpreters between us and the millions whom we govern, a class of persons Indians in blood and color but English in taste, in opinions, in morals and in intellect." Quoted in Sarabjeet Kaur, "Indigenous Education in the Punjab: An Analysis of G. W. Leitner's Report," *Proceedings of the Indian History Congress* 72, no. 1 (2011): 914.
63. Ghulam Hussain Zulfiqar, "Punjab University aur Urdu," in Faruqi and Ghaznavi, *Pākistān meṃ Urdu*, 556.
64. Razia Sultan Jan, "Ṣūbā-e Panjāb meṃ Urdu ba-taur-e sarkārī zubān kā jā'iza," *Axbār-e Urdu*, March/April 2004, 390–391.
65. Jan, "Ṣūbā-e Panjāb meṃ Urdu ba-taur-e sarkārī zubān," 390.

66. Jan, "Ṣūbā-e Panjāb meṃ Urdu ba-taur-e sarkārī zubān," 391.
67. Hamid Nizami, "Panjābī dī ibtidā'ī tᶜalīm," *Monthly Panjābī* 1, no. 3 (November 1951): 11.
68. This is largely a coincidence. The conference was scheduled to take place a month earlier but had been postponed because some of the participants had other engagements (*Axbār-e Urdu*, March/April 2004, 334).
69. Quoted in Ghulam Hussain Zulfiqar, ed. *Qaumī zubān ke bāre meṃ ehm dastāwezāt.* (Islamabad: Muqtadra Qaumī Zubān, 1986), 169.
70. *Daily Imroz*, March 28, 1948.
71. *Daily Imroz*, March 29, 1948.
72. *Daily Imroz*, March 28, 1948.
73. Quoted in Zulfiqar, *Qaumī zubān*, 195.
74. Quoted in Zulfiqar, *Qaumī zubān*, 167.
75. Quoted in Zulfiqar, *Qaumī zubān*, 187–188
76. *Daily Imroz*, March 28, 1948.
77. Quoted in Zulfiqar, *Qaumī zubān*, 179.
78. See Tariq Hashmi, *Maulānā Ṣalāḥuddīn Ahmad* (Islamabad: Muqtadra Qaumī Zubān, 2011), 103–109; Anwar Sadid, "Maulana Ṣalaḥuddin Aḥmad aur qaumī zubān Urdu," *Axbār-e Urdu*, March/April 2004, 200–214.
79. *Adabī Dunyā*, December 1948, 3.
80. Quoted in Sadid, "Maulana Ṣalaḥuddin Aḥmad," 203.
81. Quoted in Sadid, "Maulana Ṣalaḥuddin Aḥmad," 204.
82. It was later published in the yearly anthology *Behtarīn Adab 1948*.
83. K. K. Aziz, *The Coffee House of Lahore: A Memoir 1942–1957* (Lahore: Sang-e-meel, 2007), 267. Aziz uses the pejorative term *Urda* to refer to Urdu speakers from UP or Delhi.
84. Maulana Salahuddin Ahmad, "Taqsīm-e mulk kā aṡar Urdu zubān aur adab par," In *Behtarīn Adab* 1948, ed. Idāra-e Adab-e Laṭīf (Lahore: Maktaba-e Urdu): 88.
85. Ahmad, "Taqsīm-e mulk kā aṡar," 90. *Gyānī* was a Punjabi exam of the Punjab University, with a written test in *Gurumukhī* or in Urdu characters; *Urdu Fāẓil* was the Urdu exam of the Punjab University.
86. Ahmad, "Taqsīm-e mulk kā aṡar," 90–91.
87. Dialect of Urdu spoken in Old Delhi.
88. Ahmad, "Taqsīm-e mulk kā aṡar," 91.
89. Ilyas Ahmad Chattha, "Partition and Its Aftermath: Violence, Migration and the Role of Refugees in the Socio-Economic Development of Gujranwala and Sialkot Cities, 1947–1961" (PhD diss., University of Southampton, 2009), 197.
90. Oriental College's Punjabi department was closed following Partition, but surprisingly the *Panjābī Fāẓil* (University diploma in Punjabi of the university, involving a written test in Urdu characters) was maintained. Candidates could still pass the *Fāẓil* exam, even if they could not prepare for it in the university and had to do so privately. In 1951, the poet Maula Bakhsh Kushta opened a small institute, the Anglo Punjabi College, at 4 Temple Road in Lahore, where classes were taught to prepare candidates for the *Panjābī Fāẓil.* After his death in 1955, his son, Mohammad Afzal Khan, took charge of the institute (Mohammad Afzal Khan, "Pakistan te Bhārat vic Panjābī," *Panjdaryā*, September 1960, 52). The *Panjābī Fāẓil*, open to students who had not been able to continue their

studies beyond their matriculation exam, was very popular. Mohammad Afzal Khan reported that in 1955, 190 candidates appeared for the *Panjābī Fāẓil* exam and 49 cleared it; in 1956, 185 appeared and 58 cleared it (52–53). According to Shafqat Tanvir Mirza, though a few Punjabi activists such as Raja Risalu, Asif Khan, and Rauf Malik passed it out of a sense of commitment to the language, for the majority of the candidates it was a mere formality, an easy exam that gave them an additional diploma and better chances on the job market. As Shafqat Tanvir Mirza explained in his interview with Maqsood Saqib: "The candidates were not committed to Punjabi. It was just a means for them to find a better job, to progress, and even to become civil servants." Shafqat Tanvir Mirza, "Interview," in *Puchāṃ dasāṃ*, ed. Maqsood Saqib (Lahore: Suchet, 2013), 195.

91. Raja Risalu, *Lā prīt ajehī Moḥammad* (Lahore: Pakistan Punjabi Adabī Board, 2008), 127.
92. Ain ul-Haq Faridkoti, "Khoj," in *Āzādī magroṃ panjābī adab*, ed. Asif Khan (Lahore: Pakistan Punjabi Adabī Board, 1985), 16.
93. Rashid Jebi, "Panjābī zubān te radio Pākistān," *Panjdaryā*, June 1966, 34.
94. Rahman, *Language and Politics in Pakistan*, 112. "The Urdu-speaking *Mohajir* elite was perceived as having a cultural and ideological arrogance that further aggravated the issue. It believed its own language to be far superior to the regional languages spoken in the areas that now constituted Pakistan." Rashid Abbas and Farida Shaheed, *Pakistan: Ethno-Politics and Contending Elites* (Geneva: United Nations Research Institute on Social Development, 1993), 14.
95. Qamar uz-Zaman, Letter, *Monthly Panjābī*, February–March 1952, 86.
96. Noor Bijnauri, Letter, *Daily Imroz*, October 6, 1951.
97. *Daily Imroz*, July 10, 1955.
98. Faqeer Mohammad Faqeer, "Qayām-e Pākistān toṃ bʿad Panjābī bolī la'ī kīte ga'e jatan," *Bābā-e Panjābī Number, Timāhī Panjābī*, July–December 2000, 39.
99. Aziz, *The Coffee Houses of Lahore*, 266–267. Aziz coined the derogatory term *Urda* to designate intellectuals belonging to the Urdu-speaking *Mohajir* community. The halqa refers to weekly meetings of the *Ḥalqa-e Arbāb-e Żauq* (Circle of the Men of Good Taste).
100. Abdul Haq Khammi, ed., *Panjāb Rang* (Lahore: Panjābī Majlis, 1958), 7.
101. Jebi, "Panjābī zubān," 33–34.
102. Mehmood, *Panjābī maẓmūn*, 18–20.
103. Jebi, "Panjābī zubān," 34–35.
104. Mehmood, *Panjābī maẓmūn*, 20–21.
105. Mushtaq Gazdar, *Pakistan Cinema 1947–1997* (Karachi: Oxford University Press, 1997), 6–10.
106. Naveed Shahzad, *Išārya pākistāni panjābī filmī gīt* (Lahore: PILAC, 2017), 1–21.

3. Lahore's Intellectual Landscape

1. Intizar Hussain, *Cirāġoṃ kā dhu'āṃ* (Lahore: Sang-e-meel, 2012); K. K. Aziz, *The Coffee House of Lahore: A Memoir 1942–1957* (Lahore: Sang-e-meel, 2007); Anis Nagi,

Ek adhūrī sarguzašt (Lahore: Jamāliyāt, 2008); Ahmad Salim, *Sawāneḥ-e 'umrī Ḥamīd Axtar* (Lahore: Book Home, 2010); Kamran Asdar Ali, *Surkh Salam: Communist Politics and Class Activism in Pakistan 1947–1972* (Karachi: Oxford University Press, 2015); Sadia Toor, *The State of Islam: Culture and Cold War Politics in Pakistan* (London: Pluto, 2011).

2. Khizar Humayun Ansari, *The Emergence of Socialist Thought Among North Indian Muslims, 1917–1947* (Karachi: Oxford University Press, 2015), 204–213.
3. Sajjad Zaheer, *Rūšnā'ī* (New Delhi: Qaumī Council Barā-e Furūġ-e Urdu, [1956] 2006), 205–206.
4. Irfan Waheed Usmani, "Print Culture and Left-Wing Radicalism in Lahore, Pakistan, c.1947–1971" (PhD diss., National University of Singapore, 2016), 253.
5. Abdullah Malik, *Mustaqbil hamārā hai* (Lahore: People's Publishing House [PPH], 1950), 52, 98–101.
6. Usmani, "Print Culture," 253. Kamran Asdar Ali reproduced the deliberations of one such meeting in *Surkh Salam*, 137–140.
7. Usmani, "Print Culture," 255.
8. Ali, *Surkh Salam*, 93.
9. Ali, *Surkh Salam*, 93, 100.
10. Rauf Malik, *Surx syāsat* (Lahore: Jamhūrī, 2017), 275.
11. Ali, *Surkh Salam*, 100–103.
12. Ali, *Surkh Salam*, 184.
13. Ali, *Surkh Salam*, 185–186.
14. Usmani, "Print Culture," 62–63.
15. Usmani, "Print Culture," 266, 463.
16. Malik, *Surx syāsat*, 288.
17. Usmani, "Print Culture," 189–191.
18. See Rakhshanda Jalil, *Liking Progress, Loving Change: A Literary History of the Progressive Writers' Movement in Urdu* (New Delhi: Oxford University Press, 2014); Ansari, *The Emergence of Socialist Thought Among North Indian Muslims*; Hafeez Malik, "The Marxist Literary Movement in India and Pakistan," *Journal of Asian Studies* 26, no. 4 (1967): 649–664.
19. Majid Nizami, *The Press in Pakistan* (Lahore: Department of Political Science, University of the Punjab, 1958), 7.
20. The *Majlis-e Eḥrār-e Islām* was a political party founded in 1929 and led by Ata Ullah Shah Bukhari. The party, an avowed enemy of the Ahmadi faith since 1933, launched an anti-Ahmadi movement in 1953 that culminated in riots in Lahore.
21. Anwar Sadid, *Urdu adab kī teḥrīkeṃ* (Karachi: Anjuman-e Taraqqī-e Urdu Pakistan, 1996), 545.
22. Sadid, *Urdu adab kī teḥrīkeṃ*, 543.
23. Hussain, *Cirāġoṃ kā dhu'āṃ*, 47.
24. See Ali Usman Qasmi, *The Ahmadis and the Politics of Religious Exclusion in Pakistan* (London: Anthem, 2015), 65–164; Shorish Kashmiri, *Teḥrīk-e Xatam-e Nubuwwat* (Lahore: Caṭṭān, [1974] 2011), 131–145. Anti-Ahmadi activists demanded that Ahmadis be declared non-Muslims and that Foreign Minister Zafarullah Khan, who happened to be Ahmadi, be replaced.

25. Nizami, *The Press in Pakistan*, 59.
26. Shamsuddin Siddiqui, "Qaumī Šāʿirī," in *Pākistān meṃ Urdu*, ed. Mohammad Tahir Faruqi and Khatir Ghaznavi (Peshawar: University Book Agency, 1966).
27. Wasi Raza, "Urdu Novel," in Faruqi and Ghaznavi, *Pākistān meṃ Urdu*, 368–369.
28. Raza, "Urdu Novel," 369.
29. Sadid, *Urdu adab kī teḥrīkeṃ*, 600–610, 612.
30. Malik, *Mustaqbil hamārā hai*, 76–77.
31. Nagi, *Ek adhūrī sarguzašt*, 115–116.
32. Anis Nagi, *Nayā š'erī ufaq: 1960 kī na'ī šāʿirī kī teḥrīk* (Lahore: Jamāliyāt, [1969] 1988); Salim Akhtar, *Urdu adab kī muxtaṣartarīn tārīx* (Delhi: Kitābī Duniyā, 2005), 608–613.

4. The Marxist Punjabi Movement (1947–1959)

1. Ahmad Salim, *Sawāneḥ-e 'umrī Ḥamīd Axtar* (Lahore: Book Home, 2010), 115.
2. Salim, *Sawāneḥ-e 'umrī Ḥamīd Axtar*, 116.
3. Salim, *Sawāneḥ-e 'umrī Ḥamīd Axtar*, 119–120. The event was also narrated by Aftab Ahmed in his collection of portraits *Ba-yād-e ṣoḥbat-e nāzuk xyālāṃ* (Islamabad: Dost, 1997), 82.
4. M. D. Taseer, "Rūdād-e Urdu," in *Maqālāt-e Tāśīr*, ed. Mumtaz Akhtar Mirza (Lahore: Majlis-e taraqqī-e adab, [1948] 1978), 266.
5. M. D. Taseer, "Ištirākiyat-pasandoṃ kā naẓāriya-e 'ilm-o adab," in *Maqālāt-e Tāśīr*, ed. Mumtaz Akhtar Mirza (Lahore: Majlis-e taraqqī-e adab, [1949] 1978), 293. Taseer is undoubtedly referring to Stalin's "Marxism and the National Question" (1913), an important pamphlet that also discussed the right to education in mother tongues; an Urdu translation was published by the People's Publishing House (PPH). This pamphlet is analyzed by Hélène Carrère d'Encausse in "Unité prolétarienne et diversité nationale: Lénine et la théorie de l'autodétermination," *Revue française de science politique* 21, no. 2 (1971): 227–229.
6. Mohammad Hasan Askari, "Taqsīm-e Hind ke bʿad," *Caṭṭān*, October 1948, reprinted in *Majmū'a-e Ḥasan 'Askarī* (Lahore: Sang-e-meel, 2008), 1132.
7. Abdullah Malik gave a detailed account of this conference in his pamphlet *Mustaqbil hamārā hai* (The Future Is Ours) published by PPH in 1950. A selection of the speeches delivered and poems read during the conference was published in *Saverā* 7–8 (1950).
8. Malik, *Mustaqbil hamārā hai*, 70.
9. Malik, *Mustaqbil hamārā hai*, 82–83. An expanded version of this resolution was published in *Saverā* 7–8 (1950): "Unfortunately the progressive movement has so far been primarily confined to Urdu writers. While the vast majority of progressive writers' mother tongues is Punjabi, Pashto, Bengali or Sindhi, they hesitate to write in these languages . . . Write in Urdu as much as you want, try to promote Urdu as much as you can, but remember that as long as you don't write in the languages of the peoples of Pakistan your movement will remain confined to the cities! It will not be able to take roots among the masses. By not

writing in the languages of the People you are not only depriving them of revolutionary ideas, you are also not allowing them to develop their literary talents . . . If we launch a movement in favor of writing in the languages of the masses then we can be joined by a large number of peasant and worker writers. If you don't follow this your movement will remain confined to the middle class. The masses will not manage to understand many of your ideas, which could be useful to them and you will not succeed in making your movement part of the class struggle" (245).

10. Malik, *Mustaqbil hamārā hai*, 65.
11. *Saverā* 7–8 (1950): 47–48.
12. Malik, *Mustaqbil hamārā hai*, 84.
13. Malik, *Mustaqbil hamārā hai*, 92. Abdullah Malik did not name the essay in his report; he simply mentioned that Sharif Kunjahi read an essay "in Punjabi in favor of the Punjabi language." Nevertheless, Rauf Malik, who attended the conference, confirmed that the essay was *Ūṃṭ te baddū*. A version of it was published on the Punjabi page of *Daily Imroz* on March 13, 1955, and another (slightly edited) version was included in Sharif Kunjahi's collection of essays *Jhātyāṃ* (Overviews), published in 1960 by Rauf Malik. Sharif Kunjahi, *Jhātyāṃ* (Lahore: Azeez Book Depot, [1960] 1994), 19–22.
14. The version quoted here is the version that was published on the Punjabi page of *Daily Imroz*, March 13, 1955.
15. Maulana Salahuddin Ahmad, "Taqsīm-e mulk kā aṡar Urdu zubān aur adab par," in *Behtarīn Adab* 1948, ed. Idāra-e Adab-e Laṯīf (Lahore: Maktaba-e Urdu), 90.
16. Malik, *Mustaqbil hamārā hai*, 93.
17. Sajjad Zaheer, *Rūšnā'ī* (New Delhi: Qaumī Council Barā-e Furūġ-e Urdu, [1956] 2006), 303–304.
18. Abid Hassan Minto, interview by the author, March 14, 2018. Rauf Malik, another Marxist veteran, also remembered these Punjabi sessions and remembered that he too heard Ahmad Rahi for the first time at one of them (Rauf Malik, interview by the author, March 16, 2018).
19. Irfan Waheed Usmani, "Print Culture and Left-Wing Radicalism in Lahore, Pakistan, c.1947–1971" (PhD diss., National University of Singapore, 2016), 253.
20. Usmani, "Print Culture," 253.
21. K. K. Aziz wrote: "Everyone spoke in Punjabi but wrote in Urdu. To take this irrationality one step further, he spoke Urdu at the Halqa, though he continued the discussion on the same subject in the coffee house or tea house in Punjlish." *The Coffee Houses of Lahore: A Memoir 1942–1957* (Lahore: Sang-e-meel, 2007), 266.
22. This was confirmed by Rauf Malik (interview by the author, July 27, 2018). In the course of this research, we found only one transcript of a discussion that took place during the weekly meetings of the progressives. It is a transcript of the meeting held on December 11, 1948, which was published in *Nuqūš* 6 (January 1949): 179–185.
23. Malik, interview, July 27, 2018.
24. The poems were *Kaṇkāṃ de gīt* (Harvest Songs) by Amrita Pritam, *Idhar odhar* (Here and There) by Tanvir Naqvi, *Sac ka'o pare be'o* (Tell the Truth and Step Aside!) by Sharif Kunjahi, *Jaṭṭā pagṛī sambhāl* (O Farmer, Don't Drop Your Turban!)

by Afzal Parvez, *Canān ve terī cannī* (My Love I Am Your Moonlight) by Ahmad Rahi; *Iqrārāṃ wālī rāt* (The Night of Confessions) by Amrita Pritam, *Kaṇkāṃ te chankāṃ* (Harvests and Tinklings) by Abdul Majeed Bhatti, *Lamyāṃ syālī rātāṃ* (These Long Winter Nights) by Sharif Kunjahi, and *Navāṃ navāṃ bor* (New Buds) by Ahmad Rahi; *Akhyāṃ* (The Eyes) by Amrita Pritam, *Lehriye dūpaṭṭe* (Wavy Scarf) by Abdul Majeed Bhatti, *Mahīṭ* by Sharif Kunjahi, *Gīt* (Song) by Tanvir Naqvi, and *Dilāṃ de saude* (The Sold Hearts) by Ahmad Rahi.

25. Minto, interview.
26. Minto, interview.
27. Abid Hassan Minto, "Pākistān meṃ zubān kā masla," in *Nuqta-e Naẓar* (Lahore: Multimedia Affairs, 2003; first published in *Adab-e Laṭīf*, October 1951), 285.
28. Minto, "Pākistān meṃ zubān kā masla," 285–287.
29. See Malik, *Mustaqbil hamārā hai*, 93.
30. *Daily Imroz*, February 28, 1953.
31. Rauf Malik, *Surx syāsat* (Lahore: Jamhūrī, 2017), 273–274. Malik (1926–2021) was born into a respectable and religious family in the Old City of Lahore. He embraced communism in 1942 under the influence of his brother Abdullah Malik and of communist veteran Fazal Ilahi Qurban (Malik, *Surx syāsat*, 75). In 1944, while studying at Lahore's Islamia College, he became a member of the CPI. In the early 1950s, he became interested in Punjabi and passed the *Panjābī Fāẓil*. He started writing essays in *Daily Imroz* to introduce modern Punjabi literature, but his greatest contribution to Punjabi literature was his initiative to publish *Tirinjan* and *Navī rut*. Arrested in 1954 and freed in 1955, he resumed editorial activities in the early 1960s, publishing a few important Punjabi books including Abdul Majeed Bhatti's *Theḍḍā* (A Blow)—the first Punjabi novel written in Pakistan after independence—and *Jhātyāṃ* (Overviews), a collection of seminal essays by Sharif Kunjahi.
32. Malik, *Mustaqbil hamārā hai*, 110; Firozuddin Mansoor and Sibte Hasan, *Pākistān meṃ qaumī zubān kā masla* (Lahore: PPH, 1953), 56, 58.
33. Malik, *Surx syāsat*, 283–285.
34. Malik, interview, March 16, 2018. In reality, it took some six or seven months for Ahmad Rahi to write enough poems for the publication of a collection to be considered.
35. Malik, interview, March 16, 2018.
36. Malik, *Surx syāsat*, 287.
37. Malik, interview, July 27, 2018.
38. Malik, interview August 3, 2018.
39. Malik, interview, August 3, 2018.
40. Sibte Hasan was a member of the CPP's Politburo; Firozuddin Mansoor was in charge of the CPP for a while after the Rawalpindi conspiracy in 1951 and was secretary of its regional committee between 1952 and 1954. Kamran Asdar Ali, *Surkh Salam: Communist Politics and Class Activism in Pakistan 1947-1972* (Karachi: Oxford University Press, 2015), 93, 202, 303.
41. Malik, interview, July 27, 2018.
42. Mansoor, and Hasan, *Pākistān meṃ qaumī zubān kā masla*, 50–52.
43. Usmani, "Print Culture," 269.

44. The title refers to a verse of the Sufi poet Sultan Bahu *Dil daryā samundroṃ ḍūnghe* (The rivers of the heart are deeper than the ocean).
45. Born in 1907 in Lahore, into a family of landowners, Mian Iftikharuddin studied at Oxford (where he was a classmate of Sajjad Zaheer) and adopted Marxist ideas during that time. Back in India, he embraced a political career and joined the Congress Party. In 1945, he joined Muhammad Ali Jinnah's Muslim League and was elected to the Provincial Assembly of Punjab. He launched the English daily *Pakistan Times* in 1947, and the Urdu daily *Daily Imroz* in 1948, with the aim of supporting the Muslim League. But after the death of Muhammad Ali Jinnah, Iftikharuddin started to distance himself from the Muslim League, and his two newspapers quickly became opposition newspapers. After independence, Iftikharuddin became a member of Pakistan's Constituent Assembly and minister for refugees in the provincial government of Punjab. A dispute with the new leadership of the Muslim League led to his expulsion from the party in 1951. He subsequently founded his own party, the Azad Pakistan Party, whose program is summarized as follows by Kamran Asdar Ali: "Similar to the Communist Party's manifesto Iftikharuddin's Azad Pakistan Party called for real freedom, democracy and social justice along with the rejection of the Commonwealth and British presence in the country" (Ali, *Surkh Salam*, 185). Iftikharuddin was elected to the second Constituent Assembly in 1955 and sat with the opposition in the Punjab assembly between 1956 and 1958.
46. Mian Iftikharuddin, *Selected Speeches and Statements*, ed. Abdullah Malik (Lahore: Nigārishāt, 1971), 391–392.
47. Rauf Malik said: "He was a very good Punjabi orator, he would make fiery speeches in Punjabi in the rural areas, among the peasants, and even in the assembly, in the middle of a speech in English, he would suddenly switch to Punjabi." Malik, interview, July 27, 2018.
48. Usmani, "Print Culture," 243.
49. Usmani, "Print Culture," 113.
50. The political orientation of *Daily Imroz* mirrored that of Mian Iftikharuddin and his party. *Daily Imroz* was a vocal critic of Anglo-American imperialist interference in national and international politics and of the Western bloc's intrusive role in newly independent countries in the Middle East and Asia. As an opposition newspaper, it often attacked the wealthy landowners who had infiltrated the Muslim League and were manipulating it from within, attempting to keep the working classes and their representatives away from power. Usmani, "Print Culture," 114–119, 122–140.
51. The March 27, 1948 editorial endorses this support: "We are happy that Muhammad Ali Jinnah has in the debate over the Official language reiterated the supremacy of Urdu and it is quite fair to say that there is no language apart from Urdu which can be declared an Official language of Pakistan . . . and it is time for the Urdu-Bengali controversy which has started in East Pakistan to end."
52. Probably out of solidarity with Faqeer Mohammad Faqeer, who had started a movement for the reopening of this department.
53. The Lahore fort was used as a prison and interrogation center.

54. Malik, interview, March 16, 2018.
55. Zaheer Babur (1928–1998), originally from Angah, Khushab district, was Ahmad Nadeem Qasmi's nephew. The latter had taken charge of his education and his career. He had brought him to Lahore, helped him finish his studies (he passed an MA), and hired him at *Daily Imroz*. Babur quickly rose through the ranks to become assistant editor, then editor, and finally editor-in-chief of the newspaper. He was detained in 1951 for a short period during the anti-Marxist purges. He was notorious for his uncompromising editorials. He published a few essays of literary criticism and short stories, but he remained above all a journalist. His career began with his writing/editing of the Punjabi column *Gall-bāt*, and he remained so committed to Punjabi that even after the government nationalized *Daily Imroz* in 1959, he ensured that *Gall-bāt* (which was by then spread over an entire page) did not disappear. For details on Zaheer Babur's career and politics, see Ahmad Nadeem Qasmi, *Mere hamqadam* (Lahore: Sang-e-meel, 2007), 38–47; Hameed Akhtar, *Pursiš-e aḥwāl* (Lahore: Afra, 1999), 66–68.
56. The author is referring here to Mian Iftikharuddin, a "genuine senior member" of the Muslim league, who had just left it.
57. The writer was most probably Muhammad Tufail (1923–1986), editor-in-chief of literary journal *Nuqūš*.
58. Jean-François Courouau, "Les apologies de la langue française (XVIe siècle) et de la langue occitane (XVIe–XVIIe siècles): Naissance d'une double mythographie: Première partie," *Nouvelle Revue du XVIe Siècle* 21, no. 2 (2003): 35–51; "Les apologies de la langue française (XVIe siècle) et de la langue occitane (XVIe–XVIIe siècles): Naissance d'une double mythographie: Deuxième partie," *Nouvelle Revue du XVIe Siècle* 22, no. 2 (2004): 23–39.
59. Courouau, "Les apologies: Première partie," 48–51. Further examples of the masterpiece argument are found in the writings of conservative group members such as Abdul Majeed Salik and Shorish Kashmiri. Salik, "Sānūṃ Panjābī bolī te faxr ai," *Monthly Panjābī* 1, no. 2 (October 1951): 9–10; Kashmiri, "Panjābī dī taraqqī," *Monthly Panjābī* 1, no. 2 (October 1951): 45–46.
60. Courouau discusses this confusion between language and literature, which was common among the apologists of French during sixteenth century, in his 2003 article "Les apologies: Première partie," 46. His analysis owes much to the chapter titled "On croit qu'on parle de la langue, mais on parle de la littérature," in Henri Meschonnic, *De la langue française* (Paris: Hachette, 1997), 89–110.
61. Sadia Toor writes: "The progressives tended to speak in terms of *awam* ('the people') while the nationalists preferred the term *qaum* ('nation'). The choice between these two terms was not a semantic one. It represented a world of difference between two political philosophies and two incommensurable sets of interests." Toor, *The State of Islam: Culture and Cold War Politics in Pakistan* (London: Pluto, 2011), 69.
62. The June 5 column discussed the corrupt milieu of cinema; the June 12 column, corrupt politics; the June 19 column, the low moral standards of Pakistani people; and the July 3 column, corruption in the literary milieu.
63. Ahmad Nadeem Qasmi, "Doctor Faqīr Moḥammad Faqīr," *Bābā-e Panjābī Number, Timāhī Panjābī*, July–December 2000, 46.

64. Each column by Mirza Sultan Baig reads like a series of disconnected jokes. The only reason for featuring such material seems to be the wish to attract the popular public who listened with fervor to the program *Dehātī bhāyoṃ ke liye*.
65. *Šeryā ve šeryā!* (Lion, O Lion!) was published on July 22, 1958, *Pinḍ dā bāo* (The "Sir" of the Village) on October 25, 1958, *Dil dā parchavāṃ* (The Reflection of the Heart) on April 4, 1959, *Sadā suhāgan* (May Your Husband Live Forever) on June 6, 1959, and *Ikk sī rāni te ikk sī bādšāh* (Once Upon a Time There Was a King and a Queen) on July 25, 1959.
66. The essays on the Punjabi language were Sharif Kunjahi, *Ūṃt te baddū* (The Camel and the Bedouin), March 13, 1955; Shaukat Ali, *Sāḍḍī Panjābī zubān* (Our Punjabi Language), May 29, 1955; Agha Sadiq, *Panjābī dī taraqqī dā masla* (The Issue of Development of Punjabi), August 21, 1955; Mohammad ud-Din Dilgir, *Panjābī adab dī ẓarūrat* (The Need for a Punjabi Literature), November 13, 1955; Ahmad Nisar, *Adabī Panjābī dī ẓarūrat* (The Need for a Literary Punjabi), January 8, 1956; Mohammad Alam, Kapurthalvi *Panjābī likhaṇ dā navāṃ ṭarīqa* (A New Way of Writing Punjabi), February 1, 1958; Sadiq Ali, Ajiz *Sāḍḍī bolī* (Our Language), June 10, 1958; and Akmal Aleemi, *Mʿeyārī Panjābī dā masla* (The Issue of Standard Punjabi), August 23–30, 1958. The essays on Waris Shah were Sharif Kunjahi, *Rāṃjhā ikk vigṛyā hoyā bāl* (Ranjha, a Spoiled Child), 27 March 1955; Faqeer Mohammad Faqeer, *Hīr Wāriṡ Šāh vic taṣawwuf te jog mat* (Spirituality and the Sect of Yogis in Waris Shah's Heer), August 28–September 4, 1955; Abdullah Asri, *Hīr Rāṃjhe dā qiṣṣa* (The Heer Ranjha Epic), December 25, 1955–January 1, 1956; Rafiq Chaudhry, *Wāriṡ de ikk miṣrʿe dī tašrīḥ* (Analysis of a Verse by Waris Shah), August 3, 1957; Mohammad Alam, Kapurthalvi *Wāriṡ Šāh dā ʻišq* (The Love of Waris Shah), October 5, 1957; Ahmad Nisar, *Wāriṡ Šāh dī ikk talmīḥ* (A Mythological Allusion of Waris Shah), June 8, 1957; Rafiq Chaudhry, *Wāriṡ Šāh de ikk miṣrʿe dī tašrīḥ* (Analysis of a Verse of Waris Shah), August 3, 1957; and Faqeer Mohammad Faqeer *Rāṃjhā te Mirzā* (Ranjha and Mirza), July 14, 1956. Essays on aspects of classical literature were Sharif Kunjahi, *Ṣūfyāṃ dī šāʿirī* (Poetry of the Sufis), May 1, 1955; Afzal Parvez, *Myāṃ Moḥammad ṣāḥab dī Mirzā Ṣāḥibāṃ* (Mian Muhammad's *Mirza Sahiban*), June 12 1955; Afzal Parvez, *Panjābī beḥrāṃ* (Punjabi Poetry's Meters), January 22 and 29 and February 25, 1956; Rafiq Chaudhry, *Panjābī qiṣṣyāṃ dā sabb toṃ vaḍḍā kirdār Mirzā* (The Greatest Character in Punjabi Epics: Mirza), May 26, June 2, and July 7–14, 1956; Faqeer Mohammad Faqeer, *Panjābī qiṣṣyāṃ dā sabb toṃ vaḍḍā kirdār Mirzā ai ki na'īṃ?* (Could the Greatest Character of Punjabi Epics be Mirza?), June 16–23, 1956; and Sadiq Ali Ajiz, *Faẓal Šāh Navāṃkotī*, April 18, 1959. Essays on contemporary poets were Ahmad Rahi, *Ustad Fīroz Dīn Šarf Marḥūm*, March 27, 1955; Arshi, *Fīroz Sa'īṃ*, October 2–22, 1955; Arshi, *Fīroz Sa'īṃ dī āšiqāna šāʿirī* (Firoz Sain's Love Poems), November 20, 1955; Majid Siddiqi, *Šāh Šarf Marḥūm*, December 20, 1958; Majid Siddiqi, *Myāṃ Maula Baxš Kuštā Amritsarī*, June 4, 1959; and Raja Risalu, *Maulā Baxš Kuštā Amritsarī*, July 7, 1959.
67. Folk songs from the central regions of Punjab were discussed in Nasim Akhtar, *Panjāb de lok gīt* (Punjab's Folk Songs), April 24, 1955; and Saif Anjum Dar, *Lok gīt te sāḍḍā mʿoāšra* (Folk Songs and Our Society), August 24, 1957. Folk songs from Pothohar were the subject of Afzal Parvez, *Šāhlā musāfir koī na thīve* (May God

Let No One Become a Traveller!), July 21, 1957; Zya Rizvi, *Chabbe lok gītāṃ dī ikk šāx* (*Chabbe*, a Type of Folk Songs), February 21, 1959; Majid Siddiqui, *Lok gītāṃ vic muzāḥ* (Humour in Folk Songs), May 2, 1959; Zya Rizvi, *Challe, lok gītāṃ dī ikk šāx* (*Challe*, a Type of Folk Songs), May 16, 1959; Zya Rizvi, *Ilāqā Dhanī de lok gīt* (Folk Songs of the Dhani Area), August 29, 1959; and Zya Rizvi, *Māhyā lok gītāṃ dī šāx* (*Mahya*, a Type of Folk Songs), December 24, 1959.

68. *Monthly Panjābī* was the first Punjabi journal published in Pakistan after independence. Its editors-in-chief was Faqeer Mohammad Faqeer and Abdul Majeed Salik. It began publication in September 1951.
69. This reference is probably to Abdul Majeed Salik's Punjabi Cultural Society.
70. Examples of this approach are Zaheer Kashmiri, *Adab ke mādī naẕariye* (Lahore: Kamal, 1945), especially the essay *Urdu šāʿirī kā samājī pasmanẕar* (Social Context of Urdu Poetry) included in this book; and Ehtisham Hussain's essay *Ġālib kā tafakkur aur uskā pasmanẕar* (Ghalib's Thought and Its Context), in *Behtarīn Adab 1950*, ed. Idāra-e Adab-e Laṯīf (Lahore: Maktaba-e Urdu, 1951), 11–40.
71. The 1949 manifesto of the progressive writers states: "On the contrary, we progressive writers do not see literature as only the mirror of life, but as a means of changing and improving life. We consider as the foundation of our movement the notion that literature should change lives, contribute to the class struggle and pave the path for revolution" (Malik, *Mustaqbil hamārā hai*, 79).
72. He wrote in his essay *Jadīd urdu adab mein inḥeṭāṭī rujḥānāt* (Decadent Tendencies of Modern Urdu Literature): "A last tendency is that of pessimism . . . in poetry this tendency is largely inherited from the ancients. But at the time when our classical poetry was being produced there was no scope for the betterment of society, life was stagnating and that is the reason why one sees at that time such a grip of pessimism." Abid Hassan Minto, "*Jadīd Urdu adab meṃ inḥeṭāṭī rujḥānāt*," in *Nuqta-e Naẕar* (Lahore: Multimedia Affairs, 2003; first published in *Šāhrāh*, New-Delhi, 1956), 211–212.
73. The four essays on Pakistani literature are Jameel Malik, *Afẓal Parvez kī panjābī šāʿirī ke seḥtmand pehlū* (Healthy Aspects of Afzal Parvez's Punjabi Poetry), May 10 and 17, 1954; Faqeer Mohammad Faqeer, *Šumālī maġrībī Pakistan ke tīn panjābī šāʿir* (Three Punjabi Poets of North Western Pakistan), August 15, 1954; Faqeer Mohammad Faqeer, *Panjābī ġazal kā ek jā'izā* (An Assessment of the Punjabi *ġazal*), November 4, 1956; and Ahmad Sharif, *Aḥmad Ẓafar kī panjābī šāʿirī* (Ahmad Zafar's Punjabi Poetry), June 23 and 30, 1957. The other four are Abdul Rauf Malik, *Mašrīqī Panjāb kā nayā panjābī adab* (East Punjab's New Punjabi Literature), August 21, 1955; Somar Anand, *Panjābī kī nāmvār šāʿirā Amritā Prītam* (A Famous Poetess of Punjabi: Amrita Pritam), September 2, 1956; Sharif Kunjahi, *Amritā Prītam ke na'e šʿerī majmu'e par ek naẕar: 'Sunehṛe'* (A Look at the New Poetry Collection of Amrita Pritam: 'The Messages'), March 17, 1957; and Sharif Kunjahi *Jagtār Papīhā, Panjābī kā ek nauxez gītkār* (An Emerging Punjabi Songwriter: Jagtar Papiha), August 4, 1957.
74. Abdul Majeed Bhatti, *Panjāb kā ek munfarid šāʿir Wāriṡ Šāh* (A Unique Poet of Punjab, Waris Shah), August 20 and 27, 1951; Afzal Parvez, *Rāṃjhā aur Wāriṡ Šāh* (Ranjha and Waris Shah), September 17, 1951; A Hameed, *Wāriṡ Šāh kā ek kirdār* (A Character of Waris Shah), February 25, 1952; Afzal Parvez, *Hīr Wāriṡ Šāh aur*

kahāvaṭeṃ (Heer Waris Shah and Proverbs), March 3, 1952; Ahmad Rahi, *Panjāb ke 'awāmi adab aur saqāfat kā ṣaḥīḥ tarjumān Wāriṡ Šāh* (A True Spokesperson for Punjab's Popular Literature and Culture: Waris Shah), February 28, 1953; Sufi Ghulam Mustafa Tabassum, *Wāriṡ kī Hīr* (Waris Shah's Heer), February 28, 1953; Abdul Majeed Bhatti, *Wāriṡ Šāh aur bhāg bharī* (Waris Shah and 'the Lucky One'), August 31, 1953; Arshi, *Wāriṡ, ek muballiġ-e Islām* (A Preacher of Islam: Waris Shah), May 31, 1959.

75. Arshi, *Panjāb kā ek ātišbayāṃ šāʿir Ġulām Rasūl* (A Flamboyant Poet of Punjab: Ghulam Rasool), April 19, May 17 and 24, July 12, 1954; Arshi, *Panjābī ke 'aẓīm šāʿir Ġulām Rasūl ke kalām meiṃ hajw-o żam* (Satire in the Poetry of the Great Poet of Punjabi Ghulam Rasool), January 17 and 24, 1955; Faqeer Mohammad Faqeer, *Panjābī kā šʿola-nawā šāʿir Ġulām Rasūl* (A Flamboyant Punjabi Poet: Ghulam Rasool), July 8, 1956; Afzal Parvez, *Qiṣṣa Saif ul-Mulūk* (The Epic of Saif ul-Mulook), October 8, 1951; Abdus Salam Khurshid *Sassī Punnū*, July 21, 1952; Maulana Mohammad Afzal Qadir *Ḥaẓrat Sultān Bāhū*, June 26 and July 2, 1955; Arshad Multani, *Panjābī zubān ke 'aẓīm šāʿir Xwaja Ġulām Farīd* (A Great Poet of the Punjabi Language: Khwaja Ghulam Farid), July 7, 1957; Peer Ghulam Dastgir *Sayed Bulle Šāh*, December 15 and 22, 1957; Abu Yahya Imam Khan *Sayed 'Alī Ḥaidar kā kalām* (The Poetry of Syed Ali Haidar), July 26, 1959.
76. Asghar Ali's statement quoted in *Gall-bāt* on September 22, 1951 is a good example of this negative perception: "And as far as a work like Waris Shah's Heer is concerned, it's a simple love story, written in a corrupted language full of old-fashioned words derived from Sanskrit."
77. The folklore of Majha and Doab is discussed in Abdul Qadir Rashk, *Ḍholak gīt* (Tambourine Songs), July 2, 1951; Rahat Gujrati, *Māhyā*, October 22, 1951); Afzal Parvez, *Mahye ke rūp* (Forms of *Mahyas*), November 26, 1951; Abdul Majeed Bhatti, *Panjābī gīt jo pāṃc daryāoṃ kī zamīn par basne wālī behneṃ gātī haiṃ* (Some Punjabi Songs That the Sisters Who Live in the Land of the Five Rivers Sing), October 1, 1952; Abdul Qadir Rashk, *Panjāb ke lok gītoṃ meṃ 'auratoṃ kā ḥiṣṣa* (The Role of Women in the Folk Songs of Punjab), May 3, 1954; Abdul Qadir Rashk, *Panjāb meṃ behnoṃ ke gīt* (Songs of the Sisters in Punjab), January 18 and 25, 1954. The articles on Siraiki folk songs were all written by Dr. Mehr Abdul Haq: *Faṣloṃ ke git multānī zubān meṃ* (Harvest Songs in the Multani Language), February 22, 1959; *Loryāṃ* (Lullabies), March 1, 1959; *Mail gīt aur jhumreṃ multānī zubān meṃ* (Songs of Gatherings and the *Holi* Songs in the Multani Language), March 8, 1959; *Baccoṃ ke khel ke gīt aur bol multānī zubān meṃ* (Songs in the Multani Language Sung by Children During Games), March 15, 1959; *Muzāḥya gīt multānī zubān meṃ* (Humorous Songs in the Multani Language), April 12, 1959; *Jagrāte ke git multānī zubān meṃ* (Night Vigil Songs in the Multani Language), April 26, 1959; *Māhye aur ḍhole multānī zubān meṃ* (*Mahyas* and *dholas* in the Multani Language), May 17, 1959. The articles on Pothohar's folk songs were: Aziz Ibn Kamil, *Poṭhohār ke nāc gāne* (Dances and Songs of the Pothohar Region), November 14, 1955; Afzal Parvez, *Thāl aur kiklī*, October 14, 1956; *Gandum ke gīt* (Wheat Songs), June 2, 1957; *Ek poṭhohārī gīt: 'Sāwṇī'* (A Pothohari Song: *Sāwṇī*), May 1, 1958; *Poṭhohār kā lok nāc: "Sammī"* (*Sammi*: a Folk Dance from Pothohar), August 14, 1959.

78. Devendra Satyarthi, *Maiṃ hūṃ xāna-ba doš* (I am a Nomad), published in 1941, and de *Gāe jā Hindūstān* (India, Keep Singing!) published in 1946; Saadat Hasan Manto, *Dehātī bolyāṃ* (Countryside Lyrics), in *Manṭo ke maẓāmīn*, originally published in 1942 (New Delhi: Sāqī Book Depot, 1997), 51–58 and 59–66.
79. A *Māhyā* is a Love poem that consists of three lines. The first line rhymes with the third. The two rhyming lines are the same length, while the second line is usually shorter. Here is an example:

    Ikk gabhrū madānāṁ dā
    Ikk can merā māhī
    Dūjā can asmānāṁ dā

    A young man from the plains
    A moon is my beloved
    And the second moon is in the sky

    Quoted in Gibb Schreffler, "Western Punjabi Song Forms: *Māhīā* and *Ḍholā*," *Journal of Punjab Studies* 18, no. 1–2 (2011): 81.
80. Dr. Mehr Abdul Haq's *Daily Imroz* essays were collected and published in 1964 in a book, *Siraikī lok gīt* (Multan: Bazm-e Saqāfat, 1964). Note that his and Afzal Parvez's systematic collection of folkloric material was contemporary with Bengali and Sindhi folklorists' first endeavors at collecting material in their respective areas: the Bengali Academy's folk project began in 1955 and Dr. Nabi Bakhsh Baloch's folk project in 1957.
81. Usmani, "Print Culture," 189–191.
82. Salim, *Sawāneḥ-e 'umrī Ḥamīd Axtar*, 253–254.
83. Pascale Casanova writes that literary capital "depends on prestige, on the literary beliefs attached to a language, and on the literary value which is attributed to it. These factors depend on the age of a language, the prestige of its poetry, the refinement of the literary forms developed in it, traditions, the literary 'effects' associated, for example, with translations and their volume, etc." Casanova, "Consécration et accumulation de capital littéraire [La traduction comme échange inégal]," *Actes de la recherche en sciences sociales* 144 (September 2002): 8.
84. We have borrowed this dichotomy from Gisèle Sapiro, *La Guerre des écrivains 1940–1953* (Paris: Fayard, 1999).
85. Raja Risalu, *Lā prīt ajehī Moḥammad* (Lahore: Pakistan Punjabi Adabī Board, 2008), 13.
86. Risalu, *Lā prīt ajehī Moḥammad*, 13.
87. Ahmad Salim, "Tirinjan dī kuṛī," *Saver*, September 1999, 17.
88. Salim, "Tirinjan dī kuṛī," 18; Ahmad Salim, *Aḥmad Rāhī bātāṃ mulāqātāṃ* (Islamabad: Kūnj, 2005), 60–61.
89. Salim, *Aḥmad Rāhī*, 67–72.
90. Salim, "Tirinjan dī kuṛī," 19.
91. Salim, *Aḥmad Rāhī*, 66.

92. Salim, "Tirinjan dī kuṛī," 19.
93. Salim, *Aḥmad Rāhī*, 66–67. "*Yeh dāġ dāġ ujālā* (These tarnished rays)" is the first line of Faiz Ahmad Faiz's famous poem *Subḥ-e āzādī* (The Dawn of Freedom), included in his collection *Dast-e ṣabā* (Hand of Breeze) published by PPH in 1952.
94. A trauma made stronger by the fact that his own sister had been also abducted and didn't return to Pakistan until 1952 (Salim, *Aḥmad Rāhī*, 70).
95. Salim, *Aḥmad Rāhī*, 67–68.
96. Risalu, *Lā prīt ajehī Moḥammad*, 13.
97. Risalu, *Lā prīt ajehī Moḥammad*, 11–12.
98. Khalid Humayun, *Vīr tūṃ Kunjāh dā ai? Professor Šarīf Kunjāhi nāl gall-bāt* (Lahore: Sangat, 1999), 29–30, 37.
99. Humayun, *Vīr tūṃ Kunjāh dā ai?*, 37.
100. Humayun, *Vīr tūṃ Kunjāh dā ai?*, 37, 100.
101. Humayun, *Vīr tūṃ Kunjāh dā ai?*, 37, 88, 126.
102. Humayun, *Vīr tūṃ Kunjāh dā ai?*, 30, 36–37, 100.
103. Humayun, *Vīr tūṃ Kunjāh dā ai?*, 126.
104. Humayun, *Vīr tūṃ Kunjāh dā ai?*, 63.
105. Malik, interview, July 27, 2018. On Prof. Mohan Singh's innovations and *Sāve pattar*'s importance in Punjabi poetry, see Denis Matringe, *Littérature, histoire et religion au Panjab, 1890–1950* (Paris: Collège de France, 2009), 139–158.
106. Quoted in Aslam Rana, *Rang-sang, nave panjābī adab dā tanqīdī jā'iza* (Lahore: Azeez Book Depot, 1991), 32.
107. Sharif Kunjahi, *Jagrāte* (Lahore: Azeez Book Depot, [1965] 1984), 46–48, 58–59, 107–110.
108. Abdul Majeed Bhatti, *Theḍḍā* (Lahore: Hūnhār Book Depot, 1960), 2–3.
109. Bhatti, *Theḍḍā*, 4–5.
110. Bhatti, *Theḍḍā*, 7–9.
111. Zaheer, *Rūšnā'ī*, 303.
112. Bhatti, *Theḍḍā*, 10.
113. Afzal Parvez, *Kikrāṃ dī chāṃ* (Rawalpindi: Maktaba-e Xarābāt, 1971), 11.
114. This movement was initiated by Allama Mashriqi in Lahore in 1931; its goal was to deliver India from the influence of the English and to establish a unified Hindu and Muslim government.
115. Parvez, *Kikrāṃ dī chāṃ*, 17.
116. Sajjad Zaheer wrote: "The circle of progressive writers in Rawalpindi consists of a few young employees from government offices, a few college teachers and a few students. . . . Among the employees I met a young poet (his pen name was if I remember well "Parvez") in whom one felt a revolutionary and popular ardour. He had just started writing, his poetry was still immature." Zaheer, *Rūšnā'ī*, 309.
117. Parvez, *Kikrāṃ dī chāṃ*, 12.
118. Parvez, *Kikrāṃ dī chāṃ*, 12.
119. Parvez, *Kikrāṃ dī chāṃ*, 16–17.
120. *Lok Virsa* (National Institute of Folk and Traditional Heritage) is a government institution established in 1974 in Islamabad whose aim is the preservation of Pakistani folklore and crafts.

121. *Saverā* 9 (1951): 95, 101.
122. For example, poems in Urdu by Sharif Kunjahi, Ahmad Rahi, Abdul Majeed Bhatti, and Afzal Parvez can be found in the yearly anthology *Behtarīn Adab* (The Best Literature) published by the journal *Adab-e Laṭīf* in 1947, 1948, 1949, 1951, and 1952.
123. Aysha Nyaz Malik, "Salīm Kašir dī panjābī ġazal" (master's thesis, Lahore Oriental College, 2012), 24.
124. Amrita Pritam, "Ustād Dāman," *Panjābī Adab* 27 (July–September 1993).
125. Hameed Akhtar, *Pursiš-e aḥwāl* (Lahore: Afra, 1999), 72.
126. Minto, interview.
127. Pritam, "Ustād Dāman," 17.
128. Malik, interview, July 27, 2018.
129. Faiz Ahmad Faiz, *Salībeṃ mere darīce meṃ* (Karachi: Maktaba-e Danyāl, [1976] 1992), 103. Rauf Malik said: "Faiz's interest in Punjabi is the result of our efforts to promote our language." Malik, interview, July 27, 2018.
130. Shafqat Tanvir Mirza, "Interview," in *Puchāṃ dasāṃ*, ed. Maqsood Saqib (Lahore: Suchet, 2013), 194.
131. Safdar Mir, "Panjābī adībāṃ dī żehnī fiẓā," *Panjābī Adab*, September 1963, 8.
132. Saʿadat Hassan Manto, *Manṭo ke maẓāmīn* (New Delhi: Sāqī Book Depot, [1942] 1997), 51–58, 59–66.
133. Malik, interview, July 27, 2018. A manifestation of Manto's keen interest in Punjabi is his participation in a memorable session of the Punjabi Cultural Society (an organization for the promotion of Punjabi) in 1954, discussed in the next chapter.
134. Quoted in Malik, *Surx syāsat*, 232.
135. Khizar Humayun Ansari, *The Emergence of Socialist Thought Among North Indian Muslims, 1917–1947* (Karachi: Oxford University Press, 2015), 245. A *ġazal* is a single-rhymed lyrical poem ideally composed of five to twelve verses, with the first two hemistichs rhyming between them.
136. The critic Naveed Shahzad designates these "message" poems as *Maqṣadī* (goal-oriented) and *Tašhīrī* (disseminating an ideology). Shahzad, *Naẕm aur na'ī panjābī naẕm* (Lahore: Faculty of Oriental Learning, Punjab University, 2015), 61.
137. Salim, *Aḥmad Rāhī*, 69–70.
138. Kunjahi, *Jhātyāṃ*; Rana, *Rang-sang*; Arif Abdul Mateen, *Parakh paṛcol* (Lahore: Azeez Book Depot, 2000); Inam-ul Haque Javed, *Panjābī adab dā irtiqā, 1947–2003* (Lahore: Azeez Book Depot, 2004).
139. Kunjahi, *Jhātyāṃ*, 86.
140. Ahmad Rahi, *Tirinjan* (Lahore: Al-Hamd, [1953] 2005), 25.
141. Rahi, *Tirinjan*, 27, 30, 33.
142. Rahi, *Tirinjan*, 35.
143. Rahi, *Tirinjan*, 70.
144. Rahi, *Tirinjan*, 72, 83.
145. Rahi, *Tirinjan*, 96, 98.
146. Rahi, *Tirinjan*, 117.
147. Rahi, *Tirinjan*, 126, 130, 133.

148. Rahi, *Tirinjan*, 136.
149. Rahi, *Tirinjan*, 141.
150. Salim, *Aḥmad Rāhī*, 70.
151. Rahi, *Tirinjan*, 88. *Bolyāṃ* are series of *ṭappās*. A *ṭappā* is a poetic form composed of two lines. Here is an example from *Tirinjan*:

    Bārīṁ barsīṁ khaṭaṇ gayā te khaṭke lyā yā gajre
    Soṇ maiṁnūṁ akhyāṁ dī mere hoṁṭh ajjai tā'īṁ sajre

    You left twelve years ago to earn your living and brought back Flower Garlands
    I swear on my eyes that my lips have not lost their freshness. (61)
152. Abdul Majeed Bhatti, *Dil daryā* (Lahore: Nayā Idāra, 1955), 11–12, 43, 129.
153. Bhatti, *Dil daryā*, 11–12.
154. Bhatti, *Dil daryā*, 13–14.
155. Bhatti, *Dil daryā*, 19, 21, 25.
156. Bhatti, *Dil daryā*, 49, 73.
157. Bhatti, *Dil daryā*, 103.
158. Bhatti, *Dil daryā*, 111, 119, 121.
159. *Saverā* 9 (1951): 99, 100; *Saverā* 12 (1952): 260; *Saverā* 10–11 (1951): 396.
160. *Daily Imroz*, June 19, 1955.
161. *Daily Imroz*, May 29, 1955.
162. *Daily Imroz*, July 17, 1955.
163. *Daily Imroz*, May 22, 1955; July 24, 1955.
164. *Monthly Panjābī* 1, no. 1 (September 1951): 36–39.
165. *Monthly Panjābī* 1, no. 10 (June 1952): 29–30.
166. *Daily Imroz*, July 22, 1958; October 25, 1958.

5. The Conservative Punjabi Movement (1950–1960)

1. The issues of *Monthly Panjābī* published between 1951 and 1960 are valuable documents on the activities of the conservative group, its program, its discourse, and its literary production. In addition, Junaid Akram, a grand-nephew of Faqeer Mohammad Faqeer, compiled and published several collections of essays discussing Faqeer Mohammad Faqeer, his personality, and his contribution. Some essays included in these collections were written by members of the conservative group (Shafi Aqeel, Mohammad Baqir) and constitute reliable testimonies on the activities of the group. These combined sources have helped us trace the history of the conservative movement year after year. Junaid Akram, ed., *Bābā-e Panjābī, Doctor Faqīr Moḥammad Faqīr* (Lahore: Pakistan Punjabi Adabi Board, 1992); Junaid Akram, "Bābā panj daryāvāṃ dā," *Saver*, June 2000: 10–16; Junaid Akram, ed., *Kaccī munḍer par ek cirāġ, Bābā-e Panjābī Doctor Faqīr Moḥammad Faqīr kī zindagī ke aḥwāl-o āṡār ham-ʿaṣar šaxṣiyāt ke qalam se* (Lahore: Bazm-e Faqīr Pākistān, 2011).

2. Faqeer Mohammad Faqeer, "Qayām-e Pākistān toṃ bʿad Panjābī bolī la'ī kīte ga'e jatan," *Bābā-e Panjābī Number, Timāhī Panjābī*, July–December 2000, 36.
3. Faqeer, "Qayām-e Pākistān toṃ bʿad Panjābī bolī la'ī kīte ga'e jatan," 36.
4. Faqeer Mohammad Faqeer wrote that this meeting was held during the first week of July 1951 ("Merī āpbītī," *Bābā-e Panjābī Number, Timāhī Panjābī*, July–December 2000, 35; "Qayām-e Pākistān toṃ bʿad Panjābī bolī la'ī kīte ga'e jatan," 37), and this information was reproduced by Tariq Rahman in *Language, Ideology and Power* (Karachi: Oxford University Press, 2008), 231. But the year 1951 is erroneous because, according to the testimonies of Faqeer Mohammad Faqeer and Abdul Majeed Salik ("Xuṯba-e ṣadārat, Panjābī Conference," *Monthly Panjābī* 5, no. 8 [April–May 1956]: 4–5), M. D. Taseer, who passed away in December 1950, had participated in the meeting. Since Taseer was still alive in July 1950, that seems the more likely date. Junaid Akram confirmed that the year 1950 seemed to him the most likely (interview, July 26, 2018). Taseer's presence at this meeting two years after he expressed in the press his contempt for Punjabi—see "Rūdād-e Urdu," in *Maqālāt-e Tāṡīr*, ed. Mumtaz Akhtar Mirza (Lahore: Majlis-e taraqqī-e adab, [1948] 1978), 266—is surprising to say the least, but his position seems to have changed at the end of his life. Arshad Mir, a close associate of Faqeer Mohammad Faqeer, recounts in an essay that a meeting took place between Faqeer and Taseer in the months preceding Taseer's death during which the latter allegedly challenged Faqeer to translate one of Ghalib's *ġazals* into Punjabi. Faqeer immediately improvised a beautiful translation, thus convincing Taseer that Punjabi was not an inferior language and was capable of expressing complex poetic ideas. Arshad Mir, "Bābā-e Panjābī Faqīr Moḥammad Faqīr, kujh yādāṃ kujh gallāṃ," *Kārwān*, July 1976, 160. Taseer would have participated in the Dyal Singh College meeting soon after this encounter.
5. Salik, "Xuṯba-e ṣadārat," 4.
6. Akhtar Hussain Jafri, *Bābā-e Panjābī, Doctor Faqīr Moḥammad Faqīr dī ḥayātī te fan* (Lahore: Azeez, 1991), 44; Junaid Akram, interview by the author, July 29, 2018.
7. Jafri, *Bābā-e Panjābī*, 23.
8. Akram, *Bābā-e Panjābī*, 114.
9. Akram, interview.
10. The *Anjuman-e Ḥimāyat-e Islām* was established in Lahore in 1884 by Qazi Hameeduddin to educate young Muslims, defend Islam against attacks by Hindu missionaries and revivalists of the *Arya Samaj* and *Brahmo Samaj*, and to counter any propaganda against Islam. Its meetings provided a platform for Indian Muslim politicians as well as poets (Allama Iqbal, Zafar Ali Khan, Hafeez Jalandhari) who wanted to convey a message to the Muslims of the country.
11. Jafri, *Bābā-e Panjābī*, 126; Faqeer Mohammad Faqeer, "Merī āpbītī," *Bābā-e Panjābī Number, Timāhī Panjābī*, July–December 2000, 35.
12. Arshad Mir, "Bābā-e Panjābī" in *Kaccī munḍer par ek cirāġ, Bābā-e Panjābī Doctor Faqīr Moḥammad Faqīr kī zindagī ke aḥwāl-o āṡār ham-ʿaṣar šaxṣiyāt ke qalam se*, ed. Junaid Akram (Lahore: Bazm-e Faqīr Pākistān, 2011), 55–56.
13. Akram, *Bābā-e Panjābī*, 52.
14. Akram, "Bābā panj daryāvāṃ dā," 10; Jafri, *Bābā-e Panjābī*, 131.

15. Mir, "Bābā-e Panjābī," 57. The manuscript was probably "A Short History of the Sikhs" by Teja Singh and Ganda Singh (1950). The 1947 event—which left a lasting impression on Pakistan's collective consciousness—is described as follows by Subhash Chander Arora: "On March 23, 1947 a reunion of Panthic Assembly Party was held in the Assembly hall. Master Tara Singh after the brief meeting asked the non-Muslim members to follow him outside the assembly hall. Mian Iftikharuddin and other Muslim leaders were getting ready to hoist the Muslim League flag over the assembly building thereby proving their power of holding supremacy in Punjab. Master Tara Singh drew the sword and boldly shouted that nobody could install the Muslim League flag as long as the Punjab was not divided. He tore the Muslim League flag into pieces. He declared that nobody could be permitted to install the Muslim League flag by force." Subhash Chander Arora, *Turmoil in Punjab Politics* (New Delhi: Mittal, 1990), 22.
16. Shorish Kashmiri, *Nau rattan* (Lahore: Caṭṭān, [1967] 2010), 36.
17. On the rivalry between *Zamīndār* and *Inqilāb*, see Ayesha Jalal, *Self and Sovereignty: Individual and Community in South Asian Islam Since 1850* (Delhi: Oxford University Press, 2001), 287–288.
18. The Unionist Party was secular party founded in 1923 by Sir Sikandar Hayat, Sir Fazli Hussain, Sir Shahabuddin, and Sir Chotu Ram to represent the interests of the landowners of Punjab. Allama Iqbal was affiliated with it in the 1920s. This party was dissolved in August 1947. Mohammad Hamza Farooqi, "Urdu ṣaḥāfat kā inqilāb-afrīṃ numā'inda: Rozmarra 'Inqilāb' aur uskā syāsī kirdār," *Bunyād* (LUMS) 4 (2013): 94.
19. Farooqi, "Urdu ṣaḥāfat kā inqilāb-afrīṃ numā'inda," 93.
20. Kashmiri, *Nau rattan,* 37.
21. Kashmiri, *Nau rattan,* 20.
22. Kashmiri, *Nau rattan,* 39.
23. Aslam Rana, "Jošua Faẓal Dīn, ḥayātī, fikr te fan," *Khoj* 45–46 (2001): 247.
24. Abdul Majeed Salik, "Sānūṃ Panjābī bolī te faxr ai," *Monthly Panjābī* 1, no. 2 (October 1951): 9.
25. See his essay *Urdu dā navāṃ daur* in *Monthly Panjābī* 1, no. 1 (September 1951): 8–10).
26. Mohammad Baqir, "Interview," in *Puchāṃ dasāṃ*, ed. Maqsood Saqib (Lahore: Suchet, 2013), 206–207.
27. Baqir, "Interview," 213.
28. Baqir, "Interview," 212.
29. Shafi Aqeel, "Doctor ṣāḥab, kujh purānyāṃ yādāṃ," *Bābā-e Panjābī Number, Timāhī Panjābī*, July–December 2000, 85–86.
30. Akram, interview.
31. Faqeer Mohammad Faqeer, "Kašmīr dī mālikī," *Monthly Panjābī* 1, no. 1 (September 1951): 6–7; Sain Sachyar, "Jaṭkyāṃ gallāṃ," *Monthly Panjābī* 1 no. 1 (September 1951): 25–27; Ibrahim Adil, "Qaumī quwwat," *Monthly Panjābī* 1, no. 1 (September 1951): 29–32; *Monthly Panjābī* 1, no. 1 (September 1951): 32; *Monthly Panjābī* 1, no. 1 (September 1951): 43–44, 54; Waqar, Ambalvi, "Daulat zindabād," *Monthly Panjābī* 1, no. 1 (September 1951): 11–13; *Savāṇyāṃ la'ī* (For Women), *Monthly Panjābī* 1, no. 1 (September 1951): 54.

32. Maula Bakhsh Kushta, *Hīr Wāriṡ Šāh vic milāvaṭī š'er* (Apocryphal Verses in Heer Waris Shah), *Monthly Panjābī*, 1, no. 1 (September 1951): 48–51; Joshua Fazal Din, *Behišt dī taṣwīr* (An Image of Paradise) *Monthly Panjābī*, 1, no. 1 (September 1951): 45–46; Lal Din Qaisar, *Pāk Panjābī dohṛe* (Pakistani Punjabi Couplets) *Monthly Panjābī* 1, no. 1 (September 1951): 27; Peer Fazal Gujrati, *Ġazal*, *Monthly Panjābī*, 1, no. 1 (September 1951): 16; Abid Ali Abid, "Panjābī ġazal," *Monthly Panjābī* 1, no. 1 (September 1951): 42–43; Sufi Ghulam Mustafa Tabassum, *Naẕm* (Poem), *Monthly Panjābī*, 1, no. 1 (September 1951): 21; Ambalvi, "Daulat zindabād."
33. Faqeer, "Qayām-e Pākistān toṃ b'ad Panjābī bolī la'ī kīte ga'e jatan," 37.
34. Faqeer, "Qayām-e Pākistān toṃ b'ad Panjābī bolī la'ī kīte ga'e jatan," 37–38.
35. The triumphant account of this stay was published in *Monthly Panjābī*, February–March 1952, 17–23, under the title *Karācī vic Panjābī dī āwāz* (The Voice of Punjabi in Karachi).
36. Faqeer, *Karācī vic Panjābī dī āwāz*, 22–23.
37. Akram, interview.
38. Shorish Kashmiri, "Panjābī dī taraqqī," *Monthly Panjābī* 1, no. 2 (October 1951): 45–46; Hamid Nizami, "Panjābī dī ibtidā'ī t'alīm," *Monthly Panjābī* 1, no. 3 (November 1951): 11–12; Akhtar Ali Khan, "Paiġām-e tabarīk," *Monthly Panjābī* 1, no. 4 (December 1951): 11; Zafar Ali Khan, "Merā chuṭpanā," *Monthly Panjābī* 1, no. 4 (December 1951): 7–10; Ghulam Rasool Mehr, "Bolī dī taraqqī," *Monthly Panjābī*, September–October 1955, 9–10.
39. Abid, "Panjābī ġazal"; Taj Mohammad Khayal, "Ṣūbe dī ṣaḥīḥ xidmat," *Monthly Panjābī*, January 1952, 13–14; Mian Bashir, "Vice-chancellor Punjab University dā paiġām," *Monthly Panjābī* 3, no. 2 (November–December 1953): 8.
40. The expression comes from Pierre Bourdieu, "La production de la croyance: contribution à une économie des biens symboliques," *Actes de la recherche en sciences sociales* 13 (1977): 6.
41. Kashmiri, "Panjābī dī taraqqī," 46.
42. Bashir, "Vice-chancellor Punjab University dā paiġām," 8.
43. Quoted in Anwar Sadid, "Maulana Ṣalaḥuddin Aḥmad aur qaumī zubān Urdu," *Axbār-e Urdu*, March–April 2004, 211.
44. "Tributes Paid to Warris Shah," *Pakistan Times*, February 27, 1953; Mohammad Afzal Khan, "Pakistan te Bhārat vic Panjābī," *Panjdaryā*, September 1960, 54.
45. Ahmad Rahi's paper, *Panjāb ke 'awāmī adab aur ṡaqāfat kā ṣaḥīḥ tarjumān Wāriṡ Šāh* (A True Spokesperson for Punjab's Popular Literature and Culture: Waris Shah), and Sufi Ghulam Mustafa Tabassum's paper, *Wāriṡ kī Hīr* (Waris's Heer), were both published in *Daily Imroz*, February 28, 1953.
46. "Punjabi Mushaira in YMCA Hall," *Pakistan Times*, February 28, 1953.
47. Faqeer Mohammad Faqeer, "Idārya," *Monthly Panjābī* 1, no. 1 (September 1951): 2.
48. Salik, "Sānūṃ Panjābī bolī te faxr ai," 9.
49. Faqeer, "Idārya," *Monthly Panjābī* 1, no. 1, 3. Faqeer was probably referring here to a resolution adopted during the second Urdu conference in Karachi (held on April 14 and 15, 1951), according to which "Urdu's development should not be at the expense of regional languages." Abdul Majeed Salik, *Panjābī adab te Sālik* (Lahore: Punjabi Academy, 1964), 39–40. This tolerant position contrasted with

that of the first Urdu conference (held in Lahore in March 1948), during which Maulvi Abdul Haq called for the abandon of regional languages in favor of Urdu.
50. Salik, "Sānūṃ Panjābī bolī te faxr ai," 9.
51. Faqeer, "Idārya," *Monthly Panjābī* 1, no. 1, 2.
52. Salik, "Sānūṃ Panjābī bolī te faxr ai," 9.
53. Salik, "Sānūṃ Panjābī bolī te faxr ai," 10.
54. Nizami, "Panjābī dī ibtidā'ī tᶜalīm," 11.
55. Nizami, "Panjābī dī ibtidā'ī tᶜalīm," 12.
56. Nizami, "Panjābī dī ibtidā'ī tᶜalīm," 12.
57. It is probably no coincidence that this description fits perfectly with Faqeer's own poetry—nationalist poetry and poetry of action.
58. Faqeer Mohammad Faqeer, "Panjābī adab vic inqilāb dī loṛ," *Monthly Panjābī* 1, no. 1 (September 1951): 18.
59. Mehr, "Bolī dī taraqqī," 10.
60. Mohammad Baqir, "Panjāb te Panjābī." *Monthly Panjābī* 1, no. 1 (September 1951): 15–16.
61. Faqeer Mohammad Faqeer, "Idārya," *Monthly Panjābī* 1, no. 4 (December 1951): 5.
62. Sardar Khan, "Panjābī luġat," *Monthly Panjābī* 3, no. 2 (November–December 1953): 25–30.
63. Khan, "Panjābī luġat," *Monthly Panjābī* 3, no. 2, 26.
64. *Afardu* is a neologism created by joining the words *Arabi* (Arabic), *Fārsi* (Persian), and *Urdu*.
65. Khan, "Panjābī luġat," *Monthly Panjābī* 3, no. 2, 26–27.
66. Rauf Malik, *Surx syāsat* (Lahore: Jamhūrī, 2017), 252.
67. Khan, "Pakistan te Bhārat vic Panjābī," 54.
68. Unfortunately, we have not been able to find *Daily Jang*'s issues from this period, so we only know these allegations from Abdul Majeed Salik's response (Salik, *Panjābī adab te Sālik*, 38–39).
69. This statement was accurate: Safdar Mir was indeed a sympathizer of the Communist Party but not a card-carrying member.
70. The Islam League was founded in Lahore in October 1947 by Inayatullah Khan Mashriqi ("Allama Mashriqi") to continue the political action of the Khaksar Movement, which had been dissolved by its founder in July 1947.
71. Salik, *Panjābī adab te Sālik*, 41–42.
72. Salik, *Panjābī adab te Sālik*, 37–39.
73. Salik, *Panjābī adab te Sālik*, 39–43.
74. Salik, *Panjābī adab te Sālik*, 40–41.
75. Khan, "Pakistan te Bhārat vic Panjābī," 54.
76. Khan, "Pakistan te Bhārat vic Panjābī," 54–55.
77. Raja Risalu, *Lā prīt ajehī Moḥammad* (Lahore: Pakistan Punjabi Adabī Board, 2008), 60.
78. Khan, "Pakistan te Bhārat vic Panjābī," 55.
79. Safdar Mir, "Daggā te agg," *Panjābī Adab*, April 1966, 163.
80. Akmal Aleemi, *Lāhor ke ahl-e qalam* (Lahore: Sang-e-meel, 2014), 31–32.

81. According to *Monthly Panjābī* 5, no. 8 (April–May 1956): 3, the *Panjābī Bazm-e Adab* of Lyallpur was founded by the poet Umar Din Ulfat. In 1931, Ulfat created an organization in Jalandhar, the *Doābā Kavi Sabhā* (Association of the Poets of Doab). After Partition, he migrated to Lyallpur and re-created this organization, of which he was the president, under the name *Panjābī Bazm-e Adab*. The general secretary was Agha Mohammad Siddiq Saqi, and its executive committee included Syed Fazal Hussain Pasha and Lal Din Asir.
82. A conference had a symbolic role; it was a means of asserting the strength of a linguistic movement. Urdu supporters had organized two Urdu conferences in 1948 and 1951, Sindhi supporters two Sindhi conferences in 1956 (in Mirpur Bathoro and Larkana), and Bengali supporters two Bengali conferences (in Dhaka in 1954 and Mymensingh in 1956).
83. Sadaf Jalandhari, "Interview," *Bābā-e Panjābī Number, Timāhī Panjābī*, July–December 2000, 131.
84. Sadaf Jalandhari, who attended this poetic symposium, stated that it was a great success. It started at 8:30 p.m. and ended at 2:30 a.m., before a packed stadium. He mentioned among the Indian participants Ustad Khudmukhtar, Jalandhari Ram Daman, Harbans Lal Mujrim, Kans Ram Gauhar, Hari Ram Gustakh, Gordari Lal Khudsar, Inderjit Singh Tulsi, Anant Ram Bhor, and Barkat Ram Barkat, and among the Pakistani participants Faqeer Mohammad Faqeer, Abdul Majeed Salik, Hakim Nasir, Ustad Daman, Peer Fazal Gujrati, Ulfat Warsi, Agha Rafiq Saqi, Fazal Hussain Pasha, Asir Sohlvi, Aziz Fidai, Khaliq Qureishi, Ismail Safari, and Umar Din Ulfat (Jalandhari, "Interview," 130–131). It should be noted that the Indian participants were all minor Punjabi poets. Major poets like Amrita Pritam, Prof. Mohan Singh, and Pritam Singh Safir did not participate in this symposium. Among the Pakistani participants, apart from Ustad Daman, no progressive poets participated.
85. Salik, "Xuṯba-e ṣadārat"; Faqeer Mohammad Faqeer, "Panjābī adab," *Monthly Panjābī* 5, no. 8 (April–May 1956): 13–17.
86. Faqeer, "Panjābī adab,"
87. Baqir, "Panjāb te Panjābī."
88. Salik, "Xuṯba-e ṣadārat," 7.
89. Faqeer, "Panjābī adab," 12.
90. Faqeer, "Panjābī adab," 12.
91. Abdul Majeed Salik, "Panjābī conference de resolution," *Monthly Panjābī* 5, no. 8 (April–May 1956): 9–10.
92. Salik, *Panjābī adab te Sālik*, 35–43.
93. Mohammad Baqir, "Ikk ṣalāḥ," *Monthly Panjābī* 6, no. 10 (July 1957): 8.
94. Baqir, "Interview," 208.
95. Levesque, Julien, *Etre sindhi au Pakistan: Nationalisme, discours identitaire et mobilisation politique 1930–2016* (PhD diss., EHESS, 2016), 321.
96. Mohammad Baqir, "Doctor Faqīr Moḥammad Faqīr," in *Kaccī munḍer par ek cirāġ, Bābā-e Panjābī Doctor Faqīr Moḥammad Faqīr kī zindagī ke aḥwāl-o āṡār ham-ʿaṣar šaxṣiyāt ke qalam se*, ed. Junaid Akram (Lahore: Bazm-e Faqīr Pākistān, 2011), 60.

97. Faqeer Mohammad Faqeer, letter to Shafi Aqeel, January 11, 1959, in *Bābā-e Panjābī Number, Timāhī Panjābī*, July–December 2000, 393.
98. Junaid Akram stated that one reason for publishing books in Persian is that Mohammad Baqir also received grants from Lahore's Iran Culture Center (Akram, interview).
99. List of publications of the *Panjābī Adabī Akādemī* in *Monthly Panjābī*, February–March 1960, 56.
100. Baqir, "Interview," 209.
101. Faqeer, letter to Shafi Aqeel, 394.
102. Aqeel, "Doctor ṣāḥab," 89; Akram, interview.
103. Mohammad Baqir and Faqeer Mohammad Faqeer continued their activities in favor of Punjabi after 1960. Mohammad Baqir supervised the Punjabi Academy until the 1980s, and Faqeer Mohammad Faqeer became in 1963 editor-in-chief of *Ḥaqullah* (a journal founded by Masud Khadarposh) and in 1965 editor-in-chief of *Lehrāṃ* (a journal founded by Akhtar Hussain Akhtar).
104. Akram, "Bābā panj daryāvāṃ dā," 10.
105. Faqeer, "Idārya," *Monthly Panjābī* 1, no. 1, 2–3.
106. Abdus Salam Khurshid, "Panjāb dī tārīx te adab," *Monthly Panjābī* 1, no. 2 (October 1951): 27–29; Maula Bakhsh Kushta, "Panjābī de pehle āṭh sau sāl," *Monthly Panjābī* 1, no. 3 (November 1951): 37.
107. Faqeer Mohammad Faqeer, *Poṭhohārī gīt* (The Songs of Pothohar), *Monthly Panjābī*, September–October 1959, 2–4.
108. Faqeer, "Poṭhohārī gīt."
109. Faqeer, "Poṭhohārī gīt," 3.
110. Faqeer Mohammad Faqeer, "Idārya," *Monthly Panjābī* 5, no. 6 (February 1956): 2–3.
111. Faqeer Mohammad Faqeer, "Idārya," *Monthly Panjābī*, September–October 1955, 5. The One Unit Scheme, approved by Pakistan's National Assembly on September 30, 1955, merged the four provinces of West Pakistan (Punjab, Sindh, NWFP, and Balochistan) into a single province to parallel the province of East Pakistan. It met with harsh opposition in Sindh.
112. Faqeer Mohammad Faqeer, "Idārya," *Monthly Panjābī*, November–December 1958, 2.
113. Faqeer Mohammad Faqeer, "Idārya," *Monthly Panjābī*, August 1957, 6; June–July 1958, 7.
114. Faqeer Mohammad Faqeer, "Idārya," *Monthly Panjābī*, August 1959, 3. *Sacyār* (man of truth) is the nickname that Faqeer Mohammad Faqeer gave to himself.
115. Faqeer, "Idārya." *Monthly Panjābī* 5, no. 6, 2.
116. Faqeer, "Idārya." *Monthly Panjābī* 5, no. 6, 2. Faqeer's indignation at Bengali's getting an official status and not Punjabi is surprising, because he had denied in an earlier editorial that he wanted Punjabi to become an official language (Faqeer, "Idārya," *Monthly Panjābī* 1, no. 1). It is possible that he changed his position later.
117. This silence baffled the writer and scholar Ahmad Salim, who wrote: "If one browses through the pages of *Panjābī* journal, one finds no reference to the fair linguistic demands of the other provinces, and there is no trace of any support

either." Ahmad Salim, "Panjābī zubān dī teḥrīk te Doctor Faqīr Moḥammad Faqīr," *Bābā-e Panjābī Number, Timāhī Panjābī*, July–December 2000, 216.

118. Adil, "Qaumī quwwat."
119. Adil, "Qaumī quwwat," 32.
120. Hamid Nizami, "Jamhūrī mulk," *Monthly Panjābī*, August 1952, 68.
121. Ghulam Jilani Barq, "Futūḥāt-e Islām," *Monthly Panjābī* 2, no. 4 (December 1952): 23–27; Ghulam Rasool Mehr, "Islāmī ḥukūmat dā pehlā naqša," *Monthly Panjābī*, February–March 1952, 5–8; Ghulam Rasool Mehr, "Islāmī ḥukūmat dā dūjā naqša." *Monthly Panjābī*, August 1952, 10–14.
122. Faqeer Mohammad Faqeer, "Āṇ wālā moṛ," *Monthly Panjābī* 1, no. 2 (October 1951): 2–3; "Qalmāṃ sidhyāṃ kar lo!" *Monthly Panjābī* 1, no. 10 (June 1952): 3–5; "Mirzā Moḥammad Rafī: Saudā dī panjābī šāʿirī," *Monthly Panjābī* 5, no. 9–10 (June–July 1956): 3–6; Salik, "Urdu dā navāṃ daur"; Salik, "Sānūṃ Panjābī bolī te faxr ai"; Baqir, "Panjāb te Panjābī"; Akhtar Ali Khan, "Urdu dī māṃ, Panjābī," *Monthly Panjābī*, August 1952, 16; Kashmiri, "Panjābī dī taraqqī"; Sardar Khan, "Panjābī luġat," *Monthly Panjābī*, September–October 1955, 25–32; Sardar Khan, "Zubān te bolī," *Monthly Panjābī* 5, no. 6 (February 1956): 6–9; Sardar Khan, "Panjābī dī gatayyā," *Monthly Panjābī* 5, no. 8 (April–May 1956): 34–40; Sardar Khan, "Standard Panjābī," *Monthly Panjābī* 5, no. 9–10 (June–July 1956): 46–48; Sardar Khan, "Panjābī nāqadrī kyoṃ?" *Monthly Panjābī* 6, no. 12 (September 1957): 25–30; Mohammad Yusuf, "Panjābī dī pukār," *Monthly Panjābī*, October 1958, 12–13; Khayal, "Ṣūbe dī ṣaḥīḥ xidmat"; Aziz ul-Hassan Abbasi, "Asīṃ te sāḍḍī bolī," *Monthly Panjābī* 3, no. 2 (November–December 1953): 50–54.
123. Khan, "Urdu dī māṃ," 16.
124. Faqeer, "Āṇ wālā moṛ," 3.
125. Khan, "Panjābī luġat," *Monthly Panjābī*, September–October 1955; Khan, "Zubān te bolī"; Abbasi, "Asīṃ te sāḍḍī bolī"; Salik, "Urdu dā navāṃ daur."
126. Khan, "Panjābī luġat," 31.
127. Khan, "Zubān te bolī," 8.
128. Abbasi, "Asīṃ te sāḍḍī bolī."
129. Faqeer Mohammad Faqeer, "Nīm firangī," *Monthly Panjābī* 2, no. 3 (November 1952): 4.
130. Abbasi, "Asīṃ te sāḍḍī bolī," 50.
131. Abbasi, "Asīṃ te sāḍḍī bolī," 50.
132. Abbasi, "Asīṃ te sāḍḍī bolī," 50–51.
133. Abbasi, "Asīṃ te sāḍḍī bolī," 53.
134. Abbasi, "Asīṃ te sāḍḍī bolī," 53.
135. Salik, "Urdu dā navāṃ daur."
136. Salik, "Urdu dā navāṃ daur," 9–10.
137. Salik, "Urdu dā navāṃ daur," 10.
138. Taj Mohammad Khayal, "Panjābī dī benaṣībī." *Monthly Panjābī* 3, no. 2 (November–December 1953): 15–16; Nawabzada Mehdi Ali Khan, "Shakespeare dī angrezī te sāḍḍī Panjābī," *Monthly Panjābī* 1, no. 4 (December 1951): 25–26; Khurshid, "Panjāb dī tārīx te adab"; Faqeer, "Panjābī adab."
139. Khayal, "Panjābī dī benaṣībī."

140. On the ambiguity regarding the gender of the beloved in classical Urdu poetry, see Frances Pritchett, "Convention in the Classical Urdu *Ghazal:* The Case of Mir," *Journal of South Asian and Middle Eastern Studies* 3, no.1 (Autumn 1979): 60–77.
141. Khayal, "Panjābī dī benaṣībī," 15–16.
142. Khan, "Shakespeare dī angrezī."
143. The author is paraphrasing verses 23–25a of act 2, scene 2 of *Romeo and Juliet.* The original verses are:

> See, how she leans her cheek upon her hand.
> O, that I were a glove upon that hand,
> That I might touch that cheek!

144. Khan, "Shakespeare dī angrezī," 26.
145. Khurshid, "Panjāb dī tārīx te adab."
146. Faqeer, "Mirzā Moḥammad Rafīᶜ Saudā," 5.
147. Faqeer, "Panjābī adab," 16–17.
148. Khan, "Panjābī luġat," *Monthly Panjābī* 3, no. 2; Khan, "Panjābī luġat," *Monthly Panjābī*, September–October 1955); Khan, "Zubān te bolī"; Khan, "Panjābī dī gatayyā"; Khan, "Standard Panjābī"; Khan, "Panjābī nāqadrī kyoṃ?"
149. Sardar Khan, "Panjābī luġat dā ikk warqa," *Monthly Panjābī* 5, no. 9–10 (June–July 1956): 46–48; "Panjābī luġat dā ikk warqa," *Monthly Panjābī* 6, no. 12 (September 1957): 33–38.
150. P. D. Raphael, "Panjābī ᶜilm," *Monthly Panjābī,* unnumbered issue (February/March 1952): 74–76.
151. Raphael, "Panjābī ᶜilm," 75.
152. Khan, "Panjābī luġat," *Monthly Panjābī* 3, no. 2.
153. Khan, "Panjābī luġat," 26. The letters correspond to the sounds [tˤ], [ʕ] and [ɣ̥].
154. Khan, "Panjābī luġat," 31.
155. Sardar Khan, "Panjābī de ḥurūf," *Monthly Panjābī* 5, no. 5 (January 1956): 6–13.
156. This is another reference to the views of Hafiz Mehmood Shirani.
157. Khan, "Panjābī de ḥurūf," 6–7. The letters correspond to the /ʈ/ sounds /ɖ/ /ɽ/.
158. Khan, "Standard Panjābī," 43.
159. Sardar Khan is clearly referring here to the classical Sufi authors. See Denis Matringe, "L'Utilisation littéraire des formes dialectales par les poètes musulmans du Panjab de la fin du XVIe au début du XIXe siècle," in *Dialectes dans les littératures indo-aryennes,* ed. Colette Caillat (Paris: Publications de l'Institut de Civilisation Indienne, Collège de France, 1989), 527–556.
160. Khan, "Standard Panjābī," 44.
161. Neologism created by combining the words *'Arabī* (Arabic), *Fārsī* (Persian), and *Urdū.*
162. Neologism created by combining the words *Panjābī* and *Hindī.*
163. Khan, "Standard Panjābī," 41.
164. Waqar Ambalvi, "Pāk Panjābī." *Monthly Panjābī* 5, no. 3 (November 1955): 9.
165. Khan, "Panjābī dī gatayyā," 35.
166. Khan, "Panjābī dī gatayyā," 40.
167. Khan, "Panjābī luġat," *Monthly Panjābī* 3, no. 2, 26.

168. Khan, "Panjābī de ḥurūf."
169. Khan, "Panjābī luġat dā ikk warqa," *Monthly Panjābī* 6, no. 12.
170. The total number of Pakistani writers who contributed to *Monthly Panjābī* was 284, but the majority were amateur writers who contributed only once. We have included here only the writers who contributed to *Monthly Panjābī* on a regular basis and/or whose literary activities were acknowledged by conservative historians of Punjabi literature like Maula Bakhsh Kushta or Faqeer Mohammad Faqeer. Maula Bakhsh Kushta, *Tażkira panjābī šāʿirāṃ dā* (Lahore: Azeez, [1960] 1988); Faqeer Mohammad Faqeer, *Panjābī zubān-o adab kī tārīx* (Lahore: Sang-e-meel, 2002).
171. Mohammad Baqir supervised the Punjabi Academy till the 1980s; Abdus Salam Khurshid was, with Shafqat Tanvir Mirza, one of the conveners of the Punjabi branch of the "writers' guild" of Lahore in 1961; the Punjabi essays, poems, and translations of Sufi Ghulam Mustafa Tabassum were published throughout the 1950s in *Monthly Panjābī* and in the 1960s in Punjabi journals such as *Panjābī Adab* and *Panjdaryā*.
172. To know these positions, we consulted Maula Bakhsh Kushta's *Tażkira panjābī šāʿirāṃ dā* and Faqeer Mohammad Faqeer's *Panjābī zubān-o adab kī tārīx*, as well as various theses defended in the Punjabi department of Oriental College, Lahore. Anwarul Haq, "Pākistān vic panjābī adab dā irtiqā" (master's thesis, Lahore Oriental College, 1974); Lyaqat Hussain, "Allama Ġulām Yaqūb Anwar, ḥayātī fikr te fan" (master's thesis, Lahore Oriental College, 1983); Shahzad Ahmad, "Ḥakīm Tayeb Riẓvī, ḥayātī te šāʿirī" (master's thesis, Lahore Oriental College, 1988); Mohammad Tariq Zafar, "Xalīl Ātiš dī šāʿirī te kalām" (master's thesis, Lahore Oriental College, 1988); Sania Zafar, "Aḥmad Ẕafar dī panjābī šāʿirī" (master's thesis, Lahore Oriental College, 2010); Anwar Ahmad Qazi, "Ṣeḥrā'ī Gurdāspūrī, ḥayātī te kalām" (master's thesis, Lahore Oriental College, 1988); Nasrullah Mughal, "Ismaīl Matwālā ḥayātī fikr te fan" (master's thesis, Lahore Oriental College, 1989); Asya Ehsan, "Teḥrīk-e Pākistān te Ẕahīr Nyāz Bīgī" (master's thesis, Lahore Oriental College, 1999); Arifa Kausar, "Bašīr Manẓar dyāṃ panjābī adab la'ī xidmatāṃ" (master's thesis, Lahore Oriental College, 2002); Faiza Zaidi, "Niẓām Dīn Tawakkulī te ohnāṃ dī inšāya-nigārī" (master's thesis, Lahore Oriental College, 2008); Muhibullah Malik, "Hanif Caudhrī ḥayātī te fan" (master's thesis, Lahore Oriental College, 2010).
173. The doors of the radio and the civil service were closed to them, they were under constant surveillance, they spent long periods in prison, and the salaries granted by the Communist Party and the newspapers or journals were just enough to make ends meet. Ahmad Salim, *Sawāneḥ-e 'umrī Ḥamīd Axtar* (Lahore: Book Home, 2010), 163; Hameed Akhtar, *Pursiš e aḥwāl* (Lahore: Afra, 1999), 15–17.
174. Ahmad Hussain Qaladari, "Ġulām Yaqūb Anwar," *Panjābī Adab*, May 1961, 26.
175. Ghulam Yaqub Anwar, *Can dī khārī* (Gujranwala: Self-published, 1976), 10–12.
176. Faqeer, *Panjābī zubān-o adab kī tārīx*, 157–159.
177. Miraji's book *Mašrīq-o maġrīb ke naġme* (Songs of the East and the West) includes Urdu translations of Whitman, Villon, Heine, and Mallarmé, among others.
178. Anwar, *Can dī khārī*, 12–14.

179. Anwar, *Can dī khārī*, 7.
180. Sajjad Hyder, "Interview," in *Puchāṃ dasāṃ*, ed. Maqsood Saqib (Lahore: Suchet, 2013), 215–216.
181. He explained in an interview with Maqsood Saqib: *Punjabī vall mainūṃ Panjābī nāl moḥabbat nahīṃ leke ā'ī* (It was not love for Punjabi that brought me to this language). Hyder, "Interview," 234.
182. Hyder, "Interview," 220–221.
183. Hyder, "Interview," 217, 219.
184. Hyder, "Interview," 218–219.
185. K. K. Aziz, *The Coffee House of Lahore: A Memoir 1942–1957* (Lahore: Sang-e-meel, 2007), 11.
186. Rauf Malik, interview by the author, July 27, 2018.
187. Sajjad Hyder, *Hawā de hūke* (Lahore: Qaumī Kutub-Xāna, 1957).
188. We find illustrations of the concept of *Mard-e Momin* in Iqbal's poems *Ṯulūʿ-e Islām* (The Rise of Islam) and *Momin* (The Believer). Allama Iqbal, *Bāng-e darā* (Lahore: Sheikh Mubarak Ali, [1905] 1939), 303–315; Allama Iqbal, *Zarb-e kalīm* (Aligarh: Aligarh Book Depot, [1936] 1975), 45–46. Analyzing the concept of *Mard-e Momin*, Denis Matringe writes that Allama Iqbal proposes an ideal that "aims to produce not a Nietzschean superman, but a new subject aware of his responsibilities within a community in motion, a true believer who, here again, reworks the Perfect Man of Sufism and whose model is the Prophet with the first dynamic Muslim community gathered around him." Denis Matringe, " 'L'appel de la cloche': spiritualité, écriture poétique et vision politique chez Muhammad Iqbal (1877–1938)," in *Convictions religieuses et engagement en Asie du Sud depuis 1850*, ed. Catherine Clémentin (Paris: École Française d'Extrême-Orient, 2011), 13.
189. Faqeer Mohammad Faqeer, *Muwāte* (Lahore: Bazm-e Faqīr Pākistān/Sānjh, [1956] 2015), 37.
190. Faqeer, *Muwāte*, 96.
191. Faqeer, *Muwāte*, 47. In glorifying passion over reason, Faqeer follows Iqbal, whose poems *'Aqal-o dil* (Reason and Heart) and *'Ilm-o 'išq* (Knowledge and Passion) praise the merits of passion. Iqbal, *Bāng-e darā*, 28–29; Iqbal, *Zarb-e kalīm*, 20–22. Denis Matringe, analyzing this reason/passion binary, writes: "To sacrifice oneself for a freely chosen cause is still a form of true life, and it is this self-sacrifice to the ideal that Iqbal, reworking in a new sense an old Sufi binary, calls 'love' ('išq), which he often present as the opposite of *ʿaql*, the 'intellect,' the 'rationality' connected to selfish calculation and selfish interest.' " Matringe, "L'appel de la cloche," 13.
192. Faqeer, *Muwāte*, 123.
193. Faqeer, *Muwāte*, 86.
194. Faqeer, *Muwāte*, 46, 118.
195. Faqeer, *Muwāte*, 38, 75. Mansur Hallaj was a Sufi who was crucified in Baghdad in 922 for saying *Ana'l-Ḥaqq* ("I am the Truth/God/Allah!"). He had therefore reached the supreme stage of Sufism, which is fusion with God.
196. Faqeer, *Muwāte*, 30.
197. Faqeer, *Muwāte*, 105, 128.

198. *Panjābī rānī* (The Queen Punjabi). *Bābā* (Father), *Cannī rāt* (Moonlight), *Uḍīk* (The Wait). Faqeer, *Muwāte*, 27, 103, 34, 78.
199. Some examples of nocturnal poems by Akhtar Shirani are *Gujrāt kī rāt* (A Night in Gujrat), *Āj kī rāt* (Tonight), *Šabhā-e rafta* (Nights Gone By), and *Wādī-e Gangā meṃ ek rāt* (A Night in the Valley of the Ganges). Akhtar Shirani, *Intixāb-e kalām* (Aligarh: Anjuman-e Taraqqī-e Urdu-e Hind, 1959), 10, 20–21, 24–25, 55–56.
200. The metaphysical poem was also going out of fashion in Urdu, and by the 1950s it was only used by a few conservative poets like Hafeez Jalandhari and Shorish Kashmiri.s
201. *Monthly Panjābī* 7, no. 1 (October 1957): 21; *Monthly Panjābī* 7, no. 2 (November 1957): 48.
202. *Monthly Panjābī*, March–April 1953, 57; *Monthly Panjābī* 5, no. 4 (December 1955): 19.
203. *Monthly Panjābī* 5, no. 4 (December 1955): 6.
204. *Monthly Panjābī* 2, no. 1 (September 1952): 29
205. *Monthly Panjābī* 7, no. 1 (October 1957): 6–7. On Faiz Ahmad Faiz's political statements disguised in poetic language, see Irfan Waheed Usmani, "Print Culture and Left-Wing Radicalism in Lahore, Pakistan, c.1947–1971" (PhD diss., National University of Singapore, 2016), 346–347.
206. Romanticism was severely criticized by Marxist intellectuals like Abid Hassan Minto, who, in his essay *Nayā manšūr aur uske bʿad* (The New Manifesto and After), specifically warned writers against the romantic trend as it systematically ignored social issues and power relationships. Minto, *Nayā manšūr aur uske bʿad*, in *Nuqta-e Naẕar* (Lahore: Multimedia Affairs, 2003), 301–326, first published in *Saverā* 13–14, 1953.
207. *Monthly Panjābī* 2, no. 5–6 (January–February 1953): 23; *Monthly Panjābī* 5, no. 9–10 (June–July 1956): 7; *Monthly Panjābī* 6, no. 10 (July 1957): 33; *Monthly Panjābī*, February–March 1960, 40.
208. *Monthly Panjābī* 2, no. 3 (November 1952): 16; *Monthly Panjābī* 6, no. 12 (September 1957): 40. A *Sarāpā* is a detailed and metaphorized description of the beloved.
209. *Monthly Panjābī*, March–April 1953, 49.
210. Khizar Humayun Ansari, *The Emergence of Socialist Thought Among North Indian Muslims, 1917–1947* (Karachi: Oxford University Press, 2015), 245–246; Minto, *Nayā manšūr aur uske bʿad*, 323.
211. Abid, "Panjābī ġazal."
212. This corpus is limited to short stories as no conservative writer wrote and published a novel in those years.
213. Waqar Ambalvi, "Kūhjā," *Monthly Panjābī*, February–March 1952, 33–34.
214. Shafi Aqeel, "Jhanāṃ dyāṃ rohṛyāṃ," *Monthly Panjābī*, February–March 1952, 57–60.
215. Sadiq Qureishi, "Jalālpur dā Caudhrī," *Monthly Panjābī*, April 1952, 17–23.
216. Sajjad Hyder, "Kāng," *Monthly Panjābī* 1, no. 1 (September 1951): 38–41.
217. Noor Kashmiri, "Moḥabbat," *Monthly Panjābī*, February–March 1952, 45–48.
218. Shafi Aqeel, "Kaṇak de siṭṭe," *Monthly Panjābī* 2, no. 4 (December 1952): 18–21.
219. Suhail Yazdani, "Muhāṇe dī dhī," *Monthly Panjābī*, August 1952, 41–46.
220. Waqar Ambalvi, "Sāvā līrā," *Monthly Panjābī* 1, no. 4 (December 1951): 13–15.

221. Akbar Lahori, "O kauṇ sī?" *Monthly Panjābī*, August 1952, 22–24.
222. Ahmad Bashir, "*Gujhyā rog*," *Monthly Panjābī*, August 1957, 12–16.
223. Chaudhry Mohammad Asghar Khan, "Ġarīb de bhāg," *Monthly Panjābī* 1, no. 10 (June 1952): 47–48.
224. Faqeer Mohammad Faqeer, "Oh milke na mil sake," *Monthly Panjābī* 1, no. 4 (December 1951): 20–23.
225. Nazr-e Fatima, "Jannat de meḥl," *Monthly Panjābī* 1, no. 3 (November 1951): 49–50.
226. The romantic (or *Rūmāniyat*) movement started in the 1920s and promoted a form of sentimental fiction inspired by the English romantic novel (Jane Austin, the Brontë sisters). Romantic fiction counted among its early Urdu proponents Syed Sajjad Haider Yaldram, Qazi Abdul Ghaffar, Majnun Gorakhpuri, and Nyaz Fatehpuri. Its Pakistani proponents were Mirza Adib and A Hameed. Romanticism was introduced in Punjabi fiction by Joshua Fazal Din, who wrote romantic short stories in Punjabi in the 1930s. On the *Rūmāniyat* movement, see Anwar Sadid, *Urdu adab kī teḥrīkeṃ* (Karachi: Anjuman-e Taraqqī-e Urdu Pakistan, 1996), 431–443; on Joshua Fazal Din's fictional output, see Rana, "Jošua Faẓal Dīn," 370–371.
227. Hyder, *Hawā de hūke.*
228. Sajjad Hyder, "Dilāṃ de rogī," *Monthly Panjābī*, February–March 1952, 25–32; Faqeer, *Panjābī zubān-o adab kī tārīx*, 430.
229. Nazr-e Fatima, "Rāh dā ghaṭṭā," *Monthly Panjābī*, January 1952, 21–25; Hyder, *Hawā de hūke*, 31–48, 49–71; Nazr-e Fatima, "Takkar," *Monthly Panjābī*, February–March 1952, 38–40.
230. Agha Ashraf, "Sa'īṃ Dino," *Monthly Panjābī*, January 1956, 41–48.
231. Sultan Masud Mirza, "Ranḍī," *Monthly Panjābī*, March–April 1959, 48–52.
232. Hyder, "Dilāṃ de rogī."
233. Ghulam Rasool Mehr, "Merā safarnāma," *Monthly Panjābī* 1, no. 10 (June 1952): 7–10; Sadiq Ali Ajiz, "Pūran dā khūh," *Monthly Panjābī*, February–March 1952, 68–69.
234. Waqar Ambalvi, "Pāṇī vic panj din," *Monthly Panjābī* 5, no. 3 (November 1955): 11–14.
235. Khan, "Merā chuṭpanā."
236. Khan, "Merā chuṭpanā," 10.
237. Noor Kashmiri, "Haḍbītī," *Monthly Panjābī* 1, no. 4 (December 1951): 36–38.
238. The *Khalsa* is the purified and reconstituted Sikh community instituted by Guru Gobind Singh on March 30, 1699.
239. Saqib Zeervi, "Rabb jāne," *Monthly Panjābī*, February–March 1952, 62–64.

6. The Punjabi Modernist Movement (1957–1959)

1. Raja Risalu, *Lā prīt ajehī Moḥammad* (Lahore: Pakistan Punjabi Adabī Board, 2008), 61–69.
2. Risalu, *Lā prīt ajehī Moḥammad*, 61.

3. Risalu, *Lā prīt ajehī Moḥammad*, 62.
4. Risalu, *Lā prīt ajehī Moḥammad*, 64.
5. Risalu, *Lā prīt ajehī Moḥammad*, 65.
6. Risalu, *Lā prīt ajehī Moḥammad*, 63.
7. Abdul Haq Khammi, ed., *Panjāb Rang* (Lahore: Panjābī Majlis, 1958), 76.
8. Risalu, *Lā prīt ajehī Moḥammad*, 61–62.
9. Akmal Aleemi's short story *Vohṭī* (The Wife) was published in the February 1958 issue of *Panjdaryā*, Safdar Mir's play *Nīle dā aswār* in the March 1958 issue, Akbar Lahori's short stories *Ṭāṃke* (Repairs) and *Moyāṃ dī manḍī* (The Market of the Dead People) in the March and December 1958 issues, and Anis Nagi's short story *Daldal* (A Swamp) in the February 1959 issue.
10. Abdus Salam Khurshid's short story *Vāṃjhlī* (The Flute) and Nazr-e Fatima's short story *Rondyāṃ akhāṃ* (Weeping Eyes) were featured in the April–May 1958 issue of *Panjdaryā*, and Nizamuddin Tawakkuli's humorous essay *Juttī cor* (A Shoes Thief) was featured in the November–December 1958 issue.
11. Mohammad Afzal Khan, "Pakistan te Bhārat vic Panjābī," *Panjdaryā*, September 1960, 56.
12. Risalu, *Lā prīt ajehī Moḥammad*, 65.
13. Khammi, *Panjāb Rang*, 5–6, 7–10. Conceptual and stylistic similarities between the unsigned editorial and some articles by Safdar Mir published a few years later—*Panjābī kyoṃ?* (Why Punjabi?) and *Panjābī adībāṃ dī żehnī fiẓā* (The Intellectual Atmosphere of Punjabi Men of Letters)—suggest that he might be the anonymous editorialist. Safdar Mir, "Panjābī kyoṃ?," *Panjābī Adab*, January–February 1963: 7–8; Safdar Mir, "Panjābī adībāṃ dī żehnī fiẓā," *Panjābī Adab*, September 1963: 3–8.
14. Khammi, *Panjāb Rang*, 5.
15. Khammi, *Panjāb Rang*, 5–6.
16. Khammi, *Panjāb Rang*, 6.
17. Khammi, *Panjāb Rang*, 7–10.
18. Raja Risalu means that Punjabi Muslims used Urdu to assert their identity when confronted with Punjabi-speaking Sikhs and Hindi-speaking Hindus.
19. Khammi, *Panjāb Rang*, 7.
20. Khammi, *Panjāb Rang*, 7.
21. Khammi, *Panjāb Rang*, 7.
22. Khammi, *Panjāb Rang*, 9.
23. Khammi, *Panjāb Rang*, 9.
24. Khammi, *Panjāb Rang*, 6.
25. Rauf Malik, in his article *Nave panjābī adab dyāṃ lehrāṃ* (Movements in New Punjabi Literature), echoes this criticism of Punjabi senior writers: "There is a group of old writers who have spent most of their lives producing literature in Punjabi. They are now only busy listening to people sing the praises of their great works. They regard no one but themselves as true Punjabi lovers, laugh with contempt at the efforts of new writers, and discourage them." Rauf Malik, "Nave panjābī adab dyāṃ lehrāṃ," *Panjābī Adab*, December 1961, 18.
26. Khammi, *Panjāb Rang*, 6.

27. The reference is to the literary Bohemians who used to hang out in Mall Road's restaurants and tea stalls.
28. *Monthly Panjābī*, February 1959, 51.
29. *Monthly Panjābī*, March–April 1959, 56. *Vaisakhi* is a traditional harvest festival specially celebrated by the Sikhs.
30. Risalu, *Lā prīt ajehī Moḥammad*, 66.
31. Risalu, *Lā prīt ajehī Moḥammad*, 66–67.
32. Risalu, *Lā prīt ajehī Moḥammad*, 65.
33. Risalu, *Lā prīt ajehī Moḥammad*, 65–66.
34. Intizar Hussain, *Cirāġoṃ kā dhu'āṃ* (Lahore: Sang-e-meel, 2012), 145–148.
35. Risalu, *Lā prīt ajehī Moḥammad*, 67.
36. Anis Nagi, ed., *Sajre phull* (Lahore: Panjābī Majlis, 1959), 11–16.
37. Nagi, *Sajre phull*, 19–43.
38. Nagi, *Sajre phull*, 44–81, 82–128.
39. Nagi, *Sajre phull*, 12.
40. Nagi, *Sajre phull*, 14–15.
41. Anis Nagi, *Ek adhūrī sarguzašt* (Lahore: Jamāliyāt, 2008), 116.
42. Risalu, *Lā prīt ajehī Moḥammad*, 69.
43. We were unable to clarify this point because we did not have access to the issues of the newspapers for the year 1959 in which the official announcement of the ban would have appeared. The Punjabi journals of the time (*Monthly Panjābī* and *Panjdaryā*) do not offer any information on the subject because their editors-in-chief were careful not to mention such a sensitive matter.
44. Irfan Waheed Usmani, "Print Culture and Left-Wing Radicalism in Lahore, Pakistan, c. 1947–1971" (PhD diss., National University of Singapore, 2016), 301.
45. Irfan Waheed Usmani, "Print Culture and Left-Wing Radicalism in Lahore, Pakistan, c. 1947–1971" (PhD diss., National University of Singapore, 2016), 301. Arif Abdul Mateen, a former member of the Progressive Writers' Association, had in 1954–55 established an association of Marxist orientation under the name of *Anjuman- e Āzād-xiyāl Muṣannifīn*, which was banned in 1958 after the rise to power of Ayub Khan and the enactment of martial law; see Arif Abdul Mateen, *Imkānāt* (Lahore: Technical Publishers, 1988), 398–399. Veterans of the progressive movement such as Qateel Shifai, Bedil Hyderi, and Zaheer Kashmiri attended its meetings, along with emerging writers such as Azhar Javed, Nasir Zaidi, Khwaja Mohammad Zakariya, Iqbal Sajid, and Javed Shaheen. Dr. Kanwal Feroze, interview by the author, October 11, 2017.
46. K. K. Aziz, *The Coffee House of Lahore. A Memoir 1942–1957* (Lahore: Sang-e-meel, 2007), 31.
47. Anver Sajjad, interview by the author, August 1, 2018.
48. Nagi, *Ek adhūrī sarguzašt*, 116.
49. Malik, *Nave panjābī adab dyāṃ lehrāṃ*, 19; Rauf Malik, interview by the author, October 16, 2018.
50. Abdullah Malik, *Mustaqbil hamārā hai* (Lahore: PPH, 1950), 78.
51. Aziz, *The Coffee House of Lahore*, 30–31; Nagi, *Sajre phull*, 141.
52. Hameed Akhtar, *Rūdād-e Anjuman* (Lahore: Book Home, 2011), 14.

53. Noman Nasir, "Moḥammad Ṣafdar Mīr de Panjāb te Panjābī bāre chape angrezī columnāṃ dī bibliography" (master's thesis, Lahore Oriental College, 2007), 21.
54. Aziz, *The Coffee House of Lahore*, 32–33; Nagi, *Ek adhūrī sarguzašt*, 115; Zahid Dar, interview by author, October 6, 2018.
55. Mir, "Panjābī kyoṃ?," 7–8.
56. Aziz, *The Coffee House of Lahore*, 31.
57. Safdar Mir, "Kālī," *Panjābī Adab*, November 1961, 26–30; Pušpā," *Panjābī Adab*, February 1962, 27–35; "Panjābī kyoṃ?"; "Panjābī adībāṃ dī żehnī fiẓā"; "Daggā te agg," *Panjābī Adab*, April 1966, 161–164.
58. His production in Urdu includes a poetry collection, *Dard ke phūl* (Flowers of Pain, 1964), and a collection of plays, *Āxir-e šab* (The End of the Night, 1978), as well as the essay collections *Maudūdiyat* (Maududi's Ideology, 1970), *Taṣawwurāt* (Concepts), and *Adab aur syāsat* (Literature and Politics, 1997). He wrote countless columns for the *Pakistan Times* and *Dawn*—some of which were collected and published in 1998 under the title *Modern Urdu Prose*—as well as a book, *Iqbal the Progressive* (1990).
59. Nagi, *Ek adhūrī sarguzašt*, 12–13.
60. Nagi, *Ek adhūrī sarguzašt*, 96, 102.
61. Nagi, *Ek adhūrī sarguzašt*, 112.
62. Hussain, *Cirāġoṃ kā dhu'āṃ*, 140–141.
63. Nagi, *Ek adhūrī sarguzašt*, 143, 157, 128.
64. Anis Nagi analyzes this movement in detail in his book *Nayā š'erī ufaq: 1960 kī na'ī šā'irī kī teḥrīk* (A New Poetic Horizon: The Movement of New Poetry of 1960) (Lahore: Jamāliyāt, [1969] 1988), 1–70.
65. Shaheen Mufti, *Anīs Nāgī, šaxṣyat aur fan* (Islamabad: Pakistani Academy of Letters, 2009), 33, 145.
66. Khammi, *Panjāb Rang*; Nagi, *Sajre phull*.
67. Nagi, *Sajre phull*, 94, 99, 101, 120, 124, 125, 127, 111, 113, 116, 118; Khammi, *Panjāb Rang*, 23.
68. Khammi, *Panjāb Rang*, 23.
69. Nagi, *Sajre phull*, 94.
70. Nagi, *Sajre phull*, 116.
71. Nagi, *Sajre phull*, 94, 99, 107.
72. Nagi, *Sajre phull*, 107.
73. Nagi, *Sajre phull*, 121.
74. Khammi, *Panjāb Rang*, 43–53; *Panjdaryā*, August 1959, 25–38.
75. Sajjad Zaheer, "Nīnd nahīṃ ātī," in *Angāre*, ed. Sajjad Zaheer (Lucknow: Mirza Mohammad Jawad Nizami, 1932), 1–19; Mohammad Hasan Askari, *Jazīre* (New Delhi: Saqi Book Depot, 1943); Intizar Hussain, *Din aur dāstān* (New Delhi: Arshia, [1957] 2013).
76. Safdar Mir, "Nīle dā aswār," in *Ṣafdar Mīr dyāṃ likhatāṃ*, ed. Sheema Majeed (Lahore: Pakistan Punjabi Adabī Board, 2002), 69–99 (first published in *Rāvī Magazine*, Lahore, 1957).
77. Mir, "Nīle dā aswār," 70–86, 86–99.
78. *Panjābī Adab*, August 1961, 59.

79. Najm Hosain Syed, *Kāfyāṃ* (Lahore: Majlis Shah Husain, 1965). For a detailed analyzis of *Kāfyāṃ*, its modernism and literary significance, see Denis Matringe, "Disguising Political Resistance in the Sufi Idiom: The Kafian of Najm Husain Sayyid of Pakistan," in *The Islamic Path: Sufism, Politics and Society in India*, ed. Saiyid Zahir Husain Jafri and Helmut Reifeld (Ahmedabad: Rainbow, 2006), 110–130.

Conclusion

1. *Panjābī Adab*, January 1961, 3.
2. *Panjābī Adab*, January 1961, 3.
3. Encyclopedia of Punjabi Poets: Maula Bakhsh Kushta, *Tażkira panjābī šāʿirāṃ dā* (Lahore: Azeez, [1960] 1988).
4. *Panjābī Adab*, August 1961, 59.
5. *Panjābī Adab*, January 1962, 43.
6. *Panjābī Adab*, August 1963, 29.
7. L. V. Khokhlova, "The Role of Punjabi Language in Self-Identification of Punjabi Community," *Journal of Pakistan Vision* 10, no. 1 (2010): 9.
8. Tariq Rahman, *Language and Politics in Pakistan* (Karachi: Oxford University Press, 1996), 209.
9. Alyssa Ayres, *Speaking Like a State: Language and Nationalism in Pakistan* (Cambridge: Cambridge University Press, 2009), 190.
10. Harnik Deol, *Religion and Nationalism in India: The Case of the Punjab* (London: Routledge, 2000), 94–95.
11. Deol, *Religion and Nationalism in India*, 96.
12. Fateh Mohammad Malik, "Idārya," *Axbār-e Urdu*, March–April 2004, 5–7.
13. A Punjab Institute of Language, Art & Culture (PILAC) was established in September 2004; a Dr. Faqeer Research Chair was established in the Punjabi department of Oriental College, Lahore in 2013 (held by Junaid Akram, grandson of Faqeer Mohammad Faqeer); and in February 2019, a Guru Nanak Research Chair was established at Punjab University, Lahore.
14. Mohammed Hanif, interview by the author, April 3, 2019.

Bibliography

Abbas, Rashid, and Farida Shaheed. *Pakistan: Ethno-Politics and Contending Elites*. Geneva: United Nations Research Institute on Social Development, 1993.
Abbasi, Aziz ul-Hassan. "Asīṃ te sāḍḍī bolī." *Monthly Panjābī* 3, no. 2 (November–December 1953): 50–54.
Abid, Abid Ali. "Panjābī ġazal." *Monthly Panjābī* 1, no. 1 (September 1951): 42–43.
Adil, Ibrahim. "Qaumī quwwat." *Monthly Panjābī* 1, no. 1 (September 1951): 29–32.
Aftab Ahmed. *Ba-yād-e soḥbat-e nāzuk xiyālāṃ*. Islamabad: Dost, 1997.
Ahmad, Maulana Salahuddin. "Taqsīm-e mulk kā aṡar Urdu zubān aur adab par." In *Behtarīn Adab* 1948, ed. Idāra-e Adab-e Laṭīf, 82–101. Lahore: Maktaba-e Urdu.
Ahmad, Shahzad. "Ḥakīm Tayeb Riẓvī, ḥayātī te šāʿirī." Master's thesis, Lahore Oriental College, 1988.
Ajiz, Sadiq Ali. "Pūran dā khūh." *Monthly Panjābī*, February–March 1952, 68–69.
Akhtar, Hameed. *Pursiš-e aḥwāl*. Lahore: Afra, 1999.
——. *Rūdād-e Anjuman*. Lahore: Book Home, 2011.
Akhtar, Salim. *Urdu adab kī muxtaṣartarīn tārīx*. Delhi: Kitābī Duniyā, 2005.
Akram, Junaid, ed. *Bābā-e Panjābī, Doctor Faqīr Moḥammad Faqīr*. Lahore: Pakistan Punjabi Adabi Board, 1992.
——. "Bābā panj daryāvāṃ dā." *Saver*, June 2000, 10–16.
——, ed. *Kaccī munḍer par ek cirāġ, Bābā-e Panjābī Doctor Faqīr Moḥammad Faqīr kī zindagī ke aḥwāl-o āṡār ham-ʿaṣar šaxṣiyāt ke qalam se*. Lahore: Bazm-e Faqīr Pākistān, 2011.
Aleemi, Akmal. *Lāhor ke ahl-e qalam*. Lahore: Sang-e-meel, 2014.
Ali, Kamran Asdar. *Surkh Salam: Communist Politics and Class Activism in Pakistan 1947–1972*. Karachi: Oxford University Press, 2015.
Ambalvi, Waqar. "Daulat zindabād." *Monthly Panjābī* 1, no. 1 (September 1951): 11–13.
——. "Kūhjā." *Monthly Panjābī*, February–March 1952, 33–34.
——. "Pāk Panjābī." *Monthly Panjābī* 5, no. 3 (November 1955): 9.
——. "Pāṇī vic panj din." *Monthly Panjābī* 5, no. 3 (November 1955): 11–14.

——. "Sāvā līrā." *Monthly Panjābī* 1, no. 4 (December 1951): 13–15.
Amstutz, Andrew. *Finding a Home for Urdu: The Anjuman-i Taraqqī-yi Urdu, 1903–1971* (AIPS Final Report). AIPS, 2013.
Ansari, Khizar Humayun. *The Emergence of Socialist Thought Among North Indian Muslims, 1917–1947.* Karachi: Oxford University Press, 2015.
Anwar, Ghulam Yaqub. *Can dī khārī.* Gujranwala: Self-published, 1976.
Aqeel, Shafi. "Doctor ṣāḥab, kujh purānyāṃ yādāṃ." *Bābā-e Panjābī Number, Timāhī Panjābī*, July–December 2000, 84–92.
——. "Jhanāṃ dyāṃ rohṛyāṃ" *Monthly Panjābī*, February–March 1952, 57–60.
——. "Kaṇak de siṭṭe." *Monthly Panjābī* 2, no. 4 (December 1952): 18–21.
——. "Tāhlī de pattar." *Monthly Panjābī* 1, no. 10 (June 1952): 13–15.
Arora, Subhash Chander. *Turmoil in Punjab politics.* New Delhi: Mittal, 1990.
Ashraf, Agha. "Sa'īṃ Dino." *Monthly Panjābī*, January 1956, 41–48.
Askari, Mohammad Hasan. *Jazīre.* New Delhi: Saqi Book Depot, 1943.
——. "Taqsīm-e Hind ke bʿad." *Caṭṭān* (October 1948), repr. in *Majmū'a-e Ḥasan 'Askarī*, 1126–1137. Lahore: Sang-e-meel, 2008.
Ayres, Alyssa. *Speaking Like a State: Language and Nationalism in Pakistan.* Cambridge: Cambridge University Press, 2009.
Azim, Anisa Nargis. "Anjuman-e Taraqqī-e Urdu Pakistan." In *Pākistān meṃ Urdu*, ed. Mohammad Tahir Faruqi and Khatir Ghaznavi, 513–518. Peshawar: University Book Agency, 1966.
Aziz, K. K. *The Coffee House of Lahore. A Memoir 1942–1957.* Lahore: Sang-e-meel, 2007.
——. "Interview." In *Puchāṃ dasāṃ*, ed. Maqsood Saqib, 103–143. Lahore: Suchet, 2013.
Baqir, Mohammad. "Doctor Faqīr Moḥammad Faqīr." In *Kaccī munḍer par ek cirāġ, Bābā-e Panjābī Doctor Faqīr Moḥammad Faqīr kī zindagī ke aḥwāl-o āšār ham-ʿaṣar šaxṣiyāt ke qalam se*, ed. Junaid Akram, 58–64. Lahore: Bazm-e Faqīr Pākistān, 2011.
——. "Ikk ṣalāḥ." *Monthly Panjābī* 6, no. 10 (July 1957): 7–8.
——. "Interview." In *Puchāṃ dasāṃ*, ed. Maqsood Saqib, 206–214. Lahore: Suchet, 2013.
——. "Panjāb te Panjābī." *Monthly Panjābī* 1, no. 1 (September 1951): 15–16.
Barq, Ghulam Jilani. "Futūḥāt-e Islām." *Monthly Panjābī* 2, no. 4 (December 1952): 23–27.
Bashir, Ahmad. "*Gujhyā rog.*" *Monthly Panjābī*, August 1957, 12–16.
Bashir, Mian. "Vice-Chancellor Punjab University dā paiġām." *Monthly Panjābī* 3, no. 2 (November–December 1953): 8.
Bausani, Allessandro. "Recenti notizie dal Pakistan sulle literature bahui e beluci." *Oriente Moderno* 54, no. 4 (1974): 43–52.
——. "Storia e attività della Anguman-I Taraqqī-I Urdu dī Karaci." *Oriente Moderno* 35, no. 7 (1955): 331–345.
——. "Storia e attività della "Anguman-I Taraqqī-I Urdu dī Karaci." *Oriente Moderno* 35, no. 11 (1955): 536–548.
Bhatti, Abdul Majeed. *Dil daryā.* Lahore: Nayā Idāra, 1955.
——. *Theḍḍā.* Lahore: Hūnhār Book Depot, 1960.
Bourdieu, Pierre. *Ce que parler veut dire: L'économie des échanges linguistiques.* Paris: Éditions Fayard, 1982.
——. "La production de la croyance: contribution à une économie des biens symboliques." *Actes de la recherche en sciences sociales* 13 (1977): 3–44.

——. "Le champ littéraire." *Actes de la recherche en sciences sociales* 89 (1991): 3–46.
——. *Les règles de l'art: genèse et structure du champ littéraire.* Paris: Seuil, 1992.
Breseeg, Taj Mohammad. *Baloch Nationalism: Its Origin and Development.* Karachi: Royal , 2004.
Buzdar, Wahid. "Balocī šā'irī by taraqqī-pasand teḥrīk ke aṡrāt." In *Pākistān meṃ Urdu, dūsrī jild: Balocistān*, ed. Fateh Mohammad Malik, Syed Sardar Ahmad Pirzada, and Tajammul Hussain, 396–401. Islamabad: Muqtadra Qaumī Zubān, 2006.
Caldwell, Robert. *A Comparative Grammar of the Dravidian or South-Indian Family of Languages.* London: Kegan Paul, Trench, Truebner, [1856] 1913.
Carrère d'Encausse, Hélène. "Unité prolétarienne et diversité nationale: Lénine et la théorie de l'autodétermination." *Revue française de science politique* 21, no. 2 (1971): 221–255.
Casanova, Pascale. "Consécration et accumulation de capital littéraire [La traduction comme échange inégal]". *Actes de la recherche en sciences sociales* 144 (September 2002): 7–20.
Chattha, Ilyas Ahmad. "Economic Change and Community Relations in Lahore Before Partition." *Journal of Punjab Studies* 19, no. 2 (2012): 193–214.
——. "Partition and Its Aftermath: Violence, Migration and the Role of Refugees in the Socio-Economic Development of Gujranwala and Sialkot Cities, 1947–1961." PhD diss., University of Southampton, 2009.
Cheema, Sadia Nawaz. "Sajjād Haydar, šaxṣiyat fikr te fan." Master's thesis, Lahore Oriental College, 1996.
Choudhry, Kabir. *Bengali Academy: A Summary of its Achievements and Aspiration.* Dhaka: Bengali Academy, 1970.
Commission on National Education (Sharif Commission). *Report of the National Education Commission.* Karachi: Government of Pakistan, Ministry of Education, 1959.
Courouau, Jean-François. "La plume et les langues: Réflexions sur le choix linguistique à l'époque moderne." *L'Homme* 177/178 (2006): 251–278.
——. "Les apologies de la langue française (XVIe siècle) et de la langue occitane (XVIe–XVIIe siècles): Naissance d'une double mythographie: Première partie." *Nouvelle Revue du XVIe Siècle* 21, no. 2 (2003): 35–51.
——. "Les apologies de la langue française (XVIe siècle) et de la langue occitane (XVIe–XVIIe siècles): Naissance d'une double mythographie: Deuxième partie." *Nouvelle Revue du XVIe Siècle* 22, no. 2 (2004): 23–39.
Daman, Ustad. Interview with Munnu Bhai and Nawaz for Radio Pakistan, June 29, 1974. Accessed June 12, 2025. https://www.youtube.com/watch?v=ltIXLeSzQGM.
Daudi, Maqbul Anwar. "Išā'atī idāre." In *Pākistān meṃ Urdu*, ed. Mohammad Tahir Faruqi and Khatir Ghaznavi, 635–638. Peshawar: University Book Agency, 1966.
Deol, Harnik *Religion and Nationalism in India: The Case of the Punjab.* London: Routledge, 2000.
Ehsan, Asya. "Teḥrīk-e Pākistān te Ẕahīr Nyāz Bīgī." Master's thesis, Lahore Oriental College, 1999.
Faiz, Faiz Ahmad. " 'Going to jail was like falling in love again'—Faiz Ahmad Faiz." *Herald*, March 1984. Accessed June 12, 2025. https://herald.dawn.com/news/1153696.

—. *Salībeṃ mere darīce meṃ*. Karachi: Maktaba-e Danyāl, [1976] 1992.

Faqeer, Faqeer Mohammad. "Āṇ wālā moṛ." *Monthly Panjābī* 1, no. 2 (October 1951): 2–3.

—. Faqeer Mohammad Faqeer to Shafi Aqeel, January 11, 1959. In *Bābā-e Panjābī Number, Timāhī Panjābī* (July–December 2000), 393–394.

—. "Idārya." *Monthly Panjābī* 1, no. 1 (September 1951): 2–3.

—. "Idārya." *Monthly Panjābī* 1, no. 4 (December 1951): 3–6.

—. "Idārya." *Monthly Panjābī* 5, no. 6 (February 1956): 2–3.

—. "Idārya." *Monthly Panjābī*, September–October 1955, 3–6.

—. "Idārya." *Monthly Panjābī*, August 1957, 3–7.

—. "Idārya." *Monthly Panjābī*, June–July 1958, 3–8.

—. "Idārya." *Monthly Panjābī*, November–December 1958, 2–7.

—. "Idārya." *Monthly Panjābī*, August 1959, 2–3.

—. "Karācī vic Panjābī dī āwāz." *Monthly Panjābī*, February–March 1952, 17–23.

—. "Kašmīr dī mālikī." *Monthly Panjābī* 1, no. 1 (September 1951): 6–7.

—, ed. *Lehrāṃ*. Lahore: Qureishi Book Agency,1953.

—. "Merī āpbītī." *Bābā-e Panjābī Number, Timāhī Panjābī*, July–December 2000, 34–35.

—. "Mirzā Moḥammad Rafīᶜ Saudā dī panjābī šāᶜirī." *Monthly Panjābī* 5, no. 9–10 (June–July 1956): 3–6.

—. *Muwāte*. Lahore: Bazm-e Faqīr Pākistān/Sānjh Publisher, [1956] 2015.

—. "Nīm firangī." *Monthly Panjābī* 2, no. 3 (November 1952): 3–4.

—. "Oh milke na mil sake." *Monthly Panjābī* 1, no. 4 (December 1951): 20–23.

—. "Panjābī adab." *Monthly Panjābī* 5, no. 8 (April–May 1956): 13–17.

—. "Panjābī adab vic inqilāb dī loṛ." *Monthly Panjābī* 1, no. 1 (September 1951): 17–20.

—. "Panjābī mušāᶜire dī ṣadāratī taqrīr." *Monthly Panjābī* 5, no. 8 (April–May 1956): 11–12.

—. *Panjābī zubān-o adab kī tārīx*. Lahore: Sang-e-meel, 2002.

—. "Poṭhohārī gīt." *Monthly Panjābī*, September–October 1959, 2–4.

—. "Qalmāṃ sidhyāṃ kar lo!" *Monthly Panjābī* 1, no. 10 (June 1952): 3–5.

—. "Qayām-e Pākistān toṃ bᶜad Panjābī bolī la'ī kīte ga'e jatan." *Bābā-e Panjābī Number, Timāhī Panjābī*, July–December 2000, 36–39.

—. "Savānyāṃ la'ī." *Monthly Panjābī* 1, no. 1 (September 1951): 54.

Faridkoti, Ain ul-Haq. "Khoj." In *Āzādī magroṃ panjābī adab*, ed. Asif Khan, 9–37. Lahore: Pakistan Punjabi Adabī Board, 1985.

Farooqi, Mohammad Hamza. "Urdu ṣaḥāfat kā inqilāb-afrīṃ numā'inda: Rozmarra 'Inqilāb' aur uskā syāsī kirdār." *Bunyād* (LUMS) 4 (2013): 85–105.

Fazil, Abdul Rashid. "Urdu College." In *Pākistān meṃ Urdu*, ed. Mohammad Tahir Faruqi and Khatir Ghaznavi. Peshawar: University Book Agency, 1966, 591–610.

Gazdar, Mushtaq. *Pakistan Cinema 1947-1997*. Karachi: Oxford University Press, 1997.

Ghaznavi, Khatir. "Dīgar muqtadar idāre." In *Pākistān meṃ Urdu*, ed. Mohammad Tahir Faruqi and Khatir Ghaznavi, 539–554. Peshawar: University Book Agency 1966.

—. "Peshawar University aur Urdu." In *Pākistān meṃ Urdu*, ed. Mohammad Tahir Faruqi and Khatir Ghaznavi, 579–584. Peshawar: University Book Agency, 1966.

Ghosh, Papiya. "The Changing Discourse of the Muhajirs." *India International Center Quarterly* 28, no. 3 (2001): 57–68.

Grierson, George A. *Linguistic Survey of India*, vol. 8, part 1, *Sindhi and Lahnda*. Delhi: Motilal Banarsidass, [1916] 1968.

——. *Linguistic Survey of India*, vol. 9, part 1, *Western Hindi and Punjabi*. Delhi: Motilal Banarsidass, [1919] 1968.

Gyan Chandani, Subho. Interview with Mazhar Jamil, Muslim Shamim, and Rahat Saeed. In *Guftagū. Taraqqī-pasand teḥrīk ke naẕrī masā'il, aśrāt aur muxālifīn ke aʿitrāẓāt par mašāhīrīn-e adab se bātchīt*, ed. Mazhar Jamil, 197–223. Karachi: Maktaba-e Danyāl, 1986.

Hamdani, Raza. *Pašto afsāne*. Peshawar: Nayā Maktaba, 1961.

Haq, Anwarul. "Pākistān vic panjābī adab dā irtiqā." Master's thesis, Lahore Oriental College, 1974.

Haq, Mehr Abdul. *Multānī zubān aur uskā Urdu se tʿalluq*. Bahawalpur: Urdu Academy, 1967.

——. *Sirā'īkī lok gīt*. Multan: Bazm-e Saqāfat, 1964.

Hashmi, Tariq. *Maulānā Ṣalāḥuddīn Ahmad*. Islamabad: Muqtadra Qaumī Zubān, 2011.

Humayun, Khalid. *Vīr tūṃ Kunjāh dā ai? Professor Šarīf Kunjāhi nāl gall-bāt*. Lahore: Sangat, 1999.

Hussain, Ehtisham. "Ġālib kā tafakkur aur uskā pasmanẓar." In *Behtarīn Adab 1950*, ed. Idāra-e Adab-e Laṭīf, 11–40. Lahore: Maktaba-e Urdu, 1951.

Hussain, Intizar. *Cirāġoṃ kā dhu'āṃ*. Lahore: Sang-e-meel, 2012.

——. *Din aur dāstān*. New Delhi: Arshia, [1957] 2013.

Hussain, Lyaqat. "Allama Ġulām Yaqūb Anwar, ḥayātī fikr te fan." Master's thesis, Lahore Oriental College, 1983.

Hussain, Shumaila. *Sirā'īkī dāniš ke sāth mukālma*. Multan: Multan Institute of Policy and Research, 2015.

Hyder, Sajjad. "Dilāṃ de rogī." *Monthly Panjābī*, February–March 1952, 25–32.

——. *Hawā de hūke*. Lahore: Qaumī Kutub-Xāna, 1957.

——. "Interview." In *Puchāṃ dasāṃ*, ed. Maqsood Saqib, 215–236. Lahore: Suchet, 2013.

——. "Kāng." *Monthly Panjābī* 1, no. 1 (September 1951): 38–41.

Iftikharuddin, Mian. *Selected Speeches and Statements*, ed. Abdullah Malik. Lahore: Nigārishāt, 1971.

Iqbal, Muhammad. *Bāng-e darā*. Lahore: Sheikh Mubarak Ali, [1905] 1939.

——. *Zarb-e kalīm*. Aligarh: Aligarh Book Depot, [1936] 1975.

Ishaq, Fauzia. "Afẓal Parwez dyāṃ Panjābī zubān-o adab la'ī xidmatāṃ." Master's thesis, Lahore Oriental College, 2006.

Islahi, Sharfuddin. "Sindh University aur Urdu." In *Pākistān meṃ Urdu*, ed. Mohammad Tahir Faruqi and Khatir Ghaznavi. Peshawar: University Book Agency, 1966, 561–578.

Jabeen, Musarrat, Amir Ali Chandio, and Zarina Qasim. "Language Controversy: Impacts on National Politics and Secession of East Pakistan." *South Asian Studies* 25, no. 1 (2010): 99–124.

Jafri, Akhtar Hussain. *Bābā-e Panjābī, Doctor Faqīr Moḥammad Faqīr dī ḥayātī te fan*. Lahore: Azeez, 1991.

Jahani Carina. *Standardization and Orthography in the Balochi Language*. Uppsala: Acta Universitatis Upsaliensis, 1989.

Jalal, Ayesha. *Self and Sovereignty: Individual and Community in South Asian Islam Since 1850*. Delhi: Oxford University Press, 2001.
Jalandhari, Sadaf. "Interview." *Bābā-e Panjābī Number, Timāhī Panjābī*, July–December 2000, 130–132.
Jalil, Rakhshanda. *Liking Progress, Loving Change: A Literary History of the Progressive Writers' Movement in Urdu*. New Delhi: Oxford University Press, 2014.
Jamaldini, Mir Abdullah. Interview with Mazhar Jamil and Muslim Shamim. In *Guftagū. Taraqqī-pasand teḥrīk ke nazrī masā'il, aṡrāt aur muxālifīn ke aʿitrāẓāt par mašāhīrīn-e adab se bātchīt*, ed. Mazhar Jamil, 225–238. Karachi: Maktaba-e Danyāl, 1986.
——. *Laṭxāna*. Quetta: Sangat Academy, 2002.
Jan, Razia Sultan. "Ṣūbā-e Panjāb meṃ Urdu ba-taur-e sarkārī zubān kā jā'iza." *Axbār-e Urdu*, March–April 2004, 389–394.
Javed, Inam-ul Haque. *Panjābī adab dā irtiqā, 1947-2003*. Lahore: Azeez Book Depot, 2004.
Jebi, Rashid. "Panjābī zubān te radio Pākistān." *Panjdaryā*, June 1966, 33–36.
Kalra, Virinder Singh, and Waqas Butt. "In One Hand a Pen in the Other a Gun, Punjabi Language Radicalism in Punjab, Pakistan." *South Asian History and Culture* 4, no. 4 (2013): 538–553.
Kamran, Tahir. "Early Phase of Electoral Politics in Pakistan: 1950s." *South Asian Studies* 24, no. 2 (2009): 257–282.
——. "Urdu Migrant Literati and Lahore's Culture," *Journal of Punjab Studies* 19, no. 2 (2012): 173–92.
Kashmiri, Noor. "Haḍbītī." *Monthly Panjābī* 1, no. 4 (December 1951): 36–38.
——. "Moḥabbat." *Monthly Panjābī*, February–March 1952, 45–48.
Kashmiri, Shorish. *Ḥamīd Niẓāmī*. Lahore: Caṭṭān, [1966] 2010.
——. *Nau rattan*. Lahore: Caṭṭān, [1967] 2010.
——. "Panjābī dī taraqqī." *Monthly Panjābī* 1, no. 2 (October 1951): 45–46.
——. *Teḥrīk-e Xatam-e Nubuwwat*. Lahore: Caṭṭān, [1974] 2011.
Kashmiri, Zaheer. *Adab ke mādī naẓariye*. Lahore: Kamal, 1945.
Kaur, Sarabjeet. "Indigenous Education in the Punjab: An Analysis of G. W. Leitner's Report." *Proceedings of the Indian History Congress* 72, no. 1 (2011): 913–924.
Kausar, Arifa. "Bašir Manẓar dyāṃ panjābī adab la'ī xidmatāṃ." Master's thesis, Lahore Oriental College, 2002.
Kausar, Inam ul-Haq. "Balocistān kī adabī anjumaneṃ aur Urdu mušāʿire." In *Pakistan meṃ Urdu, dūsrī jild: Balocistān*, ed. Fateh Mohammad Malik, Syed Sardar Ahmad Pirzada, and Tajammul Hussain, 350–382. Islamabad: Muqtadra Qaumī Zubān, 2006.
Kazmi, Sara. "The Marxist Punjabi Movement: Language and Literary Radicalism in Pakistan." *Sudasien chronik-South Asia Chronicle* 7 (2017): 227–250.
Khammi, Abdul Haq, ed. *Panjāb Rang*. Lahore: Panjābī Majlis, 1958.
Khan, Akhtar Ali. "Paiġām-e tabarīk." *Monthly Panjābī* 1, no. 4 (December 1951): 11.
——. "Urdu dī māṃ, Panjābī." *Monthly Panjābī*, August 1952, 16.
Khan Asif, ed. *Āzādī magroṃ panjābī adab*. Lahore: Pakistan Punjabi Adabī Board, 1985.
Khan, Chaudhry Mohammad Asghar. "Ġarīb de bhāg." *Monthly Panjābī* 1, no. 10 (June 1952): 47–48.

Khan, Mohammad Afzal. "Pakistan te Bhārat vic Panjābī." *Panjdaryā*, September 1960, 52–66.
Khan, Nawabzada Mehdi Ali. "Shakespeare dī angrezī te sāḍḍī Panjābī." *Monthly Panjābī* 1, no. 4 (December 1951): 25–26.
Khan, Sardar. "Panjābī de ḥurūf." *Monthly Panjābī* 5, no. 5 (January 1956): 6–13.
——. "Panjābī dī gatayyā." *Monthly Panjābī* 5, no. 8 (April–May 1956): 34–40.
——. "Panjābī luġat." *Monthly Panjābī* 3, no. 2 (November–December 1953): 25–30.
——. "Panjābī luġat." *Monthly Panjābī*, September–October 1955, 25–32.
——. "Panjābī luġat dā ikk warqa." *Monthly Panjābī* 5, no. 9–10 (June–July 1956): 46–48.
——. "Panjābī luġat dā ikk warqa." *Monthly Panjābī* 6, no. 12 (September 1957): 33–38.
——. "Panjābī nāqadrī kyoṃ?" *Monthly Panjābī* 6, no. 12 (September 1957): 25–30.
——. "Standard Panjābī." *Monthly Panjābī* 5, no. 9–10 (June–July 1956): 41–44.
——. "Zubān te bolī." *Monthly Panjābī* 5, no. 6 (February 1956): 6–9.
Khan, Zafar Ali. "Merā chuṭpanā." *Monthly Panjābī* 1, no. 4 (December 1951): 7–10.
Khayal, Taj Mohammad. "Panjābī dī benaṣībī." *Monthly Panjābī* 3, no. 2 (November–December 1953): 15–16.
——. "Ṣūbe dī ṣaḥīḥ xidmat," *Monthly Panjābī*, January 1952, 13–14.
Khokhlova, L. V. "The Role of Punjabi Language in Self-Identification of Punjabi Community." *Journal of Pakistan Vision* 10, no. 1 (2010): 1–11.
Khurshid, Abdus Salam. "Panjāb dī tārīx te adab." *Monthly Panjābī* 1, no. 2 (October 1951): 27–29.
Kunjahi, Sharif. *Jagrāte*. Lahore: Azeez Book Depot, [1965] 1984.
——. *Jhātyāṃ*. Lahore: Azeez Book Depot, [1960] 1994.
Kushta, Maula Bakhsh. "Panjābī de pehle āṭh sau sāl." *Monthly Panjābī* 1, no. 3 (November 1951): 35–37.
——. *Tażkira panjābī šāʿirāṃ dā*. Lahore: Azeez, [1960] 1988.
Lahori, Akbar. "O kauṇ sī?" *Monthly Panjābī*, August 1952, 22–24.
Leitner, G. W. *History of Indigenous Education in the Punjab Since Annexation and in 1882*. Lahore: Republican, [1882] 1991.
Levesque, Julien. *Etre sindhi au Pakistan: Nationalisme, discours identitaire et mobilisation politique 1930–2016*. PhD diss., EHESS, 2016.
Mahar Ibn-e Akbar, Ajmal. *Ḥāfiẓ Meḥmūd Širānī aur Doctor Mehr ʿAbdul Ḥaq, lisānī naẓāryāt. Taqābulī muṭālʿa*. Islamabad: Idāra-e Furūġ-e Qaumī Zubān, 2012.
Malik, Abdullah. *Mustaqbil hamārā hai*. Lahore: PPH, 1950.
Malik, Aysha Nyaz. "Salīm Kašir dī panjābī ġazal." Master's thesis, Lahore Oriental College, 2012.
Malik, Fateh Mohammad. "Idārya." *Axbār-e Urdu*, March–April 2004, 5–7.
Malik, Hafeez. "The Marxist Literary Movement in India and Pakistan." *Journal of Asian Studies* 26, no. 4 (1967): 649–664.
Malik, Muhibullah. "Ḥanif Caudhrī ḥayātī te fan." Master's thesis, Lahore Oriental College, 2010.
Malik, Rauf. "Nave panjābī adab dyāṃ lehrāṃ." *Panjābī Adab*, December 1961, 9–19.
——. *Surx syāsat*. Lahore: Jamhūrī, 2017.
Mansoor, Firozuddin, and Sibte Hasan. *Pākistān meṃ qaumī zubān kā masla*. Lahore: PPH, 1953.
Manto, Saʿadat Hassan. *Manṭo ke maẓāmīn*. New Delhi: Sāqī Book Depot, [1942] 1997.

Marwat, Fazal ur-Rahim. "Pashto Literature: A Quest for Identity in Pakistan." *Faultines* 18 (2007). Accessed June, 18, 2025. https://www.satp.org/satporgtp/publication/faultlines/volume18/Article3.htm.

Mateen, Arif Abdul. *Imkānāt*. Lahore: Technical Publishers, 1988.

——. *Parakh paṛcol*. Lahore: Azeez Book Depot, 2000.

Matringe, Denis. "Disguising Political Resistance in the Sufi Idiom: The Kafian of Najm Husain Sayyid of Pakistan." In *The Islamic Path: Sufism, Politics and Society in India*, ed. Saiyid Zahir Husain Jafri and Helmut Reifeld, 110–130. Ahmedabad: Rainbow, 2006.

——. "L'Apparition de la nouvelle et du roman en panjabi 1930–1947." *Journal Asiatique* 273, no. 3–4 (1985): 425–454.

——. " 'L'appel de la cloche': spiritualité, écriture poétique et vision politique chez Muhammad Iqbal (1877–1938)." In *Convictions religieuses et engagement en Asie du Sud depuis 1850*, ed. Catherine Clémentin, 49–82. Paris: École Française d'Extrême-Orient, 2011.

——. *Littérature, histoire et religion au Panjab, 1890-1950*. Paris, Collège de France, 2009.

——. "L'Utilisation littéraire des formes dialectales par les poètes musulmans du Panjab de la fin du XVIe au début du XIXe siècle." In *Dialectes dans les littératures indo-aryennes*, ed. Colette Caillat, 527–556. Paris: Publications de l'Institut de Civilisation Indienne, Collège de France, 1989.

Mehmood, Bazl-e Haq. *Panjābī maẓmūn*. Lahore: Sang-e-meel, 2003.

Mehr, Ghulam Rasool. "Bolī dī taraqqī." *Monthly Panjābī*, September–October 1955, 9–10.

——. "Islāmī ḥukūmat dā dūjā naqša." *Monthly Panjābī*, August 1952, 10–14.

——. "Islāmī ḥukūmat dā pehlā naqša." *Monthly Panjābī*, February–March 1952, 5–8.

——. "Merā safarnāma." *Monthly Panjābī* 1, no. 10 (June 1952): 7–10.

Meschonnic, Henri. *De la langue française*. Paris: Hachette, 1997.

Minhas, Miran Bakhsh. "Panjābī nūṃ vādhā kiveṃ hove?" *Panjābī Darbār* 1, no. 6 (November 1928): 9–17.

Minto, Abid Hassan. "Jadīd Urdu adab meṃ inḥeṭāṭī rujḥānāt." In *Nuqta-e Naẓar*, 201–215. Lahore: Multimedia Affairs, 2003. First published in *Šāhrāh*, New-Delhi, 1956.

——. "Nayā manšūr aur uske bʿad." In *Nuqta-e Naẓar*, 301–326. Lahore: Multimedia Affairs, 2003. First published in *Saverā* 13–14 (1953).

——. "Pākistān meṃ zubān kā masla." In *Nuqta-e Naẓar*, 277–289. Lahore: Multimedia Affairs, 2003. First published in *Adab-e Laṭīf*, October 1951.

——. "Rūmāniyat, farār aur ḥaqīqat." In *Nuqta-e Naẓar*, 327–359. Lahore: Multimedia Affairs, 2003. First published in *Adab-e Laṭīf*, 1953.

Mir, Arshad. "Bābā-e Panjābī." In *Kaccī munḍer par ek cirāġ, Bābā-e Panjābī Doctor Faqīr Moḥammad Faqīr kī zindagī ke aḥwāl-o āšār ham-ʿaṣar šaxṣiyāt ke qalam se*, ed. Junaid Akram, 53–57. Lahore: Bazm-e Faqīr Pākistān, 2011.

——. "Bābā-e Panjābī Faqīr Moḥammad Faqīr, kujh yādāṃ kujh gallāṃ." *Kārwān*, July 1976, 155–167.

Mir, Farina. *The Social Space of Language: Vernacular Culture in British Colonial Punjab*. Berkeley: University of California Press, 2010.

Mir, Safdar. "Daggā te agg." *Panjābī Adab*, April 1966, 161–164.

——. "Kālī." *Panjābī Adab*, November 1961, 26–30.

——. "Nīle dā aswār." In *Ṣafdar Mīr dyāṃ likhatāṃ*, ed. Sheema Majeed, 69–99. Lahore: Pakistan Punjabi Adabī Board, 2002. First published in *Rāvī Magazine*, Lahore, 1957.

——. "Panjābī adībāṃ dī żehnī fiẓā." *Panjābī Adab*, September 1963, 3–8.

——. "Panjābī kyoṃ?" *Panjābī Adab*, January–February 1963, 7–8.

——. Pušpā." *Panjābī Adab*, February 1962, 27–35.

Mirza, Shafqat Tanvir. "Interview." In *Puchāṃ dasāṃ*, ed. Maqsood Saqib, 189–205. Lahore: Suchet, 2013.

Mirza, Sultan Masud. "Ranḍī." *Monthly Panjābī*, March–April 1959, 48–52.

Mufti, Shaheen. *Anīs Nāgī, šaxṣyat aur fan*. Islamabad: Pakistani Academy of Letters, 2009.

Mughal, Nasrullah. "Ismaīl Matwālā ḥayātī fikr te fan." Master's thesis, Lahore Oriental College, 1989.

Mushtaq, Kanwal. "Pāk Panjābī League te Punjabi Cultural Society." *Saver*, December 1997, 11–14.

——. "Panjāb vic 1951 dyāṃ conāṃ te Panjābī zubān." *Saver*, October 1997, 9–12.

——. "Panjābī bolcāl te likhnā paṛhnā." *Saver*, September 1997, 13–16.

——. "Panjābī dī pehlī conference." *Saver*, August 1997, 12–14.

——. "Panjābī lehr te tanẓīmāṃ." *Saver*, March 1998, 14–16.

——. "Sarkārī tanẓīmāṃ te idāre." *Saver*, June 1998, 14–16.

Nagi, Anis. *Ek adhūrī sarguzašt*. Lahore: Jamāliyāt, 2008.

——. *Nayā š^cerī ufaq: 1960 kī na'ī šā^cirī kī teḥrīk*. Lahore: Jamāliyāt, [1969] 1988.

——, ed. *Sajre phull*. Lahore: Panjābī Majlis, 1959.

Nasir, Noman. "Moḥammad Ṣafdar Mīr de Panjāb te Panjābī bāre chape angrezī columnāṃ dī bibliography." Master's thesis, Lahore Oriental College, 2007.

Nazr-e Fatima. "Jannat de meḥl." *Monthly Panjābī* 1, no. 3 (November 1951): 49–50.

——. "Rāh dā ghaṭṭā." *Monthly Panjābī*, January 1952, 21–25.

——. "Takkar." *Monthly Panjābī*, February–March 1952, 38–40.

Nizami, Hamid. "Jamhūrī mulk." *Monthly Panjābī*, August 1952, 67–69.

——. "Panjābī dī ibtidā'ī t^calīm." *Monthly Panjābī* 1, no. 3 (November 1951): 11–12.

Nizami, Majid. *The Press in Pakistan*. Lahore: Department of Political Science, University of the Punjab, 1958.

Nomani, Sharar. "Ilāqā Sarḥad meṃ Urdu." In *Pākistān meṃ Urdu*, ed. Mohammad Tahir Faruqi and Khatir Ghaznavi, 113–138. Peshawar: University Book Agency, 1966.

Owaisi, Mohammad Arshad. "Panjāb assembly meṃ Urdu." *Axbār-e Urdu*, March–April 2004, 362–384.

Parvez, Afzal. *Kikrāṃ dī chāṃ*. Rawalpindi: Maktaba-e Xarābāt, 1971.

Pritam, Amrita. "Ustād Dāman." *Panjābī Adab* 27 (July–September 1993): 13–18.

Pritchett, Frances. "Convention in the Classical Urdu *Ghazal:* The Case of Mir." *Journal of South Asian and Middle Eastern Studies* 3, no. 1 (Autumn 1979): 60–77.

Qadir, Nahid. "Nawāz šaxṣiyat fikr te fan." Master's thesis, Lahore Oriental College, 1995.

Qaiser, Iqbal. "Sārang, ikk m^ceyārī panjābī risāla." *Saver*, November 1997, 9–11.

Qaladari, Ahmad Hussain. "Ġulām Yaqūb Anwar." *Panjābī Adab*, May 1961, 26–27.
Qasmi, Ahmad Nadeem. "Doctor Faqīr Moḥammad Faqīr." *Bābā-e Panjābī Number, Timāhī Panjābī*, July–December 2000, 46.
——. *Mere hamqadam*. Lahore: Sang-e-meel, 2007.
Qasmi, Ali Usman. *The Ahmadis and the Politics of Religious Exclusion in Pakistan*. London: Anthem, 2015.
Qazi, Anwar Ahmad. "Ṣeḥrā'ī Gurdāspūrī, ḥayātī te kalām." Master's thesis, Lahore Oriental College, 1988.
Qureishi, Akbar Hussein. "Balocistān meṃ Urdu." In *Pākistān meṃ Urdu*, ed. Mohammad Tahir Faruqi and Khatir Ghaznavi, 92–100. Peshawar: University Book Agency, 1966.
Qureishi, Mohammad Arif. "Adabī-o 'ilmī rasā'il." In *Pākistān meṃ Urdu*, ed. Mohammad Tahir Faruqi and Khatir Ghaznavi, 461–492. Peshawar: University Book Agency, 1966.
Qureishi, Sadiq. "Jalālpur dā Caudhrī." *Monthly Panjābī*, April 1952, 17–23.
Rahi, Ahmad. *Tirinjan*. Lahore: Al-Hamd, [1953] 2005.
Rahman, Tariq. *From Hindi to Urdu, a Social and Political History*. Karachi: Oxford University Press, 2011.
——. *Language and Politics in Pakistan*. Karachi: Oxford University Press, 1996
——. *Language, Ideology and Power*. Karachi: Oxford University Press, 2008.
——. "The Learning of Punjabi by Punjabi Muslims: A Historical Account." *International Journal of Punjab Studies* 8, no. 2 (2001): 187–224.
——. "The Urdu-English Controversy in Pakistan." *Modern Asian Studies* 31, no. 1 (1997): 177–207.
Rammah, Safir. "West Punjabi Poetry: From Ustad Daman to Najm Hosain Syed." *Journal of Punjab Studies* 13, no. 1–2 (2006): 215–228.
Rana, Aslam. "Jošua Faẓal Dīn, ḥayātī, fikr te fan." *Khoj* 45–46 (2001).
——. *Rang-sang, nave panjābī adab dā tanqīdī jā'iza*. Lahore: Azeez Book Depot, 1991.
Rana, Nasir. "Panjābī lisāniyāt." *Saver*, September 2004, 14–22.
Raphael, P. D. "Panjābī 'ilm." *Monthly Panjābī*, February–March 1952, 74–76.
Raza, Wasi. "Urdu Novel." In *Pākistān meṃ Urdu*, ed. Mohammad Tahir Faruqi and Khatir Ghaznavi, 347–376. Peshawar: University Book Agency, 1966.
Risalu, Raja. *Lā prīt ajehī Moḥammad*. Lahore: Pakistan Punjabi Adabī Board, 2008.
——. "Rabb kare koī hor rāhī na hove." *Saver*, October 2002, 11–15.
Sachyar, Sain. "Jaṭkyāṃ gallāṃ." *Monthly Panjābī* 1, no. 1 (September 1951): 25–27.
Sadid, Anwar. "Maulana Ṣalaḥuddin Aḥmad aur qaumī zubān Urdu." *Axbār-e Urdu*, March–April 2004, 198–215.
——. *Urdu adab kī teḥrīkeṃ*. Karachi: Anjuman-e Taraqqī-e Urdu Pakistan, 1996.
Salich, Mohammad Munir Ahmad. *Pīr Faẓal Gujrāti, ḥayātī te bāqī kalām*. Lahore: Punjab Institute of Language, Art and Culture (PILAC), 2012.
Salik, Abdul Majeed. *Panjābī adab te Sālik*. Lahore: Punjabi Academy, 1964.
——. "Panjābī conference de resolution." *Monthly Panjābī* 5, no. 8 (April–May 1956): 9–10.
——. "Sānūṃ Panjābī bolī te faxr ai." *Monthly Panjābī* 1, no. 2 (October 1951): 9–10.
——. "Urdu dā navāṃ daur." *Monthly Panjābī* 1, no. 1 (September 1951): 8–10.

——. "Xuṯba-e ṣadārat, Panjābī conference." *Monthly Panjābī* 5, no. 8 (April–May 1956): 4–8.

Salim, Ahmad. *Aḥmad Rāhī bātāṃ mulāqātāṃ*. Islamabad: Kūnj, 2005.

——. "Panjābī zubān dī teḥrīk te Doctor Faqīr Moḥammad Faqīr." *Bābā-e Panjābī Number, Timāhī Panjābī*, July–December 2000, 215–222.

——. *Sawāneḥ-e ʿumrī Ḥamīd Axtar*. Lahore: Book Home, 2010.

——. "Tirinjan dī kuṛī." *Saver*, September 1999, 15–20.

Sapiro, Gisèle. "De l'usage des catégories de droite et de gauche dans le champ littéraire." *Sociétés et representations* 11 (2001): 19–53.

——. "Forms of Politicization in the French Literary Field." *Theory and Society* 32 (2003): 633–652.

——. *La Guerre des écrivains 1940–1953*. Paris: Fayard, 1999.

——. "Le champ littéraire français." In *Art et société, savoirs croisés en sciences humaines et sociales Brésil / France*, ed. Alain Quemin and Glaucia Villas Bôas, 69–84. Marseille: Open Edition, 2016.

——. "Modèles d'intervention politique des intellectuels, le cas français." *Actes de la recherche en sciences sociales* 176–177 (2009): 8–31.

Saqib, Maqsood, ed. *Puchāṃ dasāṃ*. Lahore: Suchet, 2013.

Sattar, Mohammad Iffat. "Akbar Lahorī, ḥayātī fan te fikr." Master's thesis, Lahore Oriental College, 1987.

Schieffelin, Bambi, Kathryn Woolard, and Paul Kroskrity. *Language Ideologies, Practice and Theory*. New York: Oxford University Press, 1998.

Schimmel, Annemarie. "The Activities of the Sindhi Adabi Board, Karachi." *Die Welt des Islams* 6, no. 3 (1961): 223–243.

Schreffler, Gibb. "Western Punjabi Song Forms: *Māhīā* and *Ḍholā*." *Journal of Punjab Studies* 18, no. 1–2 (2011): 75–95.

Sehsarami, Kalim. "Mašriqī Pākistān meṃ Urdu." In *Pākistān meṃ Urdu*, ed. Mohammad Tahir Faruqi and Khatir Ghaznavi, 73–91. Peshawar: University Book Agency, 1966.

Serebryakov, I. *Punjabi Literature*. Moscow: Nauka, 1968.

Shackle, Christopher. *An Introduction to the Sacred Language of the Sikhs*. London: School of Oriental and African Studies, University of London, 1983.

——. "Punjabi in Lahore." *Modern Asian Studies* 4, no. 3 (1970): 239–267.

——. "Siraiki: A Language Movement in Pakistan." *Modern Asian Studies* 11, no. 3 (1977): 379–403.

Shah, Syed Ali. "Panjābī dā multānī rūp." *Monthly Panjābī*, September–October 1959, 9–19.

Shah, Syed Wiqar Ali. "Abdul Ghaffar Khan, the Khudai Khidmatgars, Congress and the Partition of India." *Journal of Pakistan Vision* 8, no. 2 (2007): 86–115.

Shahzad, Naveed. *Išārya pākistāni panjābī filmī gīt*. Lahore: Punjab Institute of Language, Art and Culture (PILAC), 2017.

——. *Naẕm aur na'ī panjābī naẕm*. Lahore: Faculty of Oriental Learning, Punjab University, 2015.

——. *Urdu-Hindī tanāzʿa aur Panjābī zubān*. Lahore: Sānjh, 2016.

Shirani, Akhtar. *Intixāb-e kalām*. Aligarh: Anjuman-e Taraqqī-e Urdu-e Hind, 1959.

Shirani, Hafiz Mehmood. *Panjāb meṃ Urdu*. Islamabad: Muqtadra Qaumī Zubān, [1928] 1998.
Sibte Hasan, Syed. "Urdu zubān faqīroṃ ke takyoṃ aur ġarīboṃ ke jhompṛoṃ meṃ palī. Bombay meṃ pehlī Urdu Conference." *Qaumī Jang*, March 11, 1945.
Siddiqui, Shamsuddin. "Qaumī Šāʿirī." In *Pākistān meṃ Urdu*, ed. Mohammad Tahir Faruqi and Khatir Ghaznavi, 307–319. Peshawar: University Book Agency, 1966.
Slade, E. H. "Census of Pakistan, 1951." Karachi: Government of Pakistan, 1951.
Sohail, Mohammad, Syed Munir Ahmad, and Hafiz Muhammad Inamullah. "The Educational Services and Philosophy of Bacha Khan." *Journal of Applied Environmental and Biological Sciences* 4 (2014): 157–165.
Soomro, Khadim Hussain. *The Path Not Taken. G. M. Syed, Vision and Valor in Politics*. Sehwan Sharif: Sain, 2004.
Spooner, Brian. "Balochi: Towards a Biography of the Language." In *Language Policy and Language Conflict in Afghanistan and Its Neighbors: The Changing Politics of Language Choice*, ed. Harold Schiffman, 319–336. Leiden: Brill, 2012.
Syed, Najm Hosain. *Kāfyāṃ*. Lahore: Majlis Shah Husain, 1965.
Talbot, Ian. *Pakistan: A Modern History*. London: Hurst, 1998.
——. "A Tale of Two Cities: The Aftermath of Partition for Lahore and Amritsar 1947–1957." *Modern Asian Studies* 41, no. 1 (2007): 151–185.
Taseer, M. D. "Ištirākiyat-pasandoṃ kā naẕāriya-e 'ilm-o adab." In *Maqālāt-e Tāṡīr*, ed. Mumtaz Akhtar Mirza, 291–297. Lahore: Majlis-e taraqqī-e adab, [1949] 1978.
——. "Rūdād-e Urdu." In *Maqālāt-e Tāṡīr*, ed. Mumtaz Akhtar Mirza, 265–272. Lahore: Majlis-e taraqqī-e adab, [1948] 1978.
Toor, Sadia. *The State of Islam: Culture and Cold War Politics in Pakistan*. London: Pluto, 2011.
Usmani, Irfan Waheed. "Print Culture and Left-Wing Radicalism in Lahore, Pakistan, c. 1947–1971." PhD diss., National University of Singapore, 2016.
Yazdani, Suhail. "Muhāṇe dī dhī." *Monthly Panjābī*, August 1952, 41–46.
Yusuf, Mohammad. "Panjābī dī pukār." *Monthly Panjābī*, October 1958, 12–13.
Zafar, Mohammad Tariq. "Xalīl Ātiš dī šāʿirī te kalām." Master's thesis, Lahore Oriental College, 1988.
Zafar, Sania. "Aḥmad Ẕafar dī panjābī šāʿirī." Master's thesis, Lahore Oriental College, 2010.
Zaheer, Sajjad. "Nīnd nahīṃ ātī." In *Angāre*, ed. Sajjad Zaheer, 1–19. Lucknow: Mirza Mohammad Jawad Nizami, 1932.
——. *Rūšnā'ī*. New Delhi: Qaumī Council Barā-e Furūġ-e Urdu, [1956] 2006.
Zaidi, Faiza. "Niẕām Dīn Tawakkulī te ohnāṃ dī inšāya-nigārī." Master's thesis, Lahore Oriental College, 2008.
Zeervi, Saqib. "Rabb jāne." *Monthly Panjābī*, February–March 1952, 62–64.
Zulfiqar, Ghulam Hussain. "Punjab University aur Urdu." In *Pākistān meṃ Urdu*, ed. Mohammad Tahir Faruqi and Khatir Ghaznavi, 555–560. Peshawar: University Book Agency, 1966.
——, ed. *Qaumī zubān ke bāre meṃ ehm dastāwezāt*. Islamabad: Muqtadra Qaumī Zubān, 1986.

Index

Abbas, Rashid, 50
Abbasi, Aziz ul-Hassan, 155–159
Abid, Abid Ali, 120, 122, 128–129, 149, 170, 177–178
Abro, Jamal, 21
Adam, Abdul Hameed, 106
Adib, Mirza, 250n226
Adil, Ibrahim, 124, 128, 153–154, 170
Afghanistan, Pashto as national language of, 220n53
Afzal, Chaudhry Mohammad, 141
Ahmad, Maulana Salahuddin, 43, 45–48, 60–61, 65, 69, 89, 131; conservative Punjabi movement and, 133–134
Ahmad, Mian Bashir, 130–131, 169
Ahmad, Shehzad, 5, 62, 190, 199, 203–204
Ahmad, Zubair, 1
Ahmed, Chaudhry Nazir, 57, 80, 101, 102
Ahsan, Akhtar, 63
AIPWA. *See* All India Progressive Writers' Association
Ajiz, Sadiq Ali, 183, 188
Akbar, Abdul Akbar Khan, 24
Akbar, Syed, 41
Akhtar, Hameed, 55, 57, 59, 81
Akram, Junaid, 5, 147, 238n1
Alampuri, Maulvi Ghulam Rasool, 37, 98
Aleemi, Akmal, 5–6, 142, 188
Ali, Anwar, 51
Ali, Ashgar, 89, 234n76
Ali, Kamran Asdar, 9, 55, 219n38
Ali, Maratib, 169
Ali, Mirza Zafar, 149
Ali, Shaukat, 57–58, 64, 76, 85–86; on Punjabi language, 93–95
Ali, Sheikh Karamat, 41
Alig, Bari, 56, 102, 173
Allahabad (Allahabad Address), Allama Iqbal, 125
All India Progressive Writers' Association (AIPWA), 56
All India Radio, 53
All Pakistan Literary Conference, 62, 66–71
All Pakistan Progressive Writers' Association (APPWA), 27; Marxist Punjabi movement and, 67–68, 75, 79–80; Marxist writers and, 56–59
Amar, Abdul Hamid, 177
Ambalvi, Waqar, 59–60, 120, 128–129, 149, 167, 170; rural/urban stories by, 179–180; travelogues by, 183

Amritsari, Sadiq, 102
Amritsari, Shad, 131
Amritsari, Ustad Karam, 120, 122, 124, 149, 168–169, 196
Anand, Mulk Raj, 56
Anjuman-e Taraqqī-e Urdu, promotion of Urdu through, 14–16
Anqa, Muhammad Hussain, 25–26, 211
Ansari, Khizar Humayun, 5
anti-Ahmadi activists, 226n24
anti-Ahmadi movement, 61
Anwar, Ghulam Yaqub, 149, 169; as new generation poet, 171–172, 178
Anwar, Yaqub, 194, 197, 200–201
APP. *See* Azad Pakistan Party
APPWA. *See* All Pakistan Progressive Writers' Association
Aqeel, Shafi, 5, 129, 147, 149, 169–70, 179, 217n17, 238n1
Arora, Subhash Chander, 240n15
Aryans, 158–159
Ashk, Upendranath, 31
Ashraf, Agha, 169
Askari, Mohammad Hasan, 61–62, 66–67, 208
Aslam, M., 62
Athar, Abbas, 63
autobiographies (in Punjabi), 183–184
Awami League, 19, 27
Awara, Darshan Singh, 35, 150, 163
Ayaz, Shaikh, 21
Ayres, Alyssa, 3–4, 9, 213
Azad Pakistan Party (APP), 58, 230n45
Azad Schools, 23
Aziz, K. K., 6, 46, 52–53, 55, 147, 203, 224n83, 225n99, 228n21
Aziz, Sheikh Abdul, 147, 211

Baba, Rahman, 24
Babur, Zaheer, 57–58, 64, 81, 95, 101, 231n55; *Gall-bāt* column, 86–92, 151
Bahu, Sultan, 29, 98
Baig, Mirza Sultan, 53–54, 92, 232n64
Bailey, Grahame, 40, 127
Bakhsh, Mian Muhammad, 29, 36, 98
Baloch, Nabi Bakhsh, 22
Balochi language, 11; language movement for, 25–26, 211; national consciousness and, 25; typology for, 26
Baqir, Mohammad, 120, 122, 127, 130–131, 135–136, 143, 155; *Monthly Panjābī* and, 184; Punjabi Academy and, 145–147, 244n103, 247n171
Barkhurdar, Hafiz, 37, 137
Barq, Ghulam Jilani, 154–155
Bashir, Ahmad, 170, 180
Batalvi, Shiv Kumar, 208
Baudelaire, Charles, 190, 204
Bedi, Rajinder Singh, 31, 173
Beg, Ishfaq, 57
Bengali language: activists for, 18; administrative applications for, 11; in constitution of Pakistan, 20; criticism of, 119; language movement for, 18–20, 119; Linguistic Action Committee and, 18; as official language in Pakistan, 12–13; UNESCO and, 19; United Front, 19–20
Bhai, Munnu, 5–6, 92, 101, 108, 115–116, 149
Bhasani, Maulana Abdul Hamid Khan, 19, 211
Bhatti, Abdul Majeed, 3, 57, 64, 72–73, 98–99, 101; in conservative Punjabi movement, 122, 131, 138; *Dil daryā*, 79–80, 113–114, 174–175; early career of, 173; fictional works of, 117, 210, 229n31; in Marxist Punjabi movement, 105–107; poetry of, 206
Bhatti, Azim, 101
Bhatti, Mohammad Azam, 92, 116–117
Bhatti, Nasreen Anjum, 209
Bhutta, Saeed, 1
Bijnauri, Noor, 50
bilingual Urdu-Punjabi writers, 1, 8, 107–108, 170, 180
Bourdieu, Pierre, 9–10, 26, 241n40
Brahui language, 11
Bukhari, Z. A., 77
Butt, Waqas, 3–4, 9

Camus, Albert, 204
Carey, William, 39
Casanova, Pascale, 235n83
Caṭṭān group, of conservative writers, 62
Chandani, Subho Gyan, 21, 221n55
Chander, Krishan, 31, 102
Chatrik, Dhani Ram, 37, 150
Chatterjee, P. C., 33
Chaudhry, Mohammad Ismail Bhatti, 138
Chishti, Talib, 177–178
Christian-Muslim-Punjabi activism, 8, 35–39
Christian Punjabi writers, 2
Chughtai, Abdur Rahman, 77, 131
Chughtai, Ismat, 102
cinema, films and: in Punjabi, 53–54; in Urdu, 54
Circle of the Men of Good Taste (*Ḥalqa-e Arbāb-e Zauq*), 2, 5, 46, 60–61
civil servants: British, 32–33, 40; Pakistani, 16, 42, 49, 139, 170, 189
classical poetry, in Sindhi language, 22
colonial era: Punjabi language during, 31–41; Punjab province during, 29–41
colonialism, language of, in Pakistan, 11
commercial writers, 170
communist initiatives, in Marxist Punjabi movement, 65–80
Communist Party of India (CPI), 57; PPH Publishing and, 76–77
Communist Party of Pakistan (CPP), 57–59
conservative Punjabi movement: Salahuddin Ahmad and, 133–134; analysis and overview of, 184–185; autobiographical production within, 183–184; Baqir as leader of, 127; beginning of activities of, 121–123; civil servants in, 170; commercial writers in, 170; conceptual approach to, 120–121; creators of, 168–169; decline and end of, 145–147; defense of Punjabi literature, 161–163; Dyal Singh College and, 122–123; establishment of, 121–122, 168; expansion of, 130–131; Faqeer as leader of, 122–125, 127; fictional production within, 178–181; *First Punjabi Conference of Lyallpur*, 143–145; ideology of, 121–123; journalists in, 170; Lahore Resolution and, 124; landowners in, 170; lawyers in, 170; leaders of, 123–127, 168; literary production of, 174–184; modernist movement compared to, 193–194; multigenerational nature of, 169; new discourse in defense of Punjabi, 131–133; new literary generation within, 171–173; Pak Punjabi League, 120, 131, 137, 168, 193–194; prestigious supporters of, 169; programs of, 121–123, 134–137; Punjabi Academy and, 145–147; Punjabi Cultural Society and, 137–143; radio dramas as genre for, 182; Salik as leader of, 125–127; social capital of, 169–170; structure of, 168–171; subgroups of, 168–170; traders in, 170. *See also* conservative writers; *Monthly Panjābī*; Punjabi Cultural Society; *specific people*; *specific topics*
conservative writers: Askari and, 61–62; autobiographical production by, 183–184; *Caṭṭān* group, 60; fictional production by, 178–181; *Ḥalqa-e Arbāb-e Żauq* group, 60–61; ideological differences with Marxist writers, 55–56; *Jamā'at-e Islāmī* group, 60; literature for, 55–56; nationalist veterans group, 59; *Nawā-e Waqt* group, 60; poets as part of, 62; post-Partition stories, 180–181; radio dramas, 182; rural/urban stories, 178–180; Taseer and, 61–62. *See also specific people*
Courouau, Jean-François, 90, 231n58, 231n60
CPI. *See* Communist Party of India

CPP. *See* Communist Party of Pakistan
Cummings, Thomas F., 40

Daily Imroz, 54, 58–59, 229n31; *Gall-bāt* column in, 86–92; Marxist Punjabi movement and, 80–93, 97–98, 100–101, 148; official language issue in, 81–84; poems published in, 92, 115–117; political orientation of, 230n50; Punjabi language in, 84–86; *Punjabi Page*, 92–93; Taseer and, 65–66
Daily Jang, 138–140, 145
Dakhini dialect, for Urdu, 223n59
Daman, Ustad, 3, 36, 101, 108–109, 131, 142
Dar, Zahid, 1, 62
Dard, Gyani Hira Singh, 35
Datta, Dhirendranath, 12
Daultana, Mian Mumtaz, 42, 60
Daultana, Nawab Mumtaz, 85
dictionaries: Faqeer on, 167–168; in *Monthly Panjābī*, 167–168; for standardized Punjabi, 166–168
Dil daryā (Rivers of the Heart) (A.M. Bhatti), 113–114, 174–175; Marxist Punjabi movement, 79–80
Din, Joshua Fazal, 2, 36–37, 128, 138, 185; as traditionalist writer, 5
Dostoevsky, Fyodor, 190, 204
Duggal, Kartar Singh, 2, 35, 49, 173, 222n32
Dyal Singh College, 122–123

East Pakistan Congress Party, 12
Eisenhower, Dwight, 116
Ejaz, Manzur, 1
Elahi, Chaudhry Perwaiz, 214
English, as language: replacement in Pakistan, 11–14; replacement in Punjab province, 41–42; triglossia and, 50–53
existentialism genre, 63, 201, 205

Faiz, Faiz Ahmad, 5, 56–59, 76, 81; imprisonment of, 198; use of Punjabi language, 108–111
Faqeer, Faqeer Mohammad, 3, 36, 77, 87, 91–92, 244n103; defense of Punjabi literature, 162–163; as leader in conservative Punjabi movement, 122–125, 127; Muslim League and, 124; *Muwāte*, 174–176; Partition's negative impact on, 125; poetry collections of, 124, 174–176; post-Partition fiction by, 180–181; Punjabi Academy and, 146–147; on Punjabi language dictionary, 167–168; in Punjabi Movement, 4; *Qadiriyya* brotherhood and, 124; on standardization of Punjabi language, 165; Sufism and, 123–124; in traditionalist group, 5; on triglossia of languages, 52. *See also Monthly Panjābī*; Punjabi Cultural Society
Farid, Baba, 29, 36, 89, 109
Farid, Khwaja Ghulam, 29, 36, 98
Faridabadi, Syed Mutalibi, 59
Faridkoti, Ain ul-Haq, 49
Fatehpuri, Nyaz, 250n226
Fatima, Nazr-e, 149, 169, 181–182
feminine poetry, 103
fiction, by conservative Punjabi writers: by Marxist Punjabi writers, 117–118; by modernist Punjabi writers, 207–208; post-Partition narratives, 180–181; rural/urban stories, 178–180. *See also specific genres; specific writers*
First Punjabi Conference of Lyallpur, 143–145
folklore, folks songs and, in Punjabi language, 99–101

Gall-bāt column, in *Daily Imroz*, 88–92; origins of, 86–87
Gamon, Ghulam Hassan Khan, 171–172
Gargi, Balwant, 2, 49
ġazal genre, of poetry, 177–178
gender: language education by, 38. *See also* girls
Ghaffar, Qazi Abdul, 250n226
girls, language education for, 38
Gorakhpuri, Majnun, 250n226

Grierson, George, 40, 165
Gujrati, Peer Fazal, 36, 128, 148, 170
Gujrati, Rahat, 85–86, 88, 99–100
Gurumukhi script, for Punjabi language, 144, 163–165

Haider, Ali, 98
Haider, Dada Amir, 57, 73
Hairat, Ghulam, 131
Hali, Altaf Husain, 36
Hamdam, Ustad, 3, 36, 140
Hameed, A., 62, 250n226
Hameeduddin, Qazi, 239n10
Hanif, Mohammad, 214
Haq, Maulvi Abdul, 14, 16, 43–47, 69, 121; as "father of Urdu," 15, 78, 126, 132. *See also* Urdu
Haq, Mehr Abdul, 100, 234n77, 235n80
Haq, Qazi Fazl-e, 3, 37, 222n46
ul-Haq, Shuja, 1
Hasan, Mumtaz, 146
Hasan, Sibte, 57–59, 77–79, 95, 118, 229n40; imprisonment of, 198
Hashmi, Hamid, 81
Hasrat, Chiragh Hasan, 58, 60, 81
Hassan, Zahid, 1
Hayat, Sikandar, 240n18
Hayat, Umar, 43–44
Hijazi, Naseem, 61–62
Hindiization, of Punjabi language, 167
Hoshiarpuri, Hafeez, 131
Humayun, Khalid, 5, 104
Huq, A. K. Fazlul, 19, 211
Hussain, Abdullah, 1
Hussain, Fazli, 240n18
Hussain, Intizar, 1, 55, 196, 204
Hussain, Mohammad, 77
Hussain, Sanober, 24
Hussain, Shah, 29, 188
Hyder, Sajjad, 53, 129, 169; as new generation poet, 171–173; radio dramas, 182; Radio Pakistan and, 173; rural/urban fiction, 179

Ibn Ziyad, Tariq, 176
Ibrahim, Mirza, 57
Iftikharuddin, Mian, 185, 230n45, 230n50; in Marxist Punjabi movement, 64, 80–84, 101, 118; Marxist writers under, 58–59. *See also Daily Imroz*
Ikramullah, 1
Imagism, as literary genre, 197
India: Communist Party of India, 57, 76–77; political tensions with Pakistan, 87–88. *See also* Partition; pre-Partition era
Indian People's Theater Association (IPTA), 202
Inqilāb (newspaper), 59
instruction, education and, languages of: *Anjuman-e Taraqqī-e Urdu* and, 14–16; by gender, 38; Karachi University, 14–15; in schools, 13–14; Sharif Commission and, 15; in universities, 14–15; Urduization process, 14; Urdu language as, 13–15, 51
intellectuals, intellectual movement and: Pashto use by, 24; Sindhi language movement and, 21. *See also specific people*
IPTA. *See* Indian People's Theater Association
Iqbal, Muhammad (Allama), 29, 36, 59, 124, 174–175, 240n18, 248n188
Iqbal, Zafar, 62, 205–206, 217n17
Ishaq, Major, 4
Islam League, 138, 242n70

Jahan, Rashid, 56
Jahangir, Mian Saleem, 4
Jail Road, 2
Jain, Banarsi Das, 37
Jalal, Ayesha, 32–33
Jalandhari, Hafeez, 65, 105, 107, 124, 140
Jalandhari, Sadaf, 243n84
Jalandhari, Talib, 177
Jalandhari, Zya, 205
Jalees, Ibrahim, 65
Jalib, Habib, 190, 196, 199–200
Jalib, Iftikhar, 62, 187, 199, 203–204

Jamā'at-e Islāmī group, of conservative writers, 60
Jamaldini, Abdullah Jan, 25–26
Jamaldini, Azat, 25–26
Jebi, Rashid, 50, 53–54
Jinnah, Muhammad Ali, 13, 19, 43, 81–82, 124, 154, 176
journalists: in conservative Punjabi movement, 170. *See also Monthly Panjābī; specific people*

Kaiser, Shahidullah, 221n55
Kalra, Virinder, 3–4, 9
Kamran, Jilani, 62, 190, 199–200
Kapoor, Kanhaiya Lal, 31
Karachi, Pakistan, demographic change after 1947, 20–21
Kardar, A. R., 54
Karim, Abdul (Prince), 26, 211
Karīmullah, Khwaja Mohammad, 124
Kashir, Saleem, 5, 92, 101, 108, 115, 117, 149
Kashmiri, Noor, 149, 169, 179, 183, 217n17
Kashmiri, Shorish, 5, 31, 60–61, 65–66, 126, 130
Kashmiri, Zaheer, 57, 59, 65, 80, 103, 233n70, 252n45
Kaur, Prabhjot, 49
Kazmi, Nasir, 204
Kazmi, Sara, 3–4, 9
Khadarposh, Masud, 138
Khadim, Chaudhry Ali Mohammad, 217n17
Khammi, Abdul Haq, 62, 188, 190, 196
Khan, Abdul Ghaffar, 18, 23–24, 27, 152, 211. *See also* Pashto language
Khan, Abdul Ghani, 24
Khan, Akbar (General), 58
Khan, Akhtar Ali, 59–60, 130, 155
Khan, Asif, 141–142, 196, 210, 224n90
Khan, Ayub, 15, 22, 125, 152–153, 187, 194
Khan, Liaquat Ali, 12–13
Khan, Mazhar Ali, 58–59, 108
Khan, Mohammad Afzal, 138, 140–141, 187–189, 199–200, 224n90
Khan, Nawabzada Mehdi Ali, 162, 170
Khan, Sardar, 37, 137, 155–156, 169–170; on standardization of Punjabi language, 163–168; on Urdu alphabet, 164–165
Khan, Syed Ahmad, 183
Khan, Tahira Mazhar Ali, 72
Khan, Yahya, 219n38
Khan, Zafar Ali, 43, 59–60, 124–125, 129–130, 183
Khan, Zafarullah, 226n24
Khattak, Ajmal, 24
Khayal, Taj Mohammad, 130, 149, 155, 161–162
Khokhlova, L. V., 212
Khosla, G. S., 49
Khowar language, 11
Khursand, Khushhal Chand, 31
Khurshid, Abdus Salam, 126, 162, 211, 247n171
Krishan, Mahashay, 31
Kunjahi, Ghanimat, 147
Kunjahi, Sharif, 5, 64, 117, 131, 149, 210–211; Marxist Punjabi movement and, 68–73, 76, 95–97, 104–105, 118; poetry of, 135, 206
Kushta, Maula Bakhsh, 5, 36–37, 92, 128, 131, 140, 150, 224n90; in conservative Punjabi movement, 169–170; publication of works for, 149

Lahore, Pakistan: conservative writers in, 59–62; Marxist writers in, 55–59; modernist writers in, 62–63; pre-Partition literary scene in, 2–3; Punjabi Cultural Society in, 193–194; Punjabi literary journals in, 3; Radio Pakistan, 7, 173, 202; radio station in, 173; Urdu language use in, 41–42
Lahore Literary School (*Dabistān-e Lāhore*), 2

Lahore Press Club, demonstrations at, 1
Lahore Resolution, 124
Lahori, Akbar, 129, 149, 169, 180, 188, 195–196, 200
Lahori, Majeed, 128–129, 170
landowners, in conservative Punjabi movement, 170
language movements: analysis and overview of, 210–214; for Balochi language, 25–26, 211; for Bengali language, 18–20, 119; in Pakistan, 17–27; for Pashto language, 23–24; politicization of, 17–18, 26–27; for Sindhi language, 20–23; typology of, 26–27; for Urdu language, 42–48
languages: administrative, 11; compulsory, 23; ideology of, 215n1; national, 43–44; official, 11–13
lawyers, in conservative Punjabi movement, 170
Lehr, Ustad Ishq, 3, 36
Levesque, Julien, 22
Linguistic Survey of India (Grierson), 40
Lok Virsa, 236n120
Ludhianvi, Sahir, 57, 59, 65, 173

Macauley, Thomas Babington, 223n62
Mahi, Chaudhry Ali Mohammad, 217n17
Mahir, Mohan Singh, 49
Malhi, Gobind, 21
Malik, Abdullah, 56–59, 71, 74, 81–83, 87, 91, 173; defense of Punjabi language, 228n13, 228n22, 229n31; as Marxist activist, 221n55
Malik, Anushay, 9
Malik, Fateh Mohammad, 214
Malik, Jameel, 92, 98, 101, 108, 115, 233n73
Malik, Rauf, 58, 72, 76–77, 98, 101, 109, 173, 201; criticism of Punjabi literature, 251n25; early life of, 229n31; as Punjabi activist, 224n90
Malik, Shahbaz, 6, 169–170
Mamdot, Nawab Iftikhar Hussain Khan, 60
Mansoor, Firozuddin, 57–58, 77–79, 95, 118, 229n40
Manto, Saadat Hasan, 77, 99, 102–103, 142; short story *Khol do!*, 182; use of Punjabi language by, 108–111
Manzar, Bashir, 149
Manzoor, Khwaja, 203
Mard-e Momin concept, 248n188
Marwat, Fazal ur-Rahim, 24
Marxism: Punjabi language and, 55–56. *See also* Marxist writers; *specific topics*
Marxist Punjabi movement: All Pakistan Literary Conference, 66–71; analysis of, 118–119; APPWA and, 67–68, 75, 79–80; Askari and, 67; Bhatti in, 105–107; communist initiatives in, 65–80; creators in, 102; *Daily Imroz* and, 80–93, 97–98, 100–101, 148; *Dil daryā* and, 79–80; dominated writers in, 107–111; early development of, 64–65; Hasan program and, 77–79; Iftikharuddin and, 64, 80–84, 101, 118; Kunjahi and, 68–73, 76, 95–97, 104–105; literary output in Punjabi language, 111–119; literature essays for, 98–99; Mansoor and, 77–79; mentors in, 101; Minto program and, 73–74, 78–79; *Panjābī Majlis* and, 199; poetic works, 111–117; PPH publishing house and, 76–77; progressive initiatives in, 65–80; Progressive Writer's Conference, 65–66; publishers in, 102; Punjabi language use in, 70–73; Rahi and, 64, 72–73, 75–77, 80, 92, 97–99, 102–103; *Saverā* and, 70–73, 79–80; Waris Shah and, 75–76; Sikhs in, 64; Taseer and, 65–67, 69; Urdu language adoption as part of, 82. *See also specific people*

Marxist writers: AIPWA and, 56; All Pakistan Literary Conference and, 57; APPWA and, 56–59; Communist camp, 57–58; Communist Party of Pakistan and, 57–59; fiction produced by, 181; ideological differences with conservative writers, 55–56; in Lahore, 55–59; literature for, 55–56; Mian Iftikharuddin's group, 58–59; *Monthly Panjābī* and, 150–151; progressive camp in, 56–57. *See also specific people*
Mashriqi, Inayatullah Khan, 236n114, 242n70
Masih, Rehmat, 37
Masroor, Hajira, 57, 59
"masterpiece argument," for Punjabi literature, 161
Mastoor, Khadija, 57, 59
Mateen, Arif Abdul, 57, 59, 65, 198, 200, 252n45
Matringe, Denis, 9–10, 248n188, 248n191
Matwala, Ismail, 92
Maududi, Syed Abu Ala, 60
Mazdoor Kisan Party, 4
Mehr, Ghulam Rasool, 59–60, 125, 129, 135, 154–155, 170; travelogues by, 183
Meschonnic, Henri, 231n60
Minhas, Miran Bakhsh, 36–38
Minto, Abid Hassan, 59, 72–74, 78–79, 81, 108, 249n206
Mir, Farina, 9
Mir, Safdar, 5, 57, 110, 138, 141; *Panjābī Majlis* and, 187–188, 195, 199–203; poetic works of, 205–206
Miraji, 172, 205
Mirza, Shafqat Tanvir, 101, 107–110, 115, 149, 209, 211; interviews of, 4–5; as Punjabi activist, 224n90; "Punjabiness" ('Panjābiyat') in works of, 4; *Sangat* and, 7
Mirza, Sultan Masud, 182
modernist writers, 55–56; in Lahore, 62–63. *See also* Punjabi modernist movement; *specific people*
modern poetry: in Punjabi language, 35. *See also* classical poetry
Mohajirs, 218n22; dissemination of Urdu through, 16–17; migration to urban areas, 20–21; in *Monthly Panjābī*, 158–159; Mughal culture, 17; population demographics for, 17; in Punjab province, 50; Urdu language use by, 225n94
Monthly Panjābī (literary journal), 54, 120, 238n1, 243n81; Abbasi essay in, 157–159; autobiographies in, 183; conservative tone of, 151–155; defense of Punjabi language use in, 131–133, 155–161; establishment of, 147–148; Faqeer editorials in, 136–137, 148–149, 151–153; format of, 148–151; illustration of Punjabi language in, 155–161; Islamic essays in, 153–155; S. Khan and, 155–156; Marxists and, 150–151; *Mohajirs* in, 158–159; objectives of, 148–151; One Unit Scheme in, 151–152; Pakistani contributors in, 247n170; patriotic essays in, 153–155; patriotic themes in, 128; poetry in, 149–150, 176–178; prose works in, 129; publication of, 127–130; public reception of, 127–130; Punjabi language dictionary in, 167–168; Salik essay in, 159–161; shutdown of, 120, 147; Urduization and, 158; Urdu writers in, 129
Murphy, Anne, 9
Mushtaq, Kanwal, 4
Muslim League, 23, 58, 60, 88, 124, 230n45
Muslim Punjabi writers, 2–3
Muslims, in Punjab province (before 1947), 33–34
Muwāte (Faqeer), 174–176

Nadvi, Maulana Khair Mohammad, 25
Nagi, Anis, 5, 55, 62, 188, 194; *Panjābī Majlis* and, 198–200, 203–208; poetic works of, 205–207; *Sajre phull*

anthology, 196–197; stream of consciousness in works by, 207–208
Naī šāʿirī movement, 204
Nanak, Guru, 29, 69–70, 96
Nanda, I. C., 2, 37, 49
Naqvi, Ashfaq, 176–177
Naqvi, Mahfuz ul-Hasan Shah, 149
Naqvi, Tanvir, 4, 72–73, 101, 114
Nasir, Gul Khan, 25, 221n75
Nasir, Hakim, 131, 138, 200
Nasr, Nasrullah Khan, 24
nationalism: Pakistan and, 185; Pashto, 24; passive, 24; Punjabi movement and, 27, 216n10
nationalist veterans group, of conservative writers, 59
national languages: in Afghanistan, 220n53; definition of, 43–44
Nawā-e Waqt group, of conservative writers, 60
Nawaz, 101, 108, 117
Nazar, Qayyum, 60, 140, 170, 172
Nazimuddin, Khawaja, 12–13, 18, 125
Nehru, Jawaharlal, 108, 152
neologisms: in Punjabi language, 166–168; standardization of language and, 166–168; in Urdu language, 16
Newton, John, 40
Niazi, Munir, 63, 190, 196, 199–200, 204–206, 211
Nishtar, Abdur Rabb, 43
Nizami, Hamid, 5, 130, 134, 154; in conservative writer group, 55, 60–61
Nizami, Majeed, 31
Nizami, Siraj, 173
Nizam of Hyderabad, 15
Nomani, Sharar, 23
Noon, Feroz, Khan, 140
Nooruddin, Fakir Syed, 147
North West Frontier Province (NWFP), in Pakistan, 11, 14, 18, 23–24, 28, 47–48, 69, 74, 78–79, 127, 152, 219n38, 220n52, 244n111
One Unit Scheme, 21, 151–152, 219n38, 244n111

Paisā Axbār, in Punjabi language and, 33–34
Pakistan: Azad Pakistan Party, 58; colonial language policy in, 11; Communist Party of Pakistan, 57–59; creation of, 11; East Pakistan Congress Party, 12; English language replaced in, 11–14; language movements in, 17–27; nationalism in, 185; 1956 Constitution, 13; official languages of, 11–13; One Unit Scheme in, 21, 151–152, 219n38, 244n111; political tensions with India, 87–88; Sikhs' exodus from, 126; vernacular languages in, 43, 47–48. *See also* Bengali language; Partition; pre-Partition era; Urdu; *specific languages*
Pakistan Times, 58–59, 81, 100–101, 198, 203, 230n45, 253n58
Pak Punjabi League, 75, 120, 123, 131, 137, 168, 193–194
Panjābī Adabī Sangat. See Sangat
Panjābī Majlis: anniversary for, 195–196; banning of, 197–199; foundation of, 187–188; history of, 186–187; language ideology in, 189–192; literary influences on, 188; Marxist group within, 199; S. Mir and, 187–188, 195, 199–203; Nagi and, 198–200, 203–208; *Naī šāʿirī* movement and, 204; *Panjāb Rang* and, 189–192; *Panjdaryā* monthly, 188–189; Punjabi Cultural Society and, 199; in Punjabi modernist movement, 186–194; among Punjabi writers, 5; reorganization of, 188; *Sajre phull* anthology, 196–197; second year of, 194–199; structure of, 199–201
Panjāb Rang, 189–192
Panjdaryā monthly, 188–189
Panjwani, Ram, 21

Partition, of India and Pakistan: Faqeer traumatized by, 125; linguistic situation in Pakistan after, 41–54; post-Partition fiction, 180–181; Sindhi language after, 20–21
Parvez, Afzal, 64, 72, 92, 98, 100–101, 106–107, 114
Pashto language, 11; after independence, 23; intellectuals' use of, 24; language movement for, 23–24; literary journals in, 24; nationalism and, 24; as national language of Afghanistan, 220n53; Perso-Arabic morphemes, 24; schools for, 23; typology for, 26
Peelu, 37
Peerzada, Rafi, 53, 173
PILAC. *See* Punjab Institute of Language, Art & Culture
poetry, poets and: in *Daily Imroz*, 92, 115–117; by Faqeer, 124; feminine, 103; ġazal genre, 177–178; Kunjahi and, 95–97; Marxist Punjabi movement and, 111–119; in *Monthly Panjābī*, 149–150, 176–178; new generation poets, 171–173; obscenity in Urdu poetry, 162; pederasty in Urdu poetry, 162; in Punjabi modernist movement, 205–207; in *Saverā*, 114; Sufi, 36, 95–97; *Tirinjan* poetic cycle, 111–114; Urdu, 162. *See also* classical poetry; modern poetry; *specific people*
post-Partition fiction, 180–181
Pound, Ezra, 188
PPH Publisher, 76–77
pre-Partition era, in Pakistan and India, Punjabi literary scene in, 2–3
Pritam, Amrita, 2, 35, 72–73, 77, 109, 113, 150; literary legacy of, 163, 192; relationship with other writers, 173
Pritlari, Gurbaksh Singh, 2, 35, 104
progressive group, among Punjabi writers, 5
Progressive Writers' Association, 2, 21, 62, 103, 105–106, 201, 222n32; banning of, 186, 199; Bombay branch of, 202; manifesto of, 233n71; Punjabi Cultural Society and, 139–141
Progressive Writer's Conference, 65–66
Punjabi Academy, 27, 41–54, 161, 244n103, 247n171; creation of, 145–147
Punjabi Cultural Circle, 217n17
Punjabi Cultural Society, 4, 168, 185; activities of, 140–142; creation of, 137–140; inactivity of, 186; in Lahore, 193–194; Pak Punjabi League and, 137; *Panjābī Majlis* and, 199; Progressive Writers' Association and, 139–141
Punjabi language: Shaukat Ali on, 93–95; biblical missions and, 39–40; Christian initiatives for, 35–39; during colonial period, 31; in *Daily Imroz*, 84–86; defense in *Monthly Panjābī*, 131–133, 155–161; defense of, 34–41; demographics of, 11; dialects for, 38–39; dictionary creation for, 166–168; English civil servants' use of, 32–34; in Faiz works, 108–111; folklore, 99–101; foreign words in, 167; *Gurumukhi* script for, 144, 163–165; Hindiization of, 167; lack of literary works in, 70; limitations of, 33–34; as low language, 51; in Manto works, 108–111; marginalization of, 28–29; Marxism and, 55–56; in Marxist Punjabi movement, 70–73; Marxist Punjabi movement literary works in, 111–119; modern poetry in, 35; Muslim initiatives for, 35–39; neologisms in, 166–168; in newspapers, 34; opponents of, 32–34; in *Paisā Axbār*, 33–34; perception of, 48–50; philology of, 39–41; promotion of, 34–41; Punjab Institute of Language, Art & Culture, 254n13; in radio and cinema, 53–54; *Shahmukhi*

script, 40; Sikhs and, 29–30, 34–35, 75–76, 95; social status of users, 52–53; standardization of, 163–168; Taseer objections to, 69; triglossia and, 50–53; as "undeveloped" language, 1, 74, 95; Urduization of, 167; Urdu language as replacement for, 47–48; Urdu writers' contempt for, 1. *See also* conservative Punjabi movement; Marxist Punjabi movement

Punjabi modernist movement: analysis of, 208–209; conceptual approach to, 186–187; conservative movement compared to, 193–194; dramatic narratives in, 207–208; length of, 186–187; literary production of, 204–208; *Naī šāʿirī* movement and, 204; *Panjābī Majlis* and, 186–208; poetic production in, 205–207; short story collections, 207–208. *See also* Progressive Writers' Association

Punjabi movement: Faqeer and, 4; historians of, 3–4; history of, 8; methodological approach to, 4–10; nationalism and, 27, 216n10; Syed and, 4. *See also* conservative Punjabi movement; Marxist Punjabi movement

"Punjabiness" ('Panjābiyat'), 4

Punjab Institute of Language, Art & Culture (PILAC), 254n13

Punjabi Society of the Government College of Lahore, 3

Punjabi writers, Punjabi literature and, 49; defense of, 161–163; Faqeer's defense of, 162–163; fictional output of, 117–118; fictional production by, 178–181; literary journals, 3; literary school for, 2; "masterpiece argument" for, 161; modernization of, 205; *Panjābī Majlis* group, 5; poetic output, 111–119; political affiliation of, 3; progressive group of, 5; Progressive Writers' Association and, 2; in Punjabi Marxist movement, 98–99; *Tirinjan* poetic cycle, 111–114; traditionalist group of, 5; Urdu language use by, 30–31; Urdu literature compared to, 162–163; Urdu writers compared to, 1. *See also specific people; specific topics; specific works*

Punjab province, linguistic status in: annexation of, 29–30; during colonial period, 29–34; conceptual approach to, 28–29; early literary texts in, 29; English replaced by Urdu in, 41–42; *Mohajirs* in, 50; Muslim ruling class in, 33–34; *Paisā Axbār* in, 33–34; after Partition, 41–54; Urduization of, 29–31, 41–42; Urdu language movement in, 42–48. *See also* Punjabi language; Punjabi modernist movement; Punjabi movement

Qadir, Maulana Abdul, 24

Qadir, Sheikh Abdul, 43

Qadiriyya brotherhood, 124

ul-Qadri, Mahir, 62

Qaisar, Lal Din, 124, 128, 149, 170

Qaiser, Iqbal, 1, 5

Qasmi, Ahmad Nadeem, 5, 77, 80, 92–93, 100–101, 107, 110–111; imprisonment of, 198; in Marxist writers group, 55–59, 81; poetry of, 140; *Sajre phull* anthology and, 196–197. *See also Daily Imroz*

Qasmi, Ali Usman, 9, 216n12

Qazi, I. I., 21

Qureishi, Sadiq, 179

Raaz, Shaikh Razaq, 21

radio dramas, as literary genre, 54, 182, 208

Radio Pakistan, 7, 173, 202

radio shows, radio industry and: conservative writers and, 182; Punjabi language and, 53–54; radio dramas, 182

Rafiqi, Salim, 92

Rahi, Ahmad, 3, 5, 54, 57, 87, 117, 131; literary legacy of, 192; in Marxist Punjabi movement, 64, 72–73, 75–77, 80, 92, 97–99, 102–103; in Marxist writers group, 55, 59; poetry of, 135, 149, 206; *Tirinjan* poetic cycle and, 13, 111–114, 174
Rahi, Aslam, 169, 177
Rahman, M. Salim-ur-, 1
Rahman, Tariq, 4, 9, 17, 23, 29–30, 50, 212–213
ur-Rahman, Salim, 5, 63, 188, 205
Rai, Lala Lajpat, 31
Ram, Chotu, 240n18
Ramay, Hanif, "Punjabiness" ('Panjābiyat') in works of, 4
Randhawa, Afzal Ahsan, 5–6, 209–210
Raphael, P. D., 163–164
Rashk, Abdul Qadir, 99–100
Raza, Ali, 9
Rehman, I. A., 109–110
Riaz, Ahmad, 92, 101
Risalu, Raja, 49, 141, 188–192, 194–198, 210, 224n90. *See also Panjābī Majlis*
Rizvi, Asi, 169, 176–177
Rizvi, Tayeb, 169
Rizwani, Anjum, 106
Romanticism movement, 249n206, 250n226

Sachyar, Sain, 128
Safir, Pritam Singh, 49
Sain, Firoz, 92–93
Sajid, Ghulam Hussain, 1, 8
Sajjad, Anver, 62
Sajre phull (*Fresh Flowers*) anthology, 196–197
Salik, Abdul Majeed, 37, 54, 75, 77; in conservative Punjabi movement, 125–127; in conservative writer group, 55, 59–61, 120, 122–123; death of, 147; defense of Punjabi language, 132; essay in *Monthly Panjābī*, 159–161; Punjabi Academy and, 146–147; Punjabi Cultural Society and, 137–143. *See also Monthly Panjābī*; Punjabi Cultural Society
Salim, Ahmad, 1, 5, 103, 111, 209, 244n117
Sangat (*Panjābī Adabī Sangat*): S .T. Mirza and, 7; origins and foundation of, 3–4; Syed and, 7
Sapiro, Gisèle, 9, 235n84
Saqib, Maqsood, 1, 4
Sartre, Jean-Paul, 188, 204
Satyarthi, Devendra, 31, 49, 99–100
Sauda, Mirza, 162
Saverā, 70–73, 79–80; poems published in, 114
Schieffelin, Bambi, 9, 215n1
schools, educational institutions and: Azad Schools, 23; language of education and instruction in, 13–14; Pashto in, 23
Sekhon, Sant Singh, 35
Shackle, Christopher, 3–4
Shah, Baba Bulleh, 29, 98, 188
Shah, Hashim, 29, 98
Shah, Hassan, 84
Shah, Waris, 29, 36–37, 75–76, 93, 98, 188
Shahab, Qudratullah, 152
Shahabuddin, Sir, 36–37, 121–122, 124, 240n18
Shahid, Charan Singh, 35
Shahid, Farida, 50
Shahzad, Naveed, 237n136
Shamim, Mir Mohammad Ali, 128
Sharaf, Babu Firoz Din, 124
Sharaf, Firoz Din, 36–37, 54, 93, 124, 131, 140, 149
Sharif, Sheikh, 146
Sharif Commission, 15
Shifai, Qateel, 57, 59, 65, 92, 101, 149–150
Shina language, 11
Shirani, Akhtar, 176–177
Shirani, Hafiz Mehmood, 40–41, 126–127, 155
Shyam, Narayan, 21
Siddiqui, Mukhtar, 172

Siddiqui, Naeem, 62
Siddiqui, Saghar, 54
Sikhs: exodus from Pakistan, 126; hegemony of, 126; lexicography of, 166–167; in Marxist Punjabi movement, 64; Punjabi language use by, 29–30, 34–35, 75–76, 95; rioting by, 183
Simeen, Rashida Rashid, 169
Sindhi language: activists for, 18; administrative applications for, 11; classical poetry in, 22; importance of, 22–23; intellectuals and, 21; language movement for, 20–23; after Partition, 20–21; G. M. Syed and, 21–22
Singh, Amarinder, 214
Singh, Balwant, 31
Singh, Basawa, 40
Singh, Bawa Budh, 37
Singh, Bhai Sher, 37
Singh, Bhai Vir, 34, 35
Singh, Gurbaksh, 35, 104
Singh, Mohan, 2, 35–37, 49, 104, 150, 163, 222n32
Singh, Nanak, 35
Singh, Puran, 35
Singh, Tara, 240n15
Singh, Teja, 37, 240n15
social capital, of Punjabi conservative movement, 169–170
Soofi, Mushtaq, 1, 209
standardization, of Punjabi language: dictionary creation and, 166–168; Faqeer on, 165; Sardar Khan on, 163–168; neologisms and, 166–168; script issues, 163–165; selection of standard variety in, 165–166; Sikh lexicography and, 166–167
Stefanson, George, 126
Stogdon, A. W., 32
Sufis, Sufism and, 9–10, 248n188; Faqeer and, 123–124; poetry and, 36
Suhdarvi, Tariq, 178
Syahposh, Baba Alam, 54, 149
Syed, G. M., 18, 27, 118, 146, 211; Sindhi language movement and, 21–22
Syed, Najm Hosain, 2, 209; in Punjabi movement, 4; "Punjabiness" ('Panjābiyat') in works of, 4; *Sangat* and, 7

Tabassum, Ghulam Mustafa, 5, 56, 98, 128, 131, 138, 149; *ġazal* genre and, 178; *Panjābī Majlis* and, 195–196
Taimiti, Khizr, 138
Taj, Imtiaz Ali, 173
Taseer, M. D., 43–44, 56, 61–62, 122; Marxist Punjabi movement and, 65–67, 69; objections to Punjabi language, 69
Tatari, Muzmir, 92
Taunsvi, Fikr, 31
Tawakkuli, Nizamuddin, 149
Tej, Gurcharan Singh, 150
Temple, Richard Carnac, 40
Tirinjan poetic cycle, in Punjabi language, 114, 174; literary legacy of, 13; literary structure of, 111–112; Rahi and, 112–113; sexual violence as theme in, 112
Tirmizi, Mazhar, 1
Toor, Sadia, 9, 55, 231n61
traders, in conservative Punjabi movement, 170
traditionalist group, among Punjabi writers, 5
Tufail, Muhammad, 89–90

Ulfat, Umar Din, 243n81
UN. *See* United Nations
UNESCO. *See* United Nations
Unionist Party, 240n18
United Nations (UN), Educational, Scientific and Cultural Organization, 19
Urban, Fazal Ilahi, 229n31
urban areas, cities and: Hindus' migration from, 20–21; *Mohajirs*' migration from, 20–21

Urdu College, 16
Urdu Conference, 42–43
Urduization, as process: in instruction applications, 14; *Monthly Panjābī* and, 158; as public policy, 17–18; of Punjabi language, 167; in Punjab province, 29–31, 41–42
Urdu language: adoption of, 12–17; *Anjuman-e Taraqqī-e Urdu* and, 14–16; as compulsory language, 23–24; Dakhini dialect, 223n59; dominance of, 17; films in, 54; Maulvi Abdul Haq as "father" of, 15, 78, 126, 132; ideology of, 46; Sardar Khan on, 164–165; in Lahore, 41–42; language movement for, 42–48; as language of instruction, 13–16, 51; *Majlis* and, 42; in Marxist Punjabi movement, 82; *Mohajirs'* role in dissemination of, 16–17; *Mohajirs* use of, 225n94; neologisms in, 16; in North West Frontier Province, 11; as official language of Pakistan, 12–13; Pakistani identity and, 132; Punjabi language replaced by, 47–48; in Punjabi newspapers, 31; in Punjab province, 42–48; social status of users, 52–53; teachers' use of, 14–15; triglossia in, 50–53
Urdu writers, Urdu literature and: Circle of the Men of Good Taste (*Ḥalqa-e Arbāb-e Zauq*), 2, 5, 46; conservative nature of, 1; contempt for Punjabi language, 1; *Dabistān-e Lāhore*, 2; Lahore Literary School, 2; in *Monthly Panjābī*, 129; Punjabi literature compared to, 162–163; Punjabi writers compared to, 1. *See also* poetry; *specific people*; *specific topics*; *specific works*
Usmani, Irfan Wahid, 9, 252n45
Uttamchandani, Sundri, 21

Wafa, Mela Ram, 31
Waris, Bhola Nath, 2, 37
Warsi, Ufat, 217n17
Wilson, J., 32

Yaldram, Syed Sajjad Haider, 250n226
Yazdani, Suhail, 177, 179–180, 194, 197, 200
Yurish, Qamar, 84, 101, 107–108, 117, 149
Yusuf, Mohammad, 155

Zafar, Ahmad, 92, 101, 108, 115, 117
Zafar, Yusuf, 60, 172, 205
uz-Zafar, Mahmud, 56
Zaheer, Sajjad, 56–59, 71, 105–106, 207–208, 222n32, 236n116
Zairvi, Saqib, 169
Zaman, Fakhr, 4
uz-Zaman, Qamar, 50
Zeervi, Saqib, 177, 184

GPSR Authorized Representative: Easy Access System Europe, Mustamäe tee 50, 10621 Tallinn, Estonia, gpsr.requests@easproject.com

www.ingramcontent.com/pod-product-compliance
Lightning Source LLC
Chambersburg PA
CBHW032335300426
44109CB00041B/928

* 9 7 8 0 2 3 1 2 1 9 8 2 2 *